A WORLD TO WIN

A WORLD TO WIN

CONTEMPORARY SOCIAL MOVEMENTS AND COUNTER-HEGEMONY

Edited by William K. Carroll and Kanchan Sarker

ARP BOOKS WINNIPEG

ARP Books (Arbeiter Ring Publishing)
201E-121 Osborne Street
Winnipeg, Manitoba
Canada R3L 1Y4
arpbooks.org

Cover by Sébastien Aubin.
Typeset by Relish New Brand Experience.

Printed and bound in Canada by Friesens
on paper made from 100% recycled post-consumer waste.

ARP Books acknowledges the generous support of the Manitoba Arts Council and the Canada Council for the Arts for our publishing program. We acknowledge the financial support of the Government of Canada through the Canada Book Fund and the Province of Manitoba through the Book Publishing Tax Credit and the Book Publisher Marketing Assistance Program of Manitoba Culture, Heritage, and Tourism.

LIBRARY AND ARCHIVES CANADA CATALOGUING IN PUBLICATION

A world to win : contemporary social movements and counter-hegemony / edited by William K. Carroll and Kanchan Sarker.

Includes bibliographical references.
Issued in print and electronic formats.

ISBN 978-1-894037-73-0 (paperback).--ISBN 978-1-894037-77-8 (pdf)

1. Social movements. I. Carroll, William K., author, editor II. Sarker, Kanchan, editor

HM881.W67 2016 303.48'4 C2016-902070-3
C2016-902071-1

CONTENTS

SURVEYING THE CHANGING LANDSCAPE OF DISSENT

Let a hundred flowers bloom,
let a hundred schools of thought contend.
—MAO TSE-TUNG

SOCIAL MOVEMENTS AND COUNTER-HEGEMONY

William K. Carroll

Although its various chapters are entirely contemporary and (with two exceptions[1]) previously unpublished, this volume has a longish history. *Organizing Dissent* (Carroll, 1997), a collection published in two editions in the 1990s, brought together some of the same authors featured here in an effort to distill theoretical and practical insights on movement activism in a Canadian context. Like that book, this one speaks to activists, to students and to critical scholars interested not only in understanding the world, but in changing it. But while *Organizing Dissent* redressed the lack of book-length treatments of social movements in Canada, two decades later there is no such dearth. Rather, the field is now divided between traditionally academic overviews that centre around sociological theories (Staggenborg, 2012; Smith, 2014; Ramos & Rodgers, 2015) and texts that largely avoid theory in favour of practical analyses of direct use to activists and concerned citizens (Choudry, Hanley & Shragge, 2012; Harden, 2013; Shragge, 2013). Both genres have value, but what is needed—by activists and by students and scholars with a critical bent—is a less segmented approach.

This book strives for a unity of theory and practice—that is, a *praxis*-oriented examination of social movements—of value to activists whose interventions can be sharpened through theoretical reflection, and to students/scholars who may find in these chapters pathways into the world of activism. Our contributors draw upon yet reach beyond extant conceptual frameworks, to situate movements in an era of crisis and change—in Canada and the world. A defining feature of this book is its emphasis on the ways in which contemporary movements contest dominant political economic and cultural-psychological formations, as agencies of *counter-hegemony*. We read movements

1 Warren Magnusson's essay is reissued here with permission of the University of Toronto Press. Harsha Walia's essay is a condensed version of a chapter appearing in Walia's *Undoing Border Imperialism* (AK Press, 2013).

as agents of history-in-the-making that face ongoing challenges from hegemonic institutions—capital, state, media, etc.—and from the increasing resort to the repression of dissent. As collective responses to a deepening economic, ecological and indeed civilizational crisis, in which liberal-democratic values and institutions seem increasingly hollow, movements are potential agencies of deep democratization. They contest the sedimented practices that sustain injustice, and they sometimes prefigure alternative futures.

Throughout, we strive to make good on Marx's suggestion that the point in socio-political analysis is not simply to comprehend the world but to participate in its transformation. *A World to Win* offers a wide-ranging collection of reflections and resources for engaged students and scholars who seek not only to interpret the world, but to change it. As Kurt Lewin, a founder of action research, claimed, there is nothing so practical as a good theory (Greenwald, 2012: 99). Theory is what enables us to move beyond the concrete particulars of one specific situation, to see things in a wider context, to "connect the dots" between events in a meaningful way, opening the prospect for effective practice. To keep things centred upon the issue of praxis, my presentation below of contemporary perspectives in social movement studies is selective and attuned to their main implications for political practice. In this, I follow Saul Alinsky (1971), whose *Rules for Radicals* attempted to distil practical lessons for those coming of age in the 1960s wave of activism. But unlike Alinsky, I use social science as a critical cognitive resource. Our praxis-oriented approach asks how theoretical insights can inform strategies for resisting hegemony and building counter-hegemony.

This Introduction presents three paradigms within which social movements and activism can be comprehended. The first two—the pragmatic-reformist and the epochal-interpretive—represent the main traditions in social movement studies; the third applies the historical materialism of Marx and Gramsci, enriched with insights from the first two. At the close of each presentation I provide five key lessons for activists. These are offered not as doctrine or as logical deductions from abstract theory, but as strategic pointers that may be helpful in fashioning effective praxis. In the last section, I introduce subsequent chapters, noting how each conveys a distinct perspective from which we can understand social movements and the politics of counter-hegemony, in contemporary Canada and the wider world.

The first two paradigms have shaped the field of mainstream social movement studies since the 1970s. *Pragmatic-reformist* approaches focus on *how* movements emerge and pursue collective action, whereas *epochal interpretive* formulations focus on *why* specific forms of activism have appeared in late modernity. The former offer often intricate insights on the dynamics of contention but tend to take the historical context of movements as given; the latter are sensitized to the macro-sociological transformations and emergent cultural, political and economic contexts of collective action. In presenting historical materialism as a third paradigm, I argue that key insights from the first two can be brought together in a wider view that offers strategic resources to critical movements, and clarifies what is at stake.

The Pragmatic-Reformist Paradigm

This approach begins from the premises of our contemporary order—the division of social space into separate economic, political and cultural spheres (the market, the state and civil society respectively), the conflicting interests that stem from unequal power relations within these spheres and the observed tendency for aggrieved groups to organize themselves into social movements and to press for change, often through the institutional apparatuses of the liberal-democratic state. Although specific models have been developed to account for certain political outcomes,[2] the broad perspective that proceeds from these givens is known as *resource-mobilization theory* (RMT). Movement mobilization is a process by which resources useful to a group's collective action are brought under collective control. It is this pooling of resources that enables a group to transform itself from a collection of political spectators sharing a common interest to a contending group pursuing a shared goal (Tilly, 1978). In this transformation, social movements appear as instrumentally rational collective actors,

2 Korpi's (2006) power-resources approach, for instance, explains the development of more or less advanced welfare states by considering the extent to which the working class mobilizes within a strong trade-union movement and a social democratic political party.

deploying effective means to a shared end. On the basis of felt grievances stemming from common interests, the constituents of a movement pool their resources, and secure other resources, in pursuit of collective goods—such as higher wages, universal daycare and Indigenous self-determination. As resources become pooled, a group gains capacity to act on its common interest; that is to say, it becomes mobilized. An insight here is that *collective action is costly*: it requires most importantly labour (activists working for the movement, often with technical expertise in media relations, popular education, political strategizing etc.), but also land or facilities (e.g. an office and communications equipment) and money to pay for elements of the aforementioned (cf. Jenkins, 1983: 533).

Bringing such resources under collective control, in turn, involves *social organization*, in two senses. First, pre-existing social networks and collective identities are a prerequisite to mobilization. Indeed, the mobilization potential of a group is primarily determined by the extent of pre-existing social organization. Groups lacking such social networks and shared consciousness rarely mobilize, for they have no practical basis on which to pool resources. Conversely, groups sharing strong identities and dense interpersonal networks are highly organized, and can be readily mobilized (Tilly, 1978: 62-63). Often, mobilization involves co-optation of resources from pre-existing organizations such as churches or voluntary associations. Second, social organization *results from* mobilization; i.e., mobilization typically involves the creation of a *social movement organization* (SMO) or more broadly, a mobilizing structure (Stekelenburg & Boekkooi, 2013). Such structures, ranging from informal networks (think of the Occupy movement of 2011) to formal organizations (e.g. trade unions), collectivize control of resources and thus maintain the movement in a mobilized state, distinguishing it from a one-off campaign (Diani, 2003: 301). And, when the tide of activism ebbs, as it does over the course of "cycles of contention" (Tarrow, 2011), social networks and organizations provide *abeyance structures*, conserving the capacity to remobilize when circumstances permit.

Mobilizing structures are key to the "supply side" of collective action: they enable movements to act. But mobilization also has a "demand side" which shapes a movement's mobilization potential (Klandermans, 2013). For a movement to get off the ground, there must be popular demand for action: grievances must be translated into claims, identities must become politicized. "Movements don't emerge unless substantial numbers of people are invested with feelings of both urgency and efficacy" (Meyer, 2004: 169). In practice, movement mobilization involves a dynamic interaction that amplifies the demand for action as it creates the capacity to act through mobilizing structures.

Mobilization is key to movement formation, but to create change, social movements also require an *opportunity to act*. Changes in the *structure of political opportunities* can have decisive impact on the ebb and flow of movement activism (Tarrow, 2011). At different times and places the state may be particularly receptive or vulnerable to organized protest by a given contending group (McAdam et al., 1988: 699). Thus,

> In one era, the political forces aligned against the challenger may make collective action a near impossibility. In another, shifting political alignments may create a unique opportunity for political action by, or on behalf of, the same group (Marx & McAdam, 1994: 84).

The configuration of mobilized social forces—both within the state and in civil society—provides the strategic context within which a given social movement acts. Indeed, movements move in *strategic interaction* among collective actors that include SMOs, the state and other organizations and institutions. A good deal of strategic interaction involves various instances of *repression* and *facilitation*, as groups manipulate each other's costs of collective action, whether upwards (repression) or downwards (facilitation) (Tilly, 1978: 100-01). For instance, in the 1980s the peace and anti-poverty movements in Vancouver were vibrant in part because the local labour council *facilitated* these movements by providing key resources to groups like End the Arms Race and End Legislated Poverty (Carroll & Ratner, 1995). On the other hand, the United States government's outlawing of the Communist Party (CP) during the Cold War was *repressive*: it raised the CP's cost of collective action by guaranteeing that its leaders would be jailed whenever it undertook visible collective action (Tilly, 1978: 100).

Over time, the changing structure of political opportunities shapes the social movement sector of a given society. In Canada, for instance, the move since the late 1970s "from consent to coercion" in the state's management of industrial relations has had a *repressive* impact on the labour movement, obliging unions to rethink their own strategies and (sometimes) to build mutually *facilitative* alliances with other progressive movements (Panitch & Swartz, 2003). Importantly, *movements can recursively shape their own opportunity structures* (Tarrow, 2011): the cumulative impact of environmental activism in raising public awareness in the 1970s and 1980s made states and corporations more vulnerable to the claims of environmentalists relating to industrial pollution, wilderness preservation, global warming, etc. More broadly, the *effects* of movements register in changes to public policy, to the political culture surrounding policy and to activists themselves (in the last case altering the subjects available for subsequent collective action) (Meyer, 2004: 170-72).

Also subject to change over time is the *repertoire of collective action* available to a given group. Demonstrations, strikes and petition campaigns are forms of collective action that emerged with modernity. Originally a tactic by which artisans threatened with proletarianization fought back by disrupting the production process and imperilling employers' profits, in the 19th century the strike became the primary means by which workers advanced *new claims* regarding wages, working conditions and employment security (Tilly, 1978: 161). In the process, the strike became a standardized element in the modern working class's repertoire of action. Yet depending on the structure of political opportunities, "at different times, political pressure, sabotage, demonstrations, and occupations of the workplace all become alternatives to striking. The workers' repertoire of collective action includes more items than the strike" (ibid.: 166), and the same holds for other movements.

In the 1980s and onward a major lacuna in RMT, namely its deficient theorization of *consciousness and signification*, was recognized and partially remedied through the analysis of social movement framing. Although sometimes presented as a competing alternative to RMT (Buechler, 2000: 40), frame analysis is better understood within the pragmatic-reformist paradigm, supplementing RMT with an analysis of culture and social psychology (Buechler, 2011: 150-56). Snow and Benford (1992) define collective-action frames as emergent action-oriented sets of meanings and beliefs that inspire and legitimate social movement campaigns and activities. Such frames are interpretive schemata through which movements define certain conditions as unjust, attribute responsibility for the injustice and point to alternatives that might be achieved through collective action (Snow & Benford, 1992: 137; Tarrow, 2011: 144-46). Collective mobilization involves a process of "frame alignment" (Snow et al., 1986) in which SMOs play an active role in establishing a congruence between their definitions of the situation and those of their constituencies. Without such resonance, few members of the constituency are likely to participate. That is, human resources crucial to any movement cannot be pooled unless a collective will to participate is created, and such a collective will requires a common interpretive understanding of issues, goals and strategies. Research in this field has burgeoned in recent years, as studies have explored "how collective actors frame their grievances, goals, and their views of the world" (Snow et al., 2014: 29).

RMT offers a means of conceptually mapping the field of contemporary movement activism in *pragmatic* terms. It attends to mechanism rather than substance (Eyerman & Jamison, 1991: 39): to mobilization structures, political opportunities and framing processes (McAdam, McCarthy & Zald, 1996). By examining a group's interest-base (which is never purely a matter of "objective location" but is formed within lived experiences of group members), its resources and the organizational forms through which resources are mobilized, the surrounding structure of opportunities for collective action (which includes other mobilized groups with similar or opposed interests, as well as the state) and the repertoire of collective action through which a group presses its claims, one can read a movement as a rational collective actor. Depicting collective action as *rational*, RMT serves to *validate* movements as credible political agencies, and offers insights into the "logic" of collective action within the "dynamics of contention" (McAdam, Tarrow & Tilly, 2001; Tilly & Tarrow, 2007).

Key lessons

Our first paradigm offers five key lessons for activists.

1. Effective praxis requires analysis of *interests*: who benefits and who is harmed by a given arrangement, practice or relation. Shared interests provide a rudimentary answer to the questions Mao Tse-tung posed in 1926: "Who are our enemies? Who are our friends?" (Mao, 1967: 13). Effective mobilization (and effective strategic interaction with other actors) requires clarity about interests, both convergent and divergent.
2. *Mobilization* means bringing under collective control resources of various kinds, including most importantly human labour: the willingness of people to commit their own time to the movement. Mobilization requires social organization including both pre-existing networks and emergent networks and mobilizing structures, which enable collective action to be sustained over time.
3. Collective action is *costly*—it makes claims on resources that could be dispensed otherwise. Effective movements create a configuration of alliances and reciprocal relations of mutual aid (facilitation), thereby lowering costs of collective action. In some contexts low-cost mobilization of great numbers can be effective (e.g. clicktivism), but there are limits to this. Since states, corporations and other centres of power may respond to threats to their power by attempting to raise the costs of mobilization and collective action, movements need to develop strategies for dealing with such repression.
4. *Framing* is integral to mobilization. Effective movements develop collective-action frames that call attention to injustice and its socio-political sources, point toward alternatives and resonate strongly with broad publics. Movement outreach strategies need to maintain a democratic dialogue, so that frames, as they develop over time, enable an alignment between the movement and its social base.
5. Movements move in a dialectical relationship with *opportunity structures*, and success or failure in one conjuncture leads on to a new conjuncture that can open up new opportunities and threats. Activists need to be mindful of these changes as they come into view.

These insights have a *pragmatic-reformist* thrust. They comprise a recipe for effective activism, advancing reforms *within the perimeters of capitalist modernity, but generally not extending beyond them.* Indeed, "the domain assumptions of resource mobilization theory mirror the liberal, formally democratic political environment of social activism in the United States" (Buechler, 2000: 56; Eschle, 2001: 28) (not surprisingly the main exponents of RMT have been American sociologists). Social movements are seen as deeply implicated in the social and political practices of that modernity: in professionalization, in instrumental rationality, in formal organization (SMOs), in distinctively modern repertoires of collective action and in political opportunity structures that centre around the liberal-democratic state but span outward to include other agents in civil society (Buechler, 2000: 55-56). The pragmatic-reformist lens focuses on the present as it has been shaped by the past, but is relatively insensitive to emergent features of activism, tending instead toward the construction of general models of collective action (as in Opp, 2009). This paradigm conveys little sense of "the alternative oppositional forms of consciousness and action being created by contemporary social movements" (Ingalsbee, 1994: 140). Hence, when these scholars contemplate epochal changes, they think in terms of trends toward the professionalization of activism (Zald & McCarthy, 1987) which along with proliferation of movements across social space may lead to a "social movement society" (Meyer & Tarrow, 1998; Ramos & Rodgers, 2015)—not in terms of the changing "relationship between forms of domination and social movement challengers" (Armstrong & Bernstein, 2008: 81).

This observation brings us to a second paradigm: a collection of *epochal-interpretive* approaches, gathered loosely under the rubric of New Social Movement (NSM) theory, which strive to understand the specific kinds of movements—such as environmentalism and LBGTQ politics—that have emerged in the late 20th/early 21st century world.

Epochal-Interpretive Approaches

Sensitized to the growing salience of media, symbolic products and information in everyday life and in power relations, epochal-interpretive approaches replace RMT's root metaphor of "common interests" with emergent "collective identities" (Cohen, 1985). NSMs are viewed as instances of cultural and political praxis through which new identities are formed, new ways of life are tested and new forms of community are prefigured, within a context of epochal change in late or postmodernity.

New Social Movements

Alain Touraine (1971), who coined the term "new social movement," first enunciated his influential perspective in the wake of Paris's student-led 1968 May Movement (Waters, 2008). He viewed social movements as actors within "a system of social forces competing for control of a cultural field" (1981: 30), which is the focal point of *historicity*—of society's capacity "to act on itself" (Touraine, 1971: 3). Touraine discerned a post-World War II shift in the logic of the system, from the physical transformation of nature into industrial products to the "production of symbolic goods which model or transform our representation of human nature and the external world" (Touraine et al., 1987: 127)—from industrial capitalism to the "programmed society." As the focal point of struggle shifts from material objects to information, conflicts shift to arenas of information production and control—whether in mass media or in science and technology—and the central social-movement actors "are no longer classes linked to industrial production but groups with opposing visions concerning the use and destination of cognitive and symbolic resources" (della Porta, 2009: 366). More recently, in the long shadow of the 2008 global financial crisis and the seemingly permanent "new austerity," Touraine has argued that the globalization of financialized capitalism has opened a deep gulf between "the economic world and that of social institutions" (2014: 96), creating a "post-social" situation in which the central conflict pits the dominant power of the economy against "actors" who "base their desire for freedom and justice on their awareness of the human subject carried within themselves" (112).

While Touraine's formulation incorporates aspects of a critical analysis of capitalism, his student Alberto Melucci provides the best example of a clean theoretical break from the Marxist tradition. Melucci's (1989) *constructivist* theory depicts contemporary movements as "nomads of the present" creating temporary spaces and identities for themselves within the complex societies of late modernity. For Melucci, echoing Touraine, the rise of complex society has meant a displacement of material production (and with it, class) from the centre of social life, and its replacement with the "production of signs and social relations" (1989: 45). By implication, power is no longer concentrated in a materially dominant class; it is dispersed across the various fields of the social and increasingly is located in symbolic codes and forms of regulation. Melucci views social movements not as unified collective actors strategically pursuing their shared interests, but as variegated "networks of meaning" (1989: 58) whose collective identities are no more than tentative products of ongoing practices submerged in everyday life.

New social movements do not contest political power; their concern has "shifted towards a non-political terrain: the need for self-realization in everyday life" (1989: 23). Rather than adopt the modernist, state-centred quest for power, NSMs endeavour to *reveal and expose* "that which is hidden or excluded by the decision-making process. Collective protest and mobilization bring to light the silent, obscure or arbitrary elements that frequently arise in complex systems decisions" (Melucci, 1994: 185). In exposing power, movements pose "symbolic challenges that overturn the dominant cultural codes" (1989: 75). At the same time, the construction of collective identity is also the creation of new cultural practices within social movement networks. In challenging dominant codes, in constructing new identities such as the "out" gay or the independent woman, NSMs opened public spaces free from control or repression, wherein questions surrounding ecology, gender, sexuality and so on are rendered visible and collective. The upshot is a "democracy of everyday life" which has the potential, through movement activism, to become "a new transnational political arena in which people and governments can take responsibility for the dramatic choices that human beings are facing for the first time" (Melucci, 1992: 73).

Melucci's theory was criticized by Bartholomew and Mayer (1992) on two telling grounds. In his effort to overcome the "political reductionism" he discerns in theories like RMT, Melucci falls prey to a "cultural reductionism" which distinguishes too sharply between political action (which NSMs supposedly eschew) and collective identity formation (which NSMs supposedly embrace). Moreover, unlike other epochal concepts such as "post-Fordism" (Ely, 1993) or "disorganized capitalism" (Offe, 1985a), Melucci's "complex society" fails to specify any structural relations of hierarchy and unequal power, eventuating in "an analysis which treats codes/regulation as neutral in the sense of lacking inscription of relations of inequality and domination" (Bartholomew & Mayer, 1992: 148). Such a view informs Melucci's dubious claims that NSMs do not challenge power but merely render it "visible," and that "conflicts no longer have winners, but they may produce innovation, modernization and reform" (Melucci, 1989: 76-78). In parting company with the historical legacy of Marxism, Melucci cedes the possibility of situating NSMs within the admittedly complex but deeply inegalitarian orders of contemporary capitalism, in which political and economic power is substantially concentrated within identifiable state and corporate hierarchies.

In contrast to Melucci, Ernesto Laclau and Chantal Mouffe's discourse-theoretical post-Marxism located new NSMs not within a post-industrial epoch of complex society but within a longer epochal narrative, reaching back to the French Revolution—namely, the struggle for democracy in the modern world. New social movements are said to mark "the emergence of new antagonisms and political subjects as linked to the expansion and generalization of the democratic revolution" within a postwar hegemonic formation in which, "interpellated as equals in their capacity as consumers, ever more numerous groups are impelled to reject the real inequalities which continue to exist" (Laclau & Mouffe, 1985: 164-66). In a world of multiple social struggles in which identities have become unfixed, there are no necessary linkages between struggles; any "unity" across struggles must be practically constructed through discursive chains of equivalence, which Laclau and Mouffe term "hegemonic articulation":

> It follows that it is only possible to construct this articulation on the basis of separate struggles, which only exercise their equivalential and over-determining effects in *certain* spheres of the social. This requires the autonomization of the spheres of struggle and the multiplication of political spaces, which is incompatible with the

> concentration of power and knowledge that classic Jacobinism in its different socialist variants imply (178).

Laclau and Mouffe retain in their post-Marxism much in Marxism, including ultimately a commitment to the "ideal of socialism," which they subsume under their grand narrative of democratic revolution (ibid.). Yet their emphasis upon discursive articulation shifts the focus from the appraisal of concrete political-economic conjunctures to "the realm of the symbolic" (Bocock, 1986: 106) while their critique of Jacobinism leads them to a view of radical politics as an ever-shifting process of coalition formation that underplays the possibility of a coherent, counter-hegemonic alternative to the dominant order (Epstein, 1990: 51).

New anarchism

A related approach to NSMs that became influential toward the end of the 20th century is that of anarchist writers influenced by postmodern theorists of the 1970s-80s. In the 1980s, Paul Patton's call for "a nomadic social theory, pluralistic and deterritorialized" rejected Marxism's "will to totality" which "enjoins us to address society as a whole and is accompanied by a commitment to a unitary project of emancipation that may leave no room for the specific, limited concerns of 'marginal' social movements" (Patton, 1988: 130). The position of totality is, according to Patton, the perspective of the state "whose duty it is to resolve conflicting interests, establish priorities, and institute hierarchies" (133). Patton's alternative bears a close resemblance to Melucci's (1989) view of NSMs as "nomads of the present," arguing "not for moving beyond the fragments toward the global politics of a new alliance but for multiplying the fragmentary effects of...local campaigns" (Patton, 1988: 131).[3]

Patton's intervention was largely inspired by the ideas of Gilles Deleuze and Felix Guattari (1987), but equally intriguing postmodern

3 Belden Fields replied to Patton with a "defense of political economy and systemic analysis." Fields noted that the postmodern thrust toward single-issue politics fails to challenge and may even reinforce the hegemonic ideology of liberal practicality. By the same token, "Totally disconnected efforts are more likely to be frustrated or assimilated by the dominant structures than are efforts that are part of a larger social movement" (ibid.: 154).

approaches draw upon the work of Michel Foucault who saw in the contemporary resistances to the power of men over women, of medicine over population, of administration over everyday life and so on, a series of dispersed struggles revolving around the question "Who are we?" (Foucault, 1982: 210-12). Foucault endorsed the "partial transformations" such struggles portend and advised critical thinkers to "turn away from all projects that claim to be global or radical" (1984: 46). Following in this groove, Michael Wapner (1989) explored whether Foucault's thought furnishes a viable basis to envision strategies for social change. Foucault's biopolitical conception of power as web-like (without any point of origin, agent or predominant directionality)—combined with his decentred view of social reality as lacking any essential, fundamental element—opens up an alternative approach to politics. The omnipresence of power means that no one site is privileged as a locale for political activism, validating a multiplicity of resistances. Concomitantly, decentring removes the notion of necessity from social arrangements and thus "destroys the weight that guards against change: the notion that 'what is' is 'meant to be.'" (Wapner, 1989: 107). Yet this decentred conception of power as pervasive and ever-changing also renders the idea of coordinated, strategic opposition problematic and inhibits strategies for transformation, since "there is no target against which to organize or direct energy" (Wapner, 1989: 108). Likewise, a decentred conception of the social can provide no counter-vision from which to critique the status quo and towards which to orient social change—impairing the very reason to struggle for change (Wapner, 1989: 107). For Crook, such problems in postmodern anarchist thought pose a continuing threat of degeneration into a nihilism which "shows itself in two symptoms: an inability to specify possible mechanisms of change, and an inability to state why change is better than no change" (1991: 158).

In the early 21st century, movement analysts began to observe that "recent forms of collective action are more complex, more diverse, more fragmented than new social movements. Unlike the labour movement, they are not trying to create a new vision of society, just as, unlike many of the new social movements, they are not attempting to bring together forms of organization and action based on self-actualization" (Hamel & Maheu, 2004: 265). Distinct from yet resonant with NSM theory, the "new anarchism" (Graeber, 2002) addressed itself to what Richard Day (2005) termed the "newest social movements"—instances of radical activism, rooted in the new social movements, with an affinity "for non-universalizing, non-hierarchical, non-coercive relationships based [on] mutual aid and shared ethical commitments" (ibid., 9) and oriented toward direct action instead of state-centred demands. Exemplars include Reclaim the Streets, Food Not Bombs, the Black Bloc and the many non-branded affinity groups that have come and gone in North America in recent decades (ibid.).[4]

Day's intervention was a manifesto for "a non-reformist, non-revolutionary politics" responding to diverse needs and identities "without attempting to subsume them under a common project" (2005: 10). Strategically, it advocated and celebrated the impedance of institutions through blockades, the construction of temporary autonomous zones and the broad practice of "structural renewal"—rendering the system redundant by withdrawing energy from its structures (2005: 124). However, since "the masses of the First World have chosen quiescence, and nothing we can do will change their behaviour for the better" (Day, 2005: 126), the newest social movements are mainly about creating "more opportunities for more people to choose a life of autonomy over one of subservience" (Day, 2005: 13). As I have observed elsewhere, in this reading, the newest social movements devolve into "a lifestyle choice within the postmodern panoply, a niche claimed by non-masses with a taste for anarchism" (Carroll, 2006: 32).

More grounded, and more reflexive about some limitations in the newest social movements, is Chris Dixon's detailed analysis of the "anti-authoritarian current" within North American social movements.[5]

4 Key features of the newest movements—direct action and prefigurative politics (wherein a nonhierarchical future is prefigured in current activist praxis of radical democracy)—were already distinctive aspects of NSMs, as in Rosa Parks's iconic refusal to give up her seat on a bus in Montgomery, Alabama (1955), which inspired other direct actions in the civil rights movement (Aronowitz, 2003: 147) and the prefigurative praxis of the Students for a Democratic Society (Breines, 1989).

5 Dixon rejects Day's claim that contemporary radical activism is centred upon a politics of exit from the dominant order: "most of us are much more ambitious: we value prefigurative politics *and* we want a transformed world—the only real exit from the existing one" (Dixon, 2014: 283).

Dixon's work is based on in-depth interviews with dozens of activists, from which he distils insights on the "popular pre-figurative forms" (such as non-hierarchical decision-making) that enable anti-authoritarians to organize "in the world as it is while cultivating strategies toward the world that we want" (2014: 17). Counterbalancing this enthusiasm for new political practices of prefiguration is Dixon's auto-critique of the new anarchism, which inclines toward the neo-Gramscian approach I will develop later in this introduction. Dixon notes that the anti-authoritarian current lacks "deep thinking about what capitalism is and how we should go about fighting it" (ibid., 69), and that prefigurative initiatives tend (a) to be disconnected from anti-oppression mass struggles (104), (b) to fetishize purist principles and direct-action tactics, downplaying the need for effective strategy aimed at actual transformation (111-12) and (c) to reject intentional, durable organization, viewing "any organization larger than a small group as inherently hierarchical and therefore suspect" (200).

Dixon concludes that, in its present form and size, the new anarchism is "not capable of winning large-scale structural change"; indeed, viewed in its worst light, "this current is a set of fairly transient and insular activist enclaves engaged in frenetic activity that only occasionally connects to broader movements in any significant way" (2014: 223).

These limitations are in some respects not that different from long-acknowledged problems in earlier NSM formulations of "self-limiting radicalism" (Cohen, 1985) which Ellen Wood recognized as "ill equipped to confront the problems of the here and now" (Wood, 1995: 46)—such as capitalist globalization and the "race to the bottom." Today, the notions of "symbolic challenge" and of "multiplying the fragmentary effects of local campaigns" seem even less robust when set against the consolidation of authoritarian neoliberalism within capitalism's deepening global crisis (Bruff, 2014). I believe that lessons from these epochal approaches need to be formulated with sensitivity to our current times, recognizing the quaintness of many NSM and postmodern conceits, and the urgent need to develop a coherent and radical alternative, beyond episodic resistance and local, fragmented prefiguration.

Key lessons

We can summarize key lessons from the epochal-interpretive paradigm in five points:

1. Since the late 20th century, epochal changes have reshaped both the terrain on which movements move and the human beings who take up these struggles. The programmed society demands *increased reflexivity*, and activism itself has become a crucial element in a larger struggle over *historicity*—the self-production of a form of society increasingly laden with mass- (and now socially-) mediated semiosis. As heightened reflexivity develops amid conflicting codes and symbols, power loses its capacity to hide behind traditional legitimations and "all social locations become sites for multiple resistances to power" (Buechler, 2002: 39).
2. New social movements invent new identities and establish new solidarities. They are *critical* in the sense of being open and experimental—enabling them to challenge the structures and practices of contemporary society (Magnusson & Walker, 1988: 58-60).
3. Movements that contest the diverse maladies of late/post modernity practise a *politics of articulation*—constructing new codes and sometimes bridging across difference through discursive chains that respect autonomies—"a practice of thinking 'unity and difference', of 'difference *in* complex unity, without becoming a hostage to the privileging of difference as such'" (Hall, 1985: 93, quoted in Slack 1996: 122).
4. Critical movements are carriers of *democratization* (itself a key articulatory element), not only in the claims they make but in their *prefigurative practices*. If the goal is a deeply democratic society, movements need to prefigure this goal by adopting thoroughgoing democratic organization.
5. Critical movements reject *state centrism*—the routing of politics through states—and recognize the importance of direct action and of the politics of everyday life within civil society, itself a crucial field of struggle. They are committed to creating spaces "where we can live in the kinds of worlds we want to live in, here and now" (Day, 2007).

As we have seen (and with the exception of Laclau and Mouffe, who hold to a socialist imaginary), within the epochal-interpretive paradigm there is a tendency to see and even to celebrate contemporary struggles as partial, fragmented, as localized guerrilla warfare and nomadic militancy (Patton, 1988: 131). Such politics strives *to subvert* the hegemonic discourses that sustain subordination, to challenge the codes, but eschews a revolutionary project of *liberation* from systemic oppression (cf. Kaufman, 1994: 80).

In this, the epochal-interpretive paradigm arrives at a position on movement politics that curiously parallels that of the pragmatic-reformist. As Christopher Gunderson (2015: 248) has surmised, both perspectives tend to "presume not just the permanence of capitalism as a social system, but also the impossibility of the popular classes ever exercising political power." These different perspectives converge in turning away from the problematic of *structural transformation* in favour of a conceptualization of activism in terms of either single-issue reforms or the politics of everyday life, episodic resistance and local prefiguration. Yet this risks losing sight of possibilities for broader, deeper change as globalized, neoliberal capitalism descends into organic crisis (Carroll, 2010; McNally, 2011a; Cremin, 2015).

In these times it is increasingly problematic for social movement analysis to ignore issues of capital, class and strategy. Indeed, "in uncritically accepting the failure of new social movements to reach large numbers of working-class people (or treating this failure as a virtue) new social movement theory abdicates its responsibility to help the movements find direction" (Epstein, 1990: 48). Perhaps it is not surprising that the early 21st century witnessed "a weird convergence," at least in the US, "of some radical postmarxian philosophy and social theory with conventional liberalism" (Aronowitz, 2003: 162). At its limit, the identity politics of everyday life celebrated by such theorists devolves into an anti-politics, lacking collective organization, emphasizing lifestyle and thereby mirroring the ideology of the capitalist marketplace (Kauffman, 1990: 78; cf. Sharzer, 2012). What is needed is an approach that balances concerns about identity and locality "with an emphasis on solidarity, as well as with attention to other key categories like interest and needs" (Kauffman, 1990: 79).

While controversial within anarchist circles, one can see in recent work such as Dixon's an appreciation of these problems as challenges that need to be met head-on in praxis. This brings us to historical materialism, a third paradigm whose insights can be of value to activists today. This paradigm predates the first two by a century or more, yet in my view has only gained relevance as a way of rigorously clarifying, for those wanting to change the world, what Marx in 1843 called "the struggles and wishes of the age."

Historical Materialism

In their content analysis of two prominent journals, Hetland and Goodwin (2013) document the "strange disappearance of capitalism" from social movement studies, even as global justice politics mobilized from the late 1990s onward, and as activists themselves drew increasingly upon critical analyses of capitalism. Ironically, as scholars of social movements made the cultural turn, and also turned to micro- and meso-issues of framing, identity and networks, they simply ignored the elephant in the room (ibid.: 90, 102). In comparison, historical materialism (HM) presents a particularly strong contextualization of contemporary movements. Unlike resource-mobilization and NSM formulations, which claim most of the space within conventional social movement studies, historical materialism does not posit a free-standing theory of social movements but analyzes movements within a broad theorization of capitalist modernity.

HM proceeds ontologically from Marx's famous observation that people make their own history, though not in circumstances of their choosing. The circumstances in which we act include the institutional arrangements and alliances that stabilize the dominant regime, as well as the networks of alliances (or the paucity of them) among dissenting movements—the relations of ruling and the relations of struggle (Kinsman, 2006: 136). For activists, this perspective addresses an urgent strategic exigency:

> What we need most is a stronger sense of *agency*—"theirs," in understanding not just how the system works but how the *alliances* which underpin it work and how they can come to be taken apart,

> and "ours," in understanding how we can form the kinds of alliances that are capable of bringing about the change we say we want (Cox & Nilsen, 2014: 181).

In this perspective "social movements from above and below engage in struggles over historicity, that is, they engage and encounter each other in struggles over the direction and form of the development of the social organisation of human needs and capacities" (Cox & Nilsen, 2014: 96). From the start, HM positions contemporary movements within the changing conjunctures and crises of capitalism as a way of life, a mode of production. Each conjuncture is a distinct historical situation comprising a correlation of forces—political, social, economic, cultural—and offering possible lines of intervention for movements from below.

The imagery of movements from above and below helps clarify a crucial reality of our era. In neoliberal globalization we have not been witnessing the decomposition of class, or the end of class struggle, but a very effective movement from above, in conjunction with relatively weak and ineffective forms of organization and solidarity across issues and identities in movements from below. In Canada, the installation of neoliberalism in the 1980s, its consolidation in the 1990s and its further elaboration in recent years into a hegemonic project that Donald Gutstein (2014) has termed Harperism, was driven by a movement from above that mobilized leading corporate-capitalist organizations and agencies within an historical bloc with extensive ties to both the state and mainstream media (Langille, 1987; Carroll & Shaw, 2001; Gutstein, 2014). This underlines, as a central insight in HM, "that exploitation and oppression are underpinned by powerfully organized forces who will resist all serious attempts at structural change and who will, in some form, need to be taken on and defeated" (Barker et al., 2013: 20).

Our concern here is with movements from below, and the insights that historical materialism can bring to praxis-based assessments of the challenges and opportunities these movements face as potential agencies of transformative politics. What follows is a highly select and cursory digest of some key approaches within this tradition.

Rethinking movements and class

As Stuart Hall observed, "social movements are the modality in which class politics are enacted" (quoted in Aronowitz, 2003: 141). But what exactly are class politics? In approaching class and movements, we need to avoid both "class reductionism" and the tendency in social movement theory to underestimate the continuing importance of capitalism and class *within* movement processes.

Presented as a response to the post-Marxist retreat from Marx, Michael Lebowitz's efforts in this regard begin with the observation that such formulations invoke a stereotype of the abstract proletarian, reducing workers to "one-sided opposites of capital" (2003: vii), in contrast to which NSMs are posited as post-proletarian actors. This reification rests on a profound misunderstanding of class, class struggle and capital. Lebowitz begins by conceptualizing the historically formed deep structure of capital, which separates workers from the means of production, obliging them to perform alienated labour which, transmogrified as surplus value, accumulates as capital: the continuing source of social power for its owners and managers. Within capitalism, however, there is always a second process of production, articulated with the accumulation process, namely the production of capital's other, *the worker as a human being* with needs and capacities that change with the expanded reproduction of capital itself.

In creating a tendentially integrated global system, capital produces an unprecedented interdependence within production (and a shared fate for humanity), yet simultaneously, "capital requires separation and division among wage-labourers as a condition of its ability to capture the fruits of coöperation in production" (88). Capital thus functions as the great mediator, bringing together "individual, isolated owners of labour-power who enter into relations with the capitalist but not with each other" (Marx, 1977: 451; quoted in Lebowitz, 2003: 86). By implication, "only by struggling to reduce their degree of separation can workers achieve their goals. The struggle against the existence of a mediator between (and above) them is inherent in 'the workers' own need for development" (2003: 87). More broadly,

> the struggles of workers to satisfy their many-sided needs—whether they are struggles to develop "*that which is needed for the common satisfaction of needs*, such as schools, health services, etc." or to preserve Nature as a source of their wealth or to secure use-values in a commodity-form—are struggles against capital as mediator within society (Marx, 1875: 22). They are class struggles—struggles of those who are compelled to sell their labour-power to satisfy needs; and they are struggles against the results of capital's ownership of the products of labour.... Rather than directed against *particular* capitals, they are struggles against the power of capital as a whole and against the ruling principle of valorization....(186).

This formulation offers not only a wider view of class struggle, but the key dialectical insight that *struggle itself is a production process* "of producing new people, of transforming them into people with a new conception of themselves—as subjects capable of altering their world" (Lebowitz, 2003: 140). Capital's logic is to reproduce its economic premises in capitalist form, but workers as human beings with many needs and with capacities that emerge with those needs "transform themselves through their struggles into *other than capital's products* and thus into the historic presuppositions of a new state of society" (206). Prefiguration, on this account, is not an activity "outside" capitalism (as in new anarchism) but is built into the multiform struggles of workers, broadly understood, under capitalism (Sharzer, 2012: 150); and new social movements, rather than an opposition to class struggle, "should be seen as expressing *other* needs of workers and as the development of *new* organizing centres of the working class," pointing toward its complete emancipation (2003: 186).[6]

6 Importantly, a Marxist class analysis can yield key insights on the "information society" that has been so central to NSM formulations. Here, the recent work of Jodi Dean is exemplary. She has discerned in the protests associated with the Occupy movement, the Québec "Maple Spring" of 2012 and European anti-austerity protests "the revolt of the knowledge class," of "those whose work is exploited and lives are expropriated by communicative capitalism" (2014: 1). Through an intricate analysis of the political economy of communicative capitalism—the commodification of communication for capital, particularly in digital form—Dean offers a window on changes in class struggle's "mode of appearance," with the proliferation of distributed, precarious and unpaid communicative labour, and a way to place the revolts of the past few years within a coherent framework of historical-materialist analysis.

Accumulation by dispossession and anti-colonial struggles

In his voluminous work, David Harvey has in the past decade and a half offered some deep insights that locate recent revolts within the epochal moorings of late capitalism, postmodernity and neoliberalism. Especially important has been his analysis of how neoliberalism accentuates the tendency, ever-present within capital, to accumulate not only via *expanded reproduction* of the capital-labour relation (i.e., exploitation of wage-labour and reinvestment of the surplus into expanded production) but by *dispossession*: creating capital and profit by enclosing the commons—whether through privatization of public assets, financialization or commodification of nature, knowledge and communication. Because accumulation by dispossession takes fragmentary, inchoate forms—"destruction of habitat here, privatization of services there, expulsion from the land somewhere else"—movements opposing it tend to be variegated and diffuse, creating a new dynamic of social action across the whole spectrum of civil society (Harvey, 2005b: 174). This opens up an opportunity, on the basis of convergent anti-capitalist interests, to link the politics of labour with the multifaceted project to reclaim the commons, an opportunity that must be seized if the opposition to neoliberal capitalism is to gain traction. "The divide-and-rule politics of ruling-class elites must be confronted with alliance politics on the left sympathetic to the recuperation of local powers of self-determination" (Harvey, 2005a: 203).

In his *Seventeen Contradictions and the End of Capitalism* Harvey expands this analysis, charting the "foundational," "moving" and "dangerous" contradictions of capital, so that oppositional and anti-capitalist movements "will be better positioned to take advantage of, rather than be surprised and stymied by, the way the contradictions move around and deepen...in the course of crisis formation and resolution" (2014: 14). He notes the tendency for movements to take a piecemeal approach, addressing one contradiction at a time, as in anti-neoliberal politics. While sometimes efficacious in an immediate sense, this approach

> does not tell us how highly fragmented though numerous oppositional movements might converge and coalesce into a more unified solidarious movement against capital's dominance. The piecemeal

> approach fails to register and confront how all the contradictions of capital relate to and through each other to form an organic whole. There is a crying need for some more catalytic conception to ground and animate political action (2014: 266-67).

Harvey finds hope in the prospect of a secular *revolutionary* humanism, open to alliance with religiously based humanisms, "to counter alienation in its many forms and to radically change the world from its capitalist ways": a humanism that, with Marx and Fanon (1967), refuses the idea of a fixed human essence "and forces us to think hard about how to become a new kind of human" (2014: 287).

Harvey's thinking on the multifarious struggles against accumulation by dispossession that characterize the neoliberal era also has purchase in illuminating much longer histories of struggle. In this, Marx's (1976) analysis of how the premises of capitalism were actually established—through enclosing the commons within Europe while colonizing much of the rest of the world (also a process of enclosing commons)—is indispensable. HM has long seen colonialism and imperialism, and struggles for self-determination by colonized peoples (Nimtz, 2002; Barker, 2013), as part and parcel of world capitalism.[7] What Marx (and work that followed his lead, including Lenin's 1914 essay, "The right of nations to self-determination") took from his support for Irish independence and other struggles for self-determination, was a primary principle: "a movement that did not struggle for *general emancipation*, against *all* forms of oppression, would be neutered" (Barker, 2013: 60). Although NSM theories tended to view anti-colonial and national struggles (along with class politics) as relics—"old" social movements of decreasing salience in complex societies—we find quite the reverse in the early 21st century.

Indeed, in Canada, the struggles of Indigenous peoples—whose land and livelihoods were stolen in the process of creating capitalist

7 See Nimtz's (2002) vigorous disputation of the myth of Marx's Eurocentrism. Marx saw the struggle against *national oppression* in non-industrial societies as "a condition for advance by 'the social movement in general'" (Barker, 2013: 53). He similarly came to support the nascent anti-colonial movement in India and was crystal clear on modern slavery: "Labour cannot emancipate itself in the white skin while in the black skin it is branded" (Marx, 1976: 414).

Canada—are arguably at the cutting edge of critical movement praxis today, and scholarship in this field has begun to engage productively with historical materialism. Taiaiake Alfred has observed that under postmodern imperial conditions, "oppression has become increasingly invisible," constituted no longer by military occupations and land theft but in a "confluence of politics, economics, psychology and culture" (2009b: 58, 30). Central to the new regime is "an ideology of accumulation [that], even if it's collective rather than individual, plays right into the consumptive commercial mentality shaped by state corporatism that has so damaged both the earth and human relationships around the globe" (Alfred, 1999: 114).

Glen Coulthard has recently delineated the dual basis for "the particular form of domination" he calls the *settler-colonial* relationship (2014: 6), combining Marx's analysis of colonization as primitive accumulation with Frantz Fanon's analysis of subjection in *Black Skin, White Masks* (1967). In concordance with Harvey and others, Coulthard sees this relationship as "structured into a relatively secure and sedimented set of hierarchical social relations that continue to facilitate the *dispossession* of Indigenous peoples of their lands and self-determining authority" (2014: 7). The subjective aspect of the settler-colonial relation is grounded in what Fanon called the production of "colonized subjects"—modes of desire, behaviour and thought that "commit the colonized to the types of practices and subject positions that are required for their continued domination" (Coulthard, 2014b: 16). Just as Fanon urged those struggling against colonialism to *turn away* from the colonial state and "find in their own *decolonial praxis* the source of their liberation" (Coulthard, 2014b: 48), Coulthard discerns and advocates an Indigenous resurgence, a self-transformative ethics of desubjectification directed not toward recognition by the state but "toward our own on-the-ground struggles of freedom" (2014b: 48). Given that the settler-colonial relationship has at its heart an ongoing process of dispossession,

> Indigenous struggles against capitalist imperialism are best understood as struggles oriented around the question of *land*—struggles not only *for* land but also deeply *informed* by what the land as a mode of reciprocal relationship...ought to teach us about living our

> lives in relation to one another and our surroundings in a respectful, nondominating and nonexploitative way (2014: 60).

Strategically, this means that "for Indigenous nations to live, capitalism must die"; but for the latter to occur, those opposing colonialism must construct Indigenous alternatives within broader relations of solidarity with movements struggling against "the imposed effects of globalized capitalism," including the labour, women's, GBLTQ$_2$S, environmental and anti-racist movements (2014: 173).

World-system and anti-systemic movements

Complementing recent Indigenous analyses is a tradition of work within world-system theory which brings the analysis of colonialism and imperialism into a global perspective, emphasizing the role of anti-systemic movements that have developed in resistance to system-induced privations (Arrighi et al., 1989). Based on the premise that "global structures are often essential in defining the arenas within which social conflicts and social movements unfold," this approach notes that

> a cohesive and coherent international economic system that transcends national boundaries has existed for several centuries. This system is comprised of a single economy and a global division of labor that incorporates numerous cultures and nation-states. This economic system is quintessentially capitalist in nature, and it organizes economic activities through the institutions of private property, the process of commodification, and the practice of exploitation. Although this form of economic organization is unitary and global, it nevertheless includes distinct economic zones that comprise the world system (Buechler, 2000: 64).

The "developed" zone of the system's core is distinct from, and interdependent with, the low-wage zone of the periphery, and between these a semi-periphery forms a hybrid zone. Although all zones are pierced by class and other social struggles, within the world-system the advanced-capitalist core is economically affluent, relatively stable and politically dominant. Its position is predicated on colonial and neo-colonial relations with the periphery (which in settler states like Canada include relations with the "colony within" (Watkins, 1977)).

Within HM, world-system analysis thus identifies another relation in historical and contemporary capitalism, the core/periphery division, and explores its implications for critical social movements. Among the research programs this approach has spawned, the Research Working Group on Waves of Antisystemic Movements has sought to uncover "clusters of movement activity on a world scale," from the 18th century into the 21st, within an analysis of transitions in the world-system (Martin, 2008b: 7). A striking finding from the 18th century "was the rise of attempts to defend the possibility of a life outside the clutches of capitalism"—particularly the emergence, in the Americas and Asia, "of new communities and states" from anti-colonial struggles "against capitalist invaders" (Agartan, Choi & Huynh, 2008: 47). In this perspective, the recent trend toward global movement politics has a deep history, and "the present search for alternatives to communities organized by capital accumulation, accelerating commodification, and the national state demonstrates in part a broad return to the search for non-capitalist alternatives," which may be strongest outside core zones of the world-system (Martin, 2008a: 177). Indeed, survival of Indigenous communities is intrinsically anti-systemic, as it instantiates the right to live in ways not favoured by capitalism (Hall & Fenelon, 2005: 206).

Other contributions by world-system researchers include Chase-Dunn's analysis of how the structure of the world system produces within the semi-periphery a unique combination of motivation and opportunity, which undermines cross-class collaboration (as in welfare-state regimes of the North) yet provides "a fruitful terrain for strong challenges to capitalism" (2010: 53). Thus, from the Russian Revolution onward, the semi-periphery has been the zone where movements have mounted revolutionary challenges to capitalism and imperialism. Another systemic tendency, as global capitalism has extended its reach, has been "for social movements to develop and to focus attention on cross-sector organizing and transnational alliance-building"—as evidenced by initiatives like the World Social Forum (Smith & Wiest, 2012: 10).

System, lifeworld, democratization

The theme of *colonization and resistance*, salient in Indigenous and world-system perspectives, also holds a central place in the reconstruction of historical materialism Jürgen Habermas produced in the 1970s and 1980s.[8] For Habermas, however, colonization is a process internal to advanced capitalism itself, deepening the intrusion of the capitalist *system* (including its hierarchical state) into the *lifeworld* that vitalizes meaningful human existence and ultimately offers the basis for a democratic way of life. He holds that the formation of capitalism and of modern states, initially in Europe and tendentially (through colonization and imperialism) throughout the world, brought an "uncoupling" of system from lifeworld, with the former becoming detached from the lifeworld practices of communicatively shared experience, and organized around the instrumental logic of money and power. In the 20th century, as monopoly capitalism and its culture industries arose, the system cumulatively colonized the lifeworld, bringing its system-rationality of commodification and bureaucratic regulation into both the private sphere of everyday life and the public sphere of political debate and opinion-formation. Within a reconstructed HM, the lifeworld/system relation becomes a third architectonic feature of late capitalism structuring the field of movement praxis, distinct from capital/labour and core/periphery relations.

Habermas recognizes certain gains in the development of complex, rationalized systems, including markets, science/engineering and administrative/professional practices that enable action to be coordinated across vast expanses of space and time. His is a vision of emancipation through *lifeworld decolonization*: "the expansion of democratic social control over markets and bureaucracies through extended public spheres, combined with a critical attitude towards the normative bases of authority" (Ray, 1993: viii). Such decolonization (for which critical social movements are key agents) is feasible precisely within a parallel process of lifeworld rationalization Habermas discerns in the making of global modernity.[9] Within this variegated learning process the lifeworld has been partially transformed from a sphere of meaning

8 Habermas's theory is highly complex; here I appropriate only a few elements of it that are immediately germane to a historical materialist analysis of contemporary movements.

9 Although Habermas has sometimes been accused of Eurocentrism, his thesis of lifeworld rationalization, while based in the first instance in reflections on the European Enlightenment, is more broadly applicable. For a defence of this perspective against charges of Eurocentrism see Morrow (2013).

and identity based upon unexamined conventions and identifications to an increasingly post-conventional discursive formation, open to critical reason through dialogue and deliberation—that is, "communicative rationality." A rationalized lifeworld entails a distinctive ethics based not upon hierarchical authority (including nationalist and ethno-religious loyalties) but upon self-reflexive subjects able to take the standpoint of others, aware of the relativity of personal values, and committed in their interactions and collaborations to finding ways forward through open discussion of issues. It is precisely these practices and sensibilities that furnish the basis for a democratic way of life, as distinct from today's degraded liberal-democratic institutions that have been colonized by corporate (including corporate-media) and bureaucratic power. Like Marx, Habermas argues that the possibilities for emancipation are immanent in modernity itself, but instead of a revolutionary proletariat Habermas emphasizes the cumulative potential for releasing cognitive and moral learning processes within an increasingly rationalized lifeworld. "The task for Critical Theory, then, is to locate those social movements which are potential carriers of new learning potentials, which offer the capacity for widening the scope for a critical politics whilst defending endangered ways of life against systemic encroachment" (ibid.).

Habermas's perspective enriches HM by emphasizing that in making history, people develop not only technical capacities to transform the physical world (as in the classic concept of forces of production), but cognitive-moral capacities necessary to "those normative practices and moral relationships within which reasoned agreement *as a way of life* can flourish" (Benhabib, 1990: 346). In his initial formulation, Habermas emphasized the role NSMs play at the "seam" between system and lifeworld, defending the latter from further colonization by the former. But beyond defending particular features of the lifeworld (e.g. local community) from further colonization by money and bureaucratic power, movements may take the offensive, in *attempting to extend the field of action for communicative reason*—to transform hierarchical and instrumentalized social relations in the direction of communicative rationality, and thereby to democratize society while challenging the power of capital, the state and nondemocratic survivals of precapitalist formations (such as traditional patriarchies) in human relations.

For Habermas, offensive movement politics strives to "conquer new territory" for equality, justice and communicative rationality. Although feminism is the example he cites, Ray (1993: 63) points out that the defensive/offensive distinction does not refer to whole movements but to specific tendencies; thus "collective action may occupy a broad continuum, from defensive neo-conservative protests to campaigns that expand fluid, post-conventional identities." Within ecological politics, for instance, wilderness preservation is a defensive movement, but climate justice is offensive as it struggles to win new space for democratic praxis.

The major weaknesses in Habermas have been noted by Ray (1993), who goes on to advance a more adequate formulation. First, Habermas trains his analysis on the nation-states of Europe and North America. Yet as we have seen, capitalism and states comprise a *world*-system, and likewise, networks of communicative action (including social movements themselves) often cross national borders (Smith & Wiest, 2012; Carroll, 2016). Second, in asserting that NSMs are primarily concerned with symbols and identity, Habermas veers toward a cultural reductionism not unlike Melucci's (Ray, 1993: 177). Conversely, the demands of "offensive" movement currents represent more than a "border dispute" between system and lifeworld. In pressing for social action based on inclusive, communicative reason rather than money and power they point to structural transformation of the system itself (ibid.). Contemporary examples of such offensive praxis include "solidarity economies" and "decentralized participatory planning." The former refer to "self-management, collective ownership and bottom-up processes led by ordinary people," which create foundations for a new way of life built around "an ethos of reciprocity, redistribution and engaged citizenship" (Williams, 2014: 53-54). The latter, embracing a principle of subsidiarity[10] empowers citizens to "discuss and decide upon their priorities, elaborate, where possible, their own projects and carry them out if they are in the condition to do so without having to depend on superior levels" (Harnecker, 2014: 2). Such challenges to the dominance of system rationality, evident in

10 Namely, preferring local decision-making processes to disembeddded, extra-local ones, wherever feasible, but recognizing the need for extra-local coordination.

countries of the Latin American pink tide as well as in the Indian province of Kerala, reclaim space for lifeworld-based communicative action, embodying practices of prefiguration that are expansive rather than self-limiting, as in localist projects (Sharzer, 2012).

With regard to the charge of cultural reductionism, Nancy Fraser (2013) argues that Habermas neglects the persistence of gendered power in both lifeworld and system. She insists that the household, central within the lifeworld's private sphere, is a site of labour, not simply acculturation, and that the system/lifeworld relation has been deeply gendered, with men cast in the public roles of workers and citizens and women relegated to private roles as consumers/homemakers—reinforcing a patriarchal order against which feminism has struggled (2013: 13-52). In turn, social-reproduction feminists have registered limits in both Habermas and Fraser: their entrapment in a social-democratic perspective focused more on the terms of the "border dispute" than on the possibilities for radical transformation of both system and lifeworld. If labour is conceptualized as creative agency (whether in alienated or unalienated form) "through which we reproduce and change our social relations" (Ferguson, 2008: 49-50), and if we recognize those very social relations as extending extra-locally as a world-system or capitalist totality (Bakker & Gill, 2003: 17), then the struggle over historicity becomes discernible as a multiform process of reproduction/transformation—in class/gender/racialized relations, in core/periphery, in system/lifeworld. The analytical gain is that "real and systemic connections between the endlessly varied struggles of the oppressed become apparent, between, for instance, a childcare worker strike in Vancouver, the struggle to protect schooling for girls in Kabul and the environmental movement against mega-dams along India's River Narmada" (Ferguson, 2008: 55). These considerations propel us toward a broadly neo-Gramscian analysis of critical social movements and transformative politics.

Hegemony and counter-hegemony

Like Habermasian theory, neo-Gramscian analysis carries forward the project of *critical theory*, combining an analytical project of interpreting the world with a normative interest in its emancipatory transformation. Just as for Habermas communicative rationality is an ever-present possibility (even if colonizing processes of capital accumulation and bureaucratic power systemically repress it), within a neo-Gramscian vision counter-hegemony[11] is less an *explanatory construct* than it is a *normative guide* for constructing lines of collective action. Both approaches combine socio-political assessment of power/resistance with normative-strategic commentary on the possibilities for transforming resistance in the direction of emancipatory outcomes. But if both Habermasian and neo-Gramscian perspectives share a concern with not only analyzing the social world but consciously participating in its emancipatory transformation, they differ in other respects. Whereas Habermas's theory turns on his dual conception of *rationalization* (of system and lifeworld), neo-Gramscian thought emphasizes the duality of hegemony.

On the one hand, in modern capitalist democracies "formal freedoms and electoral rights exist alongside the class inequalities of the bourgeois state; therefore relations of domination need to be sustained with the consent of the dominated" (Carroll & Ratner, 1994: 5). Hegemony in this first sense refers to the practices, cultural codes and social relations through which that consent is organized and the "system" stabilized. The bourgeoisie does not rule directly and singularly but participates as a *leading* social force in an ensemble of alliances with other groups, including intellectuals such as liberal economists and journalists who articulate perspectives that are consonant with the interests of capital. This ensemble of alliances constitutes a *hegemonic bloc*[12] that governs as a movement-from-above by presenting its interests as universal while selectively dispensing material concessions to pre-empt effective opposition from below.

11 It should be noted that Gramsci himself did not employ the term counter-hegemony but viewed the epochal conflict between capital and labour as a struggle for hegemony, i.e., for decisive leadership within state, civil society and economy. Contemporary neo-Gramscians have employed the term "counter-hegemony" to refer to both the opposition to established apparatuses and practices of domination and the advocacy and construction of emancipatory alternatives. For an account of Gramsci's perspective see Thomas (2008); for a discussion of contemporary approaches to hegemony, counter-hegemony and anti-hegemony see Carroll (2006).

12 On the use of this concept in the analysis of political-economic structures and transformative movements see especially Cox (1987: 298-391).

In this way, a "general interest" or collective identity is constructed that unites dominant and subordinate alike as members of the same political community. Hegemony is never merely or even primarily a matter of state control. In neo-Gramscian analysis, *power is both concentrated in the state and dispersed throughout the organizations of civil society* such as the school, the church, the family, and other agencies of socialization which diffuse hegemonic world views into daily life (ibid.: 6). To the extent that this prevailing consciousness is widely internalized as reflecting the natural order of things it becomes part of "common sense." Where hegemony gains this kind of self-evident validity it fulfills a role that direct coercion can never perform: it mystifies power relations and public issues; it encourages a sense of fatalism and passivity toward political action; it justifies all manner of system-serving sacrifice and deprivation.

Under contemporary postmodern conditions, as culture becomes "in effect, coextensive with the economy" (Anderson, 1998: 55), popular consent is secured less through formation of a cultural consensus and more through distraction and fragmentation: a popular-cultural fascination with spectacular superficiality distracts people from envisaging a transformative project for an alternative future while the proliferation of diverse subcultural discourses disable subaltern groups from understanding each other and constructing solidarities (Tetzlaff, 1991: 29-30). Concomitantly, experiences of precarity and injustice can be co-opted into right-wing populist codes, as in anti-immigrant othering and the demonizing of environmentalists as "disloyal" to the (extractivist) state. In these and other ways, hegemony works "to induce the oppressed to accept or 'consent' to their own exploitation and daily misery" (Boggs, 1976: 40).

Hegemony in this top-down sense, however, captures only part of the complex political and cultural realities of contemporary life. People's lives are permeated not only by hegemonic practices and movements-from-above that legitimate the prevailing order, but also by acts of subversion and resistance that amount to a continuing guerrilla warfare. By maintaining a sense of the oppositional—of the "we" who are not "them"—popular-cultural resistances form "a necessary precondition, if not a necessary cause, of populist radical movements" (Fiske, 1989: 161). But were it the case that opposition remained fragmented and episodic one would have little reason to entertain the possibility of an alternative, *counter*-hegemony, with its hopeful prognosis for social and political transformation.

Here, Peter Thomas's typological efforts have purchase. In Gramsci, according to Thomas, the concept of hegemony makes "a contribution to the development of a prefigurative theory of a politics of another type of the subaltern social groups, intent upon forging their own conception of the world and founding their own new 'integral civilisation'" (2013: 25). The four moments in Thomas's typology comprise a "dialectical chain" based in the "non-unitary nature of hegemony, divided between 'bourgeois' and 'proletarian' practices of leadership that are substantively incommensurable" (26). Although it is the ruling class that, along with its organic intellectuals, occupies dominant positions, the possibilities for building a progressive hegemony, based in broad working-class political organization and agency, are always imminent:

> Gramsci's fully articulated concept of hegemony involves four integrally and dialectically related "moments": first, hegemony as social and political leadership; second, hegemony as a political project; third, the realization of this hegemonic project in the concrete institutions and organizational forms of a "hegemonic apparatus"; and fourth, ultimately and decisively, the social and political hegemony of the workers' movement. These four moments constitute a "dialectical chain" along which Gramsci deepens his researches throughout the *Prison Notebooks*; beginning from the "primordial fact" of hegemony as leadership, an immanent and expansive dynamic leads him to uncover the determinations of hegemonic political practice as the foundation for a new type of politics that could move beyond the forms of domination of political modernity (24-25).

For movements from below, the challenge is to develop forms of leadership that "help the masses to express, deepen and strengthen their self-engagement for socio-political transformation," enabling the leaders to learn from the masses "in an ongoing process in which the educators themselves are educated" (Thomas, 2013: 26). Such democratic and dialogical leadership facilitates the formation of an alternative political project through "an ongoing dialectical exchange and interchange between the existing political conjuncture and attempts to transform it," and even more crucially, between movement leaders and participants (27). Such a project gains traction within alternative hegemonic apparatuses dedicated to opening the way towards the abolition of oppressive and exploitative social relations. Given the totalizing power of capital as "the all-dominating economic power of bourgeois society" (Marx, 1857), a crucial element in counter-hegemonic movement is *dis*-alienation, a shift from labour as subaltern and in the service of capital, to labour as the leading creative force within an emerging post-capitalist way of life.[13]

Contemporary social movements testify to the continuing relevance of counter-hegemony as an orienting concept in social and political studies. As Cox and Nilsen note, movements often arise out of a *militant particularism*—a defensive, local struggle, which may become generalized across locales into a *movement campaign*, as in the campaign against genetically modified foods. Campaigns, however, do not take aim at "the generative mechanisms inherent to a social totality," which produce injustice and ecological maladies (2014: 82). However, if activists connect localized struggles, and "engage in a critical interrogation of the structures that engender the problems they seek to address" (ibid.), they may come to formulate a *social movement project*. As they address the social totality, such projects, such as La Via Campesina's project of food sovereignty,[14] move toward radical transformation:

> Social movement projects can be defined as *(a) challenges to the social totality which (b) aim to control the self-production of society and (c) have or are developing the potential for the kind of hegemony—leading the skilled activity of different social groups—that would make (b) and hence (a) possible* (Cox & Nilsen, 2014: 83).

13 The potential for this shift resides in the dual character of labour under capitalism, noted initially by Marx: on the one hand, the "activity that produces the master, that produces capital," on the other, "conscious life-activity," the basis for self-determination (Holloway, 2010: 89).

14 See http://www.viacampesina.org/en/index.php/organisation-mainmenu-44/what-is-la-via-campesina-mainmenu-45, accessed July 6, 2015.

My own research program—a neo-Gramscian exploration of social movements and counter-hegemony spanning four decades—can illustrate both the potential and the weaknesses of movement from below within the Canadian setting. Based initially in participant observation and intensive interviews with activists in Vancouver between 1983 and 2001, this research first traced the defensive responses of the labour and aligned social movements to a Thatcher-inspired neoliberalism that created a momentary basis of unity in the summer of 1983. Although the movement campaign that gathered under the identity of the Solidarity Coalition was able to mobilize great numbers of protesters from a wide range of critical social movements, it failed to define a counter-hegemonic project and to develop democratic, dialogical forms of leadership. The campaign reached an ignominious end when top labour leadership destroyed the campaign's conjunctural basis of unity by cutting a deal with the provincial government that betrayed human rights and other claims of the Coalition's constituency in exchange for retaining certain trade-union rights for public servants (Carroll & Ratner, 1989).

In subsequent research Bob Ratner and I discovered several tendencies germane to the issues of social movements and counter-hegemony. Our interviews with labour and other activists showed a concordance of perspectives and priorities rather than a divergence, with both groups keen to build cooperative relations across diverse movements (Carroll & Ratner, 1996). In other respects we noted strong commonalities and grounds for political cohesion across movements, where the theoretically prescribed differences between labour and NSM activists would have predicted otherwise. Most activists understood domination and injustice not as codes and discourse but in political-economic terms, as structural, systemic and materially grounded—enabling them to speak a common language in framing collective action. When we mapped out the network of cross-movement activism created by "cosmopolitans" active in multiple movements, we found that cosmopolitans understood injustice within a political-economic frame, and that movements in which political economy framing predominated—labour, peace, feminism and the urban/anti-poverty sector—tended to be tied to each other as well, forming a loose socio-political bloc. The network was carried by cosmopolitan activists with a political-economic understanding of injustice, implying that "wider participation fosters more holistic political views, leading to recognition of commonalities that cut across different movements, so that activists from diverse constituencies are better able to grasp the interconnectedness of resistance struggles" (Carroll & Ratner, 2010: 11).

Other case-study investigations highlighted the need for an ongoing war of position, to open space for "new spatio-temporal totalities" (Joseph, 2002: 218), thereby creating the conditions under which a democratic culture and new social order can emerge. Movement groups contribute to this process by carrying out three analytically distinct tasks: (1) *community building*, in the sense of elaborating collective identities and ethical-political frameworks that are oppositional to dominant conceptions; (2) *meeting needs* of constituents in ways that empower them and prefigure alternative ways of life; and (3) *mobilizing and engaging in collective action* to press for tangible changes in social relations and cultural discourses. The manner in which each group pursues these three tasks defines the horizons of its project (Carroll & Ratner, 2001: 605). Our analysis suggested that "a counter-hegemonic war of position requires a political synergy of aims and practices across the three task domains that constitute oppositional culture," enabling both "short-term material and assimilative gains" as well as "long-term disarticulation of systemic hegemony" (Carroll & Ratner, 2010: 14).[15]

Notwithstanding these counter-hegemonic potentialities, movements from below in Canada have for the most part been organized around militant particularisms, extending only occasionally to defensive movement campaigns (such as the Solidarity Coalition of 1983). Attempts to go beyond these, to propose counter-hegemonic social movement projects and to begin to establish counter-hegemonic apparatuses through which such projects might thrive, have not gained traction, although current efforts (such as the Green Economy

15 Since 2011 my research on counter-hegemony has inquired into the roles that alternative policy groups play in dialogue with critical social movements as centres of "cognitive praxis," building capacity for resistance and alternatives to neoliberal capitalism and in national (Carroll & Huxtable, 2014) and transnational (Carroll, 2015a, 2016) contexts.

Network, the Socialist project, the People's Social Forum and *Québec solidaire*) are not without promise.[16]

The task of building an alternative hegemony affords a useful comparison between neo-Gramscian HM and RMT. One major practical barrier to counter-hegemonic formation is the permanent *scarcity of resources* with which subaltern groups must cope, which as RMT emphasizes, leads each movement to priorize the immediate interests of its constituency. On this score, RMT is instructive in depicting relationships between social movement organizations as a *competition* for resources and strategic advantage (Zald & McCarthy, 1987). So long as interests are defined sectorally this dynamic will prevail, and cross-movement coalitions will tend to have an opportunistic, instrumental and fleeting character (Carroll & Ratner, 1989: 46). However, this state of affairs should not be reified as a sociological law. It is by consciously promoting broadly resonant counter-hegemonic discourses and practices—a shared counter-hegemonic project—that such competition can be significantly reduced if not overcome. Building an alternative hegemony thus implies a protracted "war of position" in which a coalition of oppositional movements wins space and constructs mutual solidarities in civil society, in the state and in workplaces, creating alternative hegemonic apparatuses capable of displacing the hegemony of the dominant class and its allies.

To take up a second comparison, the difference between Gramscian HM and the epochal perspective that currently resonates with many activists—new anarchism—turns on the analysis of the state. Anarchism holds to a narrow and rigid notion, not unlike some "orthodox" Marxist formulations, according to which the state appears as a coercive, oppressive force. However, for anarchists the strategic implication is not an instrumentalist "capture of state power" (as in certain readings of Marx) but an anti-statist refusal of power, an exodus, a "walking away" (Day, 2007). In contrast, the Gramscian concept of "integral state"—a complex ensemble of institutions of social reproduction entailing both coercion and consent, force and persuasion—depicts state and civil society as interpenetrating fields. The

16 See, respectively, http://www.greeneconomynet.ca, http://www.socialistproject.ca, http://www.peoplessocialforum.org, http://www.quebecsolidaire.net, accessed July 6, 2015.

strategic implication is that critical social movements need to "walk on both legs" (Carroll, 2006: 21), addressing both moments of the integral state and recognizing that "there is no exit from patriarchal capitalism and colonialism without a transformation of both state and society" (Carroll, 2015b: 4). The counter-hegemonic war of position implicit in this perspective is distinct from both pragmatic-reformist and epochal-interpretive paradigms—although it incorporates elements of these into an ongoing struggle to democratize all aspects of state and civil society through popular participation.

Key lessons

Integrating insights from our other two paradigms, a Gramscian historical materialism offers these five lessons for activists.

1. Given that exploitation and oppression are underpinned by organized forces that will resist transformative change, movements from below must, if they are to be effective, *address and ultimately defeat the sedimented power of movements from above*, as it traverses civil society, state and the capitalist economy.

2. Critical movements need, over time, to transform militant particularisms into alternative *counter-hegemonic projects* that contest historicity and that create structures prefiguring a socially just and ecologically healthy world—welding the present to the future, as Gramsci (1977: 65) put it.

3. Emancipatory politics advances simultaneously along several axes—class, ecology, gender/sexuality, race, (dis)ability—and involves struggles at different scales, from local to global. Activists need to fashion their initiatives on the basis of an analysis of how these intersect in a given conjuncture (cf. Doetsch-Kidder, 2012: 3): *how can the forces for emancipation be strengthened through widening and deepening relations of solidarity across differences?* Across conjunctures, the movement of movements needs to build a system of alliances that, through a war of position, wins space in civil society, the state and workplaces for emancipatory alternatives.

4. *Critical movements move against alienation* in its various modalities. They aspire to strengthen the "flow of doing" (Holloway, 2010) by transforming alienated work into creative agency within democratized relations of production (including cultural production and the (social re-)production of human beings). Given capital's central position as the great mediator, critical movements need to move toward eliminating the mediation that divides humanity against itself. The struggle for this is itself a production process, creating new people with new needs and capacities, capable of transforming their world.
5. Critical movements strive to *decolonize* lifeworlds from the logic of commodification, accumulation and statist hierarchy, to *reclaim commons* for communities (including Indigenous ones), to *democratize* the full scope of human relations within widening circles of participation and self-determination. This includes struggling against power vested in arbitrary traditionalism (as in social conservatism and religious fundamentalism), as well as placing the cognitive advances from system rationalization (science, engineering, etc.) at the service of human development and ecological health.

What Follows

The following chapters convey a diversity of perspectives from which we can understand social movements and the politics of counter-hegemony in Canada today. Although our contributing authors occasionally address social movement theory directly, they draw upon many disciplines and formulations, from political economy, political ecology, historiography and political philosophy to feminist theory, Indigenous thought, media studies and other relevant frameworks of knowledge.

Six essays grouped immediately below this Introduction survey the changing landscape of dissent and explore the implications for our understanding of movements as a diverse category of praxis. Chapters collected into Part 2 focus on specific histories, practices, discourses, strategies and forms of organization that comprise key contemporary movements. Given the importance of counter-hegemony for movements as agencies of socio-political transformation, Part 3 features four essays probing the challenges and possibilities for solidarity across contexts of collective action.

In the discussions that immediately follow this Introduction, some of the most pressing issues bearing upon contemporary movements are explored. Barry Adam provides a wide-angle view of the contingent relations linking social inequities, through movement activism, to social change. He argues that emergent tendencies are inconsistent not only with classic left analyses of working-class mobilization and cumulative socialist transformation but with such NSM analyses as Melucci's positing of a shift from political-economic to culturally oriented movements. Adam notes the epochal significance of neoliberalism as a paradigm of globalizing capitalism, whose injustices have in recent years inspired a host of popular movements that have attracted younger generations, from Latin America's pink tide and the Arab Spring to Occupy and the movement-parties of southern Europe—all of which take up political-economic issues at their core. For Adam, the analytic challenge is to explore how political-economic conditions and the "subjectivity of subordination" interact within movements that often carry a collective impulse toward democratic inclusion, and to discover effective strategies for disrupting the hegemonic projects that sustain domination.

David McNally's detailed account of the global crisis of 2008 and its aftermath in the so-called "new austerity" takes up the political-economy thread, and ties it to the subjectivity of subordination with the observation that one of neoliberalism's greatest accomplishments is a cultural transformation whose signature is the self-reliant, competitive individual— a bulwark in the further neoliberalization of society and a barrier to movement mobilization. Although the success of this movement-from-above in inaugurating an age of austerity has provoked resistance, the opposition has been unable to transit from militant-particular moment to durable movement. What remains to be seen, McNally concludes, is whether the protests to come will, through the work of organizing and learning, create forms of struggle conducive to an exit from both austerity and capitalism.

Laurie Adkin, viewing dissent's changing landscape through the lens of political ecology, discerns three global transformations that have reshaped the conditions and relations of struggle in Canada and elsewhere. Neoliberal globalization has shifted the balance of power away from communities and workers, toward transnational capital. Deepening environmental crisis, tied especially to the long-range impact of fossil capitalism, has crystalized in the existential threat of catastrophic climate change. These challenges have led movements to connect the dots across previously siloed issues and to strive for stronger alliances; and new framings such as "climate justice" signal a third, hopeful transformation, within movements themselves. Taking us well beyond the wilderness-preservation framings of earlier environmentalism, political ecology is now integral to a counter-hegemonic agenda as it provides a basis for building coalitions across movements (including labour), for negotiating transnational plans and transitions, and for creating new institutions.

Warren Magnusson also ponders the changes wrought by globalization, but links them to the metatheoretical issue of the political. His essay reminds us that distinctions we take as foundational—between the political and the social, between social order and social movements—are no more than scientifically ratified sedimentations from earlier struggles. Magnusson invites us to think of our world not in terms of fixed categories—as in the state as the container for "the political"—but as a multiplicity of movements, all of them political in the Aristotelian sense of seeking to establish or maintain distinctive ways of life. Movements move in relation to each other, thereby creating their own spaces in ways that often transcend the reified boundaries of modern politics. Ultimately, Magnusson's plea is for a critical theory that can guide political judgment in an era of new challenges and opportunities raised by the global city and the decentred state.

Lesley Wood and Craig Fortier pull us back to the problem of the state, and specifically the repression of dissent and militarization of protest policing. Rather than reify the state, they historicize it, as a formation that in Canada emerged through settler colonialism and extractivism, elaborating layers of repressive authorities to pacify oppositional forces. Although the post-1945 social accord brought an emphasis on liaison policing, with subsequent neoliberalization a new policing strategy of *strategic incapacitation* arose, directed against protests that appear to pose a risk of disruption to the smooth functioning of institutions. Along with deployment of militarized technologies of repression, construction of an integrated national security infrastructure and the legislated blurring of distinctions between protest and terrorism, these developments have shrunk the space for dissent while relations between state, surveillance, security and economy have deepened. In the circumstances, critical movements need to challenge the repressive authorities that are criminalizing dissent and militarizing policing.

Finally, in considering how the transformative aspirations that live within activist enclaves can be articulated with the wider working class whose mobilization is necessary to realize those aspirations, Stephen D'Arcy homes in on a discursive shift in recent decades, from New Left to post-New Left, in how injustice is understood and opposed. Many contemporary activists in North America view the world and their own agency through a lens that trades keywords like "oppression," "exploitation," "solidarity," "the people" and "liberation" for (respectively) "privilege," "classism," "positionality," "folks" and "safe spaces." Underpinning the differences in vocabulary are significant shifts in political vision and strategy (from ultimate liberation to everyday resistance, from system dynamics to interpersonal dynamics and from a politics of commonality to one of difference), offering both gains and losses for the Left. Activists intent on building bridges into broad publics need to reflect on those gains and losses, to resist the temptation to over-identify with either vocabulary and to redouble efforts to break out of the Left's longstanding marginality.

The seven case studies in Part 2 explore the strategies and practices movements adopt within specific relations of struggle. For Xavier Lafrance and Alan Sears, Québec's remarkably successful student strike, the "Maple Spring" of 2012, illustrates the importance of rebuilding the Left's infrastructure of dissent from its current weakened state. This infrastructure includes the manifold practices that enable people to forge collectivity grounded in solidarity, including a shared analysis and a collective memory that opposes hegemonic narratives. In the 1960s, influenced by a rising labour movement, Québec student activists adopted a syndicalist perspective and framed their identities as young intellectual workers. This opened up the language and strategies of student *union*, *strike* and active *solidarity*. The infrastructure that took root underwrote collective actions across the decades, which in turn vivified the infrastructure, building popular capacity to become one of the most dynamic and democratic social movements in North America. There are lessons in this sustained mobilization for student activists elsewhere and indeed for activists in other sectors.

Elaine Coburn and Cliff (Kam'ayaam/Chachim'multhnii) Atleo's account of Indigenous resistance and resurgence notes the remarkable tenacity of Aboriginal communities in sustaining infrastructures of dissent over centuries of dispossession and colonization. Coburn and Atleo highlight recent efforts to oppose colonial capitalism and to promote alternatives by reinventing diverse Indigenous ways of being, knowing and doing. Resistance/resurgence occurs at many sites and scales—at direct actions around dispossession and land claims (often in complex alliances with kindred movements), within Indigenous Studies academic programs, in cultural and artistic production, in the courageous hunger strike of Chief Theresa Spence (December 2012-January 2013) which inspired many activists in the ongoing Idle No More movement, and so on. Indigenous communities are of course crucial infrastructures of dissent but they are also sites of struggle between on the one hand a heartless vision of neoliberal capitalism, now advocated by some Aboriginal leaders as a pragmatic exit route from immiseration, and on the other hand a dis-alienated, Indigenous vision in which relationality, solidarity and respect apply both to human relations and to relations between humanity and the rest of nature.

If Québec's "Maple Spring" offers an exemplar of collectivity grounded in solidarity, the disability movement, explored by Pamela Moss, Michael Prince, Beth De Volder and Catriona Johnson, presents an especially variegated politics, grounded in the particularity of individual bodies yet ultimately united against ableism. This diversity recommends a granular analytic strategy, to illuminate the specific contexts in which power/knowledge configurations shape the meaning and experience of disability, the conditions of marginalization and oppression as well as the forms that resistance take. Vignettes describing four such contexts—contested illness, veterans' rights, compulsory heroism and politicized parenting—reveal a jagged, prickly politics whose diverse ends necessitate multiple organizing strategies. Amid the differences, the hegemony of biomedical knowledge and power relations figures significantly, offering both a basis for individual claims to resources and a target for counter-hegemonic challenges to prevailing beliefs about bodies, difference and deviance, as disability activists struggle against stigma, discrimination and exclusion.

Gary Kinsman's analysis of the long journey from counter-hegemonic queer resistance in the 1980s to the contemporary quest for respectability *within* neoliberal hegemony presents a particularly sharp contrast with Québec's student movement. In exploring the ascent of the neoliberal queer, Kinsman takes up the problematic of how "the world we won" turns out not to be "the world we were fighting for." His research extends to: (1) the adoption, in the aftermath of the early-1980s resistance to sexual policing, of a minority-group injustice frame that glossed class differences, allowing a gay class project to become hegemonized as "*the* 'gay' political project"; (2) the rise of a neoliberalism, detached from moral conservatism, in which a new white middle-class gay stratum could become invested; (3) hegemonic management of AIDS activism, which steered it away from direct action and into professionalized, bureaucratic venues; and (4) the shift, after the enactment of the 1982 Canadian Charter of Rights and Freedoms, to a legalistic strategy of Charter challenges which narrowed the movement's vision to a "settler homonationalism" identified with the existing Canadian state—as in acceptance of the social form of "spouse" as a normalizing template. Kinsman's chapter, linking historical analysis to the contemporary scene, shows how, within an archetypal NSM, class formation has powerfully shaped movement strategies, practices and visions—including what counts as "success."

In James Rowe, Jessica Dempsey and Peter Gibbs's analysis of the fossil-fuel divestment movement, we find a sanguine application of the Gramscian insight that ruling-class hegemony is only effective to the extent that ordinary people consent to the dominant project. As climate change becomes "a civilizational wake-up call" (Klein, 2014: 25), the carboniferous capitalism that has held sway since the Industrial Revolution becomes vulnerable to mass withdrawal of consent. Divestment thereby gains ground as a political strategy. Targeting as climate villain the fossil-fuel industry, divestment mobilizes culturally powerful institutional investors with arguments that combine the ethico-political (the ethics of profiting from wrecking the planet, the interests of future generations) with the economic (carbon resources as overvalued, stranded assets). Although any one divestment may not weaken the position of a fossil-fuel corporation (the divested shares are bought by other investors), as increasing numbers of universities and other public institutions divest, this weakens the social licence of the industry—its legitimacy within capital's hegemonic project. In concert with growing alliances against pipelines and extractivism, the divestment movement can also serve as a gateway into broader anti-capitalist and anti-colonial politics.

Divestment campaigns, while typically "local" in their focus on a given university or city government, ultimately articulate with the circuits of transnational capital. By the same token, Mark Stoddart, Jillian Smith and David Tindall's analysis of protest and media coverage at the 2009 Copenhagen COP15 Climate Summit shows how environmental movements used a global arena as a protest venue to convey their claims, via mainstream media, to more local publics in Canada. By drawing international attention to the Harper government's pathetic foot-dragging on climate change, activists created a "boomerang effect," as international shaming of Canada questioned the legitimacy of local state policy and the fossil-fuel sector. Still, there are limits to this approach. The environmental groups that get media play are the big, professionalized ones whose political frames are congruent with hegemonic discourses of ecological modernization and "Mainstream Sustainability." More radical challenges are left to the side, in a process that blames laggard regimes such as Canada's while reinforcing the hegemonic project of "green capitalism" (Goodman & Salleh, 2013). Ultimately, Stoddart and his colleagues suggest that climate activism needs to move beyond blame games that reduce political complexity to the calling-out of "climate villains." They recommend a multi-scalar approach, a "localized cosmopolitanism" balanced between transnational initiatives and more sub-national and community-based praxis.

Next, Harsha Walia revisits the question of the state and counter-hegemony, while pointing ahead to the theme of solidarity which is explored further in Part 3 of this volume. Recounting the rich record of migrant-justice activism within No One is Illegal (NOII), and reflecting on her own experiences as an activist within that movement,

Walia shows how NOII's praxis extends from a focal point in migrant justice, to contest "the systemic structuring of global displacement and migration through and in collusion with capitalism, colonial empire, state building and hierarchies of oppression" (Walia, 2013: 8). In the process, NOII breaks out of single-issue politics and contributes to anti-capitalist, Indigenous solidarity, feminist, Palestinian self-determination and workers movements. Its practical emphasis on empowering organizers from racialized and immigrant backgrounds has made NOII an important school for the development of organic intellectuals and leaders in a key sector of social-justice politics, whose salience will likely increase as transnational accumulation, militarized conflict and ecological crisis create more refugees and migrants. The five overlapping forms of praxis that Walia discerns within NOII, ranging from community organizing and direct support work through strenthening anti-capitalist resistance and building long-term alliances with Indigenous communities, offer indispensable insights to activists across a wide range of struggles.

Chapters in our third section focus a critical eye on the issue of solidarities across national borders, social positionalities and identities—a matter of signal import in the politics of counter-hegemony. In his critique of calls for global unions, the universalization of labour standards and transnational collective bargaining, Sam Gindin brings a pragmatic perspective into play. Such initiatives depend in the first place on vibrant labour movements within each national space, mobilizing strong class capacities vis-à-vis capital and states. Paradoxically (though consistent with a well-known phrase in the *Communist Manifesto*), international solidarity requires national foundations. Without strong working-class cultures and movements challenging neoliberal individualism and injustice and pushing for democratic alternatives within national spaces, internationalism gets reduced to slogans and cheerleading. This is not to downplay specific efforts at international solidarity, in opposition to imperialist aggression or in support of progressive struggles abroad, which in Gindin's view should be maintained and expanded. The labour Left needs to build a national movement with internationalist sensibilities, open to participation and learning at the international level, but focused on developing capacities domestically.

Matthew Corbeil and Jordan House also address the issue of solidarity and the future of labour, but their focus is more localized. Pointing to the ways in which actually existing unionism is constrained within the hegemonic structure of industrial relations, they see a requirement in labour movement renewal for creative agency that reaches beyond that system. Solidarity networks provide an exemplar. Using direct action casework as a singular strategy, they conduct focused campaigns against wage theft, unpaid overtime and other indignities. Besides empowering unorganized workers, such campaigns serve as a "crash course in class," developing new organic intellectuals for labour. Yet solidarity networks seem unable to scale up to deal with structural issues, and they show a weak capacity to sustain themselves over time. Even so, the principles informing solidarity networks and the practices that thrive within them need to be adopted by unions as part of a renewal of labour militancy and a rebuilding of an anti-capitalist Left.

Michael Bueckert's interrogation of the horizontalist practice of solidarity within the Occupy movement of 2011-12 offers a similarly critical reading of a signature practice within new anarchism. Horizontal solidarity rejects leadership and representation as statist authoritarian practices, and advocates a solidarity that places individual autonomy at its centre—as in Occupy's participatory practices of leaderless, consensus decision-making. Yet the absolute commitment to individualism is at odds with collective struggle, while the rejection of leadership obscures the reality of divisions between core activists and others. Bueckert argues that the forced choice between horizontal and vertical modes of organizing is unproductive, since "vertical" structures and representation are crucial in strengthening solidarity through building infrastructures of dissent, enabling political interventions that express a responsibility to those not immediately present and participating. In an inequitable world that limits participation for many subalterns, purely horizontalist politics ends up perpetuating inequity rather than eroding it. If they are to foster counter-hegemonic solidarity beyond direct participants, contemporary movements must incorporate forms of leadership and representation that, as Gramsci (1971: 144) suggested, create conditions that erode the very division between "rulers and ruled."

Finally, Jacinthe Michaud explores the complex solidarities that inhere in the intersectional "double activism" through which many feminists have attempted to create a synergistic counter-hegemony by crossing movement boundaries. Two moments of synergy between feminism and the Left in Québec—that of the early 1970s and that of 2012's "Maple Spring"—highlight tensions and dilemmas, as in feminist autonomy versus absorption into a gender-blind Left, and collaboration with state institutions versus disengagement. For feminists committed to double activism, the challenge has been to integrate both sides—to become political subjects according to their own rules, maintaining a practical autonomy from both masculinist hegemony and feminist-separatist orthodoxy. Michaud's analysis challenges activists to exceed the boundaries of siloed movements—feminist, environmentalist, queer, Indigenous and so on. But it also suggests that building solidarities that cross differences—so integral to counter-hegemonic politics—will remain a daunting project.

Taking stock of the entire gamut of essays collected here, we find a wide range of perspectives on the politics of counter-hegemony, holding both affinities and tensions. The *specificity* of different political issues and grievances (and associated strategies and practices) is evident throughout, but nowhere more acutely than in Moss and her colleagues' analysis of the "dissenting bodies" that comprise the disparate politics of disability. Although the diverse currents of these politics "crave social justice in specific ways" (p. 197), there is still the prospect of cross-disability opposition to the hegemony of ableism. In a similar vein, Coburn and Atleo insist that Indigenous politics comprise "not just another social movement," and emphasize the movement's internal diversity. Walia's examination of migrant activism explores the struggle against racism and the legacy of colonialism from a different yet entirely complementary angle. These essays and others, such as Kinsman's, focus on struggles that have often been grouped, as NSMs, under the cultural politics of identity/difference, but our authors interrogate the material conditions—institutional and political-economic—under which these movements move, and the specific challenges they raise not only to hegemony but to counter-hegemony as an inclusive, ethico-political project of solidarity.

Indeed, the politics of solidarity and alliance-building, so crucial to counter-hegemony and so challenging in practice, is explored not only in Part 3 but throughout this volume. For instance, Walia sees alliance-building as integral to NOII's wide-angle migrant activism, but similarly, Adkin tasks political ecology's organic intellectuals with building coalitions, new institutions and transitional plans while rooting "political discourse in shared values and a common agenda of democratic reforms" (p. 110). Rowe, Dempsey and Gibbs speculate that the divestment movement targeting Big Carbon might forge solidarities with other divestment movements, such as the Boycott/Divest/Sanction movement against Israeli apartheid, opening a prefigurative vision of democratic control over public wealth. In Lafrance and Sears's account of the Québec student movement, a syndicalist framing of students as "intellectual workers" created a bridge to labour activism and to broader anti-capitalist politics. D'Arcy's discussion of the Left's two vocabularies—the New and the post-New—foregrounds the need for activists to construct solidaristic bridges across these dialects, and out of insular enclaves.

Insights from the resource-mobilization paradigm get reworked in several of the chapters that follow. Lafrance and Sears's core concept, the infrastructure of dissent, resonates with both RMT and Gramscian analysis as it calls attention to the combination of organizational and cultural resources that enables collectivity to be forged and sustained over time, even across generations. Stoddart and his colleagues observe that in the mediatized politics surrounding climate summits it is the professionalized and better resourced environmental groups that gain media-derived authority, with the effect that their mainstream, ecological-modernization framing of the climate crisis predominates over more radical voices. Gindin's insistence that labour's renewal requires mobilization in national theatres of contention builds on the insight that within global capitalism national states remain key players in labour's strategic interaction with capital. Although it differs with Gindin on many points, Corbeil and House's take on direct action casework and solidarity networks as an emergent strategy for labour also emphasizes the need for mobilization that is locally grounded and that contributes concretely to revitalizing the labour movement. Bueckert's critique of horizontalism in the Occupy movement deepens our understanding of how organizational forms of activism shape actual practices of mobilization and collective action, sometimes with unintended consequences. Horizontalism was meant to eliminate hierarchy, to maximize inclusion and thus to strengthen the movement, yet Bueckert concludes that it "made it impossible for [Occupy's] diverse constitutive elements to act in a collective manner" (p. 335).

At stake in the studies collected here is the struggle for what Magnusson calls political space, which includes responding effectively to state coercion and repression (the centrepiece of Wood and Fortier's chapter) while resisting co-optation and absorption into the hegemonic projects of neoliberalism, green capitalism, masculinist hegemony on the Left, etc. The struggle is not simply "out there" in the world of political economy, but within our inner worlds, over the "subjectivity of subordination." It is a struggle against subalternality—against the "normative violence of enforced sameness" which makes heroism compulsory for persons with disabilities (Moss et al., p. 203), underwrites the neoliberal queer and pressures all of us to embrace competitive individualism. Yet our studies show that this is also a struggle to win new space and to form new subjectivities, as witnessed most strikingly perhaps in an Indigenous resurgence that champions in practice a deeply relational ontology grounded in "interconnected, reciprocal and respectful relationships" (Coburn & Atleo, p. 191).

As Indigenous struggles are now at the forefront of movement praxis in Canada, it is not surprising that several of our chapters weave these struggles into the analyses. This indicates both a heightened consciousness of their relevance to counter-hegemony and an increased collective capacity of Indigenous communities and allies, as they confront various configurations of state and capitalist class power, to resist colonization as an ongoing process while enacting resurgence as a practical form of dis-alienation. These struggles in turn raise broader issues of global justice, linking decolonization, an urgent project for Indigenous peoples, to the more general decolonization of lifeworlds and dis-alienation of human and human-nature relations—which are prerequisite to a substantially democratic and ecologically healthful way of life.

Although our contributors range widely across the terrain of contemporary movement politics, our collective efforts unavoidably leave important areas of social struggle unexamined. Movements against imperialism, militarism, poverty and corporate domination of media—and groups such as the Council of Canadians and the Ontario Coalition Against Poverty[17]—exemplify a few of the silences. In focusing our case studies around struggles based in Canada we offer highly relevant analyses for Canadian activists, students and researchers. But we put to the side the many worlds of activism that thrive beyond Canada's national borders—worlds that are of increasing relevance to those who call Canada home. This volume's elisions testify to the richness of movement praxis, and to its open-ended character. I hope that the insights recorded here will be of value both in interpreting the significance of social movements in our troubled world and in suggesting liberatory pathways for remaking that world.

17 For case studies of these groups see, respectively, Coburn (2011) and Shantz (2002).

POLITICAL ECONOMY AND CULTURE IN MOBILIZING FOR CHANGE

Barry D. Adam

How are we to think analytically about collective subjectivity and social mobilization in the early 21st century? This is the latest version of a longstanding question of the modernist imagination: Is history something that just happens or can people take control of their own fate? In Marx's classic phrasing from the *Eighteenth Brumaire*, "Men make their own history, but they do not make it under conditions of their own choosing." The vision of the modern era has been to seek ways in which people might make history more as they please to benefit greater numbers of national populations. Whether Bentham's utilitarian rule of governance for the greatest happiness of the greatest number or Marx's principle from *Critique of the Gotha Program*, "From each according to his ability, to each according to his need," the modernist aspiration for greater equality and democracy has always carried with it the question of what the agent of history might be that could counteract the immense power and wealth of ruling elites.

The question taken up in this chapter is the more sociological take on this question which inquires into how social inequality may generate discontent, how discontent may lead to resistance and opposition, and how resistance may be translated into strategies that make social change. Marx set out a powerful and compelling scenario about how all this might have worked in the 19th century, when the rise of capitalist relations of production generated a social polarity between an owning class and a working class exploited for its own gain and advancement. That working class would be motivated to organize itself into a revolutionary force that could abolish the core exploitative relationship and divisions between social classes. Much of the Western Marxist tradition that followed in the 20th century dissected this formulation and opened up each step of the historical scenario to find out why history did not unfold in that way and to wonder again about how collective subjectivity and social mobilization could come about.

The complexity, ironies and deviations from the classic formulation of class mobilization turned out to be many. The European industrial working class envisioned in the 19th century proved to be only one of many forms of working or dispossessed classes generated in different capitalist formations throughout the world. How these various class formations act collectively in specific historical conditions turned out to be highly variable. Further questions arose concerning the various conditions that shape how people come to see themselves as sharing a common social location and come to identify themselves as a class. Culture and ideology played critical roles as lenses through which grievance and entitlement were conceived, goals were formulated and possibilities for change were perceived. Examination of revolutionary movements and social change showed how often people came to organize oppositional movements through multiple combinations of loyalties, identities and social perceptions affected by gender, ethnicity, nationality, region and religion, as much as (or more than) class identification.

Much of this work in the Western Marxist tradition occurred in Europe in the 20th century. In the United States, questions of social mobilization fell more often under the rubric of social movement analysis that looked at the multiple ways in which people develop mutual identification, shared identities, a sense of common fate and a will to mobilize together. Social movement analysis tended to leave behind any claim about social mobilization as a reflection of class or political economy, falling into rationalist or cultural constructions of movement formation. The rationalist view largely perceived social movements as variants of lobbies, that is, collections of self-interested individuals organized to advance their own benefit (Jasper, 2010). The question at hand was to figure out what resources they could acquire, and political opportunities they could take advantage of, in order to attain their goals. The cultural view tended to postulate gender, race and sexual identities as given and to view movements as expressions of a demand for "recognition" of cultural difference (Fraser, 1997). These views often grounded themselves in observations of new social movements of the second half of the 20th century (environmentalism, civil rights, feminism, gay liberation), seeing them as collective subjects largely unanchored in the political economy postulated by Marxism as the foundation for the grievances that would stimulate collective mobilization. As Margit Mayer (1991: 189-90) summed it up:

> European theories, still influenced by more or less explicit assumptions of a class structured society and logics of material (re)production, assume that each new reproductive stage produces and is challenged by social movements that articulate historically changing social cleavages, if not the older variety of class antagonisms. This European attitude contrasts sharply with the view of society as an unstructured ensemble of groups, of ruling classes as a relatively homogenous elite, of the state as structurally permeable or as institutionally biased against insurgency. These various elements of the American theoretical framework together produce the image of a static social arrangement that continually adapts, in the pluralist view, due to its permeability and openness or, in the social-democratic view, is only exceptionally perturbed.

The last decades of the 20th century and first of the 21st presented a new set of socio-historical circumstances that further eroded leading precepts about collective subjectivity and social mobilization. In this period, the fall of Soviet socialism in Europe made the possibility of a viable alternative to capitalism appear increasingly remote and left the idea of socialism deeply tainted by the example of undemocratic bureaucratic authoritarianism that had characterized Soviet Eastern Europe. At the same time, the conservative governments of the United States and the United Kingdom, at the behest of their corporate elites, pressed toward a neoliberal reordering of the political and economic order both at home and abroad through such international institutions as the International Monetary Fund and World Trade Organization (Arrighi, 1994; Harvey, 2005; Teeple, 1995). Samuel Bowles and Herbert Gintis (1987: 58-59) contend that the early postwar period of the 1950s and 1960s was founded on an implicit social contract among three key sectors (that they call the Keynesian compromise) consisting of:

- state economic regulation where state-supported demand impelled economic growth and profit, and regulated class conflict through trade union legislation,

- continued capitalist control of investment, and
- workers' ability to partake of the wealth generated by postwar growth through unionization; a social wage through the state provision of health, education and welfare; and the promise of individual (rather than collective) social mobility for their children, if not for themselves.

This system was maintained in the context of a Cold War imperium over the Global South.

The Keynesian compromise began to unravel in the 1970s. The Reagan and Thatcher governments, in particular, accelerated and promoted the shift toward neoliberalism, that aimed to pare back both the real and social wages of workers, managing social discontent by: (a) investing heavily in police and prisons at the expense of health, education, welfare and public transit; (b) propagating a neo-conservative ideology of lowered expectations, "family values" and individual responsibility; and (c) weakening workers' organizations by facilitating the easy worldwide transfer of capital to locations with comparatively quiescent and amenable populations (Adam, 2002). Along with neoliberal restructuring of states and economies has come a neo-hegemonic ideology that denies both collective subjectivity and social mobilization because, it contends, everyone either is or should be an autonomous, "free" individual in a marketplace of choices. The ideal neoliberal subject is the always already fully adult, rights-bearing, contract-making citizen and consumer presumed by liberal democracy and the capitalist marketplace, a subject propagated by business and government, circulating as the basic "common sense" of corporate mass media (Adam, 2005).

In these inauspicious historical circumstances the "new social movements" appeared, often as a "second wave" of movements that had precedents in the early 20th century. Though Jürgen Habermas (1987) characterized them largely as "defensive" movements to preserve community and the lifeworld from the predations of the state and corporate sectors, the new social movements have also sought to resist and reform the ways in which race, gender, sexuality and the environment have been taken up and reproduced in advanced capitalist societies (Adam, 1993; Cox, 2011: 68). Their arenas of action have not only been the workplace and the state, but also the social organization of family, education, communication media, religion and social service. They have faced formidable obstacles in challenging the neoliberal agenda by: (a) exposing and challenging the availability of environmental and social inputs taken for granted by capitalist production and expansion, (b) deconstructing the neoconservative disciplinary ideology of receiving less while working more, and (c) resisting right-wing populism rooted in the resentment of those whose social status has declined in neoliberal economies (Adam, 2002). They have also challenged how notions of Western individualism and the neoliberal subject in particular are constructed in opposition to typically nonwhite, colonized and disenfranchised others. These notions ignore how the autonomy of individuals depends a good deal on their social class status, and they presume ongoing patriarchal relations of female subordination. Certainly the new social movements have been far more than defensive agents searching for "recognition." Even gay, lesbian, bisexual and transgender (LGBT) movements, often held up as the iconic "cultural" movement for recognition (Fraser, 1997), supposedly unrelated to political economy, could never have come into existence if it were not for the profound reorganization of economy, kinship and urban mobility brought about by the capitalist world system (Adam, 2001). Nor can their demands for human rights legislation or marriage be deemed un-materialist as access to employment and legal guarantees of household economies have very real material consequences engaging questions of obligations to provide support, inheritance and so on (Adam, 1993; Butler, 1997). All the same, they have been "different" kinds of movements compared to labour movements, less interested in or less optimistic about acquiring state power, and often decentered or "rhizomatic" (Melucci, 1989) acting much more like episodic networks than the disciplined units imagined in the early 20th century. While all of these movements have had moments of envisioning profoundly reorganized societies of democratic participation and freedom, over time, their engagement with neoliberal states has tended to press them back into a human rights framework that recodes their objectives as "equal rights" contained by a liberal individualist system with little hope of overturning larger hierarchies of inequality.

Collective Mobilization in the Early 21st Century

More than three decades have now elapsed since the Reagan-Thatcher era and the claims and promises of the neoliberal agenda have been put to the test. Social inequality has not diminished; indeed a generation of Reaganomics, "trickle down" theory, and neoliberal policies have resulted in a sharp increase in inequality. Continuous tax reductions for the corporate sector have not resulted in economic growth, full employment or a "tide that lifts all boats." They have created accelerated wealth accumulation among the top 10%, and especially the top 1%, massive capitalization of the corporate sector, and increased concentration of corporate power as capital accumulation has fuelled corporate takeovers rather than investment in productive infrastructure (Brennan, 2015; Broadbent Institute, 2014). The 2008 financial crisis revealed the extent of the financialization of the economy, lack of investment in production, and the extent of rapaciousness and entitlement among ruling elites. Neoliberalism did successfully accomplish one goal by refashioning advanced industrial societies in the mould of the first "liberal" era of the late 19th century of unprecedented wealth concentrated in the fewest of hands. The nations of Europe, North America and Australia have been pressed in the direction of more extreme models of social inequality along the lines of India, Mexico or Brazil where some of the richest families on the planet live among vast impoverished populations. If there is anything to the original Marxian vision of the advance of capitalism exacerbating social fissures between exploiting and exploited classes and thus generating organized social opposition to increasing inequality, then one would think the socio-historical conditions are once again in place for social upheaval.

A decade and a half into the 21st century, there is a new array of popular mobilizations that appear to fall into approximately four broad camps:

- The nations of the *Alianza Bolivariana para los Pueblos de Nuestra América* (ALBA), consisting of five Latin American countries and six small English-language Caribbean island states, constitute a relatively mature alliance of nations where progressive, democratic coalitions of movement actors have succeeded in forming governments with the explicit aim of resisting neoliberal dictates and wresting power from traditional oligarchical families (Muhr, 2013; Rénique, 2009). In the core South American countries of Venezuela, Bolivia and Ecuador, labour organizations are but one sector of broad-based movement alliances of once-excluded populations of the "urban poor, the informal sector, religious communities, the indigenous, the Afro-descendent, and women" (Ellner, 2012: 106). Steve Ellner (2012: 97) identifies the common characteristics of these governments as having "an emphasis on social participation and incorporation over considerations of economic productivity, modifications of the Marxist notion of class, diversification of economic relations, preference for radical democracy over liberal democracy, and the celebration of national symbols." The Nicaraguan state, governed by the *Frente Sandinista para Liberación Nacional*, still owes allegiance to the original alliance of workers, peasants and intellectuals that first brought it to power in the 1979 revolution. (The election of a president in El Salvador in 2014 from the *Frente Farabundo Martí para la Liberación Nacional*, a very similar social formation, makes that country a potential candidate for ALBA.) Cuba, which also has membership in ALBA, might be considered a decaying state socialist system of the Soviet type in search of renewal. While willing to trace a lineage to the tradition of Latin American revolution and socialism, it is noteworthy that (with the exception of Cuba), the ALBA states seek to operate within liberal democratic electoral principles, have little adherence to socialist orthodoxies, but owe their existence to social mobilizations with democratizing impulses of the traditionally disenfranchised.

- The Arab Spring shook the kleptocratic dictatorships in the region beginning in 2011 in Tunisia. Manuel Castells (2012) argues that these uprisings against authoritarian and arbitrary rule were uniquely aided by access to the internet in societies with limited civil society organizations. While apparently most successful in Tunisia in establishing an electoral system, elsewhere the democratic impulse was suppressed, especially in Saudi Arabia, Bahrain and in the restored brutal dictatorship in Egypt, or it led to disintegrating states and warring factions in Syria, Yemen and Libya.

- In Canada and the United States, protest against the rule of the "one percent" took the form of anti-globalization demonstrations (especially from 1999 to 2001) outside free trade conferences that were intended to ease the free movement of capital but not of workers (Masquelier, 2013; Rowe & Carroll, 2014; Smith & Wiest, 2012). These anti- (or alter-) globalization movements have precedent in the Zapatista movement in southeastern Mexico which sought to defend Indigenous communities against the neoliberal policies of the Mexican government. The Occupy Wall Street demonstrations in North America followed on the aftermath of the 2008 financial crisis (Gitlin, 2013) which Lauren Langman (2013: 512-13) attributes directly to the "vast government bailout [that] pumped trillions of dollars into the insolvent banks and 'saved' the banking/financial system. The government rescue halted the plummet, saved the financial system and its elite prospered, yet ordinary people lost jobs, houses were foreclosed, people evicted, and many remain unemployed and/or underemployed." Sparked by a proposal by the Vancouver-based alternative magazine *Adbusters*, Occupy proved to be loosely organized, spontaneous and short-lived, but nevertheless influential in crystallizing the notion that far too much wealth and power had been taken by the "one percent" in each society. More recent Canadian manifestations of resistance to neoliberal policies and rule by the "one percent" have taken the form of the 2011-2012 Québec student movement (Bégin-Caouette & Jones, 2014) and the Indigenous people's Idle No More mobilization (Wotherspoon & Hansen, 2013).
- Also in the wake of the 2008 financial crisis and a wave of draconian austerity measures and job losses, a left populism has emerged in the form of Podemos in Spain and Syriza in Greece in European Union countries hardest hit by debt reduction policies, where they pose a challenge to old-Left socialist parties as well as mainstream liberal and conservative parties.

These contemporary mobilizations do show a link to the political economy of capitalism in its neoliberal form especially in attracting younger generations struggling to find a place in a tough labour market. They show a sense of betrayal with the implicit social contract that was to deliver a decent standard of living and a modicum of social mobility. Socialist or Marxist discourse may be one discursive strand woven into their demands and aspirations, but their overall trajectory is a loose assemblage for social inclusion and democratic participation in the face of the "one percent."

They also show that the constituencies most often identified with the new social movements are not inherently disengaged from state power. While the new social movements did demonstrate that social change could and should happen in social fields outside the state and distinguished themselves from earlier movements that presumed that social change was overwhelmingly a question of seizing state power and imposing change through instruments of the state, it is also clear that courts and legislatures were frequently social fields in which these movements worked and that, when the socio-historical circumstances were favourable, they became part of larger coalitions that transformed themselves into political parties and potentially new kinds of governments. Some of the earliest gains in LGBT civil rights, for example, came about when LGBT movements joined nationalist coalitions in Québec and Catalonia and became part of new governments. Similarly, Indigenous movements have been critical actors in broad-based alliances that succeeded in overturning the military kleptocracies that once ruled Bolivia.

Reconceptualizations

The linkages between social circumstances, subjectivity and mobilization still prove to be complex. Social researchers and theorists have moved forward on several fronts to make sense of the various ingredients that go into the processes and interactions that may lead to social change. The question of the subjectivity of subordination stands at the nexus of social circumstances and responses to them whether defeat, resignation, resilience, resistance or rebellion. Hegemonic powers and cultures have their effect in propagating discourses and pressing people into social locations where they may be confined to, and resigned to, their apparent fates at least for a time. The subjectivity of subordination requires "a phenomenology of everyday life which comprehends the choices made by people within the practical and material constraints of their subordination which, then, re-create or alter that subordination" (Adam, 1978: x). The experience of power, and the everyday knowledge and practices it generates, is a necessary piece for understanding how "governmentality" occurs well outside the direct purview of the state itself (Foucault, 1980). Sometimes that experience is of material deprivation, but it may also be about the depredation of life chances in various spheres of life.

People may find themselves caught in local contexts governed not only by the two great forces of advanced industrial societies, the state and corporate sectors, but by deprecatory attitudes, harassment and aggression by the people around them. These practices may link back to the larger political economy, especially in state and corporate exhortations to require individuals to take "responsibility" for their own well-being (Barry, Osborne & Rose, 1996) or they may take the form of local power mechanisms that intersect with, but do not necessarily originate in, political economy. Michael Omi and Howard Winant coined the useful notion of the "racial project" to talk about these processes. Pointing out that race is "an unstable and 'decentered' complex of social meanings constantly being transformed by political struggle," racial projects "connect what race *means* in a particular discursive practice and the ways in which both social structures and everyday experiences are racially *organized*, based upon that meaning" (Omi & Winant, 1994: 55-56). In racial projects, political economy and culture are mutually determining as they operate across societies in educational institutions, imagery in mass media, employment practices, housing access, mistreatment or violence in the streets and so on. "When categories become concretized in bodies, reproduced through social practices, solidified in buildings, and embedded in systems for the allocation of rewards and punishments, culture becomes both formidably powerful and, ironically, 'nearly invisible'" (Swidler, 2001: 19). The desire for social change, then, may arise on a variety of fronts and change requires identifying and disrupting the power mechanisms that operate in racial projects and in the many other projects defined by other social fault lines.

The analytic challenge is to show how political economy and culture act as different phases of a dynamic interaction that happens at the level of "racial projects" and in the world system. For Elizabeth Armstrong and Mary Bernstein (2008: 82) this means investigating "the shifting nature of domination (both material and cultural) in both governmental and nongovernmental institutions and collective efforts that arise in response to different types of domination" without privileging "economic and political disenfranchisement" as the only forms of disenfranchisement worth recognizing. Perhaps most fundamental is how people's consciousness, practices and sense of self-efficacy are constituted by an array of constraints and conditions such as: the life-chances available to them given their location in a social structure, the discursive systems circulating around them with which they make sense of their experiences, and the ways in which historical processes shift the whole array. The experience of subordination, be it material deprivation, violence or insult (Eribon, 2004), can arise in a wide range of circumstances, not least of which are those imposed by the major forces of contemporary societies, the state and capital. Even the new social movements, which have organized themselves around such social distinctions as gender, sexuality, race and disability, know well that oppressive practices are very often enmeshed in state and corporate power structures so that law and the workplace are necessarily fields of action in making social change. But the genius of these movements has been in understanding the many other social fields in which change must happen and that the cumulative effect of changes made in the governmentality of everyday life can exert irresistible pressure back on the state and corporate spheres. It is this multi-pronged, networked, decentred approach to change which frustrates radical visions of overturning and restructuring social systems but it is an approach evident in many of the latest manifestations of mobilization of the early 21st century as well.

From these multiple starting points can emerge a social constituency that has a sense of facing a shared set of discriminatory or exclusionary practices. The translation of these shared experiences to collective action runs through often lengthy socio-historical processes whereby people find sites to communicate with each other and develop some sense of commonality and thus community. Whether through 19th-century salons (Habermas, 1989), neighbourhoods and women's networks (Fraser, 1990), workplaces (Thompson, 1968), churches (McAdam, 1982) or gay bars (Weeks, 1981), much depends on the degree to which people are able to connect or are even allowed to connect. Out of these networks come writers, artists and community leaders who can begin to articulate ways of thinking that break with the orthodoxies of religion, authority or mainstream media (Cox, 2011; Gramsci, 1971). In these networks of thinking "against the grain" emerge the collective subjectivity that grounds everything from individual gestures of defiance to court suits, community institutions, alternative media and social movement organizations.

Certainly there is a wide range of possible forms of collective subjectivity that can come out of these processes and these different visions of subjectivity are reflected in different streams of social theory (Adam, 2005). Theorists like Anthony Giddens (1991), Ulrich Beck (1992) and Zygmunt Bauman (2000) tend to construct images of itinerant, uprooted, "disembedded" subjects struggling to orient themselves in social worlds without familiar signposts and facing risks at every turn. They are perhaps the clearest embodiment of neoliberal individualism: responsible for their own fate, not reliably connected to others and unlikely to think collectively. Habermas (1987), on the other hand, allows for networked community members defending their lifeworlds against the incursions of state and capital with environmentalism as the exemplary movement to spring from this social location. Third and more interesting for the analysis of social change are the emergent, newly connected identities in formation where a collective impulse toward democratic inclusion flows from communities seeking to overcome exclusion by race, gender and sexuality, but also certainly the various contemporary protest groups that push back against accelerating inequality embodied by the "one percent." Still, not all collective subjectivity and social mobilization takes a democratic or inclusive form. Social constituencies that feel their social status to be under threat and have a strong sense of entitlement to the privileges they already enjoy may indulge in a reactionary politics of resentment and repression as they lash out against "undeserving" minorities. Their historical form may be organized around a romanticism of a lost past, religious fundamentalism or authoritarianism.

Ultimately movements engaged in real political contests over time are shaped by the political opportunities and limitations that they encounter. They develop and change course through engagement and compromise with the powers that be and are pressed to take seriously the cultural frameworks of their opponents in order to make claims seen to be credible by power holders.

Conclusion

The linkages between political economy and collective subjectivity that may lead to social mobilization remain challenging both for social analysts and for strategists who seek to discover or foment a movement with the power to make social change. Theodor Adorno (1973: 17-18) argued that "the need to lend a voice to suffering is a condition for all truth." Suffering is an experience grounded in political economy but always mediated by an intersection of social statuses and by discourses circulating in local culture that define legitimate and shameful grievances, worthy and unworthy victimhood, entitlement and just desserts. While the state and capital are the primary power centres of advanced industrial societies, and as such exert tremendous control over who gets what, experiences of suffering may stem not only from deprivation but from derision, bullying, harassment, violence or social exclusion. In these arenas, the state and capital may play reinforcing or diminishing roles depending on how these social practices are taken into existing institutions. The challenge for social analysts is how these social forces hold together in "projects," whether racial or defined by other social fault lines. It is then a question of discovering what may be effective in disrupting these projects by finding points of leverage that may prove to be multiple and diverse.

The link between capitalism and its opposition has proven to be neither as direct nor sure as imagined by the early Marxists. Karl Polanyi's (1957) magisterial overview, *The Great Transformation,* posited that the destructive effect of market forces extending across whole societies must stimulate social and state responses to limit that destructiveness as fully marketized societies are too damaging and intolerable to be sustained. Yet neoliberal political economy has over time generated a culture where success comes to be defined by market rules, the good citizen is the "responsible" person who expects neither support nor protection from the collectivity, and in turn has limited need to contribute to a greater good. People prove themselves to be remarkably adaptable, and the demands of competitive individualism propagated by neoliberal culture come to be internalized by many and even incorporated into modern forms of masculinity. The generation of a subjectivity compatible with the current array of dominant forces goes far in damping dissent or resistance. Nevertheless, the benefits of capitalist and other intersecting systems of domination are always distributed unevenly with the very few benefitting enormously, many struggling not to fall behind and many more excluded, disciplined or contained. The social mobilizations of our era show the limits of neoliberalism as political economy and culture as it generates the pain that stimulates new opposition in the long run. Resistance and mobilization, in turn, do influence state and corporate practices, undermine racial and other projects, and enlarge the realms of human rights (Bowles & Gintis, 1987) even as states and corporations expand into new territories of computerized and electronic surveillance in the name of good marketing or fighting terrorism. The social fields in which social movements work have consolidated popular disapproval of, for example, sexual harassment, smoking, water pollution or police violence against black people, and they have prefigured new ways of living, like same-sex families. Labour union movements have secured not only better wages but social benefits from health care to pensions that benefit societies as a whole. Many of these changes have become part of the governmentality of societies and have ultimately found their way into law and jurisprudence as well. Major change that overturns entire systems of hierarchy has proven more elusive, even in the great revolutions of the modern era (Skocpol, 1979). Still, critical incidents and moments of duress or crisis, whether rooted in pressures exerted by the global economy (like the Greek debt crisis) or repressive incidents that capture public imagination (like the police attack and self-immolation of Mohamed Bouazizi in Tunisia) continue to galvanize and coalesce discontent into new collective identities and demands for democratization.

NEOLIBERALISM AND ITS DISCONTENTS
Austerity and Resistance in an Age of Crisis

David McNally

> The global financial crisis of the late 2000s...stands as the most serious global financial crisis since the Great Depression. The crisis has been a transformative moment in global economic history whose ultimate resolution will likely reshape politics and economics for at least a generation (Reinhart & Rogoff, 2009: 208).

"The world of the last three decades is gone," wrote the *Financial Times* in early 2009 (Financial Times, 2009). How right they were. More than six years later, the world economy remains mired on a sluggish track, earning "a barely passing grade" according to a major global report card (OECD, 2015). Worldwide unemployment is persistently high; insecurity and poverty are rampant; and deep cuts to social programs remain the order of the day, as austerity policies erode services and impoverish seniors, children, women, the unemployed and the working poor. Not surprisingly, all this has provoked widespread forms of resistance to neoliberalism and austerity. Understanding how and why the world changed in 2009, what drives austerity policies, and how they might be overturned are the central objectives of this chapter.

It is a basic rule of thumb in a capitalist society that economic "good times" lay the seeds of future disasters. The last great contraction took place in the 1970s, finally ending in 1982 (at the beginning of the neoliberal period). For the next 25 years (prior to 2008), the world economy underwent a sustained expansion. During this quarter-century long boom (1982-2007), China, arguably the preeminent case of so called *globalization*, became the new "workshop of the world," as foreign investment poured into its sweatshop zones. Riding outside investment, China was transformed into a major industrial power, even as rural poverty soared, sweatshop life damaged millions, and cities became hopelessly polluted. While China boomed, the American economy underwent a new "high-tech" revolution which saw computers entering factories, schools, stores and homes on an astonishing scale. A series of "emerging economies"—from Brazil to India—also entered new growth cycles, with millions leaving the land and entering wage-work. Meanwhile, across Europe, Japan, the United States and Canada property values soared, making many ordinary homeowners feel considerably wealthier (McNally, 2011a: 2). Then in 2007, after 25 years of dynamic growth, the currents of the world economy reversed, and boom sharply gave way to slump.[18]

The Crash of 2008-09

Like most crashes, this one gave off early warning signals which the mainstream gleefully ignored. After all, there was a party going on in stock and real estate markets, and no one wanted to hear that the punch bowl had turned smelly. What did it matter that, over the course of 2007, some significant hedge funds suffered multi-billion dollar losses, all due to suspect mortgage-based investments? Or that several major banks, often with financial ties to these funds, did the same? Bankers, investors and government officials disregarded it all. Then in March 2008, Wall Street investment bank Bear Stearns disintegrated in a single week, burning through $16 billion as it desperately tried to hold off its creditors. Again, financial investors and state officials treated it like an isolated incident. Four months later, the warning signs were once more dismissed, when the US economy was rocked by the third-largest bank failure in its history, the crash of IndyMac Federal Bank. But no one, with the exception of mainstream economists, could dismiss what happened in mid-September 2008. Within a matter of days, the venerable Wall Street bank Lehman Brothers, with a market value of $635 billion, evaporated, its investments apparently vanishing into thin air. Seven years earlier, when Enron Corporation had spectacularly crashed—in the then-largest bankruptcy in US history—it carried a market value of $60 billion. With a value more than ten times greater, the shockwaves generated

18 As with every boom, the world economy saw local crises throughout the period 1982-2007. What it did not experience, however, was a generalized global slump.

by Lehman Brothers' dramatic collapse could not be ignored. As if obeying a bugle call, global investors all panicked at the same time, bringing on a monumental financial crash.

The essence of a panic is that every bank and investor frantically seeks to reduce risk. Unsure of who will topple next, they do everything to recover the cash they have advanced (at interest) to other banks and firms. They call in their loans, much like an individual demanding repayment on an IOU. Then they hoard their cash, unwilling to lend it anywhere until the panic subsides. This produces a *liquidity crisis*, in which banks and corporations find it virtually impossible to borrow money even for everyday needs. But, if the underlying economy is basically sound, government-run central banks can simply inject lots more cash into the economy and the panic will ease. The problem in 2008 was that the underlying economy was anything but sound. In fact, the global economy had been in a drunken stagger for a decade, following a mammoth crisis in East Asia in 1997, which foreshadowed crashes in Russia in 1998 and in Brazil a year later.

Frightened by these developments, from the year 2000 on Western governments, led by the US, chopped interest rates in order to entice consumers and businesses to borrow and spend. And they complied big time. Investment banks and hedge funds in particular took heaps of the cheap money, often spending it on investments tied to housing and real estate. Rarely, however, did they actually buy land or houses. Instead, they gobbled up huge amounts of the flavour of the month investment, which involved shares in big bundles of mortgages. Known as mortgage-backed securities (MBSs), these investments give their buyers a slice of mortgages (or student debts or car loans, in other cases) that have been packaged together as "securities." In fact, MBSs are as secure as the mortgages that underlie them. And since ordinary banks were instructed to do everything they could to trick and hoodwink people into taking out mortgages they couldn't afford—often by offering low-interest "teaser rates" that would kick considerably higher after a year or so—the investments based on these mortgages were anything but secure. So, as the global economy slowed down after a quarter-century of growth, many mortgage-holders lost their jobs and could no longer make their payments. Others simply couldn't meet payments when interest rates rose. Soon, hundreds of thousands of people were defaulting on mortgages. Meanwhile, some savvy investors, using instruments known as derivatives, had started to bet against mortgage-backed securities. Sensing that MBSs were going to crash, they bought a sort of insurance policy requiring the seller to pay off big if mortgage-backed securities tanked (and in today's world of high finance, they didn't need to own the MBS—they could simply buy the insurance as a sort of wager). Consequently, if a set of investments collapsed, the financial institution that insured them would not only be required to pay off the original owners; it would also be obliged to pay off scores of others who had spent millions on bets that MBSs would crash and burn. Profiting on the misery of others like this is the financial equivalent of buying insurance that pays off if California experiences a major earthquake. The institutions selling the insurance (or, to be precise, the derivatives that act like insurance) believed that such a quake could never happen—and they were proved disastrously wrong. Once real estate markets started to melt down, a catastrophic train wreck was on (see McNally, 2011c: 4).

And what a wreck it was. In the United States, all five Wall Street investment banks evaporated. Just like a line of dominoes, banks toppled one after the other in Britain, Spain, Germany, Ireland, Iceland and beyond. Meanwhile, global stock markets plunged 50%, wiping out $35 trillion in financial assets in a matter of months. Panic gripped the global economy, just as it seized world leaders. "I am really scared," US Treasury Secretary Hank Paulson told his wife on the day Lehman Brothers disintegrated (Paulson, 2010: 215). A day later, September 15, 2008, AIG, the world's largest insurance company, melted down. And the crisis was not confined to financial markets: world industrial output plummeted 13% in 2008-09, while international trade plunged a full 20%. As ice-cold fear gripped world leaders, they did one of the very few things at which they excel: giving public money to private firms. Inventing one program after another, each with a ridiculous acronym, they injected trillions of dollars into the world's banks. When a few trillion didn't do the trick, they found trillions more. In the end, something well in excess of $30 trillion was handed out via governments to the world's banks, and to global corporations like General Motors and Chrysler, or shovelled into government "stimulus" programs designed to kick-start the world economy.[19] The result has been a massive expansion in the *monetary base* of most Western countries. By "monetary base," we refer to the assets—gold, foreign currencies, government bonds, stocks and so on held by central banks—that are meant to underpin the currencies these central banks issue. In the United States, the monetary base has quadrupled since 2008, thanks to the huge quantity of MBSs and the like purchased by the central bank. This is an enormous monetary expansion which, while rescuing private banks, has done little to restart economic growth.

The Great Bank Bailout of 2008-10 (and ongoing bailouts since then, particularly in Europe) thus involved governments giving real, hard cash from the public coffers to financial institutions in exchange for the toxic junk, like MBSs, that was sinking them. Sometimes this reality was obscured by claims that a *country* was receiving a bailout. But bailouts directed at countries, like Ireland or Greece, are deliberately designed for injection into private banks. Governments merely serve as intermediaries. Eventually, however, someone had to pay for the Great Bank Bailout. After all, international lending institutions, which determine the interest rate at which governments can borrow, do not look kindly on states that generate huge deficits. Without a plan to pay down their debts, governments routinely have to pay more to borrow funds. So, states had to quickly present credible plans for how they would pay off the massive debts they incurred to rescue the banks. Like members of a chorus, they all sang the same tune: austerity, austerity and more austerity. In other words, the bank bailouts would be financed on the backs of children, seniors, single mothers, the disabled, the sick and the poor—as government funds previously targeted for schools, health care, pensions and social welfare were slashed in order to pay down the borrowing required to bail out banks.

19 In "stimulus" programs, governments deliberately invest in building roads, hospitals, airports and so on in order to boost spending and employment, as opposed to bailouts in which, rather than build anything, they simply give the money to private firms. For my calculations of $21 trillion in bailout and stimulus funds as of early 2010, see McNally, 2011a: 197n4. A year later, one US-based economist put the American Federal Reserve Bank's total banking bailout at $29 trillion (see Felkerson, 2011). Since that time, trillions more have been spent, particularly in Europe in frantic efforts to reboot the European economy and to prevent an economic collapse in Ireland, Portugal, Greece and the Ukraine, among others.

Austerity: Making the Poor Pay

> The price of this financial crisis is being borne by people who absolutely did not cause it. Now is the period when the cost is being paid, I'm surprised that the degree of public anger has not been greater than it has (Mervyn King, former Governor of the Bank of England, quoted in Inman, 2011).

In candidly admitting that "the price of this financial crisis is being borne by people who absolutely did not cause it," the Bank of England's former governor was merely stating the obvious. After all, the public had been forced to bail out banks, hedge funds and investment companies that had helped create a crisis. And these same "people who absolutely did not cause" the mess were then subjected to an age of austerity and the poverty, insecurity and diminished quality of life that comes with it. Of course, there is more to austerity than this. It is also about increasing the social power of corporations and banks, and about weakening the forces of opposition in society. Part of this involves lowering people's expectations of life, and getting them to accept the blame for society's ills—a point to which we shall return. But it is also about the sheer sadism of a ruling class that celebrates destroying the fabric that sustains people's lives.

Let there be no doubt about the brutality of the assault on working-class people. In response to the crisis and the bailouts, Latvia fired one out of every three teachers, while slashing pensions by 70%. Ireland chopped the wages of public employees by 15% (later followed by further cuts), just as Russia announced the elimination of one out of every five public-sector jobs. In Greece, wages have been cut at least 30%, and pensions chopped 30-45%, pushing nearly half of all pensioners below the poverty lines and contributing to alarming increases in poverty, homelessness and suicide rates (Henley, 2015; Penn Medicine, 2015). In the US the federal government hacked $4 trillion from social spending in a single blow, followed by trillions more in cuts at federal, state and city levels. California, for instance, chopped $2.5 billion from health care, slashing health insurance for 900,000 poor children. Meanwhile, the state of Michigan ordered Detroit to close half of its schools, bringing some class sizes to 60, at roughly the same time Chicago announced plans to close 50 schools. Looking at the effects of such cuts in Britain, the Institute for Fiscal Studies predicted "a decade of pain" for working-class households, estimating that on average they would end up $4,500 poorer each year due to higher taxes and diminished social services as 400,000 teachers, nurses, social workers and others faced job cuts (Schifferes, 2010).

Canada too is following the same trend, even if it was not hit as hard by the global slump as were other Western nations—at least not at first. With spending cuts to social programs at federal, provincial and municipal levels, economic hardship has jumped alarmingly. At least one in five children in the country now lives in poverty, up from 12.4% in 1989. Scandalously, 40% of all Indigenous children live below the poverty line, as do half of all children born to immigrant families in Ontario (Campaign 2000, 2015). As employment gets more precarious across the board—since 2009 part-time employment has been growing much more rapidly than the full-time variety—so people's finances become increasingly insecure. More than half of all workers in Canada are now living paycheque to paycheque, without the ability to make ends meet in the event of just a one-week delay in their pay (Canadian Press, 2015). And now, in mid-2015, a fundamental weakness of the Canadian economy is exacerbating all these trends. As oil prices tumbled throughout 2014, investment in oil exploration and development plummeted, particularly in Alberta, blowing up the Conservative government's strategy of pushing Canada down the path of an "energy superpower." Six years into the global slump, Canada is now among the worst performing of the major economies (Parkinson, 2015). Along with poverty and economic insecurity come stress, mental health challenges and disease. In fact, poverty is responsible for the premature deaths of 40,000 people in Canada each year (Raphael & Bryant, 2014).

All of this looks frighteningly worse when we turn to the Global South, where the global slump has contributed to escalating dislocation, hunger, malaria, tuberculosis and horrifying levels of infant mortality. Deteriorating economic conditions, corporate grabs of land, fresh water and natural resources, and the civil wars such conditions provoke, has accelerated migration of poor people around the globe (Ferguson & McNally, 2014c), often at terrible risk to life and limb. From the beginning of 2014 to mid-2015, more than 5,000 migrants died at sea, simply trying to cross the Mediterranean from North Africa in desperate bids to restart their lives in Europe. The punitive, closed-door policies of European governments—as of their counterparts in Canada and the United States—is just one more condemnation of the heartlessness of neoliberal capitalism in the age of austerity.

While drastically harming the quality of people's lives, austerity policies also fail to deliver on their ostensible promise: to generate dynamic economic growth. In fact, austerity does exactly the opposite by dampening already sluggish growth—and honest members of the elite know it. After all, if government eliminates hundreds of thousands of jobs, and if it cuts pensions and social assistance payments, it automatically reduces incomes and spending. This means fewer purchases of food, clothing, furniture, cars and more—reducing overall economic demand, production and employment. Britain's Office for Budget Responsibility, for instance, calculated that austerity policies reduced economic growth by 1.4% in 2011-12 (Chote, 2013). And for countries that have been subjected to the most vicious forms of austerity, the results have been catastrophic: the Greek economy, for instance, has contracted by a whopping 25%, while youth unemployment is well above 50%. For these reasons, many commentators have argued that austerity policies are irrational, the product of deluded right-wingers. But this criticism misses the essential point. Yes, austerity is *socially* irrational insofar as it undermines the well-being of a majority of people. But the purpose of a capitalist society is not the social good—it has never been about augmenting human well-being. Instead, it is to reward the owners of private enterprises by way of high and sustained profits. As Canadian financier and media personality, Kevin O'Leary, has put it: "A business doesn't have any feelings. Its DNA is to make money" (O'Leary, 2009). And by that, admittedly anti-social, criterion—helping corporations make money—austerity has been a success.

Profits and Inequality in the Age of Austerity

In a nutshell, then, austerity is a triumph—at least in capitalist terms—if it makes ordinary people poorer while boosting corporate profits and the incomes of the rich. One of its key effects has been to make workers more insecure and, by so doing, to lower wages and benefits. Globally, there are 30 million more people unemployed than there were in 2008. On top of that, another 40 million people have become so discouraged that they have quit looking for paid work. In addition, sluggish growth since 2008 means that 34 million fewer jobs have been created than would have been the case at previous growth rates. Overall, then, there are at least 100 million fewer people gainfully employed today than would have been expected under pre-crisis circumstances (ILO, 2015). And that breeds enormous fear and insecurity from which employers and government have been profiting no end. In particular, it enables employers to coerce workers into accepting increasingly precarious employment—part-time, casual and insecure jobs, which pay low wages and carry few or no benefits. According to the Canadian Imperial Bank of Commerce, for instance, job quality—measured in terms of full-time hours and wage levels—has fallen to its lowest-ever recorded level. More and more jobs created in Canada are of the low-wage, part-time type. In fact, in the heavily populated Ontario corridor embracing Toronto and Hamilton and the areas in between, fully 44% of workers are precariously employed, and the numbers are worse for women, Indigenous peoples and workers of colour (McMaster University & United Way, 2015: 3). In the US, more than half of all jobs created since 2009 have been in low-wage positions. Like clockwork, low wages and precarious employment have helped boost corporate profits everywhere. In the United States, wages have fallen to their lowest ever recorded share of gross domestic product while profits, which grew 20% every year between 2008 and 2013, have taken a record high share (Schwartz, 2013; Greenhouse, 2013). Similar trends have been in play in Britain (Monaghan, 2014).[20]

One of the traditional defences of capitalism is that those who make profit aid everyone by investing and creating jobs. That is a dubious claim at the best of times, but it looks downright ridiculous these days. In fact, rather than engage in job-creating investments, corporations have been hoarding cash, or using it to buy back their own shares (which simply makes shareholders richer). By the end of

20 It may now be the case that a weak global economy is curtailing profit growth, since wage compression and precarity can only do so much without a new wave of corporate investment.

2010, for instance, non-financial firms in the US were sitting on about $2 trillion in cash—a record amount (Sadowski, 2010). European firms have been hoarding even more cash, while non-financial firms in Canada had a whopping $600 billion in cash by the end of 2012 (Parkinson, 2013). Expanding profits have clearly been doing little to boost economic growth and job creation. But they have been doing wonders to make the super-rich ever richer. In fact, the redistribution of wealth away from wages and toward profits and interest payments has dramatically enriched the wealthiest people on the planet, and widened the gap between rich and poor around the world.

The Occupy movement made the global 1% an appropriate target of criticism. But in the United States a group one-tenth that size—the richest 0.1% of Americans—now has as much wealth as the bottom 90% of their fellow citizens. Not since the Great Depression of the 1930s has US society been so unequal (Saez & Zucman, 2014). According to Statistics Canada, the wealthiest 1% of families held nearly half of all the country's wealth in 2012. And globally, we have reached the obscene state in which the richest 80 people on the planet have as much wealth as the bottom half of humankind—that's right, 80 people have as much wealth as 3.5 billion of their fellow human inhabitants. And as Oxfam has shown, the top global 1% has more wealth than all the remaining people on earth (Oxfam, 2015). As grotesquely unfair as this is, it is the logical consequence of capitalist austerity.

As much as austerity is centrally about boosting profits and pleasing the financial institutions that buy government debt (the various IOUs, or government bonds and bills, which states use to finance their shortfalls), it is also a political agenda, designed to foster corporate investment, a pro-business society and personal identities tied to market expectations. When looked at from this standpoint, it becomes easy to recognize that many of the arguments made for austerity are crudely ideological, i.e. blatant attempts to pass off as economic necessity what are in fact *political* choices. Take the case of Canada.

Since the age of austerity was announced by the dominant states in 2010, governments in Canada have vigorously pursued cutback policies. Yet there is no evidence that Canada has any kind of public debt problem, let alone a crisis. This is not because, contrary to claims by government officials, Canada did not have a bailout program. In fact, banks and auto corporations received huge injections of public funds—something in the range of $300 billion (Russell, 2011). Yet, that bailout program came after more than a decade of large program cuts by Liberal and Conservative governments.[21] As a result, the federal government's debt in Canada is minimal, notwithstanding the bailouts, standing at about 35% of the country's gross domestic product—compared to a level of 58% in Germany, 70% in Britain and 180% in Greece. A country like Greece may have a debt dilemma, even if it's not for the reasons usually cited (contrary to myth, Greeks work many more hours and for lower wages than most Europeans, but corporations and banks massively evade taxes, diminishing government revenues).[22] But Canada has no meaningful debt problem. Its federal government (alongside the country's provincial governments) is merely using the political climate of global austerity in a calculated effort to promote lower wages, weakened unions, cuts to social programs and reduced corporate taxes—all in an effort to prove that Canada is a more pro-business environment for corporate investment than most other states. This is why one astute commentator has referred to the approach as *competitive austerity* (Albo, 1994). Of course, all of this has an ideological dimension. After all, states must try to convince their inhabitants that austerity is both necessary and desirable. This is done in part by false analogies about national debt being the same as families going into debt. But since when did families have the capacity to tax the whole society to raise revenues? However, another method for getting the public on board is the *shock doctrine*, in which governments deliberately engineer crises that, by producing instability and social unrest, shock the population into accepting policies that would otherwise appear unpalatable (Klein, 2008). In 1995, for instance, Ontario's education minister was filmed arguing that it was necessary to "bankrupt" the province's education system in order to

21 Those cutbacks, beginning in the 1990s, represent the consolidation of neoliberalism in Canada. For useful discussions of neoliberalism as an elite project see Seymour, 2014 and Harvey, 2005a.

22 Of course, Greece could repudiate this debt in whole or in part by claiming that it is a form of odious debt entered into without any commitment to the public good, as Argentina among other nation-states has done in recent years.

manufacture a "useful crisis" that would allow the government to radically restructure the system. In the course of producing artificial crises, neoliberalism has undertaken to reshape personal identities around the vision of people as self-reliant and competitive individuals responding to the demands of economic markets, rather than as social individuals, working together to improve society and the quality of human life, and using public resources (such as education, health care and social insurance) to that end. In the neoliberal view, we are all in it for ourselves, without commitments to others, all desperately seeking to reduce our tax burden while fashioning ourselves into the loyal, happy-to-accept-meagre-wages, no-life-outside-of-work types that corporations want of us.

There is no doubt that neoliberalism has enjoyed major victories in remaking culture and personal identities. But this has involved more than the conquests of people's minds by free-floating ideologies. Neoliberalism's cultural gains are rooted in real social-material transformations in everyday life. Consider, for instance, the massive erosion of unions over the last 40 years. There was a time when unions represented a significant counter-power to capital, one rooted in working-class communities and capable of mobilizing thousands upon thousands of people. For nearly two generations, however, unions have typically failed to deliver sustained improvements in the quality of life for most workers. Job security, standards of living, benefits and pensions have, as a general rule, all been rolled back, even if small numbers of (predominantly older, white and male) workers have held on to remnants of them. Unions have been unable to stop vicious neoliberal attacks—from US President Ronald Reagan's destruction of the air traffic controllers' union in 1981 to British Prime Minister Margaret Thatcher's assault on the miners' union in 1984-85, or from British Columbia Premier Bill Bennett's attack on that province's unions, especially teachers, in 1983 to Ontario Premier Mike Harris's "common sense revolution" against social assistance, social housing and union rights in 1995-96. And progressive social movements have been largely unable to mount the kind of militant, sustained, mass resistance that could actually reverse the neoliberal agenda. In this context, there is a *pragmatism of defeat*, which encourages people to give up on collective efforts to improve the world in favour of individualist approaches which emphasize accommodating, going with the flow and "looking out for Number One."

It is arguable that the shattering of older social solidarities and the creation of new kinds of market individualism represent among the biggest accomplishments of neoliberalism. It would be foolhardy to underestimate the scale of this cultural transformation. But there is also a danger that we lose sight of the contradictions in this new ideological and cultural landscape—and in so doing that we ignore the prospects for protest and resistance, which are the necessary soil for the generation of political movements designed to truly change the world.

Anti-Austerity and the New Protest Cycle

Let us begin this section with a sobering assessment. In 2008, capitalism entered its greatest crisis since the 1930s and yet it has produced "not the vaunted upsurge of the working class and the Left, but rather the strengthening of neoliberalism" (Seymour, 2014: 28). Put differently, the ruling groups have seized on the opportunities this crisis has created to further *neoliberalize* society. Left-wing forces have generally failed to reshape public discourse about the slump, or to mobilize mass forces for social transformation. Instead, the agenda of privatization, reduced social services, racialized social control, climate-change denial, anti-union legislation and further impoverishment of the poor has rushed ahead, consolidating one gain after another. And yet...

And yet, there has been mass resistance, sometimes on an enormous scale, as I document below. This resistance has seized streets, parks and workplaces, sometimes bringing hundreds of thousands out to challenge austerity. However, as I have written elsewhere, the *modes* of resistance have not been equal to the challenges we face (McNally, 2011c: 49). Let us start with each side of this equation: first, the evidence of mass protest; and, second, the limits of the modes of resistance on offer thus far.

Only a few months into the crisis, a mass upheaval, led by determined youth, toppled the government of Iceland, whose policies had led to a profound financial collapse. At the same time that Iceland's government was resigning, a wave of occupations erupted against plant shutdowns and job losses at factories in the US, Canada, Ireland, France and Scotland. Workers in France took things to a new level, in several cases kidnapping their bosses and holding them hostage in occupied workplaces until deals were reached to preserve jobs. Early 2009 also saw extraordinary general strikes galvanized by youth, feminists, environmentalists and trade unionists in Guadeloupe and Martinique, as well as a 77-day occupation by metalworkers in South Korea. The end of 2010 and early 2011 witnessed the heroic uprisings for Bread and Freedom in Tunisia and Egypt, as dictators were overthrown by a convergence of youth-based insurgencies in the streets and militant workers' strikes in the factories, mills, schools, hospitals and transportation systems. The uprisings of the Arab Spring inspired youth in Spain, organized under the label of the Indignants, to seize city squares in upsurges against austerity and unemployment. The movements in Tunisia, Egypt and Spain were next the inspiration for the Occupy Wall Street protests in New York, which stimulated Occupy movements in hundreds of cities.

Nobody could have predicted that the seizure of a park near Wall Street by a few hundred protesters in New York would galvanize oppositional energies. Yet, by challenging the rule of modern life by the richest 1%, and by holding up an image of democratically assembled common people, Occupy quickly made a mass impact. Within two weeks, polls in the US showed that Occupy Wall Street was twice as popular as the right-wing Tea Party movement in the Republican Party, notwithstanding the fact that the Tea Party had scores of millionaires backing it and Occupy had little more than energy, passion and imagination. In virtually no time at all, Occupy movements sprang up in 70 major US cities, and dozens more from London, England to Toronto, Canada. As important as Occupy was for its political message—opposition to organizing society for the benefit of the 1%—equally significant was its political *form*, involving an experiment in direct and participatory assembly-style democracy.[23]

23 Inevitably, participatory democracy was more an aspiration than a reality, in part because Occupy failed to draw in substantial enough numbers from diverse working-class communities, and also because it had miles to go to meaningfully address social inequities organized around race and gender.

Of course, the most inspiring experiment of this sort was the system of self-governance established by the hundreds of thousands who seized Tahrir Square in Cairo during the 2011 uprising against then-president Hosni Mubarak. The Egyptian insurgents established their own security system to guard against the police and army; they set up medical stations and food centres, along with child care facilities. And, crucially, they created regular democratic assemblies which encouraged radically democratic decision-making by tens of thousands of people gathered in the Square (McNally, 2011b). In so doing, they began to reinvent the Commune form that has been typical of working-class uprisings for nearly 150 years. Their mode of self-organization also directly challenged the style of politics central to neoliberalism. If neoliberalism excels at one thing, it is privatizing decision-making power, taking it from people and those they elect and transferring it to unelected elites, as Wisconsin Governor Scott Walker did in 2011 by turning his Department of Commerce over to business leaders. By creating a democracy of the people in the streets, the Egyptian insurgents—to be followed by the Indignants in Spain and Occupy activists in the US and beyond—were constructing elements of an alternative form of social and political life. That they failed, for many complex reasons, should not diminish their accomplishments.

Unlike the movements in Tunisia and Egypt, which overthrew dictators, the dramatic seizures of public spaces by Occupy activists tended to remain socially isolated. The Occupy actions were not accompanied by insurgent strikes of workers that threatened to paralyze large swathes of the capitalist economy. Consequently, Occupy did not become a multi-front movement, simultaneously threatening economic interests and challenging the political order. In addition, Occupy failed to develop as a movement rooted in working-class communities, schools and workplaces that could call its supporters out to public spaces when threatened. This made it much easier for police forces to isolate the activists camped out in parks, and evict them in night-time raids. The heroic activists who seized Gezi Park in Istanbul, Turkey in May 2014 did make more meaningful connections of that sort. In fact, it is estimated that 3.5 million people participated in more than 5,000 actions in solidarity with the Gezi Park uprising. Although police violence— accounting for eleven deaths, 8,000 injuries and 3,000 arrests—pushed the protesters out of the park, the spirit of Gezi had its revenge in elections just over a year later when the left-wing People's Democratic Party, running on a platform of social justice, feminism, environmentalism and justice for the Kurdish people, captured more than 10% of the vote, electing 82 members of the Turkish parliament (Genc, 2015).

Among the more successful youth-based uprisings in the age of austerity have been the mass student strikes and protests in Chile (2011-13) and in Québec (2012). These momentous student upheavals had the distinct advantage of turning university and college campuses into insurgent organizing spaces for democratic mass assemblies which steered the movements. It is much harder, after all, to push students out of colleges and universities—where they congregate, meet, work, study and sometimes live on an everyday basis—than it is to evict protesters from a downtown park. And in both the Chilean and Québec cases, this advantage gave them months (or years) to organize, assemble and reach out into communities and neighbourhoods to build broad-based support that made it difficult for governments to isolate them from the wider public. This helps explain the ability of the Chilean movement to resurge in the summer of 2015 in coordination with mass strikes by teachers. Similar dynamics were in play in the Chicago teachers' strike of 2012, which grew out of years of community organizing around education in racialized communities by a rank and file movement in the Chicago Teachers Union. Militant teachers had for years protested the system of "racial apartheid" in Chicago's school system and had resisted school closures in poor neighbourhoods. When they took strike action, those same communities rose up in solidarity with them, giving the strike aspects of a real people's movement.

There were sometimes comparable forces at work in the inspiring upsurges of youth-based Indigenous and African-American activism in the Idle No More movement in Canada (2012-13), on the one hand, and the Black Lives Matter movement in the US (2014-15), on the other. Both movements displayed the democratic, grassroots, from-below organizing methods of the current global protest cycle, contributing their own unique inflections and innovations. And both touched deep roots in their respective communities, and among layers of the predominantly white population.[24] Sometimes, they met generational challenges within their own communities. But most significantly, their pre-eminent obstacle remained the entrenched racisms within power structures and much of the white population.

All of these struggles—from factory occupations and general strikes, to mass insurgencies and anti-racist movements—are shaped by a growing anger against austerity and all the dehumanization it breeds, from poverty to gender violence, and from union-busting to the shooting of people of African descent. To be sure, there are long-standing systemic causes of all these forms of oppression. But the age of austerity has exacerbated them and galvanized insurgent forms of opposition. As prison abolitionist Ruth Wilson Gilmore, discussing the anti-police violence protests in Ferguson, Missouri, put it, "the rebellions in Ferguson and Baltimore and beyond are uprisings against austerity, sparked by police murder and about all of the relationships and conditions that made the murder possible" (Vulliamy, 2015).

Yet, we confront a dilemma. Powerful social mobilization against austerity has recorded precious few victories thus far. One key reason for this has to do with the difficulty activists and grassroots organizers have faced in making the transition from a *moment* to a *movement*. Because "infrastructures of dissent" (Sears, 2014; see LaFrance & Sears, below) largely atrophied or disappeared throughout more than three decades of neoliberalism, the inspiring energies displayed over weeks of occupations, student strikes and street protests often do not have strong and respected oppositional political spaces to sustain them when, inevitably, energies sag and the upheaval experiences setbacks. Unlike insurgent union movements with their labour halls and meeting rooms, rebellious civil rights movements with their churches or defiant community mobilizations with their neighbourhood centres, protests that converge in the streets or parks often lack rooted networks that can sustain them over years of activist work of the sort that has been crucial to the successes of anti-racist, feminist, anti-war and union movements. Without the development of real social roots in communities, workplaces and schools, anti-austerity uprisings will tend to stall, unable to translate exciting moments into

24 For an excellent account of the emergence of Idle No More, see Coulthard, 2013. On Black Lives Matter see the compelling analysis of Taylor, 2015.

sustained movements. This has been true even of momentous uprisings, like those in Tunisia and Egypt, which could momentarily generate the social power to overturn dictators. Thus far, most anti-austerity insurgencies have lacked staying power—and the forms of political organization that makes it possible.

There are, of course, some partial exceptions. Mass social struggle has thrown up some important new political formations such as Syriza (the Coalition of the Radical Left) in Greece and Podemos (We Can) in Spain, which are having a mass impact on political life. As significant as these developments are, however, they too reflect distinct weaknesses of all the radical movements that have emerged in the neoliberal period—a disconnection from earlier radical traditions, and weak institutional roots in working-class communities. This partly explains the tendency in these new political formations to curb anti-capitalism in favour of accommodation with the powers that be—a tendency that pushed the leadership of Syriza into potentially fatal compromises with the austerity agenda of the International Monetary Fund, the European Central Bank and the European Commission. We can only hope that the Greek Left will be capable of rising to the challenges before them.

The development of radical mass protest movements is invariably a long, complex and contradictory process. What always proves vital, however, is that dedicated activists build centres of learning and organization that can assist the political clarification and development of the mass struggle. If it is true, as the quotation that opens this chapter suggests, that the crisis that erupted in 2008 "has been a transformative moment in global economic history whose ultimate resolution will likely reshape politics and economics for at least a generation," then there are many years of resistance ahead in which that work of learning and organizing can be done. The crisis is not going away any time soon. Nor are the regular eruptions of mass protest. What remains to be seen is whether the *forms* of organization and struggle will emerge that could make possible a radical social transformation that leaves behind austerity, neoliberalism and the capitalist system that breed them.

POLITICAL ECOLOGY AND COUNTER-HEGEMONIC POLITICS

Laurie Adkin

> It is only in a shared belief and insistence that there are practical alternatives that the balance of forces and chances begins to alter. Once the inevitabilities are challenged, we begin gathering our resources for a journey of hope. If there are no easy answers there are still available and discoverable hard answers, and it is these that we can now learn to make and share (Raymond Williams, 1983: 268-69).

Political ecology is not an all-encompassing movement or theory of social change. It is, however, an essential element of any project to replace capitalism with societies rooted in principles of justice and respect for ecological imperatives. This is because political ecology is a way of thinking about the social and political world that consistently keeps in play the mutually constitutive relationship between human societies and nature. Political ecology combines, minimally, critical political economy with knowledge about ecological relationships. The work of political ecologists has ranged widely across disciplines, integrating concepts and methodologies from geography, sociology, anthropology, conservation science, law, history and the humanities. As it has evolved as a theoretical framework for analysing the causes of ecological and socio-economic crises, political ecology has maintained an historically informed, critical stance toward capitalism, and has integrated other radical critiques of the hegemonic order—notably, feminist, anti-racist and post-colonial (Neumann, 2005; Robbins, 2004; Rocheleau et al., 2013).

Evidently, political ecology is not equivalent to "the environmental movement" or to "environmental politics." Environmentalists may be more or less informed by a critical, political-ecological framework of analysis. One of the objectives of this chapter is to provide a rough assessment of environmentalism in Canada today in relation to counter-hegemonic coalition-building. While I view political ecology as providing core, guiding principles for counter-hegemonic politics, I argue that democratization, too, is essential to the realization of socially just and ecologically sustainable paths of development.

The priority of democratization for counter-hegemonic politics has been identified repeatedly by socialist and post-Marxist thinkers—notably, by Raymond Williams, in the British context, in response to the rise of neoliberalism in the 1980s, and by Chantal Mouffe (1988, 1993, 2000). Struggles within the liberal democracies for a socially just and ecological model of development are routinely obstructed by policy processes and political institutions that privilege private interests in short-term capital accumulation over the general interests in sustainable social well-being. In essence, liberalism has divided the political from the economic spheres, placing the economic "off-limits" to the application of the equality principle and to democratic political regulation. The political institutions of the liberal democracies are legitimated by the existence of formal rights and freedoms while permitting only restricted forms of citizenship (reduced, mainly, to periodic elections). Changing this will constitute a "radicalization" of liberal-democratic institutions so that they become more egalitarian, participatory and inclusive, allowing citizens to engage in meaningful, deliberative decision-making about societal development.

From my work on environmental conflicts, it has become clear to me that a primary consideration for the social actors engaged in counter-hegemonic struggles must be the conditions for creating and sustaining a strong civil society and a much more meaningful and participatory form of citizenship than that offered by the neoliberal "democracies" of our times. It has been precisely the project of new right ideologues and the interests they represent to erode to the greatest extent possible the resources available to citizens and to collective actors to conduct research, inform, communicate, educate, organize and generally to engage effectively in the hegemonic politics of establishing meanings, shaping public opinion and demonstrating the feasibility of alternatives to the status quo model of development. There is much terrain to reconquer here, and much new terrain to explore, as the technologies and other resources available in such a war of position continue to change. Moreover, as I have argued elsewhere

(Adkin, 1998, 2009), counter-hegemonic social movements may be articulated to one another by their common stakes in democratizing reforms. Indeed, these struggles may be recast in many respects as democratic struggles.

Political Ecology and Counter-Hegemony

Political-ecological analyses have proven to be flexible and context-sensitive in their integration of multiple scales and axes of analysis in explaining particular phenomena—from urban sprawl or inner-city decay in North America (Gonzalez, 2005; Heynan et al., 2007), to the dispossession of Indigenous peoples (Harrison, 2009), famines and violent conflicts (Peet & Watts 2004; Peluso & Watts, 2001; Watts & Bohle, 1993). However, each of these critical axes of analysis—ecological, race, gender, sexuality, class—remains distinct; one does not and cannot subsume all the others, and no such claim is made for political ecology. What is, I argue, indispensable for successful counter-hegemonic politics, is an intersectional mode of analysis that—as a matter of reflex—gives serious consideration to the causal role of every relationship of domination/subordination in the explanation of any given conflict.

Political ecology—like post-structuralist feminism, queer theory, critical race theory or post-colonial theory—has the virtue of a kind of radical openness to a diversity of explanatory relationships. Without such an intersectional mode of analysis, social movements are limited as counter-hegemonic actors. An environmental campaign to protect a territory from industrial exploitation that does not align with the needs of the Indigenous people having claims to the same territory may achieve one goal (preservation) at the expense of another (exclusion or dispossession). "Liberal environmentalism" (Bulle, 2014) may achieve some diminution of environmental harms while reinforcing the capitalist logic that makes environmental destruction inevitable. The environmental justice movement may protect a particular racialized community from exposure to "disproportionate" environmental risk, without identifying the need to restructure the capitalist economy (Harvey, 1999). A "sustainable" agricultural policy may perpetuate an unjust sexual division of labour and of the benefits of production. These are just a few examples of the problems created by a lack of "mobile positioning" (Haraway, 1991) in the analysis of conflicts and the formulation of programs of reform. In a nutshell, counter-hegemonic politics is crucially dependent for successes upon the building of coalitions—not instrumental, tactical, short-term coalitions, but mutually emancipating, transformative coalitions cemented by shared values and commitments.

What, then, are the values, principles or objectives that might knit together the coalitions needed to profoundly challenge the multi-faceted hegemonic order? At the height (or depths) of the battles with Thatcherism and the ascendance of neoliberal ideology in the 1980s, socialist thinkers were grappling with the same problem. The guiding principles that the Welsh cultural theorist Raymond Williams identified were: "movement beyond a market economy," a shift of production "towards new governing standards of durability, quality and economy in the use of non-renewable resources" and a "move towards new kinds of monetary institutions, placing capital at the service of these new ends" (1983: 256).

While these directions are as relevant today as they were 30 years ago, it is useful to drill down to the values upon which they draw, and to extend or revise these as needed in the current context of counter-hegemonic politics. For example, I argue that a much more robust set of ecological values needs to be elaborated than the conservationism embodied in Williams's call for the prudent use of "non-renewable resources."[25] The worldview labelled "ecocentrism" is both more radical and more inclusive of ecological values than the earlier discourses of conservation or preservation, or even eco-socialism, and has affinities with the kin-centric cosmologies of Aboriginal cultures (Martin-Hill, 2004). Ecocentrism was not really on the radar of socialist thinkers in the 1980s, but needs to be now, because it opens the doors to a more radical understanding of what needs to be changed in human relationships to nature than that provided by anthropocentric and promethean discourses. I agree with Robyn Eckersley (2004) that ecocentrism is consistent with egalitarian and humanist values (not misanthropic). In addition, ecocentrism accepts that the relationship of humans to other species is one of *interdependence*. Therefore,

25 Ecological economics principles are more fully elaborated in Adkin, 2003.

even human self-interest would, from any rational perspective, be sufficient grounds to protect the conditions that other species need to flourish. Ecocentrism calls into question the normalcy of the numerous hierarchies that operate in modern thought and cultural practices, beginning with speciesism, instead asking us to think of other species as different but equal in importance to the functioning of the biosphere, or as having needs that must be accommodated—even when this requires the relinquishing of privileges to which humans have become accustomed in their occupation of the planet. Beyond this, we (humans) may disagree about the ethics of various human relationships to other species, establishing our positions in different cultural or spiritual traditions as well as in changes in scientific knowledge and technologies.

Ecocentrism does not stand in, here, for a comprehensive, counter-hegemonic "value system," but does capture important guiding values with regard to human-nature relations. Clearly, deliberative democratic principles, with their emphasis upon communicative reason and inclusion, along with egalitarianism, respect for difference, solidarity and recognition of human needs for individual self-realization must all be underpinning values of counter-hegemonic politics. Notwithstanding the tensions that may arise among these values, each has a role to play in the creation of communities that can nurture and sustain a good life.[26]

New Times

Environmental movements, like other social movements, respond to new conditions of struggle, adopting new discursive frames, reshaping their own identities, and redefining their priorities. While there have been many significant changes since I mapped the Canadian environmental movement for the first edition of *Organizing Dissent*, a quarter century ago, at least three major transformations must be considered here.

26 English-speakers have, as yet, utterly inadequate vocabulary to express what I want to say here. I suspect that Indigenous cultures have superior language, such as the Kahnia-ke-haka concept *kani-kon-ri:io* (Arquette et al., 2004; Alfred, 2009b) or the Anishnawbe concept *minobimaatisiiwin* (LaDuke, 1999)

In the early 1990s the gates to the deregulated movement of capital and goods had already been opened by the reforms of the Thatcher and Reagan administrations in the early 1980s, leading to ascendance of neoliberal orthodoxy within the IFIs, and the imposition of the "structural adjustment" policies in the newly created debtor countries of the Global South. The liberalization of investment and trade rules was effected through trade agreements and the WTO (the Free Trade Agreement passed in Canada in 1988, the NAFTA in 1993). The effects of these reforms have been described in detail by David Harvey (2005), Thomas Piketty (2014), Saskia Sassen (1996, 1998, 2007, 2014) and many others. By the mid-1990s this transformed global political economy was being recognized by a new ontological concept, "globalization" (James & Steger 2014), and soon gave rise to a counter-movement—an anti- (or alter-)globalization movement that has taken such forms as the 1999 mobilization in Seattle against the agenda of the WTO (which succeeded the GATT in 1995), the annual World Social Forum, beginning in Porto Alegre, Brazil in 2001, and new NGOs/networks like ATTAC or Via Campesina. The discursive framing and strategic thinking of environmental organizations in Canada was, however, only beginning to be reshaped by these new realities in the early 1990s. More than 20 years later, environmental organizations are more globally connected, and their campaigns more transnational. Arguably, the growth of global inequality and the resistance across the Global South to new forms of colonization have radicalized many environmentalists' critiques of capitalism and have made environmentalists in the Global North more aware of their own privileges and obligations.

As corporations, investors and financial institutions have gained new rights and freedoms, workers and communities have been burdened with greater insecurity and risk. The shrinkage of government funding for public goods (education, health, environmental protection, public broadcasting) as well as governmental and private support for civil society organizations (subventions, charitable tax status, individual donations) has eroded resources important to sustaining a vibrant civil society. While the consequences of "globalization" have reconfigured the strategic and analytical frameworks of environmental organizations, the transformations wrought by neoliberal regimes locally have affected the resources and political opportunities available to ENGOs (and to all social movements). By "resources" and "opportunities" I mean not only sources of funding, but also access to media and to public spaces, availability of legal means to contest policy decisions, access to decision-makers and political rights and freedoms (of assembly and speech—essential to protest and civil disobedience).[27] That the imposition of neoliberal governance has required more authoritarian states has become evident to most social movement actors.

A second transformation which has substantially reoriented the environmental movement is ontological in a scientific sense (as compared to the shift in political-economic ontology that is captured by such concepts as globalization). Becoming salient in political discourse parallel to, or somewhat later than, the concept of globalization, are the framing of climate change as a global ecological crisis, along with the concepts of "peak oil" and "fossil capitalism." Global awareness of climate change was growing in the 1980s and resulted in the negotiation of the UNFCCC at the Rio (UNCED) Summit in 1992. Yet until that point, climate change was not the central concern of the environmental movement in Canada, and was not even mentioned in my contribution to the 1992 edition of *Organizing Dissent*. In Canada, public attention to the issue reached a peak ten years later, in 2002, with the debate about ratification of the Kyoto Protocol. ENGOs like Greenpeace, the Sierra Club and the David

27 Much attention has been given, in this regard, to the discourse and legislative agenda of the federal Conservative government. For a summary, see Voices, 2015. It is also notable that policing on the ground has changed, becoming more massive and violent in response to large mobilizations like the G20 Summit in Toronto in 2010. A June 2015 report by the Québec Ligue des Droits et Libertés (LDL) calculates almost 7,000 arrests at demonstrations in that province since March 2011 (LDL, 2015: 6). The coordinator for the LDL observed recently that the numbers of arrests—including "mass arrests"—have grown by 400% since 2011. Notably, the targets of political repression have also changed. From the 1970s to the beginning of the 2000s, most protests were organized by the separatist, union and (towards the end of that period) the alter-globalization movements. Today, the targeted movements include students, ecologists, anarchists, "anti-capitalists," anti-colonialists and groups denouncing police brutality. See Simon Van Vliet, Manifestations et répression politique : un rapport accablant, *Ricochet*, June 26, 2015, http://www.ricochet.media/fr/483/manifestations-et-repression-politique-un-rapport-accablant

Suzuki Foundation are today centrally concerned with climate change, and the ENGOs formed (outside of Québec) since 2000 have this as a primary focus (Climate Action Network, 2002; Canadian Renewable Energy Alliance, 2004; Canadian Youth Climate Coalition, 2006). Within Québec, public support for government-led action to reduce GHGs is particularly strong, and there have been effective campaigns against hydraulic fracturing ("fracking") and the Energy East pipeline (Batellier and Sauvé, 2009/10; Nature Québec & STOP, 2010; Université de Montréal, 2014). While these campaigns are driven by concerns for agriculture, water quality, human health and impacts on landscapes, they are also linked to climate change.

"Peak oil" is a concept familiar to petroleum geologists since the 1950s, but significant in political discourse only since about 2004. Predictions about the peak production of conventional oil, followed by declining rates of output as reserves deplete, have been overshadowed by the development of hydraulic fracturing and deep water drilling technologies that have permitted the exploitation of harder-to-reach sources of oil. Likewise, the use of steam to separate bitumen from sand has enabled the rapidly growing production of crude oil from "non-conventional" reserves. Needless to say, extraction from such reserves entails new environmental risks and harms for which no commensurate remedial technologies exist. Think "Deep Horizon" or the Alberta tar sands region. Fracking and bitumen extraction require enormous quantities of water, much of which becomes waste water or is removed from the hydraulic cycle. Such effects may become limiting factors for non-conventional oil production in themselves, as communities mobilize opposition in response to local environmental and health concerns. The extraction and processing of non-conventional sources of oil require, in addition, greater investment than the production of conventional oil. For this reason, economists talk about "peak oil" in the sense of costs of production that will eventually raise the price of oil to a level that triggers economic recession. According to energy economist Jeff Rubin (2009), for example, the high price of oil was the key cause of the world recession that began in the United States in 2008. In Rubin's view, we should not expect a return to earlier levels of economic growth; on the contrary, travel, consumption and other aspects of an oil-intensive lifestyle are going to be curtailed significantly. Whether or not new technologies may be found to drain existing reserves of oil and gas, or to discover new ones, the picture painted by peak oil claims is one of societies driven to ever more environmentally high-risk, self-destructive and economically costly extremes to extract every last drop of fuel from the planet. The higher the risks and the costs, the more untenable it becomes for particular interests (energy companies and their political clients) to resist calls for the adoption of already existing alternatives to the burning of fossil fuels.

"Fossil capitalism," a term associated with the German ecological economist, Elmar Altvater (2006), identifies the model of capitalist development that took root in the West following World War II as one fundamentally dependent upon oil as its fuel.[28] The unique properties of oil (such as its EROI, transportability, storability), Altvater argues, made possible rapid industrialization and the decoupling of production from natural energy cycles, as well as the expansion of industrialization to all parts of the world. The global demand for oil has, however, run up against ecological limits along with the peak oil limits described above. In Altvater's view, no other existing energy source can reproduce all of the properties and uses of oil, which means that the intensive regime of accumulation that has characterized the last 70 years is giving way to something new. If solar energy becomes the new foundation of our economies, our societies will, in Altvater's view, become far more democratic due to the nature of the technologies of production and distribution of solar energy and the social relations of production linked to these.[29] The key point with regard to the discursive shift marked by "fossil capitalism," however, is that it links struggles against capitalism to the protection of planetary ecosystems. These three ontological shifts, together, have underpinned a global

28 A similar term, thought to have been introduced by Lewis Mumford (2010) in 1932, "carboniferous capitalism," has been revived and has re-entered our political lexicon (Byrne et al., 2011; Dalby, 2002; Newell & Paterson, 2010; inter alia).

29 Similar predictions have been made by others, notably Hermann Scheer (1994). This mode of analysis, in which the roots of regime types are found in the predominant sources of energy and technologies of an era, also underpins Timothy Mitchell's theorization of the relationship between coal and social democracy (2009, 2011).

environmental movement for a societal transition that is variously labelled "post-carbon," "green" or, most recently, "decarbonization."

The third global transformation that has reconfigured the terrain of environmental politics and the identities and discourses of environmentalists is that *other* social movements, too, have been transformed by, or have grown up in, the new conditions of neoliberal globalization and deepening ecological crisis (in particular, the salience of the climate change threat). As linkages have been made among the intensive extraction of fossil fuels, existential environmental threats, political resistance to green transition, corporate power, and massive global poverty/inequality, the human rights, anti-racist, Indigenous, peace, church-based social justice and union movements have joined in struggles against "carbon colonialism," for repayment of "ecological debt"[30] and for "climate justice." The membership list of the Canadian Climate Action Network, for example, includes dozens of organizations, including ENGOs, policy think tanks, unions and other associations.[31] A Tar Sands Resistance march in the US in June 2015 was led by the African-American President of the Board of Directors of Sierra Club, Aaron Mair, Tom Goldtooth of the Indigenous Environmental Network, Winona LaDuke of Honor the Earth, Bill McKibben of 350.org and Reverend Lennox Yearwood of the Hip Hop Caucus, among others. Mair wrote that the movement rejected the fossil fuel industries' discursive framing of crude oil from Canada as the solution to "energy independence for America" as a "cynical effort to deny sovereign indigenous people their treaty rights, and deny humanity a carbon-free future."[32] Such discursive framings of root causes, solutions and the stakes of struggle identify global relationships—of exploitation and historical injustice, on the one hand, and of solidarity, on the other hand. For actors identifying themselves with these movements, then, environmental problems are no longer local; they cannot be

30 Pope Francis used this term in his encyclical letter to Catholics, published June 17, 2015 (http://www.vatican.va/content/francesco/en/encyclicals/documents/papa-francesco_20150524_enciclica-laudato-si.pdf).

31 See http://www.climateactionnetwork.ca/who-we-are/our-members/.

32 Aaron Mair, "A Diverse Nation Comes Together Against Tar Sands," June 10, 2015, http://www.sierraclub.org/change/2015/06/diverse-nation-comes-together-against-tar-sands?utm_source=insider&utm_medium=email&utm_campaign=newsletter.

resolved by local action alone, or by mere "environmental regulation" of the existing economic model. In such framings, every environmental problem is enmeshed in multiple scales and in socio-economic relationships. As the term "climate justice" suggests, the crisis of nature and the crisis of justice (Sachs, 1999) require an integrated ecological and social response.

Environmentalism and political ecology in the Canadian context

In the wake of these transformations, what kind of environmental movement do we see in Canada today? A division of labour still operates among organizations, for reasons that have not changed greatly over two decades (Adkin, 1992, 2014). Not every environmental organization is concerned with issues that cross scales in the same ways that climate change does. Wilderness conservation campaigns or mobilizations around specific pollution sources may not require support from international coalitions or be significantly determined by transnational actors (corporate or other). There are, however, significantly different ways of framing what is at stake in such relatively local conflicts, and these differences are important to any mapping of environmental movements in relation to counter-hegemonic politics.

Wilderness preservation and species protection still constitute major concerns of the movement, but ENGO campaigns no longer proceed without regard to the traditional and territorial claims of First Nations. Indeed, the most significant change since the early 1990s, with regard to social movements, has been the rise everywhere of Indigenous movements for cultural survival and self-determination. In the Canadian context, the emergence of the Indigenous Environmental Network[33] and Idle No More (in 2012) have obliged the settler environmental movement organizations to move over and work in alliance with a new generation of Aboriginal leaders. This relationship is fraught with tensions, but also holds considerable counter-hegemonic potential. The Indigenous movement for self-determination has broken through the de facto apartheid system in which ENGOs operated 30 years ago, and has asserted a leadership role in struggles that makes these no longer

33 According to its website, the IEN was founded in 1990 and began to hire staff in 1995. See http://www.ienearth.org/about/.

only about "the environment," but also anti-colonial struggles. Many ENGOs are seeking, and embracing, these new alliances, as is evident in the pipeline conflicts in Canada (Enbridge's Northern Gateway, Kinder Morgan's TransMountain Pipeline, TransCanada Pipeline's Keystone extension and Energy East Pipeline project). Governments and corporations advancing resource exploitation projects—whether these be in mining, forestry, fisheries or related construction (roads, upgraders, terminals) and transportation sectors—now confront opposition from two movements, often working together, and employing a broader range of juridical and other resources (Adkin & Courteau forthcoming; Stendie & Adkin forthcoming).

As I suggested above, numerous conflicts are now linked by environmental actors to the deepening crisis of climate change, and, concomitantly, to the need for rapid "energy transition." From the internationalized campaign for a moratorium on the expansion of oil sands production and the anti-fracking movement in Québec to municipal debates over transportation and urban sprawl, every option is measured against the associated greenhouse gas emissions as well as the mitigation and adaptation costs of various courses of action. These articulations have expanded the potential for coalition-building. For example, politicians and citizens who may be skeptical about climate change science can nevertheless see the wisdom in achieving greater energy efficiencies and thereby minimizing medium- and long-term risks for municipal taxpayers.[34] Farmers and opponents of urban sprawl are connecting food security and local economy arguments to climate change concerns (the minimization of long-distance transportation). People on the west coast worried about oil (or diluted bitumen) spills are making common cause with Aboriginal communities situated along the pipeline routes or at the shipping terminal sites, as well as with climate change activists. There is not space here to paint a bigger picture of these connections, but taken as a whole, multiplying conflicts around land use, energy, water, health, protection of other species, livelihoods, Aboriginal sovereignty, climate justice and citizenship rights are converging in unprecedented ways.

34 This is one of the lessons of the Edmonton Citizens Panel on Energy Strategy and Climate Change, a deliberative exercize conducted by Alberta Climate Dialogue, the Centre for Public Involvement and the City of Edmonton's Environment Department in 2012. See http://www.albertaclimatedialogue.ca.

To the extent that social movements do converge around a broadly shared analysis of the social and ecological crises we are facing, and around a program of reforms, each movement is radicalized. For the environmental movement, this means, for example, that the agenda of reforms that some environmental think tanks and consultants have adopted as being politically "feasible" (e.g. "putting a price on carbon," creating markets in CO_2 offsets or mandating more stringent fuel efficiency standards for private vehicles) is pulled and stretched in directions that cannot so easily be assimilated by large corporations into their investment and marketing strategies, or exploited by financial capital. Demands coming from coalitions of climate/environmental/food security/Indigenous activists and organizations that constitute a more serious threat to hegemonic interests include, for example, restrictions on new resource exploitation in the North and the extension of First Nations' control over the ownership of these resources, the pinching of Canadian oil supplies to US and Asian markets, the withdrawal of massive subsidies for fossil fuel producers and the shifting of these to publicly owned renewable energy sources, challenges to the interests of "property developers" and the reassertion of political control over investment and trade rules.

A question that other contributors to this volume will address more fully is the role of the labour movement in the formation of such coalitions and of a new, political-ecological consensus. Not surprisingly, unions and the workforces they represent are not all moving in the same direction or at the same pace with regard to an agenda of political-ecological reforms. Resource sector workers, in particular, feel most directly threatened by talk of slowdowns or shutdowns in the oil sands, the Hibernia oil field, uranium mining, shale gas production, or gold and diamond mines. Likewise, many refinery, transportation, heavy machinery production, pipeline and construction sector workers are dependent for their jobs on continuing investment in resource extraction and access to markets for these resources. Jobs in these sectors have several other things in common: they are private sector jobs, they are relatively highly paid jobs and they are jobs mainly for men. Indeed, they often require the migration of men from their home communities to other parts of the country and the construction of work camps. Women, on the other hand, predominate in the lowest-paid, casual or part-time, and service sector jobs.[35] A significant set of cleavages (cultural, as well as pertaining to income or security) exists within the working class: between private and public sector workers, non-union and unionized workers, service sector and industrial workers, and minimum-wage and high-paid workers. Each of these cleavages maps onto gender, racial and citizenship[36] hierarchies.

Political ecologists are optimistic about the creation of sustainable livelihoods in a low-carbon (or "post-carbon") economy, but resources and opportunities for serious planning, leading to a managed transition, have been inadequate. Given the governments that have been in office municipally, provincially and federally for decades, it is understandable that workers in the resource-dependent sectors have low levels of trust in promises of a job-creating green transition. Moreover, while low-carbon economies may offer citizens more secure livelihoods in healthier and more resilient communities, along with the promise of an ecologically sustainable model of development for future generations, the new forms of employment are likely to offer lower nominal wages than many of the resource sector workers are accustomed to earning. Security and quality of life are not, of course, provided solely by private income, but also by public investment in universal services and infrastructure, as well as such measures as guaranteed income pensions, and so on. One sees here the extent and the complexity of the planning that needs to occur to bring about a transition to a low-carbon economy and a redistribution of wealth that guarantees income security and a high quality of life for all.

Making Change Real

"Environmentalism" in the form of a singular focus on wilderness or landscape preservation or the protection of human health from environmental contaminants has, through the anti-globalization and ecological justice struggles of the last 20 years, become more aware

35 In Alberta, for example, 71% of minimum-wage workers are women (Kleiss, 2014). Of the 23% of Alberta workers who are low-wage earners (under $16.00/hour), 61% are women (PIA, 2014).

36 Many of the low-wage workers are recent immigrants or temporary foreign workers.

of the inter dependencies that political ecological analysis identifies. Civil society organizations across the spectrum of "issues" are recognizing the fundamentally anti-democratic nature of neoliberal, patriarchal and colonial political governance. We see this in the social media campaigns mobilizing opposition to the Harper government in Canada, the "one percent," the plutocracy that rules the United States, the European banks and international financial institutions (IFIs), and other actors or institutions associated with global inequity and ecological destruction. There is growing awareness that democratic reforms need to be at the top of the agenda for the progressive social movements. They are essential to strengthen civil society—to deepen its capacities for formulating and implementing real alternatives to the existing norms and institutions of governance.

The democratization of political institutions—referring (in Canada) to such reforms as: public subvention of political parties; rules around party funding and advertising, as well as lobbying; government budgetary transparency; improved access to information; adoption of a proportional electoral system; abolition of the Senate; measures to increase the representation of women, racialized minorities and First Nations people in legislative bodies; the institutionalization of citizen deliberation in policy-making with political accountability to citizens—can be expected to revitalize public interest in political life, empower citizens vis-à-vis political decision-makers and significantly change the rules of the game with regard to governance.

Beyond political reforms, the defence (and extension of resources for) public goods is also foundational to democracy and participatory citizenship. Think, for example, of the ways in which universal, publicly funded education from early childhood education and care to university levels underpins social equality, the participation of women in public spheres, engaged citizenship and societal problem-solving capacities. Post-secondary education institutions and independent research institutes also produce much of the research used to inform public policy debates or citizen interventions in consultation processes. It is critical that this knowledge be produced by independent researchers in the public interest, and that it be available to the public—contrary to the trends we have seen since the 1980s in which these institutions are being restructured to serve corporate interests and knowledge is being commodified. Public broadcasting is another pillar of informed, engaged citizenship as well as the critical, independent journalism that holds public authorities to account (Leys, 2001). The trend in which public broadcasting is being forcibly wizened by budgetary starvation while a handful of corporations are permitted to control vast media empires needs to be reversed. Priority reforms at the federal level, then, should include a proportional electoral system, a democratized and expanded CBC, and a strong "public interest" mandate for the post-secondary education system accompanied by the democratization of and increased resourcing for the national research funding agencies.

What do such reforms (and many more) have to do with the agenda of critical political ecology? Ecologists, like other social movement actors, lament the power of corporate interests to determine government policies (municipally, provincially, federally), as well as the neoliberal and productivist commitments of most of the governing parties. They struggle to influence policy outcomes in a system that is designed to ensure their marginality. The election of "green" governments committed to a political-ecological agenda of change, *and the successful implementation of such a transition* in the face of the predictable capitalist backlash, will require the prior existence of an educated, organized and empowered "green public."

The recent election of an NDP government in Alberta—after 44 years of one-party rule by the Conservatives—is explained not only by the combination of the incompetence of the Conservatives as fiscal managers and a period of low oil prices (hence provincial revenue shortfalls), but also by the less examined changes taking place in civil society since the mid-1990s. In particular, the establishment of public interest organizations[37] and their steady output of reports (documenting the failures of government policies and the availability of well-researched alternatives) have contributed substantially to the

37 The Pembina Institute, the Parkland Institute and Public Interest Alberta have been particularly important in countering the claims of the right-wing think tanks (like the Fraser Institute, the University of Calgary School of Public Policy), associations (e.g. Canadian Taxpayers' Federation), neoliberal economists, and corporate and Conservative Party campaigns to shape public opinion. They have had some support from counterparts like the Canadian Centre for Policy Alternatives.

reframing of conflicts and the discrediting of hegemonic discourse. Notably, at least three of these organizations (Parkland Institute, Public Interest Alberta, Friends of Medicare) have received support from the Alberta Federation of Labour or other union organizations. These labour organizations are also producing their own research. Labour leaders in Alberta appear to have learned the lessons of the crushing defeat of civil society opposition to the 1990s' "Klein Revolution." Over time, options that earlier were labelled by the governing party as "anti-Albertan" or "unrealistic" gained in credibility among larger audiences. The NDP, whose platform has drawn heavily upon the research of these organizations, has benefited from the groundwork they put in place. By moving swiftly to democratize political institutions and to provide resources for civil society organizations, the NDP can reinforce the infrastructure that will sustain a vibrant green public. The possibility of a further substantial transformation in the conditions for counter-hegemonic politics is now open.

Conclusion

Political ecology is integral to a counter-hegemonic reform agenda because it offers a substantive set of directions for a post-capitalist, ecologically sustainable model of development. Returning to the brief discussion of resource sector workers, above, and to Raymond Williams's insistence that people need to be able to believe that "practical alternatives" are available, it is clear that political ecologists must build coalitions to develop and negotiate transitional plans as well as new institutions. The starting points for such coalitions may be municipal or regional; the ways in which national and global institutions (treaties, trade and investment agreements, WTO rules, jurisdictional division of powers, etc.) constrain, obstruct (or occasionally enable) changes at the local level will become clear soon enough, and will point the way toward the coalitions and reforms needed at other scales. What is important, as Williams observed, is that: "while certain principles can be established, all actual policies have to depend on new and difficult audits of resources, which must by definition be specific. We can look first at the principles, but their full practical bearings cannot be set down except in this place and that, by this enquiry and that, in a sustained and necessarily negotiated process" (1983: 256). This conclusion directs our attention to what are, in my view, the critical tasks of the organic intellectuals of counter-hegemonic politics. There is, of course, the need to root political discourse in shared values and a common agenda of democratic reforms. Research must construct a solid account of the political, economic, cultural and ecological relationships operative within a given frame of action, including the ways in which these relationships cross multiple scales (from the local to the global). This foundation is essential to identifying the agency of change and the resources needed to strengthen civil society, and to develop a program and strategy for change. All of the social movements, including the unions, have important, necessary roles to play in such planning and negotiation.

Williams argued further that criticism of capitalism or enumeration of the many horrors of the times (salient then, the fear of nuclear war) would, alone, do little to mobilize people to undertake collective action for a better world. When he wrote these words, climate change and peak oil were hardly on our radar, nor the risks of genetically modified organisms, nor imminent mass extinctions of other species due to human demands on the planet's carrying capacity. Chernobyl hadn't happened yet. Today, more than ever, counter-hegemonic politics must be about "making hope practical, rather than despair convincing" (Williams, 1983: 240). Political ecology offers many of the tools we need to build a world in which humans and all of nature are no longer treated, as Williams put it, as "raw material for production," but in which there is a "new orientation of livelihood: of practical, self-managing, self-renewing societies, in which people care first for each other, in a living world" (1983: 262, 266).

GLOBALIZATION, MOVEMENTS AND THE DECENTRED STATE

Warren Magnusson

When we talk about social "movements," what is it that moves, and in relation to what? Do we have some "fixtures" in mind when we speak about movements? If so, what are they, and what do we mean by suggesting that they are stable? Does globalization refer to a process of *de*stabilization, and, if so, what is being destabilized: the fixtures or the movements (or both)? Why do we describe globalization as "economic," but call movements "social"? What do we mean by the economic and the social, and how do these things relate to the "political"? Is the political what relates to the state, and, if so, is *that* what is being destabilized? Is the destabilization the same as "decentring"?

My purpose here is not to answer all these questions, but instead to suggest that the answers we normally take for granted are inadequate. Ultimately, I point toward a different way of thinking about social movements. I refuse the two distinctions that enable us to talk about social movements in the traditional way: between social order and social movements and between the political and the social. These distinctions get in the way of realistic thinking about politics. The very idea of "social science" is at odds with political understanding, and we need to foreground the political if we are to make sense of the world in which we live—a world best understood as a global city, a city that is itself an ensemble of movements that make up our way of life. Following Louis Wirth (1938), I designate that way of life as "urbanism." Unlike him, I suggest that urbanism can only be understood as a political phenomenon, and that we need to relate to that political phenomenon. Recent theories of globalization (Knox & Taylor, 1995; Castells, 1996; Appadurai, 1996; Brody, 2001; Held & McGrew, 2003)—and their reverse, ideas about decentring (Hardt & Negri, 2000)—point toward that phenomenon, but give us few means for understanding it. This lack is related to the tendency to depoliticize everything we analyze scientifically. Consciously or unconsciously, we conceal the politics of our analyses—sometimes by offering misleading shows of our political commitments—in order to conceal the politics of the phenomena we are analyzing.

The Idea of a Social Movement

On most conceptions, there is a comparatively stable frame, environment or structure in relation to which social movements occur. Judging from the social science literature, it seems that the relevant fixtures are the ones that hold people in place: the laws, customs, structures of government, hierarchies of status, differences in wealth and income, and other features of society of which people often complain. Apparently, a social movement is something that challenges the "social order," whatever that is (Tarrow, 1994; Tilly, 2006).

Every social movement that has been identified as such tends to have a different conception of the fixtures it is moving against. Socialism, environmentalism and feminism are far from the same in their aims and objectives; more different still are the various religious and nationalist movements. One way of understanding this is to say that every movement defines its *own* time and space: that is, it locates itself in relation to certain fixtures of social reality, gives an account of its own origins, defines for itself a terrain of struggle, and projects a vision of what the world should be like (Touraine, 1981, 1995; Walker, 1988, 2010; Melucci, 1989, 1996; Eyerman & Jamison, 1991; Vahabzadeh, 2003).

The surprising thing is that many analysts assume that there is ultimately a *single* fixture against which contemporary social movements are struggling. In the belief of these analysts the central fixture against which all the "progressive" movements are struggling is the one that stabilizes the various forms of exploitation and oppression (Young, 1990). It might be capitalism, patriarchy, anthropocentrism or something else. Move this fixture, and everything else begins to move; keep it steady, and everything is held in place. If this is so, there is a *centre* to the politics of social movements, which has to be discovered politically. Based on this view, things really start cooking politically—qualitative change is in prospect—when the movements get their acts *together* (Butler, Laclau & Zizek, 2000; Conway, 2004; Hardt &

Negri, 2004, 2009). It is possible on this view to distinguish between fundamentally *reactionary* movements, which altogether mistake the sources of exploitation and oppression, and fundamentally *progressive* movements, which identify at least some of the real obstacles.

Within the social movements that command our attention in this book, there seems to be an oscillation between two poles. At the one extreme is what we might call a particularist radicalism, which constitutes itself within its own space and time and imagines itself capable of self-transformation (Day, 2005; De Young & Princen, 2012; Hern, 2010). Thus, we have people creating their own communities and attempting to free themselves by their own actions from the strictures imposed by the rest of the world. Such communities have a tendency to treat everyone outside them as an actual or potential enemy. Their inwardness (and potential hostility to others) limits their ability to generate more profound social change. At the opposite extreme is the feeling within social movements that everyone really is *the same*—that all people are one, in principle, and that, since what *we* believe is true for everyone, there really is nothing legitimate outside our movement (Ingram, 2013). This usually involves the idea that the fixtures that dominate us form a single ensemble, which is subject to fundamental transformation. Thus, the centring of movement activity seems to follow from a certain conception of its object.

The idea of *fundamental* social change was at the heart of the 18th century conception of a "revolution" (Tilly, 1978). The French revolutionaries thought they could overthrow the fixtures of the *ancien régime* and establish a new society. As they imagined it, nothing would remain the same once the old regime had been replaced. Moreover, they sensed that, although the revolutionary movement could proceed in many venues, the movement would remain incomplete if it did not transform the state. As the centre of sovereign authority and thus of armed force and legal regulation, the state was a nexus of resistance to revolutionary change. It had to be overcome or transformed.

To a large extent, social movement politics is caught up with the old idea of a revolution, and comes with the same intellectual baggage, especially the notion that there is a fixture that holds things together, a fixture that activists—call them rebels, revolutionaries, resisters or protesters—can transform if they get hold of it. Is this what draws activists toward the state as an object of protest, even when their theories suggest that change has to happen elsewhere or in a different way? Are activists, like earlier revolutionaries, just being realistic when they challenge the state, or is this realism an ideological reflex that needs challenging?

The Idea of the State

Whatever the 18th century revolutionists intended, they set in train a series of movements that delegitimated previous political structures and established the idea that legitimate governments derive their authority from the people (Vincent, 1987; Held, 1995; Cruikshank, 1999; Rose, 1999; Dean, 2010). The effects of these movements have been felt throughout the world. So-called progressives have been especially eager to pursue democratization and thus to work within the processes it entails. This may mean working "within the system," but at its extreme such a politics entails a revolutionary challenge to the government and hence to the state itself. Most democratic activists have believed that the people need to form a party of their own so as to make the state theirs. As an ideal, the state is a promise of justice, and so no matter how much social movement activity exists, the terrain of politics seems to slope toward it (Derrida, 1994). Serious activists are thus drawn into the domain of party politics, where the object of state power is explicit.

This centring process is always resisted within a social movement, however. By definition, a social movement is within civil society, and thus appears to be outside the state (Cohen & Arato, 1992). People in the movement are supposed to renew or revolutionize themselves. From this perspective the fixtures that prevent people from becoming what they should be are actually deep within them: it is these fixtures, above all, that must be shifted. To the extent that a social movement is informed by such a perspective, it tends to turn inward. However, in a dialectical reversal, such inward-turning often results in an outward explosion of energy, and in this context "realists" within the movement suggest that it cannot achieve its outward objectives unless it organizes itself in relation to the state. The transformation of the state thus appears as the ultimate objective of outward, political action.

Contemporary political space appears to have a particular shape, and this *ideologically shaped appearance* has profound implications for how we think about politics (Bartelson, 1995, 2001; Walker, 1993, 2010). The world is divided into sovereign states, which collide with one another in international relations, but each of these sovereign states is constituted as an autonomous political centre. Thus, to be effective (realists say), a social movement must organize itself not in accordance with its *own* conception of space and time, but rather in accordance with structures for politics that are already given. In consequence, a profound tension always exists between the timing and spacing of the movement itself—its own conception of when and where it is acting in its movement for change—and the political grid it confronts in the form of the state.

Given the other "sovereignty" that movements must confront—the sovereignty of "the individual"—the inward turning of movements is crucial to success. In the rhetoric of sovereignty, a person's or state's desires are supposed to be respected because they reflect needs or interests that are constituted from within. It is not for others to say whether these desires/needs/interests are authentic or appropriate. Thus, on this view, relations between individuals or states have to be conceived as *external* relations, in which interests are potentially at variance. For social movements, this is a problematic conception, for they wish to put what is internal to individuals or states at issue. The presumption is that states/individuals have been fixed in particular forms and are now held in relations of domination that give the lie to the idea that what is expressed by a particular individual or state is an authentic representation of what lies within. Rather, what we express is supposed to be an effect of the systems of domination that hold us in thrall. Generally, we say what is expected of us, and we also *want* what is expected of us (to the delight of advertisers). If we are to become different, we have to challenge or be challenged in terms of what we are internally. Insofar as social movements mount such challenges, they disrupt the sovereignty claims of both states and individuals, and hence are engaged in a "revolutionary" politics.

There can be no doubt that a social movement expressing an alternative vision of human life is on a dangerous and difficult political terrain. It is challenging the fixtures within both the individual and the state, and as such it is doubly at odds with the dominant order. This is why social movement activism so often conveys the sense of a life on the edge. As an activist, one is balanced precariously between the forms of life implicit in an alternative vision and the ones imposed in the dominant order. To imagine that the dominant order is on the verge of transformation, or to think oneself into a place where nothing outside really matters, is to ease the psychological tensions involved in living on the edge. However, there is liable to be a violent oscillation between political "realism" and political "idealism." Those who opt for the former are liable to be condemned for "selling out," while the rest will be accused of self-indulgent withdrawal from the real world. This tragic cycle, which forms the stuff of the morose reflections of ex-activists, is not one that can be broken by retracing the old paths under new colours. More fundamental rethinking is required, and this will take us into the domain of the state's significant other: civil society.

The Idea of Society

It may not be apparent to sociology students that the idea of "society" is parasitic upon the notion of the state, a notion that began to take shape in 16th century Europe (Skinner, 1978). The state was understood as the ultimate source of order, and hence as what *constituted* a society legally and politically. As Hegel (1991) put it in the early 19th century, the state was the ground and completion of civil society. Now we take the identification of states and societies largely for granted, and label cultures, economies, societies and even languages in state-centric terms. The other aspect of this is that we assume that everything associated with the state—law, government, political institutions and public administration—is on one side, and everything else on the other, as part of "society." So, the economy is thought to be separate from the state, as are family life, social activity, cultural expression and most of the things we associate with social movements. If we assume that life exists in a lot of separate spheres, each with its own rationale, we can develop a science for each. That has been the project of the modern social sciences. One aspect of this project has been the aim to explain everything naturalistically, and hence without reference to philosophy, politics or religion.

In ancient times Aristotle (1963, 1996) insisted that the economic had to be understood in relation to the political, and the political in relation to the philosophical, in accordance with the hierarchy of ends in human life. The displacement of this hierarchy by a naturalistic science of society—either in the guise of an independent sociology or an ensemble of social sciences, each with its specific field of interest—in itself entailed a different way of thinking about politics. In this new way of thinking (which is now so old to us that we forget that there was ever any alternative), "politics" is a special sort of activity, separated off from other things that people do. The domain of the state (or activity in relation to the state) is the home turf of politics. We identify activity in other domains as political insofar as it mimics the forms and practices of politics on its home turf. For instance, we look for conflicts of interest and value that put rules of social practice into question, examine patterns of domination and resistance, and attempt to explain cooperation and conflict. In this way, we can identify politics wherever we choose to look in civil society. Such a parasitic conception of politics leaves in place the assumption that political action is epiphenomenal—in other words, that what people do politically can be explained by forces at work outside politics. This is the tendency of all forms of naturalistic explanation, a mode of explanation implicit in the idea that a complete science of human life is necessarily social rather than political.

Aristotle (1963: 26-27) says that the science of politics is properly conceived as the *master* science. This idea follows from his understanding that politics is concerned with the development and implementation of the principles necessary for the good life. To Aristotle, a polis (what we might call a city-state) was a complete community, whose way of life or principles of organization were always at stake politically. To be active politically was to be engaged practically in the question of what form the polis should take and how that form could be preserved or implemented. Nothing was outside politics, because the question of politics was the question of how we should live. Thus we might have other sciences—he might talk of rhetoric or military leadership, we might say sociology or economics—that might properly inform our political science, but the centrality of political science followed from the fact that the other sciences were to contribute to political judgment. The need for political judgment was not only an unavoidable human need, but one that reflected the highest of human capacities: the capacity to establish a way of life for ourselves, and to govern ourselves in accordance with the principles we had established. What centred the various sciences (including what we call the natural sciences) was this need for political judgment. These sciences were useful insofar as they helped us decide what we had to do, and the greatest questions we had to decide were political (that is, they related to our lives as a whole or in their full complexity).

This suggests an important distinction between a politics centred on the state and one centred on the problem of judgment. The state is conceived as a set of institutions standing over and apart from society. As such, it appears as a fixture, and politics seems like an activity related to that fixture. By contrast, a judgment-centred politics has no necessary spatial location: or, to be more accurate, its space expands indefinitely to encompass the whole, and then folds in on itself in particular locations. A judgment-centred science or philosophy (the distinction between the two becomes immaterial in this context) tends to focus all inquiries on the ultimate question: what is to be done? This is a question that can be posed locally or globally, and, wherever it is posed, it points beyond itself to the other locations where it is addressed. Insofar as this political question is displaced in favour of naturalistic explanation, the science in which we are engaged is reified and depoliticized. The further we go along such a path, the more difficult it becomes to recognize our own political assumptions.

This brings us back to the question of a social movement. Why do we call these movements *social*? Is it that we want to repress the knowledge that these movements are political? Or, are we so attached to the state that we cannot think the political otherwise, however much we try? What are the implications of shifting the centre of political activity to civil society and separating that off from the state? If societies are just states in disguise, how can turning from politics to social action enable us to deal with economic globalization or the decentring or "hollowing out" of the state?

The Idea of the Global

An obvious difficulty with Aristotle's analysis is that he fixes politics within the polis. His ideal was a self-sufficient city-state, not too small to be independent but not too large to be known properly by its own citizens. For him, citizenship was something that should only be conferred on the masters of households—not on women or slaves or servants or dependants. Moreover, the polis was to be fiercely independent—prepared for war if necessary (one of the reasons why Aristotle thought of citizenship as naturally male). As a result, the polis was like a protected enclosure: set off from other such political communities and guarded against the intrusions of women, children, workmen and others who were deemed incapable of rational political judgment. Although open debate and considered judgment on human affairs as a whole were supposedly at the centre of politics, that centre was constituted as a citadel fortified against the wrong people (Rancière, 1995, 1998, 2006).

By comparison, the modern state *seems* more open and inclusive. Citizenship is available to everyone, and states spread out over huge tracts of territory with millions or even hundreds of millions of inhabitants. Thus, the masses and the strangers, the low-born and the poor, the feminine and the juvenile are all included within the politics of the state. But, this inclusiveness—which we call "democracy"—seems like a sham, because the fix is in from the start (Young, 2000; Isin, 2002). Formerly separate societies, economies and cultures are now so closely integrated that the putative sovereignty of states seems increasingly illusory. Although when we have an election or discuss public policy in a country like Canada, we pretend that we are sovereign, we know that we have to defer to the demands of "the market," the rules set by international agencies, and—especially—the requirements of the United States. Our national sovereignty, like the freedom we offer to the young, comes with so many conditions that it often seems like the opposite of what it is supposed to be.

Much of what people have in mind when they talk about "globalization" is the intensification of market pressures. All activities—including artistic creation, scholarly research, charitable service and public deliberation—are now considered to be marketable commodities. To merit a decent life, one must have worth on the market, and to have worth on the market one must become what the market demands. Of course, a real freedom is involved in being able to spend or give money as we choose, and being allowed to compete in any business or for any occupation that attracts us. But this freedom is the sunny side of the totalitarianism of the market: the flowers on our chains, as Rousseau (1987: 3) put it more than two centuries ago. By enslaving ourselves to the market, we get access to what the market offers, but at the price of becoming what the market demands. There is no guarantee even then that the market will have use for us: that is what faces people in what Mike Davis (2006) calls "the planet of slums."

For more than 40 years, the major governments in the Western world have been trying to cut back public expenditures, privatize public services and reorganize government on market principles (Harvey, 2005a; Panitch & Gindin, 2012; Banting & Myles, 2013). There has been a good deal of resistance to this process, and the process has been slow as a result. However, the trend has been accelerating since the 1990s. The theme of domestic politics in almost every country is the one enunciated so succinctly by British Prime Minister Margaret Thatcher in the early 1980s: "There is no alternative." Since there is no alternative, the point of political activity seems increasingly obscure, and it is not surprising that voter participation is declining, that people are becoming more alienated from their governments, and that new oppositional movements are again expressing the sort of anger and vengefulness once associated with fascism. When the popular desire for revenge is more apparent than the desire for liberation, optimistic talk about the positive features of contemporary social movements seems touchingly anachronistic. Can movements be anything other than punitive and destructive when "there is no alternative" to the totalitarianism of the market?

To put the issue so starkly is to remind ourselves that, when we invoke the "social" in the context of a political analysis, we are referring to whatever has been expelled from the realm of respectable politics. Social movements express the goals, identities, aspirations and resentments that have not been completely incorporated into the routines of day-to-day politics within the state. Thus, the movements always represent a threat of some sort to the good order of the state.

We should not delude ourselves into thinking that what has been excluded is necessarily benign, although we should be able to see that the relentless restriction of political opportunity implicit in the globalization of the market is a major source of popular desperation. In a perverse cycle, political exclusions themselves produce the desperate behaviour that justifies demands for more exclusions. One of the great themes of neoconservatism in the 1970s was that we could no longer afford democracy, because the people expected government to spend more money than capitalists were prepared to allow. The solution proposed was to put legal limits on public spending, borrowing and taxation, and to force governments to put as many services on the market as possible (Crozier, Huntington & Watanuki, 1975; Gill, 1990). *Voilà*, the politics of the 1990s and beyond. If we are to break the vicious cycle of political restrictions, we really need to globalize our politics, so that we can deal constructively with the forces that are impoverishing our lives and producing the violence that we can sense around us.

Unfortunately, it is difficult to know what such a globalized politics would involve. I have no simple answers of my own, but I do think that we have to make a conceptual shift from our state-centric conceptions of society and politics, economy and culture. For me, this process is eased when I begin thinking of the world as a huge city, with economies, cultures and systems of governance that recall the patterns of the great metropolises of the past and present (Magnusson, 1996, 2011, 2015). In such metropolises, there is no state that provides an overarching order: rather, it is the life of the metropolis that encompasses the activity of state agencies and puts them in play in relation to a variety of other activities. To analyze such political complexity, we have to remember that the phenomena we are observing are not fixtures but movements. These movements interact in complicated ways—in fact, in such complicated ways that the interaction probably cannot be conceived as occurring within familiar four-dimensional space. Since every movement creates its own space-time, we have to imagine interaction in a global *hyper*-space (Kaku, 1994; Magnusson, 2000), which has many more than four dimensions and which allows for regional autonomies that, although relative and limited, are nonetheless real. How one is to act politically in such a global hyperspace is not immediately apparent, but we may get some clues from thinking about the nature of the city (Amin & Thrift, 2002; Kingwell, 2008; Brugmann, 2009; Beaumont & Dart, 2010; Saunders, 2010)—and more particularly from reflection on urbanism as an "architectonic" social movement.

The Idea of Urbanism

In 1938 Louis Wirth wrote what was to become the most widely cited article in American sociology: "Urbanism as a Way of Life." He was trying to make sense of the difference between modern US society and the old world that was passing away. He did not necessarily applaud what was going on, but he could see that the Chicago with which he was familiar was fundamentally different from the forms of society that still existed in the US countryside. He did not think that terms like capitalism or industrialism fully represented or explained that difference; so, he hit on the notion of "urbanism as a way of life." There are several important insights buried in Wirth's concept: (1) what is dominant is not a structure but a movement (urbanism); (2) this movement is to be understood as a "way of life": that is, holistically; and (3) the movement somehow encompasses other movements like capitalism and industrialism (to which, we might add scientism, liberalism and statism). The big mistake that Wirth made was to understand the architectonic movement of urbanism naturalistically, rather than to conceive of it as a political movement. A political movement is something that can be contested from within and without.

Thinking about urbanism in the widest terms, we can see that it is at least as old as the ancient civilizations of Egypt and Iraq: it has been with us in some form for thousands of years (Mumford, 1961). Urbanism is older than modernity or capitalism. The outward explosion of the Europeans in the 16th century, the revolutions in commerce and industry in the 17th and 18th centuries, the consolidation of industrial capitalism and European imperialism in the 19th century, and the successive reorganizations of the world economy and the state system in the 20th century and since certainly have involved profound qualitative changes in the conditions of human life. In retrospect we can see that the way of life that has emerged from these changes—and that was foreshadowed long before—is urbanism (LeGates & Stout, 2016; Parker, 2004). Moreover, it is now becoming apparent that we all live in a giant city of global scale.

No one particularly intended to create a global city, and it was not apparent until recently that such a thing was possible. Nonetheless, the impetus in this direction can be detected in the processes to which Marx and Engels drew attention many years ago (Marx, 1977). Those were processes of material production, whereby successive generations of people in different parts of the world attempted to provide for their own subsistence, and developed new needs as they did. In turn these new needs induced further inventions, and so on, in a continuing cycle. Whether or not people really meant to, they have been gradually changing the world to suit themselves. Thus, they have been humanizing their own environment, so that the world in which people live today is already in large degree the effect of earlier human actions (Cronon, 1991, 1996). The semiconscious effort to make the world into a place that suits us ultimately takes the form of urbanism: a way of life in which people concentrate in cities and towns, which are connected to one another by various means, and from which people appropriate the surrounding countryside and natural wilderness. In the end, what is outside the urban is what has yet to be fully controlled. At a certain point—the point we have now reached, I think—it becomes apparent that the urban system is so dense that it no longer makes sense to think of cities as separate from one another. What we used to call cities are more like particular districts of a single, global city, which extends to the most obscure corners of the earth (McLuhan, 1964; Lefebvre, 2003).

There is little to be gained from imagining that wilderness reserves or fishing villages or tribal communities or family farms are somehow outside the urban. In fact, every one of these "places"—real or imaginary—has a vital role to play in marketing the products demanded by urbanites (Zukin, 1991, 1995, 2010). Moreover, the place of these places within the larger whole is determined by a politics that we can sensibly designate as "urban." Urban politics in this sense is not a politics confined to municipalities, nor is it peculiar to places where the density of human settlement is especially high. Rather, the politics of the urban is the politics that relates—critically or supportively—to the practices by which we humanize our environment. The urbanites who sit down in front of logging trucks or pipeline carriers are involved in a form of urban politics: they want the fact of their protest flashed across screens around the world, and hope for decisive remedial action from the urban centres of power (Magnusson & Shaw, 2003; Klein, 2014). They are acting from within to secure a natural "outside" that puts appropriate limits to human endeavour.

To think this way about what we are doing is to emphasize that none of us are outside the practices by which we are destroying the natural wilderness, enslaving ourselves to the market, excluding socially marked minorities, acting violently and otherwise behaving in ways that moralists label inhuman. Since we share in the responsibility for the dreadful things that are happening (as well as in the credit for human achievements), there can be no honest politics that fails to remind us of this responsibility. Urbanism is *our* way of life, and it is our responsibility as humans to recognize the way we are living, to take responsibility for what we are doing, and to consider what we can do politically to improve our own practices. In this context, we need to recognize that we are involved in a number of activities, the most important of which we can conceive as social movements. These movements are not necessarily directed at particular fixtures. On the contrary, they create their own spaces in relation to other ongoing activities. In truth, the human world is a world in movement in which the apparent fixtures are just sedimentations or reifications of earlier movements. Movements move in relation to one another, and not in relation to stable fixtures.

So, how are we to think of the state, or the market, or patriarchy? There is only one possible answer: as movements. Conceived as a fixture, we can imagine the contemporary economy as "the market" or "the globalized market." Conceived as a movement, the same phenomena appear as capitalism. That capitalism is a movement (and that Marx, for instance, conceived it so) is quite apparent, not only because capitalists (like other movement activists) spend huge amounts of time and money on publicizing their cause, organizing political parties, and so on, but also because the institutions and practices produced by capitalism are constantly changing (Dean, 2010; Gill & Cutler, 2014; Panitch & Gindin, 2012). Capitalism is not some fixed thing: it is a movement that brings people in relation to one another in particular ways and encourages them to respond creatively to the constraints and opportunities that arise in consequence. The forms of political, social and economic organization that are most conducive to capitalism are subject to constant revision, and so it is always a mistake for critics and opponents of capitalism to suppose that the form fixed for now will still be there in ten or 20 years. We might say the same for statism, patriarchy, racism or any of the other movements that have been subject to criticism or resistance.

To understand statism as a movement is particularly important, for it is in and through this particular movement that we come to understand politics in a particular way. It is important to recognize (*pace* Marx) that statism is not simply an effect of capitalism. Statism emerged in the context of 16th century humanism, and took particular hold on the Western political imagination as a consequence of the 17th century wars of religion. It may be well to remember in our own age of religious fundamentalism that statism was and is a movement *against* such fundamentalism and in favour of a particular form of civilized political order. One of the questions that we have to face today is whether statism remains the most adequate response to the dangers of religious warfare, or whether we must act to transcend the movement altogether. Certainly, the proliferation of states and interstate institutions in the 20th century suggests that statism will continue to be a powerful movement for the foreseeable future. It is less clear what other movements will be producing alternatives.

The Idea of the Political

Lurking in this analysis is a concept of the political that has yet to be articulated with sufficient clarity. If we accept the idea that what appears to us is an ensemble of movements—some more important than others, but none of them with the capacity to determine the whole completely—then the politics that must concern us is *within and between movements*. But, what is it to say, "politics" (Arendt, 1958; Maier, 1987; Rancière, 1995; Isin, 2002; Keane, 2003; Crick, 2005; Mouffe, 2005; Walker, 2010; Merrifield, 2013)? If politics is not simply what relates to the state or mimics it, what is it? What are we saying when we declare that a particular problem is political, or label our own actions as political interventions? What is the point of thinking politically rather than socially?

As indicated above, concepts like judgment and responsibility seem to be intimately associated with the notion of politics. To act politically is to take responsibility and to exercise judgment. But, in relation to what? The simplest answer is, "In relation to everything." The political is what exceeds the merely economic, social or moral. It is the domain in which we are obliged to relate economics, morality, religion, identity and much else to one another. It is the domain in which the rules of judgment the boundaries between one thing and another, are always in question. These matters are in question because they have no universally satisfying answers, and because the political is the locus for resolving differences that cannot be resolved by applying the established rules. The political is always a domain of uncertainty, negotiation, deliberation, compromise—and violence. That we could constitute the political as a domain without violence is a recurring dream, but violence is always in the shadows, always a problem (and an option) that must be considered (Campbell & Dillon, 1993). Politics is always difficult and dangerous (if only for the people who are excluded from it). To draw attention to the political character of our activities is to remind ourselves of our own violence, as well of the ideals we pursue. It is thus to insist on our responsibility for our own actions, and on the need for judgment in these matters.

So conceived, politics is the creator and destroyer of boundaries. Political activity may produce the boundaries between one country and another or between the state and civil society, but it is also political activity that puts those boundaries into question. If I am right about the fact that we are now living in a global city, then the familiar boundaries of modern politics are now contained within a way of life that washes over them. The world contains a proliferation of political authorities, each of them liminal; that is, every authority sits uneasily at a boundary, pointing beyond itself into the world as a whole. Few of these authorities are democratic (Archibugi & Held, 1995; Isin, 2000; Gill & Cutler, 2014; Held, 2010; Shaw, 2000; Sinclair, 2004). None is sovereign in the relevant sense. The Aristotelian idea of a self-contained polity is illusory, as activists who retreat into their own communities soon discover. Whether we like it or not, we are in a world of movements that interact with one another in complicated ways and require us to respond to them, despite the fact that we can never quite predict the consequences of our own actions. The political challenge is that we have to do this collectively. It is not a challenge that we can refuse by pretending that we are just playthings of the gods.

CONSENT, COERCION AND THE CRIMINALIZATION OF DISSENT

Lesley Wood and Craig Fortier

- In 2013 RCMP tactical units armed with assault weapons raided the anti-fracking blockade of Mi'kmaq activists in New Brunswick.
- In 2015, police tear-gassed, pepper-sprayed, surrounded, arrested and ticketed student protesters in Montreal for marching without permission.
- In 2015, the federal government passed Bill C51 that increased the power of intelligence authorities to monitor Indigenous anti-pipeline activists.

It appears that the space for dissent is shrinking. And clearly, the state response to dissent is increasingly militarized and pre-emptive. But then we remember the clubbing, shooting and killing of strikers in the Winnipeg General Strike in 1919, the armed siege, tear gas and flash-bang grenades against Mohawk protesters at Kanehsatà:ke in 1990 and the infiltration of anti-apartheid movement groups in the 1980s. So perhaps things have always been this way? What has changed? How do we understand the long histories of repression by the Canadian state, while also paying attention to recent changes?

In their analysis of changes to protest policing in Europe and the US, Donatella della Porta and Herbert Reiter (1998) suggested that protest policing strategy is determined by

1. Configurations of political power
2. Organizational features of the police
3. Public opinion
4. Police occupational culture
5. Police interaction with protesters

All of these are filtered by police knowledge, defined as "the police's perception of external reality, which shapes the concrete policing of protest on the ground" (1998: 22). This framework gives us a starting point for understanding the continuities and changes of political repression in Canada, especially if we recognize that the "configurations of political power" must incorporate the broader political economy that shapes the regime. By locating the operation of repressive authorities (police, intelligence and military) in a framework that pays attention to state formation, in a context of colonialism, capitalism and white supremacy, we can see both the continuities and the changes (Smith, 2010).

Charles Tilly's (1985) model of state formation highlights the foundational processes of resource extraction. The particular features of these processes, when combined with the elements in della Porta and Reiter, shape the form repression takes. Tilly's model, like Gramsci's, sees states as institutions that combine both coercion and consent. While liberal democratic states like Canada have emphasized consent, over the past fifteen years there appears to be a return to more visible repression of increasingly broad sections of the population. While this shift has been identified in other OECD countries, in Canada, the ways this has manifested are rooted in the history of Canada as a settler colonial state.

State Formation and Settler Colonialism

The world is divided amongst nation-states modelled on the regimes that emerged out of struggle between powerholders in 16th-18th century Europe. To subdue or co-opt challengers both inside and outside of the boundaries of their territory, they needed to extract resources. The demands of state-making, war-making and offering protection to supporters shaped the subsequent infrastructure. The organization of armed agents of the state required for war-making, state-making and protection of capital required economic, political and social infrastructure—and necessitated the extraction of resources (Tilly, 1992).

Emergent European powers obtained the resources needed to assert political sovereignty through the dispossession of the people in their own territory, the taxation of trade, contracts with allies, the expansion of the African slave trade and the colonization of people in distant lands. In North America, as in South Africa, Israel, Australia and New Zealand, settler colonial control was established through the dispossession of the Indigenous people and the theft of land (Coulthard, 2014a). Over a few hundred years, institutions and structures were imposed on decimated, displaced and marginalized Indigenous populations. At the same time, in much of the Americas, settler colonialism was also shaped by the extraction of resources and forms of social organization made possible by the exploitation of African slave labour.

Settler Colonialism and Repression

Repressive authorities play a particular role in state formation—facilitating the accumulation of wealth and power by those in control. When and how consent and coercion operate is shaped by the way that resources are extracted, by the organization of state power and by the interactions amongst settlers of different classes and Indigenous populations. Extraction had particular features that shaped the Canadian settler state. The earliest European settlers, mainly British and French, were part of a private commercial process of extracting wealth for Europe through the conquest of territory and peoples. The Hudson's Bay Company (HBC) was founded in 1670 and established settlements and treaty relationships. Canadian confederation in 1867 built off of this corporate foundation of land theft and resource extraction, one which offered "protection" and resources to allies and insiders through co-optation and treaties but sought to subdue or eliminate challengers outside the corporation (and its sponsors in the British monarchy). The first purveyors of organized force would have been the armed guards and private security of corporate interests. Employers used military, militia and "specials" appointed by local magistrates to police strike activities, plus private police such as Pinkerton's as both spies and security forces—some of whom who used beatings and summary executions (deLint & Hall, 2009: 55). But soon, colonial authorities incorporated public police into the growing state infrastructure.

Emsley (1999) argues that these models emerged in 19th century Britain and France, and spread to varying extents throughout Europe, the British Empire and the United States. "These ideal types—state civilian, municipal civilian and state military—differ in chain of command and accountability and in the way that men were recruited, equipped and deployed. In Canada, all three ideal types are represented and can account for long-standing differences among Canada's police" (in The Council of Canadian Academies, 2014).

The state military North Western Mounted Police (NWMP) and its descendants have played a key role in Canadian policing. The NWMP was organized as a paramilitary organization, in terms of rank structure, training and weapons, under central government control. The goal of the force was the pacification of the territory and the extension of the settler colonial government—through managing conflict, protecting settlers and facilitating the treaty-making process (Marquis, 1997 and 2005 in Dafnos, 2014). The approach was not simply coercive, but attempted to incorporate allies, relying heavily on surveillance, relationship building and the recruitment of Indigenous constables and scouts.

Emsley's "municipal civilian" or metropolitan policing emerged a few years later with Sir Robert Peel's London Metropolitan Police Force. This type became the main type of force handling political protest and strikes in Canadian cities. Its emergence was tied to public disorder and the subsequent outcry about police action (Mainwaring-White, 1983). There were 29 riots between 1839 and 1864. These riots and the police response led to major government inquiries into British North America policing systems and calls for reforms (deLint & Hall, 2009: 56). Thus began a long process in both Toronto and Montreal of professionalization and authorizing the rule of law within policing. Public police forces were established in Québec City (1833), in Toronto (1835), in Montreal (1843), Hamilton (1846), London (1855), etc. By 1849 all towns in Upper and Lower Canada were required to operate a police office. But local forces often became corrupt and were reluctant to "handle disturbances." As a result, in 1856 John A. Macdonald, attorney general at the time, introduced legislation for a provincial police force—Emsley's second state civilian type. In British Columbia a Provincial Police was established to provide "law and order" following the significant arrival of mostly US gold miners in 1858 (de Lint & Hall, 2009: 58). Similarly, due to the threat of US expansion the Ontario Provincial Police was formed in 1909.

Each type of police agency played a role in state building and the pacification of external and internal challengers. But as the population grew, and with it various challenges from both Indigenous and settler communities across a vast territory, authorities required a more controlled, effective and integrated national policing infrastructure. In the wake of militia and private security violence in the Winnipeg General Strike, the federal government expanded the NWMP, which became the RCMP in 1919. This new institution combined a strong relationship with ruling parties and the political system with the control and surveillance of Indigenous communities as well as immigrant and political groups considered to be dangerous to Canada's status quo—including Communists, Jews, Ukrainians and Chinese communities. The centrality of the RCMP in policing, and its roots in pacification and the extraction of resources established a model that would return.

The Good Old Days? Negotiation, Liaison, Management

From World War I until the late 1960s, Canadian political and economic infrastructure rapidly expanded. Workers struggling to defend their interests gradually gained ground, establishing collective bargaining rights, increased wages and benefits (Panitch & Swartz, 2003). While this meant that some (white, employed, unionized) protesters became incorporated into a consensual relationship with the state and capitalism, others faced ongoing coercion. Police repressed unlawful protest using a strategy of escalated force, with lawbreakers punished through arrest or violence. This strategy was called into question at the end of the 1960s; after the civil rights movements triggered police violence, and widespread riots against racism and policing led federal inquiries to condemn police strategy, US police began to rethink this protest policing strategy (deLint & Hall, 2009). Instead of "escalated force," police sought ways to manage protest that limited confrontation. Canadian police decision-makers paid close attention to these shifts. Both US and Canadian police began to communicate with protesters, presenting themselves as a neutral party between employer and workers, or between different "special interest groups" within the state. This emphasis on "consent policing" used the language of the foundations of Sir Robert Peel's Metropolitan Police. As Turk (1982: 23) argues, the "less explicit the threat of violence and the more explicit the concern for safety the more [the appearance of] effective policing" (23). Called "liaison policing" in Canada, the model emphasized negotiations, communications, permits and discretionary enforcement with the goal of maintaining public order and avoiding disruptive escalation and rioting (deLint & Hall, 2009). This approach succeeded at reducing visible repression and criticisms of police strategy.

TINA—There Is No Alterative

As neoliberal restructuring accelerated in the 1980s, this model faced increasing tensions. Proponents of neoliberalism argued that the economy would benefit by reducing regulation, by privatization of publicly owned institutions and through free trade. Economic decisions became internationalized and privatized, removed from public control. Social spending was cut, but the role of the police expanded. In 1990, the Solicitor General of Canada produced a document entitled "The Future of Policing in Canada," which included predictions on the effect of neoliberal social spending cuts on policing. Criminologists André Normandeau and Barry Leighton coolly describe the integration of the Canadian economy with the world economy, and subsequent "short term dislocations of labour" (15), noting that a "pool of poorly educated, unskilled unemployed people will grow in large cities, contributing to property crime and violence," and describing the downloading of services, the deinstitutionalization of people and the cuts to services (ibid.). As a result, the authors conclude, there will be implications for police work: "more civil unrest may be anticipated, based on more groups in society seeing themselves as disadvantaged." In response to these changes, the authors suggest more privatization of policing, increasing collaboration with public and private actors, and the use of new technologies (14, 33, 44).

Twenty-five years after that report, it is clear that neoliberal globalization has shifted the attention of political authorities away from the demands of citizens and residents and towards those of investors and shareholders. Income inequality between the richest and poorest in society has increased. In Canada, while the Charter of Rights and Freedoms established important civil and political rights, increased inequalities of wealth and power limited the influence of growing numbers of poor people. Over the past fifteen years, changes to the Canadian economy have accelerated these changes. The increasing importance of oil, gas and mining to the global economy has led to intensified resource extraction in more remote territories, territories whose Indigenous land claims are unresolved (Sawyer, 2004; Altamirano-Jiménez, 2013: 1; Gordon, 2013).

At the same time, the field of policing and security has transformed. Over the past fifteen years, the boundaries between public policing, private security, intelligence and military have blurred. The integrated approach and language of "Public Safety," "Homeland Security" and "Emergency Management" represent this shift. Repressive actors are also coordinating and communicating across national boundaries—sharing "best practices" within the heavily privatized arenas of professional policing. In these arenas, the tools and logics that once separated intelligence, private security, military actors and policing are increasingly shared. A recent report by a panel of experts on Canadian policing argues that instead of policing, there is now a "security web" (The Council of Canadian Academies, 2014). As a result, the logic, tactics and practices of security have changed. In this new merged field, policing has taken the logic of risk and threat assessment from the language of intelligence agencies. While consent remains a goal, protest policing increasingly adopts related logics of pre-emption, pacification and militarization.

Strategic Incapacitation

This new policing strategy is visible in Canada as early as the Vancouver Asia Pacific Economic Community (APEC) Summit of 1997. In the months leading up to this event, the RCMP, encouraged by political authorities, evaluated activist organizations and mobilized ethnic groups in terms of the threat they posed, and when the activists were judged unpredictable and thus threatening, they pre-emptively arrested leaders, caged protesters behind fences, and when they did not remain passive, pepper-sprayed them on national television. This strategic combination of threat assessments, pre-emptive arrests, spatial control and less lethal weapons is sometimes called strategic incapacitation (Gillham, 2011). While police manage the majority of protests and movements through negotiated management or liaison policing, if protesters are seen as unpredictable, risky or threatening, evaluations that are constructed through racialized and classed lenses, police will be likely to shift into a "strategic incapacitation" or militarized strategy—and the goal becomes incapacitating the protest and protesters. As seen in the APEC example, strategic incapacitation has a number of features.

First, the gathering of intelligence, threat assessments and pre-emptive policing underlie the strategy. Information is evaluated with the goal of avoiding "worst-case scenarios" and uncertainty. This goal is used to justify surveillance and infiltration, and in the case of mass protests, to explain pre-emptive raids on homes or organizing spaces and at times pre-emptive mass arrests of crowds.

The second element of strategic incapacitation is spatial control. There are techniques of spatial control, including security perimeters, as we saw around the G20 summit in Toronto. They also include the kettling of protesters—surrounding them with police and refusing to let them leave the area—as is often seen in Montreal. In the recent May Day marches in that city, police kettled a group of anti-capitalist activists, arresting and ticketing 647 activists for violating the city's infamous P-6 anti-protest bylaw. Meanwhile, a larger group of activists were corralled by police in riot gear, pepper-sprayed and tear-gassed (Wheeland, 2015). A third strategy of spatial control is the use of "protest pens." This technique, imported from the US, designates particular areas as "free speech zones." Despite such designation, police arrested hundreds of people in the area during the G20 protests in Toronto. The police also use a spatial control strategy that breaks up large groups of protesters through the use of barricades.

The third element of strategic incapacitation strategies is the use of less lethal weapons to disperse or control demonstrators. The earliest of these, tear gas, long used against protesters, has been adapted for the contemporary context. On March 23, 2015, 62,000 university and CEGEP students in Québec held a one-day strike. They were joined by union members and community activists to demand an end to austerity budgets that cut social spending while cutting corporate taxes. Some universities and colleges voted to go on strike for two weeks and on the designated day of action, April 9, protesters occupied Université du Québec à Montréal until the police evicted them using tear gas.

Hand-held pepper spray (OC spray) canisters began to replace tear gas in the early 1990s. Initially proposed as a tool to be used between the baton and the gun, pepper spray was first targeted at protesters in North America in Ottawa. That was on May 31, 1993 when police used it against anti-racist protesters attempting to disrupt a neo-Nazi rock concert. The third time pepper spray was used against protesters in North America was also in Canada. It was also against anti-racist activists, protesting an election rally by Preston Manning. Over the next few years, police forces across the country began to adopt the spray—pausing only slightly after the RCMP made front page news when its officers sprayed protesters at the APEC summit in Vancouver in November 1997.

Especially given the relative size of the two countries, Canadian police use of pepper spray against protesters remains disproportionately high. In 2012, according to a Lexis-Nexis search of all media sources, Canadian and US police used pepper spray 28 times against protesters, 20 of which were during Montreal's student uprising, and once in Toronto. Even in 2011 when Occupy was at its height, with mobilizations in hundreds of cities in the US, pepper spray was used eighteen times, three of which were in Canada—more than double what one would expect, given the size of the two populations, and police forces.

Techniques of strategic incapacitation are often combined. During the aforementioned 2015 protest where Montreal police tear-gassed students, they also used pepper spray before detaining protesters within a kettle and ticketing 182 demonstrators with $640 tickets for violating the controversial P-6 law that criminalizes taking part in a protest without informing the police as to the route of the march (Montreal Gazette, April 9). Since 2012, about 3,500 protesters have been charged under the bylaw.

Following a similar arc of adoption as pepper spray, Canadian police used Tasers against protesters before US police did. The first use of a Taser in a protest context in either country was in Québec City during the 2001 Summit of the Americas, when an officer used a Taser on a man lying face down, waiting to be arrested. The second time police used a Taser on a protester was a few months later at Ottawa's G20 protests. The third time was when Halifax police used it against anti-war protesters; and the fourth time was when Ottawa police attempted to dislodge Algerian refugees sitting in the Immigration Minister's office. The police use of plastic bullets to subdue protesters also has a particularly Canadian history—with police firing 900 at protesters during the Québec City protests of 2001.

These are only a few of the less lethal weapons, once used in military confrontations, now used against protesters. Others include the stun grenades/flash-bang grenades/smoke grenades/ pepper spray projectiles used on anti-police brutality protests in Oakland and Ferguson, Missouri and student protests in Montreal, Long Range Acoustic Devices (sound cannons) and rubber bullets.

Both the APEC protests of 1997 and the Seattle protests against the World Trade Organization were turning points in protest policing strategies (Gillham, Fernandez, etc.). The move towards strategic incapacitation was consolidated in the period following the attacks of September 11, 2001. After the attacks both the Canadian and US governments elaborated and integrated national security infrastructures. In the United States, this took the form of the Department of Homeland Security and in Canada, Public Safety Canada, established in 2003. These institutions incorporate state authorities, security actors and corporate leaders—particularly in key sectors—a configuration foundational to the Canadian state. Albo and Fanelli (2014) show how this relationship has been restructured since 2012, with a move towards "total privatization" and increasingly authoritarian controls over protest.

In Public Safety Canada, the distinctions between crime, political protest and terrorism become blurred. The institution uses a definition of terrorism which includes an "act or omission undertaken... for a political, religious or ideological purpose that is intended to intimidate the public with respect to its security, including its economic security, or to compel a person, government or organization (whether inside or outside Canada) from doing or refraining from doing any act, and that intentionally causes one of a number of specified forms of serious harm."[38]

Public Safety Canada uses risk and threat assessments to organize its operations and allocate its resources. It prioritizes the protection of what is called "Critical Infrastructure," a term defined as "processes, systems, facilities, technologies, networks, assets and services essential to the health, safety, security or economic well-being of Canadians and the effective functioning of government."[39] If protest is believed to target "critical infrastructure," i.e. rail or highway blockades, national security routines are launched. Such a logic attempts to gain the consent of the dominant majority, while targeting others for criminalization and coercion.

In the spring of 2015, the federal government passed Bill C51. This initiative targets any activity that "undermines the sovereignty, security or territorial integrity of Canada or the lives or the security of the people of Canada." It includes the following: "Interference with the capability of the Government of Canada in relation to intelligence, defence, border operations, public safety, the administration of justice, diplomatic or consular relations, or the economic or financial stability of Canada" (Cuthand, 2015). The government's justification for the bill as a response to the terrorist threat was largely successful, particularly within Parliament—where criticisms remained limited to questions of oversight and funding. Nonetheless, as news of the bill spread, people mobilized against the way that the bill, while officially permitting lawful dissent, allows the Canadian Security and Intelligence Service (CSIS) to carry out undefined "measures" against perceived threats, including anything that interferes with Canada's "economic or financial stability" or the country's "critical infrastructure." The bill passed nonetheless.

One can see the logic that ties dissent to "threat" in a 2014 Critical Infrastructure Intelligence Assessment by the RCMP. Entitled

38 See https://www.publicsafety.gc.ca/cnt/rsrcs/pblctns/rslnc-gnst-trrrsm/index-eng.aspx#s1.

39 See http://www.publicsafety.gc.ca/cnt/ntnl-scrt/crtcl-nfrstrctr/index-en.aspx.

"Criminal Threats to the Canadian Petroleum Industry," it describes a "growing, highly organized and well financed, anti-Canadian petroleum movement that consists of peaceful activists, militants and violent extremists who are opposed to society's reliance on fossil fuels." It uses a language of threat, risk and extremism to describe a movement that is diverse and has widespread public support, albeit one which might well be regarded by the Harper government as a threat to the country's economic stability. This same language is visible in police discussions of the Québec student protests, the Mi'kmaq anti-fracking protests and the security around the G20 summit. This conflation of economic and security interests that benefit the wealthiest has facilitated the spread of strategic incapacitation.

Conclusion

Since the first public police units formed in order to enforce private property and commerce in London, England, they have worked to maintain the status quo. However, over the past fifteen years protest policing has changed, and the space for protest has shrunk. Those challenging capitalist and state authorities are surveyed and assessed, kept behind fences and police lines, subjected to less lethal weapons and arrested before they act. More and more, public protest in Canada and elsewhere is considered threatening—especially when the protesters are Indigenous, people of colour, poor or immigrants. But to simply argue that coercion has increased ignores the way that coercion and consent have long been used to control the population.

Repressive authorities in the earliest days of settler state formation in Canada adopted a model of colonial policing that aimed to protect resource extraction, pacify populations both inside and outside of the settler nation and build the legitimacy and capacity of both business and the ruling regime. Police combined the use of force with relationship building. They monitored communities and built trust, cracking down hard on those who interfered with the mines, railways and the occupation of land. As neoliberal globalization has re-empowered corporations and transformed states and the field of security itself, contemporary security practices are similarly integrating intelligence gathering, militarization and economic interests.

However, we must pay attention to the particular configuration of coercion and consent. As economic decision-making becomes increasingly removed from democratic control, and economic interests and security interests are conflated, repressive actors are given more legitimacy, resources and autonomy. When the economic interests of the wealthy become dependent on a small number of extractive industries, priorities shift. Consent is becoming irrelevant as we're told that there is no alternative to the security state. This creeping authoritarianism is allowing police agencies to monitor activists, and to experiment with less lethal weapons and techniques of spatial control. But such incursions and innovations are neither inevitable nor unstoppable; their blatant nature can build opposition. By challenging the legitimacy, resources and autonomy of repressive authorities as they criminalize dissent, we defend the breathing spaces needed for building resistance, relationships and a better world.

THE POLITICAL VOCABULARY OF THE POST-NEW LEFT

How Activists Articulate Their Politics and Why It Matters

Steve D'Arcy

The rise of an anti-systemic social movement, when it happens, can seem quite sudden and almost effortless. But in point of fact this appearance of spontaneous generation masks a lot of very hard work, on the part of countless individuals, to produce the outpouring of creativity, cooperation and effective communication on which the movement depends for its existence. Social movements require the coordinated yet independent initiative of many thousands of people, operating in far-flung locales, and sustained over a period of years. People not previously active in public affairs have to step forth into practices of direct action, self-organization and collective decision-making, which the dominant ideology has long encouraged them to leave to supposed experts, such as professional politicians or government officials.

The emergence of an authentic people's movement can only take place if a special kind of bridge has successfully been built and then defended: a bridge between (1) the ambitious agendas for far-reaching social change that, most of the time, attract a following only in relatively marginal activist enclaves, and (2) the kind of broad-based public sympathy and popular participation that can generate "people power" on a scale which would normally be utterly unavailable to activists. In short, a social movement emerges only when radical ideas gain a base of broad, enduring and active public support. Marx put the point aptly: political radicalism, normally marginal and ineffective, "becomes a material force once it has gripped the masses" (Marx, 1844).

Loss of Credibility for the New Left Political Vocabulary

Given the difficulty of building these bridges between activist enclaves and broad publics, and considering the predictable efforts by elites to thwart movement-building at every opportunity, how is the rapid emergence and expansion of social movements even possible?

What did it take to launch the Civil Rights Movement in the 1950s, the Anti-War Movement in the 1960s, or the Women's Liberation Movement in the 1970s?

We are not particularly well positioned to answer this question today. After all, if we knew how to build broad-based, militant and enduringly effective social movements, many of us would be actively replicating in the present era the considerable successes of earlier generations. As it turns out, however, there have been very few sustained upsurges of popular protest and community organization in Canada or the United States since the 1970s, in spite of some important outbreaks and upsurges (see Harden, 2013) like the Global Justice Movement, the Occupy movement, the Québec Student Strike, Idle No More and Black Lives Matter. In spite of these bright lights and hopeful moments, however, we can see in hindsight that the movements of the 1960s-70s represent a relatively high watermark of popular mobilization and organization, never quite replicated in the decades since (Sears, 2014).

It might be tempting, then, to imagine that we could unlock the secrets of how to build movements by taking a close look at the organizing methods and styles of public engagement deployed by movement activists in the New Left era (roughly, from the early 1960s to the late 1970s). How did the Black Panther party manage to build a large, powerful and inspiring organization of radical activists, with chapters in dozens of cities across the United States (Bloom & Martin, 2013), in the course of only a few years? How did Students for a Democratic Society start out with a small group of a few dozen students in 1962, and turn itself into one of the most powerful organizations in the history of the North American student politics in about a five-year period (Sale, 1973)?

Unfortunately, this seemingly promising approach to finding a way forward for movement-building in our own time tends not to yield much insight. What we find when we look at the record of those movements is that, however nostalgic we might be for their historic achievements and their enviable dynamism and impact, we could never plausibly regard them as offering up models for us to emulate in our own time, at least not in any direct or straightforward way. The problem is that the activists of those years seem to have had ways of thinking and speaking about political activity that would be seen as manifestly unacceptable in our own time.

After all, what would happen if we tried to use a 1960s-70s style of activism as a model for political organizing today? Suppose, for instance, that a few us were to go around to activist "spaces" in the contemporary context, acting and speaking in the manner typical of organizers from the heyday of the New Left, that is, in the style familiar from the Black Panther Party or Students for a Democratic Society. We might begin by confidently asserting the need to unite "the people" in a common struggle for "liberation," proposing "alliances" based on "solidarity" and a shared commitment to promoting "the revolution" against "the system." (This might sound like a cliché or a stereotype, but these terms really did infuse the discourse of the activist Left in those years; indeed, at the time, these formulas were important departures from the "Old Left" vocabulary of "the bourgeoisie," "dual power," "dictatorship of the proletariat" and "popular fronts.") In any case, the response would be predictable. Far from this revivalist approach offering a way forward, setting the stage for a revitalization of left activism and a new impetus to broad-based movement building, we would, on the contrary, be met with either confusion or disdain, or both.

The problem would not be one of understanding, so much as credibility. The political vocabulary of the New Left era would be *understood* by activists today, at least in general terms. But it is unlikely that it would be *taken seriously*. The terms in which the New Left expressed its politics—"the people," "liberation," "alliances," "the system"—would be viewed as (and indeed, would actually be) a throwback to an earlier era. The great majority of activists, below the age of 30, just don't talk that way anymore. And it is worth stopping to think about why that is. This would not be simply because of superficial changes in terminology, but because these political formulas presuppose things about political activity and social change that would strike people today as fundamentally implausible. The result is a divide, an unmistakable chasm, between the political vocabulary of the New Left of the 1960s-70s, and the political vocabulary of today's "post-New Left."

From the New Left to the Post-New Left: A Mutation in the Activist Political Vocabulary

But before analyzing the root causes and practical implications of this transformation, we need to get a feel for these two vocabularies, and how they differ. Consider the following table. In the left column, several keywords of the New Left era are listed, along with their definitions. In the right column, each word is paired with a keyword from today's activist Left, which has largely displaced the older term.

NEW LEFT POLITICAL VOCABULARY (1960s–70s)	POST-NEW LEFT POLITICAL VOCABULARY (1990s–now)
"Oppression": a pattern of persistent and systematic disadvantage imposed on large groups of people, in many domains of social life, including employment, social status, treatment by the legal system, vulnerability to violence, and more; e.g, racial oppression, gender oppression, etc.	**"Privilege":** a set of unearned benefits that some individuals enjoy (and others are denied) in their everyday lives, by virtue of their place in a racial or gender or other "identity" hierarchy, e.g. male privilege, white privilege, cisgender privilege, etc.
"Exploitation": a feature of economic systems, including capitalism, in which unpaid labour is extracted from working people for the benefit of a relatively small number of exploiters, who comprise, in economic terms, a ruling class.	**"Classism":** an attitude of scorn, condescension or disrespect toward persons of low income, similar to what once was called "snobbery" or "class-based elitism."
"Alliances": the confluence in struggle of large-scale social forces (like social classes, or social movements), as part of a strategic orientation toward the coordinated pursuit of common aims.	**"Allyship":** a sincere commitment on the part of a privileged individual to offer ongoing support to individuals, groups or organizations that oppose that kind of privilege, and to take direction from them about the form that support should take.

"The People": a label for the totality or potential collectivity of those who are not members of the small, ruling elite; it is usually seen as including workers, the unemployed, small farmers, students, and almost all women, people of colour, and so on.

"Consciousness-Raising": a process of popular political education, in which learners are viewed as already having an implicit grasp of critical insights about injustice and social change, but invites them to participate in a collective learning process in order to become fully aware of these insights and their implications through dialogue with peers.

"Solidarity": a stance, within and between social movements, of treating "injuries to one" as if they were "injuries to all," and resisting them in common, as matters of shared priority, rather than as the concern only of those under attack. Example: The "I am Trayvon Martin" slogan used in anti-racist protests in 2013, which echoed the old labour-movement principle of solidarity ("An injury to one is an injury to all"; cf., "Injustice anywhere is a threat to justice everywhere.") (See http://iamtrayvonmartin.tumblr.com/.)

"Liberation": a term used to refer to ultimate victory in struggles against systems of oppression and/or exploitation, e.g. national liberation, women's liberation, black liberation. Cf. "emancipation," e.g. the emancipation of women, the emancipation of the working class.

"Folks": a term that refers to groups of people, in the plural, without suggesting that they comprise a singular totality that could be united in one common struggle, which may be precluded by the difference of their experiences and degrees of privilege.

"Calling Out": an approach to challenging "folks" who show a lack of insight or concern about issues of privilege, in which they are confronted by peers and urged to "check" their privilege.

"Positionality": a practice of acknowledging the specificity of one's social position, especially one's access to privilege, which may make one incapable of understanding or speaking authoritatively about the ways others are impacted adversely by the operation of privilege. Example: the "I am not Trayvon Martin" meme from 2013, which urged white people to refrain from identifying with African-American resistance, for reasons of positionality. (See http://wearenottrayvonmartin.tumblr.com/.)

"Safe(r) Space": the attempt to create occasions or locations wherein the adverse effects of privilege on marginalized people are minimized in everyday interpersonal interactions, notably by encouraging "folks" in those spaces to "check their privilege" and by "calling out" any failures to embody "allyship."

Some immediate caveats and qualifications are necessary, to ward off misunderstanding.

First, the new vocabulary is used almost exclusively by the English-speaking Left in a few countries, especially Canada, the US and (to a lesser extent) the UK. Elsewhere, such as in Latin America and southern Africa, the Left has its own distinctive vocabularies, which would have to be analyzed separately. This is important because it reminds us that the post-New Left vocabulary has not been shaped by some of the broad popular struggles that have happened elsewhere, and some of its features seem to be symptomatic of this fact. Second, the older vocabulary is still in use today. Indeed, many people use both vocabularies, or at least draw from both, even if they have a primary vocabulary that dominates their speech and writing about activism. Even so, it seems clear that the first vocabulary has faded and continues to fade from use within today's activist subcultures, as the second one continues to gain ground. Third, it is possible to use one set of words to express the other set of meanings. That is, one can retain the words "solidarity," "oppression" or "consciousness-raising," while using them in a way that is shaped by the new vocabulary, so that by "solidarity," you mean acknowledging positionality; by "oppression," you mean individual privilege; and by "consciousness-raising," you mean calling people out. Conversely, one can use the new terms, but give them the old meanings. For this reason, if one hears a contemporary activist use the word "alliance," which would be a rare thing, it is worth stopping to ask, Do you mean the confluence in struggle of large social forces like classes or social movements, or do you mean privileged people being committed as individuals to offering support to those adversely impacted by privilege, and taking direction from them? Only in this way can you confirm which vocabulary is being used, strictly speaking. Fourth, my remarks refer to "ideal types" (Weber, 1904), not the exact ways that every activist talks. In other words, although my account of the post-1990 activist vocabulary is intended to be recognizable by everyone familiar with contemporary activist subcultures, it is probably a bit more reflective of some "scenes" than others. For example, it will be immediately recognizable, I think, to anyone familiar with the work of Tim Wise, Peggy McIntosh and Melissa Harris-Perry (the last of whom

Ta-Nehisi Coates (2014) described as the US's foremost public intellectual), or many of today's most widely read "social justice blogs," such as *Everyday Feminism* (everydayfeminism.com) and *Black Girl Dangerous* (blackgirldangerous.org). Still, my core contrast (in the two columns) may appear overdrawn and exaggerated to people whose contact with activist subcultures occurs mainly through grassroots protest organizing. In organizing contexts, most activist speech is infused with a pragmatic focus on getting things done, so some of this jargon recedes into the background. Nevertheless, I would be surprised if anyone familiar with today's activist subcultures in English-speaking North America claimed not to recognize the terminology that I attribute to today's activists.

Reflecting on the gulf that divides these two styles of political speech, some (mostly, but by no means exclusively older) people—whether out of nostalgia or out of substantive reservations about the politics of this transformation, or both—will recoil from the vocabulary of today's activists. There is no shortage of critics who complain about the focus on "privilege" (Smith, 2013; deBoer, 2014) and "calling out" (Jones, 2014) in the contemporary activist scene. But we should try not to be seduced by the broad-brushed dismissal with which the most incautious critics (like Fisher, 2013) reject the politics that pervades today's activist subcultures. In many cases, the political sensibility of these critics has been shaped (for better and for worse) by the 1960s radicalization and its aftermath, and no doubt that perspective brings with it important insights. However, we should remain open to the possibility that some aspects of the new vocabulary may offer important insights as well, some of which may correct mistakes embedded in the older vocabulary. We can retain an open mind, even if we remain reluctant to embrace the new jargon wholesale.

Conversely, some partisans of the post-New Left will insist that any resistance to the new vocabulary must be rooted in an attempt to cling to privileges which, allegedly, the new discourse threatens (Khan, 2014). This dogmatic stance likewise reflects a narrow-minded sensibility that renounces the very possibility of learning from engagement with perspectives that contest one's own basic assumptions. It is this fundamentalist sensibility that has earned "the Twitter Left" and "the social justice blogging community" a sometimes well-deserved bad reputation (Stallings, 2012), but those attitudes should not be allowed to insinuate themselves into our more thoughtful political conversations, especially as they unfold in real-world, offline organizing projects.

In fact, neither of the two political vocabularies considered here should be deemed to be either above reproach or beneath contempt. Both are ways of articulating the politics of people committed to the struggle for social justice, so they deserve, if not necessarily our endorsement, at least our willingness to listen and, where possible, to learn.

The Roots of the Vocabulary Change

Granted that this chasm separating the two vocabularies exists, why are they so different? What accounts for this mutation in the mode of speech typical of left political activists in recent decades? A close examination of the two systems of terminology reveals some underlying principles that are driving the transformation. In particular, one can discern the operation, just below the surface, of three fundamental shifts.

1. **A shift in priorities from ultimate victory to challenging everyday impacts.** The older vocabulary looked at capitalism, racism and sexism (for example) as social systems or institutions that could and probably would be defeated, once and for all, in the foreseeable future. Accordingly, activists of that era defined and described their movements as struggles for "socialism," "black liberation" or "women's liberation." By contrast, the new vocabulary tends to suspend judgment on (without denying) the prospects for ultimate victory, and to focus its attention on challenging everyday impacts of capitalism, racialization and gender, in the here and now. This prioritization of resistance to everyday impacts infuses not only the way activists today talk, but also how they choose what to do. For example, what is happening in this meeting, today, is emphasized much more, because it is not seen merely in instrumental terms as a means to destroy systems of domination. The meeting itself is generating impacts that have

to be challenged as they arise. Addressing problems of "process," which once would have been seen as a "distraction" from an urgent liberation struggle, is now seen as part and parcel of what the Left is for.

2. **A shift of focus from analyzing system dynamics to analyzing interpersonal dynamics.** The old vocabulary assumed that political analysis should study large-scale, often transnational, social systems and structures, centuries in the making, e.g. systems of oppression and exploitation. In contrast, the new vocabulary assumes that race and gender and other forms of privilege are enacted in everyday, interpersonal interactions. This is key to the concept of "privilege." It is likened to "an invisible knapsack" of advantages or monopolized benefits that some receive and others are denied (McIntosh, 1988). Privileged persons gain these benefits whether or not they even know or acknowledge it. Thus, whereas activists in the late 1960s and 1970s were keen to use history and political economy to develop a sophisticated analysis of the historical process, centuries-long, that established European colonial domination of much of the world, the new vocabulary both reflects and encourages a change of focus, toward how racism (for example) is enacted or reproduced in the everyday interactions of white people with racialized people, as individuals or in groups. The analysis of the power dynamics of these everyday interpersonal interactions has tended to gain in prominence and sophistication, in parallel to the relative de-emphasis of the importance of political economy and critical sociology within the activist Left.

3. **A shift in emphasis from commonality (among social groups) to specificity.** The vocabulary of the former New Left grew out of and contributed in turn to the construction of broad-based popular movements, in which hundreds of thousands and sometimes millions of people participated. By contrast, the vocabulary of today's anglophone North American activists emerged in a completely different and arguably much less favourable context. One symptom of this is a change in emphasis from the search for commonalities that could be the basis for building alliances and expanding the base of support for militant mass movements,

to grappling with the barriers to joint organizing and common struggle. In brief, the old vocabulary emerged in a context where opportunities to encourage solidarity and collaboration were actively sought, whereas the new vocabulary emerged out of the frustration of failed efforts to bridge gaps between people and organizations that reflected real differences. There is a certain optimism in the idea of "consciousness-raising," or the concept of "the people," that seems naive and unconvincing to many of today's activists. The shift from "consciousness-raising" to "calling out," for instance, reflects (and encourages) a loss of confidence in the capacity of people to learn about, understand and oppose forms of inequality that do not adversely impact them as individuals. These doubts are, in turn, elaborated in terms of positionality and privilege.

Taken together, these three shifts go a long way toward explaining the transformation of the way activists talk, which has been noticeable at least since the 1990s.

Reflecting on this shift, and the politics implied by it, there seem to be both gains and losses, from the point of view of the fundamental challenge of movement building, which I noted at the outset. Arguably, the only justification for even having a special vocabulary for articulating the politics of left activists is that such a vocabulary might help build bridges between the transformative aspirations that animate otherwise isolated radicals operating within activist enclaves and the broad public in the wider working class whose activation and mobilization is needed to make those aspirations a reality.

Gains and Losses Associated with the Vocabulary Change

Does the shift from the New Left vocabulary to the post-New Left vocabulary help or hinder such bridge-building efforts?

There are, to be sure, important advantages for movement-builders articulating their politics in the new way. After all, the vocabulary and the practice of the Left in the 1960s-70s had several serious problems, even if these defects are hard for some to see through the fog of nostalgia-clouded historical memory. It's true that the movements of the 1960s and '70s were vastly more potent, and drew in vastly more people from all walks of life, than any political organizing that happens on the Left today in Canada or the US, with the possible exception of the Global Justice and Occupy movements during their peaks. And yet, many people entered and participated in the New Left *in spite of* serious concerns about the persistence, within movement activities, of sexist behaviours and attitudes, forms of machismo that were both misogynist and homophobic, and ways in which (in some organizations and struggles) college-educated, middle-income white people tended to dominate the proceedings and set the agendas (Morgan, 1970; Combahee River Collective, 1977). To the extent that it was plagued by problems of this kind, the New Left's practice belied the radicalism of the movement's official rhetoric, and made its universalistic claims about the "unity" of "the people" ring hollow. It seems clear that the attentiveness in today's left activist subcultures to interpersonal dynamics within the movement reflects a genuine learning process. It is a step toward beginning to address problems that were, in effect, glossed over and even actively concealed by phrases like "the people" and a complacent view of the prospects for building genuine "solidarity" and "alliances." There are real barriers to solidarity, which have to be actively addressed, rather than assumed away at the level of vocabulary choice. To its credit, the post-New Left political vocabulary excels at frank acknowledgement of those barriers.

Related to this, the post-New Left vocabulary also makes it much harder for people to dismiss or vilify groups within larger movements that find it necessary to organize independently, in order to formulate demands or critical insights about failures of movement organizations to address their specific concerns. For instance, whereas the New Left vocabulary could encourage people to denounce as "divisive" women finding it helpful to set up a women's caucus in their union, the post-New Left vocabulary makes this move seem quite sensible: it doesn't divide the people and erode solidarity, but only enables folks to organize to create a safe space where the specific concerns of women can be addressed, without the distorting influence of male privilege always getting in the way. We might disagree about how exactly to handle or describe this measure, but few of us today would want to surrender this insight, which seems to be an important advance, precisely in helping to build movements that are inclusive and welcoming, in this case to women (although the point applies to other marginalized or dominated groups, too).

On the other hand, however, it is also true that the series of shifts from the old vocabulary to the new one has entailed certain losses. I will mention three.

First, the relative de-emphasizing of system-level causation, in favour of a new emphasis on the importance of individual action or inaction, tends to weaken the integration of everyday activist discourse with the theoretical analysis of systems like capitalism and colonialism. It is true that, in exchange, we have a vocabulary that better enables us to focus on class privilege and settler privilege, understood in terms of interpersonal dynamics. But if we are to defeat colonialism and capitalism, we cannot do so one person at a time, or one interaction or relationship at a time. The systems themselves have to be named, understood, attacked and overthrown. This issue is, obviously, closely connected to the loss of a focus on liberation. A liberation focus and a systems focus share a common understanding: that the purpose of the Left is to defeat systems of exploitation and oppression. Challenging immediate impacts is important, but not enough: it is necessary, but by no means sufficient. Moreover, the way we challenge everyday impacts should be informed by our understanding that they are not produced simply by individual actions, but by the operation of large-scale systems. The Left needs a vocabulary, and a self-understanding, that highlights and foregrounds the importance of constructing and expanding anti-systemic movements that aim to defeat systems of oppressive and exploitative power. It is hard not to think that the older vocabulary better expresses this insight, even as it obstructs our access to other critical insights that are also indispensable.

Second, the post-New Left political vocabulary sometimes seems to instill or foster a generalized pessimism about the very possibility of finding common ground, becoming in effect a "self-fulfilling prophecy" in which activists are encouraged to forgo even the attempt to build broad alliances (for instance, between Indigenous people and working-class settler communities), on the pretext that anything beyond individual efforts to "be an ally" are pointless and doomed to fail, since there is not sufficient commonality of interests or experiences to make cross-movement alliances (e.g. between Indigenous sovereignty organizing and the trade union movement) feasible. To the extent that the new vocabulary has embedded within it a strategic analysis which is systematically pessimistic about broad-based alliance-building, it is arguably a barrier to building powerful social movements and a deterrent to investing the long-term energy and time needed to cultivate those cross-movement relations of mutual defence, mutual trust and mutual aid.

Finally, a third pitfall of the new vocabulary is that there is some danger, at least, that it may tend to reinforce the sense of marginality of the activist milieu, considered as a constellation of "scenes" and "subcultures." If the impulse that animates the construction and deployment of a vocabulary and a style of speech is mainly the desire to consolidate the shared culture and sense of commonality of people whose leftist values leave them alienated from the wider society, then the predictable outcome will be to solidify and further entrench the sense of distance between left activists and the wider working-class public. In short, it can function as a barrier to the bridge-building that movements rely upon for their very possibility. To some critics, the post-New Left political vocabulary shows signs of just this sort of retreat from the aspiration to break out of enclaves and subcultures to engage with wider society. These critics note, with an unmistakable skepticism, the perhaps symptomatic timing of the new vocabulary's emergence, in the wake of the Reagan/Thatcher era and the wave of defeats inflicted on the Left in those years (Carr, 1999; Choonara & Prasad, 2014). They worry that the manner in which activists articulate their politics today may have strayed in the direction of a defanged adaptation to defeat and political marginality (Reed, 2001).

Conclusion

One could certainly say more about the gains and losses associated with adopting either of these two vocabularies. But perhaps it is enough to have sketched an approach to thinking about the question. Both vocabularies have been formed to address indispensably important concerns, so we should be reluctant to give up on either one. The most important thing, I would suggest, is to refuse to allow either of these two ways of speaking, writing and thinking about left activism to evade the challenge raised by its counterpart. Those who wish to retain an expression like "the people," and who feel reluctant to take up the term "folks" in its place, are certainly entitled to do so. But one hopes that their use of the notion of "the people" will be disciplined by a certain amount of sensitivity to the motivation that has led some activists to drop that term from their vocabulary. On the other hand, those who embrace the newer way of articulating left politics should, in the same way, remain (or become) attentive to the importance of highlighting issues of system dynamics, large-scale alliance-building, and ultimate liberation, rather than letting these urgently important matters disappear from view entirely.

I have argued here that movement-building involves, crucially, an attempt to build bridges that mediate between the transformative aims of radicals and broad publics that are normally indifferent to projects of far-reaching social change. (I explore this theme further in the closing pages of D'Arcy, 2013.) The vocabularies that activists deploy, in order to understand themselves and to make themselves understood by others, can serve to construct such bridges. But they can also serve to erect barriers to the constructive work already done, notably by previous generations. It is worth paying attention, therefore, to the potential pitfalls of ill-considered elements of whatever political vocabulary one adopts.

There are limits to this, however. Notwithstanding the importance of how activists articulate their politics, we should resist any suggestion that vocabulary choice is the decisive variable determining the vitality and appeal of the Left. The weakness of the Left today is not primarily the fault of the way activists talk. What the Left lacks above all is the infusions of energy it can only receive from mass upsurges of popular struggle, of the kind that benefited left activism in generations past. The single most important difference between today's post-New Left and the New Left of the 1968 era isn't a difference of vocabulary. It is a difference in the scope and scale of popular rebellion, mobilization and organization. There were, quite simply, vastly more people flowing into anti-systemic struggles in the 1960s than there are today. Since participation in social-movement struggles is basically the only setting (other than a few university courses and a few tiny and isolated leftist groups and collectives) where most people have the opportunity to learn about leftist ideas and strategies, the radical Left is trapped in a position of chronic marginality, lacking any clear path to "mainstream" relevance, i.e., any capacity to secure a meaningful role in shaping the ideas of large numbers of people or wielding any substantive influence. What the Left of today lacks, therefore, is the expansive pool of social antagonisms and conflicts upon which earlier generations of radicals could rely for periodic injections of enthusiasm, critical insights about the nature of the systems we oppose and how to defeat them, and what Rosa Luxemburg (1919) called "the forward-storming combative energy" of broad popular movements.

With this in mind, we can hopefully see that blaming the forms of speech and styles of self-interpretation of activists for the Left's marginality is like blaming the dead fish when a pond dries up after years of catastrophic drought. The pathologies of the Left—chronic sectarianism, exaggerated levels of self-doubt about the utility of leftist politics, limited capacity to engage with a broad public outside of leftist subcultures, the all too common shift of focus from organizing against systemic racism and sexism to obsessing about racist or sexist utterances by celebrities or public figures as these are debated on social media, and so on—these are all symptoms, not underlying causes, of the fact that the levels of social struggle are so low today that much of the time the Left has no context, no "habitat" (so to speak) in which to operate on a healthy basis. Inevitably, it threatens to shrivel up and lose a lot of its former vitality and dynamism. It is cut off from the source that had once nourished its growth and vigour. While critical examination of how we understand and communicate our politics does matter, therefore, we should steer clear of the naïve hope for a tiny and isolated, yet healthy and dynamic activist Left. This is a deeply incoherent expectation.

The solution, of course, is for the activist Left to commit fully, and with a renewed sense of urgency, to breaking out of its longstanding isolation. What is needed is a reinvigorated determination to push past everything that stands between the radical aspirations of those who inhabit activist enclaves or leftist subcultures and the always formidable social power that lies dormant, but never loses its transformative potential, of the capacity of working-class people to organize themselves for the defeat of systems of domination and exploitation.

MOVEMENT STRATEGIES AND PRACTICES—SOME KEY CASES

The working class demands the right to make its mistakes and learn the dialectic of history.

—ROSA LUXEMBURG

INFRASTRUCTURE OF DISSENT

The Case of the Québec Student Movement

Xavier Lafrance and Alan Sears

There is no shortage of anger among the current generation of post-secondary students. It is no secret to them that they are paying more than previous generations for a post-secondary education that is the ticket to a very uncertain future. It is not surprising that many students feel they are getting a bad deal. Further, many of them are aware of the impact of persistent inequalities that mean that women, racialized and/or Indigenous students face specific obstacles both on campus and in society despite claims of multiculturalism and gender equality.

This sense of injustice, however, is not generally connected to political activism. Students today may be facing very similar challenges, but to date there is not much sign of a collective response. In the absence of such a collective alternative, people tend to organize their lives around personal lifeboat strategies to survive in difficult circumstances.

When an alternative does seem possible, as happened during the 2012 Québec students' strike, many are drawn into activism that seems to address their grievances and concerns. In 2012, Québec students mobilized and went on strike to defeat a 75% tuition fee increase. This important and all too rare partial[40] victory against neoliberalism did not come out of nowhere, but was the latest mobilization in a long history of student strikes and protests going back to the late 1960s. In this chapter, we argue that the Québec student movement has deliberately developed an *infrastructure of dissent* over generations that provides the basis for connecting anger to power through collective mobilization.

40 After several months, the strike forced the Liberal government to call elections, with the tuition hike and the social upsurge it had caused as one of its main issues. The Liberals lost power to the Parti Québécois, which had promised to cancel the hike. The Parti Québécois subsequently announced a milder tuition "indexation."

No Future

Students currently attending post-secondary institutions are navigating a political and economic landscape shaped by over 30 years of neoliberal restructuring. Since the early 1980s, employers and state policy-makers have developed an interconnected set of strategies to enhance the power of corporations and undercut resistance from working-class and social movements. Employers and state policy-makers developed these strategies over time through "a series of gyrations and chaotic experiments" (Harvey, 2005a: 13). The central goal of neoliberalism is "the use of state power to orient society towards the market, the buying and selling of goods, services and our capacities to work" (Sears, 2014: 88). State policy-makers have implemented neoliberal strategies by slashing social programs, introducing principles of user pay, privatizing formerly public services and spaces, and destroying the tax base required to fund the public sector. Yet this is not a simple erosion of state power, as policy-makers have also invested heavily in policing, prisons and increased immigration controls.

The neoliberal reorientation of state power has gone along with employers' implementation of lean production methods to restructure workplaces and employment relations in important ways. Lean production methods were originally developed in the Japanese automotive manufacturing sector. Employers have drawn on key elements of lean production methods and generalized them into management strategies that reach into all sectors of the economy on a global scale. The core of lean production is "the continuous search for marginal improvements in costs by constantly stressing and readjusting the production system and, above all, the labor process" (Moody, 1997: 87). The implementation of lean production has included the widespread use of information technology to deskill work, the spatial reorganization of work at a local and global level, and the increased use of precarious employment (part-time, temporary or contracted out) in a variety of sectors.

The cumulative impact of over 30 years of restructuring has been intensified by the austerity regime implemented since the current global slump began in 2007-08. The net result is a very uncertain future, with relatively high levels of unemployment for younger people, the destruction of secure jobs in the private and public sectors, and rapid economic change that makes planning difficult. At the same time, neoliberal restructuring is having a dramatic effect on post-secondary institutions themselves.

Students who are currently enrolled in post-secondary institutions confront neoliberal restructuring in many areas of their lives. They go to school in institutions that are being dramatically restructured along neoliberal lines. Tuition fee increases are often the most visible face of neoliberalism on campus, affecting not only students' educational experiences but also haunting their post-graduation lives with debt. The restructuring of colleges and universities goes much deeper than tuition increases associated with privatization and user pay. Government policy-makers and university administrators are implementing policies to transform every dimension of post-secondary education, from the experience of the classroom to the content of programs and from the governance of institutions to staff employment relations.

Students also encounter neoliberal restructuring and lean production in their own paid employment. They must work long hours in paid employment to meet the demands of increasing tuition costs (Marshall, 2010). The part-time jobs they take on to pay for their education are often in areas where lean management techniques have made great inroads, such as retail, call centres and food or beverage services. Not only are these areas defined by their use of precarious labour, but they are also characterized by the detailed regulation of work processes through information technologies and management by stress. In their paid work, students often face relatively low wages and unpredictable shift patterns. They often work in fraught situations navigating between the demands of customers and the expectations of management.

It is not only at school and work that students negotiate the world created by neoliberalism, but also in their personal lives and relationships. Governments have allowed the public realm to shrink and deteriorate, which raises the cost of leisure activities, public transportation and housing. At the same time, neoliberalism has been programmed into the mobile devices and social media that influence patterns of play, relationships and work. Further, students find themselves hemmed in by lack of economic and social autonomy due to an extended dependence on their parents or guardians, brought on by the costs of education, low pay at work and the lack of affordable housing options.

Finally, neoliberalism frames the prospects of those now in post-secondary studies. Employers have succeeded over the last 30 years in creating a two-tier workforce, where older workers with some degree of job security, benefits and pension are being replaced by younger people hired on precarious status as freelancers, part-timers or contract hires. Social services have been starved of resources, so that the safety net that was there for previous post-World War II generations is full of holes. Housing prices have been driven up by gentrification and speculation, while public housing is not being built and the existing stock is rotting from a generation of deferred maintenance. Meanwhile, climate change is creating an increasing threat to well-being in the future, driven by reliance on fossil fuels and the organization of the economy.

Many students are keenly aware of the challenges that confront them, on and off campus. Yet this burning sense of injustice is not widely associated with activism or political engagement. Today's students are often cynical about the current political system, but equally cynical about the prospects for making change through mobilization. An important exception to this perspective has been in Québec, where students won one of the few victories we have seen against neoliberal restructuring in the massive 2012 strike and popular mobilization. We will argue below that the 2012 strike is part of an ongoing pattern of general strikes and student mobilizations dating back to 1968.

The ability of Québec students to mobilize against neoliberalism at a time when many others seem paralyzed and cynical is due to an infrastructure of dissent developed and sustained by the radical wing of the movement over a long period of time. The infrastructure of dissent is the means through which people develop the capacities to turn anger into power, to mobilize. These capacities must be reproduced over political generations, which on campuses turn over in a relatively short period of time.

Infrastructure of Dissent

C. Wright Mills (1959) argued that the great value of the sociological imagination was that it allowed people to link their personal troubles to public issues. The sociological imagination provided tools to help people trace the roots of their personal situations back to the social relations and historical processes that shape the world they inhabit. This provides the basis for recognizing that it is possible to act. "By the fact of his[/her] living he [/she] contributes, however minutely, to the shaping of society and to the course of its history, even as he[/she] is made by society and by its historical push and shove" (Mills, 1959: 6). Mills argued that the sociological imagination could help people see themselves as agents capable of acting on society even as it shaped their own possibilities.

The sociological imagination in this sense is necessary for mobilization, but not sufficient. It is also important that people develop an infrastructure of dissent that allows them to forge an active collectivity, ultimately capable of building a counter-power that can confront those in charge. One student in a classroom or one employee in a workplace may have limited traction in challenging a decision by the teacher or the boss. However, once a larger number of students or workers begin to cooperate, they develop a collective power that can actually push back against the authority figures. Students demonstrate this power in a very limited way when they begin to pack their stuff away near the end of the allotted class time, sometimes even pushing the teacher to end the class a bit early.

The great social movements that have won some degree of social justice have created ways to forge collectivity. Movements such as feminism, anti-racism, queer liberation and trade unionism provide a frame that connects individual grievances to collective organization and new ways of knowing the world. The discovery of collectivity can be intoxicating. Looking back at the year 1968, a high point in global activism, Sheila Rowbotham (1981: 29-30) remembered: "In a way there was too much to absorb. You couldn't believe your own ears sometimes. Nothing seemed impossible. The experiences of 1968 opened your political eyes and ears."

The infrastructure of dissent is the means through which people forge the collectivity to challenge injustice. This infrastructure of dissent includes a wide range of formal organizations and informal networks which together provide the means for people to recognize their place in the world and work together to challenge the power of dominant groups (Sears, 2014). This can take many forms, including everything from student unions to cultural practices, from politicized identities to anti-capitalist organizations. The infrastructure of dissent provides the spaces in which people can:

- develop a shared analysis to challenge the dominant account we are offered through schools, government or the mainstream media;
- communicate news and shared analysis outside of official channels;
- develop a collective memory to challenge the official explanation for how things got to be this way; and
- forge active collectivity grounded in solidarity.

In the absence of an infrastructure of dissent, those who hold the dominant social positions shape the terrain. The employer shapes the operation of the workplace, controlling the terms of employment, the way work unfolds and the conduct of employees. The teacher runs the classroom, setting the agenda for the class, demanding silence whenever she or he speaks and allowing others to speak only when recognized. The police regulate public space, for example targeting certain people on the basis of race or other visible factors while allowing others to proceed unimpeded.

Once the subordinated population forges a collectivity, they develop capacities to resist and transform the situation, at the very least forcing formal or informal negotiations about how to proceed. When workers organize, they can use formal channels such as collective bargaining or informal methods such as spontaneous work stoppages to challenge management's power. Students who develop effective solidarity can speak out *en masse* to challenge the conduct of a class. As people on the streets become a crowd in a more organized sense, the ability of police to set the terms of engagement can be undercut.

William K. Carroll and R.S. Ratner (2001: 607) stress the importance of "oppositional culture" and the ways social movements serve as "laboratories for and carriers of such culture." We are using the term "infrastructure of dissent" to describe the combination of oppositional culture with concrete organizational practices, whether formal or informal (Sears, 2014). It is this combination of culture and organization that provides the ability to forge collectivity and sustain it over time, including processes of generational replacement as people leave the scene. It is through the infrastructure of dissent that we come to understand ourselves as a "communal body," in the words of the novelist Ben Lerner (2014: 34).

The infrastructure of dissent was taken for granted through much of the 20th century as it persisted over political generations. People developed and sustained this capacity for collectivity in the context of specific ways of living and working. In the early 20th century, for example, many working-class people lived in neighbourhoods right near a large workplace, such as a mine or a factory that employed many in the community. There was a commonality among neighbours, who often shared the same rhythms of life and cultural expectations for their futures. Children, for example, often grew up expecting to work and live much as their parents did, perhaps even working in the very same place.

In this situation, the formal collectivity of trade unions and left-wing political organizations coexisted with informal work networks and a whole range of social and cultural organizations. The dramatic changes in work and life associated with neoliberalism undercut existing forms of infrastructure of dissent. For example, the closure of factories and mines represented not only the loss of relatively secure jobs, but the destruction of a whole ecology of relationships that had sustained resistance capacities (Gindin, 1998: 80).

People interested in mobilizing against neoliberalism and austerity today will need to build an infrastructure of dissent that fits the ways of work and life that have emerged out of the past 30 years of restructuring. One of the crucial ways to do this is to learn from those places where an infrastructure of dissent has been built and sustained. The Québec student movement is an important example, as activists have been able to sustain resistance capacities over many political generations.

The Québec Student Movement and Its Infrastructure of Dissent

The Québec student movement is currently one of the most active and democratic mass social movements in North America. This situation is largely due to the movement's ability to internally reproduce an effective infrastructure of dissent. This infrastructure and the mobilization capacities it sustains have played a crucial role in the leadup to, and coordination of, the great student strike and "Maple Spring" of 2012. In that year, tens of thousands of Québec students went on strike (300,000 at the peak of the movement) and participated in huge street protests of hundreds of thousands on several occasions. These massive days of action were only the most visible of a whole range of actions, many of which were smaller but none the less impressive and often very creative.

The Liberal government of Québec tried to shut down the movement with repressive legal measures, but this led to defiant actions of mass civil disobedience, among the largest in Canadian history. The student strike was eventually flanked by a "casserole movement" that saw citizens take to the streets banging on pots in a show of solidarity with striking students.

This impressive movement was organized, led and sustained by a student movement in Québec that is not homogeneous. Since the 1960s, most student unions in the province have been informed by *student syndicalism* that aimed to advance the interests of students by building their collective power, much as trade unions and other worker organizations forge solidarity in the workplace to advance the interests of employees. Yet, there has been great debate about just how these interests should be understood within a student movement that has historically been divided between two main tendencies: *syndicalisme étudiant de concertation* (student unionism oriented around engaging with administrations and governments, for example through lobbying) and *syndicalisme étudiant de combat* (militant student unionism, oriented around mobilization and strikes).

These tendencies have historically been articulated around divergent provincial student unions to which local student unions have been affiliated.[41] Today, the Fédération étudiante universitaire du Québec

41 On the history of the student movement, which there is no space to address properly here, see Bélanger (1983), Lacoursière (2007), Leduc (2010) and Theurillat-Cloutier, Leduc & Lacoursière (2014).

(FEUQ) and the Fédération étudiante collégiale du Québec (FECQ) represent the accomodationist tendency, which was hegemonic within the student movement from the early 1990s up to the 2005 student strike. From 2005-12, the accommodationist and militant wings of the union each had considerable weight. The Association pour une solidarité syndicale étudiante (ASSÉ), the organization that played the leading role in the great strike of 2012, is presently the national organization that represents militant student unionism within the broader student movement. We will focus here on ASSÉ, which exemplifies the role of the infrastructure of dissent within the Québec student movement, and more broadly within a lively activist Left described above.

ASSÉ was founded in the context of a broader mobilizing campaign in opposition to the 2001 Summit of the Americas in Québec City. Not surprisingly, this new student union was influenced by the anti-globalization movement and adopted some of its "horizontal," decentralized democratic forms and practices (Theurillat-Cloutier, Leduc & Lacoursière, 2014). From 2001 to 2003, the ASSÉ led campaigns predominantly directed against the commodification of post-secondary education in the context of a globalizing economy.

At the same time, the ASSÉ was born out of a process of analysis and reflection upon some of the flaws of preceding organizations and movements. This process led to the realization that the new organization would need to prioritize a *syndicalist* perspective (relating broader political perspectives to concrete struggles to defend the interests of members) as well as a certain degree of organizational centralization (by allowing, for instance, the executive committee to have more powers and responsibilities) (Moysan-Lapointe, 2005; Marsan, 2005).

Beginning in the 1960s, Québec's student movement gradually adopted the principles of student syndicalism. The student movement drew on the spirit of the 1947 Charte de Grenoble, a key document of the Union nationale des étudiants de France (UNEF) that outlined the doctrine of student syndicalism.[42] The model of worker activism and the French tradition of student syndicalism served as the sources of the organizational and activist principles that the ASSÉ still embodies today.

42 On the Charte de Grenoble and student syndicalism, see Marsan (2005) and Theurillat-Cloutier, Leduc & Lacoursière (2014). The extracts from the Charte quoted below are taken from these texts.

The first article of the Charte de Grenoble declared that the student is "a young intellectual worker." As workers in formation, students have a right to "material independence," which is guaranteed by "the free exercise of union rights." Solidarity among students united within their own organizations is thus understood as a key condition for their fundamental social rights to prevail. Yet, with rights come responsibilities. Beyond the defence of their own immediate interests, the Charte insists on the students' duty to "defend liberty against all oppression, which, for the intellectual, constitutes the most sacred mission."

The definition of students as "intellectual workers" appears to be even more relevant today than it was in the immediate postwar period, particularly given that many are forced to seek paid employment to finance their education. Today, indeed, students are already workers, instead of simply being workers-in-the-making. Student syndicalism attempts to take students out of the ivory tower and to unite them with workers as part the broader working class. Students are understood as a social force capable of participating in social change alongside workers and other social movements.

To accomplish this, students need to adopt organizational structures and repertoires of contention inspired by the labour movement. In other words, they need to form their own student unions that do some of the same work as trade unions. Students share a common interest—to secure free, accessible and quality education—that can lead them to form unions and to fight not only for their own life conditions, but also for a just, equal and free society. A crucial aspect of this syndicalist perspective is that student *politics* is mediated by student *unionism*. Instead of small affinity groups alongside large, politically amorphous student unions (or student "governments"), student syndicalism recognizes the need to form unions that understand the collective defence of the material interest of their membership as a launching pad for broader social and political struggles. This allows for *mass mobilization* beyond activist circles.

Obviously, important differences remain between labour and student union movements. A very significant one is that students do not have the direct economic leverage of striking workers. Yet, beyond street demonstrations, office occupations and similar type of actions, student strikes do represent a very potent means to pressure university and college administrations, as well as governments. With sufficient participation and when successfully enforced, a student strike can largely paralyze the education system. If classes are stopped long enough, the strike jeopardizes the completion of the semester and thus the graduation of student cohorts that need to exit the system to make room for the incoming class. Student strikes affect an important sector of the process of social reproduction that is placed under the responsibility of campus administrators and government officials. Confronting these officials, student representatives can thus benefit from a real, structural balance of power—as has been demonstrated by numerous, often successful, student strikes in Québec over the last 50 years.

From a militant student syndicalist perspective, this source of power represents a crucial asset. Student unions need to go beyond lobbying governments based on well researched arguments and proposals (though, of course, well researched arguments are also very important). Confronting state officials, and intervening in the public space, student representatives must be backed by a well informed and mobilized student population. Thus, it is not sufficient for the student unions to abstractly depict themselves as representatives of their membership and as defenders of its interests. The point of student unionism as understood by ASSÉ is to actually get members to actively and massively participate in the defence of their collective interests.

Student syndicalism as practiced by ASSÉ is thus not only militant, it is also democratic. Democracy is understood as a fundamental condition for mass militancy. Regular general membership meetings (GMMs) by local student unions serve as spaces of collective exchange and debates where students assess the political context, adopt demands and decide on actions. Through GMMs, local unions also designate delegates and provide them with mandates that are relayed to ASSÉ's provincial congress. At congresses, delegates follow and interpret their mandates to work toward a synthesis of different—and sometimes clashing—local positions. Congress decisions are then relayed back to GMMs. Though in practice often imperfect, this back and forth movement between local and provincial assemblies is substantively democratic.[43] Through this democratic process, members of student

43 For an assessment of the strength and flaws of this democratic process, see Ancelovici & Roy-Allard, 2014.

unions can control their movement from below by participating in the drafting of platforms of demands and by outlining action plans needed to support these demands.

The ASSÉ normally engages in escalating campaigns, beginning with lower-stakes mobilizing activities such as circulating petitions, before moving to stronger militant actions such as street protests, office occupations, limited strikes, and eventually at times to a general, unlimited strike. Through this escalating process controlled from below by GMMs, rank-and-file members come to identify with the demands and actions attached to a specific campaign. At each step, collective assessments of the need to escalate the campaign, to launch a strike, to renew it or to stop it take place. In this way, rank-and-file members can actually appropriate the movement and make it their own. This process of self-activity can also create the context for individual and collective political radicalization. Thus, ASSÉ's campaigns are generally built around concrete demands embedded within a broader political perspective that is systematically put forward within the movement as well as in the media. Members of student unions engage in a collective fight to win concrete, immediate demands. Through this struggle, many come to embrace the broader and deeper political perspective also put forward by the campaign.

Yet, a lively democratic culture within the student movement and the well-attended and fruitful GMMs do not spontaneously grow like wildflowers in springtime. This is where an infrastructure of dissent plays a crucial role. Another important difference between the labour and student movements is the rapid membership turnover that characterizes the latter. This intense turnover, together with the fact that nothing about life in liberal capitalist democracies prepares student union members for the kind of participatory democracy that lies at the core of militant student unionism, requires that a democratic culture be built from the bottom up and carefully reproduced.[44] On their own, democratic structures such as GMMs formally enshrined within local unions' constitutions in no way insure that students will actively engage with these spaces. GMMs come alive because of other elements of the infrastructure of dissent that are also at work.

44 Alain Savard and Marie-Ève Tremblay-Cléroux (2013) developed this point in a particularly insightful manner.

Intense mobilizing work is required to create a democratic and militant culture that can sustain mass movements reaching far beyond the committed activist circles on campuses. Moreover, without specific counter-measures the social relations of oppression (such as sexism, racism, homophobia and transphobia, etc.) within the broader society will be reproduced within the student movement (Savard & Tremblay-Cléroux, 2013). Networks of activists are thus necessary both to create and sustain the conditions of mass mobilization and to address systematic oppression within the movement.[45]

Networks of activists connect across campuses and regions, sharing capacities and resources through local unions, regional committees and provincial structures. Some activists are elected onto executive committees and other formal committees at both provincial and local levels.[46] These activists play crucial roles with important powers and are consequently accountable to congresses and GMMs. This accountability and oversight of elected activists ensures that important tasks will be handled in a careful and responsible way. In parallel, many unelected activists become active through mobilizing committees, which provide a context for more spontaneous forms of engagement (for instance, passing by a local union's office to pick up some journals in order to distribute them during lunch breaks). These more flexible structures allow for the involvement of large numbers of activists supporting the work of elected officials, significantly enlarging the reach of the movement. In this and many other ways, formal and informal practices exist side by side in the student movement's infrastructure of dissent. This infrastructure creates the means for the reproduction of core layers of activists who can play a crucial role as catalysts in the making and sustaining of a broader movement.

Reaching out to the membership and keeping it as informed as possible about social and political issues, current campaigns or

45 This is not to say that activists are immune to reproducing oppressive practices—they certainly are not. The point is simply that organizing large social movements makes the task of eradicating systemic oppressions within such movements much more complex than it is within small affinity groups.

46 A presentation of the ASSÉ's internal rules, structure and committees is available in its Status and Rules document, which can be found in French at this address: http://www.asse-solidarite.qc.ca/wp-content/uploads/2014/09/statuts-et-reglements-derniere-mise-a-jour-avril-2014.pdf.

upcoming events is a priority. Websites, tracts, posters, pamphlets and other material are regularly produced by the ASSÉ's information committee and local unions, and widely distributed by activists on campuses. Members are also directly engaged by activists in classes and other spaces such as cafeterias. The ASSÉ's journal committee produces the organization's newspaper, the *Ultimatum*, which covers relevant current issues and events and provides information about decisions made and actions planned by the provincial and local unions. In these different ways, an effort is made to provide the membership with alternative sources of information not available through mainstream media and to establish direct and constant contact with the student population. Intervention within the public spaces of the broader society to promote the student movement's position is also recognized as an important task. To accomplish this, a member of the ASSÉ's executive committee works with elected spokespersons to organize press conferences and interviews with journalists.

In order to assist the production of information materials, a provincial committee as well as different local unions produce research papers on key issues pertaining to the education system and broader social and political matters. Capacity for organizational self-analysis is also maintained. Periodic orientation congresses formalize this self-evaluation, but different, often more informal initiatives, also take place. Reflection papers are thus circulated by affinity groups, as was the case in 2010, when *Force étudiante critique* produced a manifesto criticising the ASSÉ for its centralizing and undemocratic tendencies.[47] Hence, the student movement—or at least its militant and democratic wing—and its infrastructure of dissent takes shape through a process of ongoing discussion and debate which includes self-criticism.

These moments of self-analysis and reorientation, as well as mobilizing campaigns in general, are informed by a sharp knowledge of the Québec student movement history that reaches wide and deep within the movement. This historical knowledge is constantly and

47 *Force étudiante critique*'s manifesto is available online at http://www.fichier-pdf.fr/2011/02/08/bases-preliminaires-ggi-victorieuse. For an excellent reply and very sharp presentation of democratic militant student syndicalism, see Savard and Tremblay-Cléroux (2013), which was produced in preparation for the ASSÉ's 2013 orientation congress.

very carefully disseminated among activists. It is also evoked in different debates, during GMMs and elsewhere, to convince rank-and-file members of the historical efficacy of tactics and strategies currently being discussed, adopted or implemented. This collective memory is sustained in part through formation camps/retreats organized by the ASSÉ's formation committee three times a year. Books, pamphlets and other texts on the history of the student movement and on its struggles (most importantly Québec's nine unlimited general strikes) are also published and circulated. Casual conversations at bars after meetings or demonstrations, at parties or at other social gatherings also play an important role in disseminating this historical knowledge. Within student activist circles, friendships and loving relationships can also nurture a militant culture woven out of (often nerdy) historical and procedural knowledge, ongoing strategic reflections, reminiscence of epic (verging on legendary) actions, funny memories and jokes.

Active solidarity is also sustained through this infrastructure of dissent. Experienced activists, often elected at the provincial or local level, play a crucial role in crafting themes for campaigns, key demands and action plans. These themes, demands and plans are normally developed by activists in advance of their discussion, potential modification and eventual approval by GMMs. Local executive and mobilization committee members play a crucial role in activating these campaigns by informing and mobilizing members on the ground. Yet, on many campuses, only limited mobilizing capacities and democratic culture exist and flying squads organized provincially or regionally must come to help with mobilization. Activists at different levels also play a crucial role in organizing demonstrations and other type of actions. For all of these mobilizing tasks, the ASSÉ's central mobilization committee can play an important facilitating role, while the organization's legal committee provides support for activists facing police repression and legal pressures. A committee for social struggles also works to bridge the ASSÉ's struggle with those led by different labour unions, community groups and other social movements.

Active solidarity to fight oppressive relations internal to the student movement is also deployed—though the level of capacities mobilized for this often remains largely insufficient. Struggles against gender inequality, both within the movement and in society, have an important place within the ASSÉ, which has an active women's committee. Some of its tasks are to produce analysis, to prepare workshops and to organize different actions related to women's struggles for equality. This focus on gender oppression also helps to reveal sexist practices within the student movement, including within the ASSÉ itself. Thus, for instance, a recurrent gendered division of activist labour has been noted by many women activists within the organization.[48] However, less attention is given to other forms of oppression such as racism, colonialism, homophobia and transphobia. This represents an important lacuna that was identified by some activists during the 2013 orientation congress organized by the ASSÉ.

The infrastructure of dissent reproduced by the ASSÉ was actively and consciously built through a history of mass struggles. Out of each mobilization, new layers of activists emerge, militant capacities can be enhanced and individual and collective strategic intelligence can be sharpened. Successful campaigns and general strikes, such as those of 2005 and 2012, have led different local unions to distance themselves from a strategy of accommodation, while some have come to embrace militant democratic student unionism.[49] Organizing and participating in mass social mobilizations against neoliberal policies, in the face of often severe police and state repression, has also nurtured an anti-capitalist perspective among networks of Québec student activists. This sometimes latent, sometimes conscious anti-capitalist perspective expresses itself in different ideological tones within the militant wing of the student movement. Some anti-capitalist activists are closer to the Left political party Québec Solidaire, while others belong to different Marxist or anarchist groups or have no formal organizational affiliations. When these groups unite in a productive—if sometimes tense—cooperation to organize a campaign, as was the

48 On the struggles led by female activists against gendered oppression within and outside of the ASSÉ and on the limitation of the ASSÉ's effort on these issues and issues related to other forms of systemic oppression, see Delvaux, Desrosiers, Galerand and Lécuyer (2014) and Ancelovici and Roy-Allard (2014). Different texts on these issues were also produced in preparation for the ASSÉ's orientation congress of 2013. These texts are available here: http://www.orientation.bloquonslahausse.com/wp-content/uploads/2013/02/Cahier-des-me%CC%81moires.pdf.

49 This process is discussed in Lafrance (2014).

case in the leadup to the 2012 strike, their anti-capitalist perspectives can become an important asset. Indeed, this anti-capitalism plays a crucial role in informing an understanding of the systemic, pro-capital bias of the state, the fundamental limits of a lobbying strategy and, consequently, the need to build countervailing power by organizing mass student mobilizations while contributing to the development of a *class* solidarity reaching beyond the confines of the student movement.

NOT JUST ANOTHER SOCIAL MOVEMENT
Indigenous Resistance and Resurgence

Elaine Coburn and Cliff (Kam'ayaam/Chachim'multhnii) Atleo

All progressive social movements matter insofar as they challenge existing, unjust social relations and prefigure alternative, more just ways of living together with the world that sustains us all. Many forms of Indigenous resistance and resurgence do both of these things, critiquing what Kahnien'kehaka scholar Taiaiake Alfred (2009a) refers to as "colonial capitalism," while prefiguring alternatives. These movements face serious opposition from those invested in the status quo, including states, transnational capital, and many non-Indigenous people who benefit from Settler colonialism. In this chapter, however, we resist analyzing Indigenous resistance and resurgence as if Indigenous struggles were "just another social movement." We choose not to understand these movements in terms of ideational "frames" mobilized by movement actors (e.g. Bedford & Snow, 2000) for instance, or in terms of "political opportunities" seized or left unexploited (e.g. Meyer & Minkoff, 2004), which is the vocabulary of social movement theories. Instead, we emphasize insights from diverse Indigenous perspectives, drawing upon Nuu-chah-nulth concepts and struggles in particular, as formulated by Umeek, a Nuu-chah-nulth hereditary chief and retired professor. This leads to a better appreciation of Indigenous resistance and resurgence movements in their specificity, rather than as "instances" illustrating mainstream social movement concepts and theories. Moreover, this decision to work from diverse perspectives participates in Indigenous resurgence by "creating space" (Kovach, 2009) for those voices in the academy.

Defining Indigenous Resistance and Resurgence

> "(H)ow do we fit into the scheme of things?" (Umeek, 2011: 35).

This is a political as well as ontological question. Many diverse Indigenous peoples answer by situating themselves within specific places and relationships with all living things, including the sky, earth, water, other humans, animals and plants. Hence, the Nuu-chah-nulth, whose perspectives are particularly considered here, are a saltwater people from the northwest coast, a relational positionality that we explore in detail below. What is clear is that prior to colonization, there were no "Indigenous peoples," only Cree, Dene, Nuu-chah-nulth and so on, peoples who—like the Métis subsequently—constructed unique political identities through shared histories and intimate relationships with specific places and peoples (Andersen, 2014: 11-20).

After the 1492 invasion, however, the colonizers referred to all these peoples together as "Indians." This term has had specific legal meanings within colonial legislatures and courts, at least since the 1876 Indian Act. Now "Aboriginal" is commonly used in Canada. Other colonial documents make distinctions among First Nations, Métis and Inuit peoples, although colonial "recognition" of the Métis people was only achieved in 1982, as a result of long struggles by the Métis (see Coulthard, 2014b, however, regarding the limits of "recognition" politics; Andersen, 2014 on Métis histories and politics). Various Indigenous peoples have fought to establish their own pan-Indigenous concepts, challenging colonial terminologies while still retaining distinct national identities as Cree, Anishinaabe and so one. These pan-Indigenous concepts include but are not limited to terms like "original peoples," "Native" and the just-mentioned "First Nations," which makes clear that diverse Indigenous peoples are self-determining peoples who occupied lands before the colonizers. Here, we use "Indigenous" as a political concept that describes diverse original peoples with shared histories, including but not limited to the shared experience of colonialization.

Despite colonial tendencies to portray Indigenous peoples as monolithic blocs, they are diverse across and within nations. They include: millionaires, working-class people and those who are both unemployed and excluded from subsistence activities; men, women (e.g. Green, 2007; Suzack et al., 2010; McKegney, 2014) and genderqueer persons (e.g. Driskill et al., 2011); elders and the young; enabled persons and those with disabled and "defamiliar" bodies and minds (Davidson, 2008; Durst & Coburn, 2015) and sexual minorities, queer or "two-spirit" Indigenous persons (e.g. Justice, 2010;

Driskill et al., 2011). Indigenous persons may live on or off reserve or circulate among the two (Peters & Andersen, 2013) and they hold varying legal statuses with respect to the colonial state and within their own nations. They represent many different nations, from the Cree to the Dene to the Anishinaabe to the Métis, each with unique histories and contemporary politics. Indigenous nations are sites of difference, inequality and of political contest and debate.

We define Indigenous *resistance* among these diverse nations as any challenge to colonial-capitalist relationships. Historically and contemporarily, colonial-capitalist dynamics include genocide; forcible assimilation into Christianity and the English and French languages through residential schools (Alfred, 2009b); forcible incorporation into colonial political and judicial systems, where the state is both party and judge in disputes with Indigenous nations (e.g. Henderson, 2015); social "welfare" policies that place more Indigenous children in care today than during the residential school era (e.g. Crey & Fournier, 1998; Blackstock, 2003); and forcible dispossession from the land, necessitating the selling of labour power for a salary or a wage (proletarianization) (Atleo, 2015). In this context of genocide and forcible assimilation, resistance to colonial-capitalism includes basic, physical survival and the maintenance of Indigenous worldviews, languages and associated practices. Resistance is manifest in the persistence of Indigenous political institutions and relationships, including hereditary political power where it existed. Finally, Indigenous resistance includes challenges to ongoing dispossession, by the colonial state, Settlers and capital (for-profit corporations).

In contrast, Indigenous *resurgence* is the reinvention of diverse Indigenous ways of being, knowing and doing that are suggestive of transformed social relationships beyond the "necropolitics"—or death politics (Mbembe, 2006)—of colonialism. Put another way, if Indigenous resistance challenges colonial-capitalist relations in many domains, from everyday economic life to the arts, to education, to gender and sexuality politics, Indigenous resurgence renews Indigenous relationships, practices and worldviews with the land, water and other Indigenous peoples. Analytically, resurgence encompasses resistance, since the critical reinvention of Indigenous principles and practices resists assimilationist and integrationist colonial-capitalist logics and relationships. At the same time, as Umeek (2011) suggests, "resistance" is often a prelude to resurgence and more fundamental transformations of relationships with humans and the natural and spirit worlds. As he observes, "inevitably and purposefully, the very means of resistance became part of the means of transformation..." (Umeek, 2011: 161). Hence this analytical distinction between resistance and resurgence is weak rather than strong, a matter of emphasis and interpretation rather than sharply exclusive analytical categories.

"Telling Stories Away from Home"

> "(T)he setting of a story requires no introduction...because each story takes place in home territory" (Umeek, 2009: 2).

If the setting of stories may be taken for granted in "home territory," this is not true of stories told through the written word, which by its nature is decontextualized. The writer and reader rarely know each other personally and the political, social and spiritual location of both writers and readers may be unclear to the other. This anonymous quality of writing, which may seem helpful from positivist social science perspectives that ideally see the writer's biography as irrelevant to the outcomes, is problematic from many Indigenous perspectives. In a relational approach to knowledge, the reader/listener is better able to understand a story when the story and the knower are clearly positioned within relationships with the natural world and other human beings. If I explain that I, Elaine Coburn, write as a white, non-Indigenous able-bodied "straight" woman who grew up in Canada and have lived my adult life in France, this is therefore not about a personal "identity" claim. Rather, it is a reflexive epistemological statement that locates my writing from within unequal racialized and gendered colonial relationships, relationships likewise marked by inequalities around dis/ability and sexuality, as well as with respect to colonial borders. Therefore, I write as a non-Indigenous outsider from a specific, inevitably complex standpoint.

I, Cliff (Kam'ayaam/Chachim'multhnii) Atleo, contextualize my writing by specifying that I am Tsimshian and Nuu-chah-nulth, married to an Anishinaabekwe, a father of two children and a graduate student. Historically, Nuu-chah-nulth-aht have a critical relationship with the sea, whose abundance has long provided for us—both in terms of sustenance and as vitally informing our worldviews. This places my insights in the context of the histories and perspectives of my ancestors and relatives, who are northwest coastal peoples. Moreover, this assertion is a political claim in a colonial context that has forcibly sought to sever our relationships and responsibilities. My perspective is therefore that of an insider with a vested interest in the issues considered here. At the same time, although sharing aspects of the colonial experience with other Indigenous persons, I am an outsider with respect to diverse Indigenous peoples (e.g. Cree, Métis, Dene) distinct from my own heritage. Finally, I am male, able-bodied and so on, which means that, likewise, I speak from particular perspectives—being Indigenous is critical to my standpoint, but not exhaustive of it.

This chapter draws on insights from each of our distinct but complementary research approaches. Our co-authorship is based on the premise that there is a basis for dialogue across the colonial divide, not least the grounds of shared humanity (LaRocque, 2010: 13). Indeed, the Nuu-chah-nulth principle of hishookish tsa'walk ("everything is one") is a reminder that coordination with neighbours is inevitably required to achieve relations that are at once peaceful and just in an interconnected world.

Global Colonial Capitalism as Dispossession by Force

Indigenous histories do not start with colonial capitalism (King, 2015). Nonetheless, the invasion of Indigenous lands and waters by Europeans marks the beginning of a long relationship of ongoing colonial violence, including processes of dispossession, alienation and exploitation (Coulthard, 2014b). The purposeful elimination of Indigenous peoples by colonial states was a brutal and, to put it starkly, "functional" solution to Indigenous presence on lands and waters desired by the Settler colonizer (Simpson, 2014: 22). These genocidal policies were justified by colonial ideologies about the purported "savage," the ontologically imperfect or less than human Indigenous person deserving death (LaRocque, 2010: chapter two). Such policies were further supported by the self-serving colonial prophecy that Indigenous peoples were doomed.

Later assimilationist policies, while officially renouncing the physical elimination of Indigenous peoples, sought to erase Indigenous peoples as distinctive peoples. The residential school systems, where over 4,000 Indigenous children were murdered (Indian Country Media Today, 2014) and where many others suffered sexual, physical and emotional abuse, were maintained up until the 1990s in Canada (Truth and Reconciliation Commission of Canada, 2015). Although today the "Indian problem" is no longer framed explicitly as such, colonial policies continue to assume that modernity is congruent with colonial-capitalist relationships. In this view, persistence of diverse Indigenous ways of life is "archaic" and problematic. Indeed, any differences between non-Indigenous and Indigenous persons are assumed to represent a "gap" or "deficit" that must be resolved by state incentives (Walter & Andersen, 2013: chapter one). Failing that, colonial laws are meant to discipline Indigenous persons so that they assimilate into colonial standards of what constitutes "normal" and "desirable" everyday practices, not least incorporation as wage labour into the capitalist economy.

Today, hegemonic liberal understandings of the land, water, animals and plants, designated as "private property" and natural "resources," are reinforced by the colonial legal system. Indigenous relationships with the lands and sea are sundered, replaced by private property ownership by for-profit petrol, mining, logging and fishing corporations, as well as colonial settlements. Inevitably, the profits of destructive industries on Indigenous lands and waters accrue to very few, while Indigenous peoples are left to cope with the negative consequences.[50] On lands claimed as municipal, provincial and national parks, Indigenous presence and practices are criminalized. The strain of such "ordinary" colonial oppression disrupts fundamental relationships with the natural world, entails negative consequences for basic

50 For a damning report on the deleterious health effects of mercury poisoning on generations of Grassy Narrows residents, for instance, see Harada et al. (2005). Reed Paper, Dryden Chemicals and other companies that polluted Grassy Narrows have neither cleaned up nor compensated the community for the harms they have caused and continue to cause to the environment and health of the residents and their descendants.

physical well-being as well as related emotional and spiritual health (Alfred, 2009a).

Such material dispossession is allied with persistent, if changing colonial imaginaries that dehumanize Indigenous peoples. Mainstream films, books and even fashion often present Indigenous peoples as archaic, purely historical peoples. This denies contemporary Indigenous presence, especially off-reserve Indigenous realities (Adese, 2015). In popular culture, routinized forms of hate speech, as in the sports franchise "Redskins," contributes to a climate in which Indigenous peoples may be dismissed, degraded and subject to violence, when caricatural representations of Indigenous peoples are not "consumed" as entertainment. As Emma LaRocque (1996) argues, the widespread dehumanization of Indigenous women as "squaws" cannot be dissociated from the gendered, racialized violence reflected in more than 1,500 murdered or missing Indigenous women and girls (Ambler, 2013) in Canada.

"Five Hundred Years of Resistance": Indigenous Struggles in Historical Perspective

Indigenous resistance to genocide, assimilation and hate speech is centuries old. In 1992, when many colonial nations celebrated the "discovery" of the "new world" by Columbus, Indigenous peoples mourned the invasion and subsequent murderous colonialisms while at the same time honouring "500 years of Indigenous resistance" (e.g. Hill, 2010). Often, that resistance has been dramatic. In recent centuries, to remember one well-known struggle, Louis Riel led opposition to the colonial state's 1869 incursions onto Métis land around the Red River. His struggles ended in defeat nearly two decades later in 1885, when he and other Métis leaders were hanged as "traitors" by the colonial government (Métis Nation of Ontario, 2015).

In other moments, diverse Indigenous nations have sought to form pan-Indigenous alliances to negotiate more powerfully with the colonial state. The Allied Indian Tribes of British Columbia was established in 1916, for instance, in an unsuccessful effort to formalize the Nisga'a's jurisdictional rights over their lands and waters (Kulchyski, 1988). In the aftermath of World War I, the League of

Indians of Canada was founded by a Kahnien'kehaka war veteran Frederick Ogilvie Loft. These attracted considerable support, so that annual conventions were held from the 1920s through the 1930s, sometimes attracting as many as 1,300 to 1,500 delegates (Kulchyski, 1988: 99-100). The League sought to unite Indigenous peoples to protect Indigenous rights, land title and self-determination in government through the band councils. Like earlier Indigenous political organizations, the League faced sustained opposition, including efforts by Indian Affairs to revoke Loft's Indian status. In the late 1930s and early 1940s, other pan-Indigenous organizations were formed within colonial provincial boundaries, like the 1931 Native Brotherhood of British Columbia. Alongside formal political bodies, critical resistance continued informally, as generation after generation continued and continues to share traditional knowledge and to speak Indigenous languages while maintaining connections with the natural world. Many practices were maintained even when illegal. For instance, the Indian Act specifically outlawed the potlatch until 1951. Resistance efforts have involved important leadership by Indigenous women, despite laws that refused women leadership positions in colonial-sanctioned band councils until 1950.

In the contemporary period, however, the most prominent wave of Indigenous struggles arose in the aftermath of the notorious White Paper (1969). The White Paper proposed to unilaterally terminate the Indian Act and dismantle Indian Affairs. Although Indigenous peoples were critical of both, the Paper effectively represented a refusal to honour Treaties, where these had been signed, and to respect the inherent rights of Indigenous peoples to their own territories and to self-determination. Indigenous peoples were supposed to dissolve into the "just society" of the colonial state, assimilating fully as a condition of access to full citizenship rights. The White Paper generated strong opposition among Indigenous nations, who argued instead for a transformation of colonial Canada, which Harold Cardinal (1969) forcefully critiqued in his book *The Unjust Society*. These struggles for Indigenous self-determination and nation-to-nation relationships were to enduringly mark the Indigenous and Canadian political landscape, with the creation of the National Indian Brotherhood, in 1970, which later became the Assembly of First Nations and, in reaction to this patriarchal leadership, the 1974 creation of the Native Women's Association of Canada. During this same period, the first Native Studies programs were established by and for Indigenous scholars and students. In the 1970s, a very small number of Indigenous intellectuals, like Métis literary critic and feminist scholar Emma LaRocque, created whole curricula and central textbooks from scratch (LaRocque, 2015). Their approaches emphasized Indigenous knowledge and perspectives against dominant anthropological perspectives constituting Indigenous peoples as "objects" of expert study by mainly non-Indigenous professors (in a world context, see Tuhiwai & Smith, 1999).

Protest and mobilization continued through the 1980s and 1990s across many different Indigenous nations. As Rima Wilkes' (2015) research suggests, since the 1980s alone, there have been over 500 Indigenous protest "events" from fish-ins to hunger strikes, not including events associated with the Idle No More movement that began in December 2012. Some of these events have entered even the broader non-Indigenous consciousness as place names where Indigenous peoples have defended their lands against resource extraction and colonial settlement: Kahnesatake, 1990; Ipperwash, 1995; Gustafsen Lake, 1995; Grassy Narrows, 2002; Elsipogtog, 2012. These have often involved violent clashes with the colonial police and military. During the same period, Indigenous peoples, who had once been barred from law schools, led a series of landmark legal cases around Aboriginal rights and title, including *Sparrow, Gladstone, Marshall, Vad der Peet*, *Haida, Taku River Tlingit,* and perhaps most infamously *Delgamuukw* (Atleo, n.d.).[51] Of course, such legal cases were not always successful—unsurprisingly, given that the colonial state is at once party and judge. Nonetheless they are suggestive of broader

51 The 1997 Delgamuukw case recognized Indigenous title in principle, but the judge who made the decision likewise argued that it could be violated for the purposes of "the development of agriculture, forestry, mining, and hydroelectric power, the general economic development of the interior of British Columbia, protection of the environment or endangered species, the building of infrastructure and the settlement of foreign populations to support those aims" (see Atleo, n.d.: 11-12). Hence, the ruling "recognized" title, only to insist upon the wide range of circumstances in which it did not apply. In our view, this case is emblematic of the ways that colonial-capitalism is thrust upon Indigenous nations.

Indigenous agency, in all fields, represented here through attempts to bend colonial law to Indigenous purposes (Henderson, 2015). Other forms of resistance have been less visible but still critical, including water walks, often led by Indigenous women, to highlight responsibilities of all peoples to the water that sustains us all (Bédard, 2008: 102-07), the picking of medicines on traditional lands claimed as provincial parks (e.g. Corntassel, 2012: 93), and the pursuit of land-based learning, pursued alongside or instead of more formal, institutionalized learning.

The most notable and recent wave of Indigenous activism is the "Idle No More" (INM) movement. In December 2012, INM emerged in opposition to the federal omnibus Bill C-45, which gutted fundamental protections of vital waterways and attacked Indigenous sovereignty with legal terms implying the permanent "surrender" of Indigenous lands. Among the more visible of INM initiatives, round dances were held in shopping malls and around state buildings, reclaiming spaces usually given over to capitalism and colonial power. The participation of non-Indigenous actors in such dances bore witness to broader public support for Indigenous struggles, suggestive of the possibility of more enduring Indigenous and non-Indigenous solidarity (Martineau, 2015). For over a month, Chief Theresa Spence fasted on fish broth, symbolizing and embodying "hardship and sacrifice" and putting her life at risk. In so doing she called attention to the poverty of her own and many other Indigenous nations, a consequence of ongoing colonialism and the government's failure to honour Treaty relationships, where these exist. Writer, intellectual and activist Leanne Simpson (2013) referred to her as *Ogichidaakwe* Spence "a holy woman...a warrior, a leader," who risked her body and her life to dramatize the need for justice for Indigenous peoples. The Nishiyuu youth, beginning with just a few individuals and later including over 250 Indigenous persons, walked over 1,500 kilometres to Ottawa to call for action for Indigenous rights (APTN, 2013). The nascent Indigenous Nationhood Movement (www.nationsrising.org) carried out acts of self-determination, like reaffirming Indigenous title of the mountain PKOLs. Located near Victoria, British Columbia, the original name of PKOLs has been overwritten as "Mt. Douglas" on colonial maps, while Indigenous jurisdiction was erased by unilateral declarations that PKOLs was part of provincial parkland. In a ceremony, the Indigenous Nationhood Movement erected a sculpted sign at the top of PKOLs affirming historical and contemporary Indigenous presence in the area and calling for restored nation-to-nation relationships among Indigenous and Settler peoples (Martineau, 2015). These are illustrative, not exhaustive of the kinds of events and movements that together made up the Idle No More struggles.

Idle No More is not over, but continues in different forms. We offer some suggestive, further illustrations here:

- In both academic and non-academic settings, new technologies are being mobilized to enable the online learning of Indigenous languages. The First Voices website offers free mobile phone applications to help learn the basics of several different Indigenous languages. There are also grassroots examples of crowd-funded immersive language learning like those led by Khelsilem and the Skwomesh Language Academy.
- Indigenous relationships with humans and the natural world are being renewed in everyday life through the remaking of traditional foods, clothing and trading systems (Atleo forthcoming), as well as through preparation for and practices of ceremony.
- Indigenous learning is being reinvented, as in the Dechinta Centre for Research and Learning, a northern institution that proposes land-based forms of learning with Indigenous faculty with both traditional and university-based knowledge.
- Storytelling is taking on new as well as traditional forms. Films, like Kent Monkman and Gisèle Gordon's *Group of Seven Inches* (Monkman, 2005), offer playful but sharp-edged denunciation of myths of the noble savage and of binary gender and heteronormative relations. As Monkman and Gordon describe, in the film "Miss Chief Eagle Testickle" (the outrageous alter ego of Cree artist Kent Monkman), forces innocent naked white men to become her figure models, seduces them with whisky, and when she's done with them, dresses them up as more "authentic" examples of the "European male" (Monkman, n.d.). Such artistic works challenge colonial gender and sexual norms, alongside

movements of "two spirit" and queer Indigenous activists, creating new stories at once politicized and personal.

- Individuals like Doreen Demas, a blind Indigenous activist, represent the often marginalized voices of Indigenous persons with disabilities. Demas has been active at Idle No More events, at the United Nations and through academic work (e.g. Demas, 1993; Durst & Coburn, 2015). She has insisted that Indigenous persons with disabilities are self-determining and do not require pity, charity or rehabilitation but political support to dismantle barriers to their agency, including within their own Indigenous nations.

In contrast to the colonial stereotype of a frozen Indigeneity, Indigenous resurgence is not about repeating static, unchanging practices. Indigenous peoples adapt to new contexts, but also alter those contexts through human inspiration, innovation and solidarity.

Nuu-chah-nulth Experiences of Colonial-Capitalism

We have offered some shared Indigenous experiences with colonial-capitalism and of various resistances to this radically unequal and unjust world system. Here, we turn to Nuu-chah-nulth experiences, which are both distinctive and typical of Indigenous experiences with colonial-capitalism. The Nuu-chah-nulth, a word that means "all along the mountains and the sea" (http://www.nuuchahnulth.org/tribal-council/welcome.html), are northwest coast peoples. Alongside traditional hereditary forms of power, the Nuu-chah-nulth are organized today in the Nuu-chah-nulth Tribal Council, made up of fourteen distinct First Nations, all located along the west coast of Vancouver Island. Historically, Nuu-chah-nulth communities thrived off the bounty of the sea, an idea captured by the common coastal expressions of "when the tide is out, the table is set" or "Salt Water People." After contact with European and American trading ships, the Nuu-chah-nulth also hunted and traded sea otters and seals. A generation or two ago, although many of us had already been incorporated into the capitalist system as wage labourers, we were still heavily involved in commercial fishing with a Nuu-chah-nulth fleet of over 200 boats. Today, most of us can no longer claim an everyday relationship to the sea that has sustained us for countless generations. We have been alienated from our connections with the sea, a disconnection that effectively starved us into submission—and into the capitalist wage economy or, worse, the new poverty of unemployment.

As for the Ahousaht, one of the fourteen Nuu-chah-nulth First Nations, many are working for fish farm companies. Under-regulated fish farming has been shown to present a threat to natural fish stocks, and is a costly and wasteful production of fish. Ahousaht originally opposed the encroachment of fish farms into their waters, but they eventually signed a protocol agreement in 2002 with fish farm companies for an undisclosed amount of financial compensation and input into ongoing fish farming practices and site placement. The example of fish farms in Ahous waters is a complicated one that is indicative of the contemporary neoliberal political and economic climate. The Nuu-chah-nulth have long stated that they do not oppose economic development, which is not necessarily synonymous with capitalist relations of exploitation—so long as they are involved, have meaningful input and that projects do not unduly threaten ecosystem health and longstanding Nuu-chah-nulth principles. This is why, for many, the leadership's support for the fish farms and even the more recently controversial copper mine proposal have been surprising—until one grasps the full context of the situation and the very real material poverty our communities now endure. Many literally face the choice of feeding their families through fish farms, or facing serious hardship and even starvation.[52] The never-ending desire for recognition of our hereditary leaders and their rights, jurisdictions and responsibilities, means that some argue for hereditary decision-making power over mining and fish farms, which means engagement with mining and fish farms—rather than waiting for such recognition from hostile governments, likely to impose fish farms and mining on us without any input or consultation. Despite all this, there is persistent community opposition to these projects, the copper mine in particular, and the

52 We might observe that in *Capital*, Marx did not condemn 19th century tin and copper miners for despoiling the environment—he understood that engagement in such back-breaking and nature-destroying work was part of the broader capitalist system that compels human beings to sell their labour power in order to live. Indigenous peoples are no different: we are trying to survive in circumstances not of our own making and we often suffer extraordinary hardship.

Ahousaht have committed to holding a community referendum to determine whether they will support it or not. In this respect, resistance and critique still play a role in shaping community policy, so long as they also respect traditional Ahous governance. Our critique of contemporary colonial-capitalism is expressed through our hereditary governance systems, not against them.

Differing perspectives and priorities are not new to Clayoquot Sound, including the "War in the Woods" in the 1990s. This struggle began in the 1980s and became international news by the early 1990s, when Nuu-chan-nulth peoples and environmental organizations and protesters blocked the logging corporation MacMillan Bloedel, which sought to clear-cut centuries-old trees in the area with the approbation of the provincial colonial state. In 1993, over 800 individuals were arrested for such blockades (Salazer & Alper, 2000). Old-growth forests have been protected—provisionally—as a consequence of this short-lived coalition between Indigenous peoples, environmentalists and local non-Indigenous activists.

It is worth stressing that the alliance between Nuu-chah-nulth-aht and various environmental NGOs has always been fragile and precarious. Bruce Braun has written about this dynamic at length, challenging what he characterizes as an inappropriate binary logic, espoused by many ENGOs, which contrasts "pristine nature" with "destructive humanity" (2002: 1). This binary logic erases contemporary Indigeneity by perpetuating a mythological, essentialized understanding of Indigeneity that amounts to a unique form of eco-colonialism. Additionally, the work of some ENGOs has actively inhibited some Indigenous communities' abilities to develop their own contemporary economic solutions. The strategic alliance was mostly short-lived with the Nuu-chah-nulth Tribal Council accusing environmental groups of "neo-colonialism" in 1994 and the banning of Greenpeace from Clayoquot Sound in 1996 (Braun: 107-08). Since then, relations remain precarious with anyone that does not acknowledge or respect Nuu-chah-nulth jurisdiction and priorities.

Co-opting Nuu-chah-nulth resistance: Aboriginal neoliberalisms

Since contact and colonization, Nuu-chah-nulth-aht have struggled to exhibit agency and maintain some control over our interactions with the state and capitalist markets. Most recently, we have engaged in forms of Aboriginal economic development that closely resemble neoliberal capitalism, the contemporary shape of a shape-shifting, centuries-old world capitalist system. To some, this is an Indigenous adaptation to a context that we have not chosen and a way of maintaining minimum controls over our lands and "resources" on them, despite opposition from colonial states and powerful corporate actors. Others might call it a co-optation into colonial-capitalist relationships, in which all of life is instrumentalized with the aim of producing profits (typically accruing to the few). Certainly, in some cases, Aboriginal economic development, like mainstream capitalism, celebrates individualism, entrepreneurship and the generation of profits, subsuming concerns for the environment. Although there is certainly resistance, some Nuu-chah-nulth actors reproduce hegemonic neoliberal rhetorics and urge integration into a despiritualized world understood simply as a business opportunity.

The Nuu-chah-nulth Economic Development Corporation (NEDC) is an example of our participation within the dominant neoliberal economic development paradigm. The stated aim of the NEDC is to "assist Aboriginal's (sic) make their dreams come true and build a better future for business!" (www.nedc.info). By way of illustration: a recent event sponsored in part by the NEDC called "Build My Business Together" is filled with slogans that have become familiar within contemporary capitalism, including "nothing succeeds like success." The event offers "business training" and "business planning and marketing" and advice on "topics" like "rewards and risks" and "the pleasures (and pains) of entrepreneurship." Another topic is "Aboriginal cultural issues and opportunities" which reads as if Indigenous cultures are just another (business) opportunity to be exploited. The poster font has the first "s" in business replaced by the dollar sign. Business and entrepreneurship in this sense is conceived as nothing more than generating (individual) wealth, where wealth is understood in the narrowest, strictly monetary, terms. The poster also has a caption reading "'Real World' Business Skills Training," signifying both effective business skills and, possibly, suggesting that the real world is a world by and for business. If the aim of the NEDC is to make "dreams come true," events like these appear to conflate Nuu-chah-nulth "dreams" with "a better future for business."

This language reflects a neoliberal worldview that is produced and reproduced in other influential institutions and literature. The Harvard Project on American Indian Economic Development, the Royal Commission on Aboriginal Peoples, and individuals like the charismatic Clarence Louie, chief of the Osoyoos Indian band, all emphasize similar commitments to business, entrepreneurship and individualism. They share a common vocabulary of risk, exploitation, personal responsibility, and economic development. The underlying argument is that through individual initiative, Indigenous persons will become entrepreneurs and achieve personal wealth. In this way, we will close the "gap" between supposedly desirable mainstream Euro-Canadian ways of being and doing and Indigenous poverty and suffering. The latter is not considered an outcome of centuries of colonialism and capitalist dispossession, but instead attributed to individual failures to adapt to the "real world" and seize the "opportunities" provided by integration into "effective business practices." In such visions, capitalist tenets of growth and exploitation dominate and displace our own unique Indigenous worldviews and reciprocal relations.

Living Nuu-chah-nulth-aht

In our view, in contrast, the "real world" has little to do with the world imagined by—or desired by—business, which is capital. We do not live in a world of atomistic individuals whose only motivations are unsustainable growth and greed. Nor is the "real world" the one imagined by colonial states, in which civilizing Euro-Canadians finally bring "backward savages" into modernity, where modernity is imagined as synonymous with colonial-capitalist relationships. Rather, the real world is the one that is known to us as Nuu-chah-nulth peoples. This is a world of fundamentally interconnected, reciprocal and respectful relationships. Earlier, we referred to the principle of hishookish tsa'walk, or "all is one." This principle reminds us that there is no such thing as the economy, separate from humans, animals, plants and the natural world. Nor is the "real world" one of atomized, isolated individuals or "entrepreneurs" living in a financial cyberspace. Instead, we are fundamentally interconnected. We all depend upon the natural world to sustain life. We all depend upon each other to live and grow and flourish as human beings, whose values are much richer than a dream of simply more and more personalized wealth.

In a fundamentally interrelated world, other humans, and the sea and land, animals and plant life, the sun, the sky, are deserving of our respect. For Nuu-chah-nulth-aht, this idea is captured in the critical concept of iisaak. Iisaak is a complex idea, but signifies respect for all things, including for our relatives, strangers, leaders, children, elders, and all of creation, for this diversity is rooted in our common origins (Atleo, 2004: 15-160). Many Nuu-chah-nulth-aht, individually and together, are seeking ways of honouring and respecting each other and the natural and spirit worlds—of making iisaak a guiding principle for everyday life. A sea people now cut off from the sea, some of us, for instance, have turned to communal, organic farming, a way of respecting the relationships among all life rather than superexploiting and polluting the earth for short-term gain. Others have sought to revive old skills, with respect to making our traditional housing, gathering and preserving foods and medicines and trading these along once-extensive pathways (Atleo, 2015). Some of us are in academia, trying to share our stories in new ways, writing down and reflecting upon the shared knowledge that has been passed to us in other settings. Umeek has written about the complex worldviews of the Nuu-chah-nulth in his book *Tsa'walk*, for instance, while Charlotte Coté has shared stories of our whaling traditions (Coté, 2010). There are Nuu-chah-nulth language revival programs, some of them sharing basic phrases through Internet technologies. Gordon Dick, a Nuu-chah-nulth artist, has carved both celebratory and commemorative totem poles, under Tim Paul, renewing traditions of wood carving alongside painting, drawing and ceramics.

Of course, art may be abstracted from context and become just another commodity. To show their relevance and secure positions in a neoliberalizing academy that increasingly values "partnerships" with the for-profit private sector, Indigenous academics may feel pressure to share knowledges in ways that contribute to the creation of privatized "intellectual property." Organic farming may be on the margins of the normal, colonial-capitalist economy, without challenging colonial-capitalist dispossession of Indigenous lands and seas. Language lessons may be bought and sold in private for-profit academies. Combatting all of this will require transformations that do not depend on heroic individual actions, but solidarity across diverse Indigenous peoples and with non-Indigenous supporters who agree that such a world is neither desirable nor inevitable. It will mean developing creative ways of living out the idea that "all is one" and that all life and the earth, sun, sky and water are deserving of respect. These are practical guides to everyday actions, whether it is in the arts of everyday life or academia. They remind us not to treat others instrumentally and to consider how our actions reverberate with consequences for all of our relations.

Some might argue that this is romantic. We would argue that the dystopian vision of contemporary neoliberalism—a world made up of markets, formed through a thousand selfish actions of atomized individuals whose ultimate and only motive is greed—is no less idealistic (Dupuy, 2012: 64). Moreover, as Indigenous peoples, we have long enough collective memories to recall a time when our worlds were organized on different principles and so could be again.

"A Place, a Purpose, a Reason for Being"

The stories we have told here—of dispossession within world colonial-capitalism, of resistance and resurgence by diverse Indigenous peoples—are not unique to Indigenous peoples across lands claimed by Canada. Rather, they are familiar worldwide: to the Maori, to the Saami, to the Quechua and many others. We can learn from our exchanges with other Indigenous peoples, who have faced similar oppression and yet continue to live and renew their traditions and worldviews. In addition, we can learn and act in solidarity with non-Indigenous peoples, many of whom suffer from colonial-capitalist relationships that exploit many and benefit very few. Doing so will not be easy. It will mean recognizing that we occupy this world, not as atomized individuals, but as interrelated humans that share all of creation. It will mean that non-Indigenous persons will have to learn to respect Indigenous peoples who have been dehumanized for centuries. It will mean learning and inventing ways of feeding and sheltering and creating that do not rely on exploitation and the permanent destruction of the natural world, nor on the alienated labour power of other human beings.

Inevitably, this means acting where we are. We do not act globally, in the sense of acting abstractly in an undefined global space. Instead, we always act and reflect from and in specific places. It is specific places, and our relationships with them, that give meaning to our lives. It is difficult to overestimate the opposition that will arise as we seek to live out our lives according to principles of hishookish tsa'walk and iisaak. There are multibillion-dollar corporations that will bitterly oppose every relationship, every action and every worldview that threatens to cut into their profits and contests their claim to "private property ownership." They will mobilize lawyers, draft laws, use private police, and they will be supported with the full weight of the state, including the judicial system and the use of the state police and the military. We have seen this before. Moreover, the battles we win are always provisional. Clayoquot Sound, for instance, is under renewed threats, just two decades after monumental battles to preserve the land and life there. Our seas are polluted and overfished. We are routinely subject to violence, especially Indigenous women and girls. Against this, we have centuries of survival and determination. We have principles that are not just traditions, but ways forward to a more just and sustainable world. We have the possibility of solidarity, including with those non-Indigenous persons who share our dismay and anger with the world-as-it-is and who are willing to struggle alongside us for a world-that-may-be.

We are faced with a choice. We can reduce our existence to a competitive, individual struggle for more and more personal wealth. Or, we can create space so that all of us have a place and each of us has the chance for meaningful existence, in relationship to one another. As Umeek puts it: "(E)veryone, without exception, has a place, a purpose, a reason for being" (Atleo, 2004: 115). One way of understanding Indigenous resistance and resurgence is to say that it is a commitment to making this true, in our everyday lives and, when necessary, through extraordinary actions that affirm our place within a complex, interrelated world of humans, animals, plants, the earth, the sky and spirits.

PLACING DISABILITY POLITICS
Uneven Sitings of Dissenting Bodies

Pamela Moss, Michael J. Prince, Beth DeVolder and Catriona Johnson

Disability and Social Justice

The disability movement in Canada comprises a wide range of politics that at times seems incompatible with other movements based on a collective, social justice politics. In Canada, historically, disability has been associated with individual bodies supported and reinforced by the intense medicalization of physical impairment within the health care system. Deafness, blindness, and hemi- and quadriplegia have dominated popular and mainstream understandings of disability as well as those on the Left. Other types of disability including various types of neurodiversity, madness and physical difference remain hidden away, individualized and invisible to the public.

Three key events in the early 1980s brought attention to disability within mainstream Canadian audiences and social justice circles, and would frame the way in which disability gets taken up in policy and practice venues for the next three decades. First, 1981 was, as designated by the United Nations, the International Year for Disabled Persons. In Canada, this prompted a parliamentary committee to hold cross-country hearings with numerous disability groups and advocates resulting in a series of reports calling for a range of social policy reforms. Second, in 1982, the *Canadian Charter of Rights and Freedoms* guaranteed equal rights for persons with a mental or physical disability. Equality under the law for disability, alongside race, national or ethnic origin, colour, religion, sex and age, protected individuals from discrimination because of a mental or physical characteristic. Third, the designation of persons with a disability as an equity group in a landmark report in 1984 by the Honourable Rosalie Abella meant that specific practices could be put in place so that those guaranteed rights could be achieved.

These events, however, were not the types of changes needed to repair the fissures already commonplace within the movement. Living with dignity and full participation in all aspects of life, especially with regard to decision-making, became rallying cries across the country as the independent living movement strengthened throughout the 1980s. The practice of equal rights seemed to fit more snugly for those with visible disabilities who used mobility aids and assistive devices and needed changes to the built environment than for those whose impairments were invisible (i.e., arising from systemic bodily disruptions or mental illness) and needed more flexibility in the type of changes in workplace and public spaces. Equity challenges focused on groups who had been disadvantaged historically with regard to employment (women, Aboriginal peoples and visible minorities, in the language of the Abella Report). But for many persons with a disability, employment challenges took years to surface, in part because of the employment practices already in place for persons with disabilities (e.g. sheltered workshops) and in part because of the general practice of not employing persons with any type of disability. Through collective demands for access to education and public services, the Canadian landscape for persons with a disability began changing. Disability activism produced mixed results federally and provincially: While across-the-board policies on accessibility and inclusion addressed unequal access (e.g. transportation, building codes, sign language), individualized assistance programs promoted uneven support to access (e.g. the Canada Pension Plan disability benefit is tied directly to employment).

These fissures within the disability movement, however, need not suggest an insurmountable hurdle in an engagement with social justice. Rather we see them as a set of opportunities to enact a variegated politics that is both specific to individual bodies and united against ableism. We first provide a framework for understanding disability in material and discursive terms in relation to power and knowledge. We then turn to a series of vignettes, or concise descriptions, that tease out how the politics of disability comes to be practised in specific places. In these vignettes, we address contested illness, veteran rights, compulsory heroism and politicized parenting. We close with a discussion of what these vignettes do as stories about disability politics and some observations about how they can inform a wider understanding of social justice.

Framing Dissenting Bodies

Resolving the difficulties arising from organizing across types of disability to effect change is not as simple as saying, "Get on the same page and fight oppression." What may be oppressive in one context for a wheelchair user, for instance, may not affect someone who is deaf. Or, what has given rise to the marginalization of a woman diagnosed with borderline personality disorder who has been evicted from her third apartment in six months is different from the issues faced by a soldier who has completed rehabilitation for a leg amputation and who has a supportive spouse and stable housing. In approaching disability we find it useful to focus on the practices that address deployments of power *in situ*, temporally and spatially as well as discursively and materially (after Braidotti, 2011; Mol, 2002; see Roets & Braidotti, 2010).

We understand the disparate politics extant within the disability movement in Canada to be located in the specific contexts within which a specific disability or disabling condition expresses itself. These contexts hold within them various configurations of power and patterns of practices that shape what disability means, how individuals experience disability, what it is that oppresses and marginalizes persons with disabilities, and how resistance takes form. The very context within which an activist acts generates a space to engage multiple political strategies to organize dissenting bodies. These strategies simultaneously hold, and thus must work with, competing aspirations both in the sense of what to focus on and how to do it as well as what knowledge to draw on to make political claims.

The myriad politics within the disability movement crave social justice in specific ways. In the following four vignettes, we show how disability politics are informed by the specificity of the context within which the politics of disability gets taken up. These snapshots as a collection show how practices of power through knowledge systems operate to inform how oppositional politics within disability can work. They demonstrate how individual and collective positioning vis-à-vis the state shapes the means through which persons with disabilities can access benefits and entitlements. They speak to how powerful discourse is in defining what counts as disability through mobilizing affective and symbolic resources to limit specific instances of dissent. And together they disclose how politicized dissent emerges through personal and collective commitment to negotiating the boundaries of knowledge systems, material relationships and practices of power.

Placing Disability Politics

Embracing contentious relations

Contested illness poses a unique challenge for both the disability movement and social justice politics. Contested illness refers to those forms of disabling conditions that are "dismissed as illegitimate—framed as "difficult," psychosomatic or even non-existent—by researchers, health practitioners and policy-makers operating within conventional paradigms of knowledge" (Moss & Teghtsoonian, 2008: 7). Over the past couple of decades, names of contested illness—food sensitivities, fibromyalgia (FM), Lyme disease—have entered mainstream discourse, which has been a result in part of the widespread circulation of biomedical knowledge outside medical circles and of the rise in recognition of chronic forms of illness. Specific to all contested illness is a fundamental mismatch between the experience of debilitating illness and the categories used by medicine to capture what is going on. Important in understanding the conflict between people with disabling conditions seeking help and medicine as a knowledge system is that going to the doctor is the principal resource available to people in need of fixing an ill body.

An effect of this mismatch is to place both the people living with illness and the illness itself at the margins of medical knowledge systems. Take for example myalgic encephalomyelitis (ME). Struggles among researchers and clinicians over whether the entity exists have made it difficult to set up effective treatment options. Historically, the groups of symptoms thought to comprise the illness have variously been known as atypical poliomyelitis, Royal Free disease, Tapanui flu, Epstein-Barr, chronic fatigue syndrome (CFS), chronic fatigue and immune deficiency syndrome (CFIDS), and, as of 2015, systemic exertion intolerance disease (SEID). Indeed, past successes in naming and recognition have positioned ME as a diagnosable entity (Fukuda et al., 1990; Holmes et al., 1988; Institute of Medicine, 2015), even among front-line general practitioners. Such successes have brought peace of mind to many living with ME for their experience of ill health has been acknowledged by those in positions of power who can offer treatment to alleviate the distress of illness as well as sign off on an application for a claim to both state and private disability benefits.

While a diagnosis is increasingly part of clinical practice, there is still discord in determining the boundaries of the illness among activists themselves. For example, within the international ME community, a large group of individuals living or diagnosed with ME are huge supporters of ME Research UK, a charity dedicated to raising money for biomedical research. The working assumption for the group is that ME is a specific disease and although many have been diagnosed with ME, only a small percentage of them actually have the disease (Abbot, 2009). ME is considered a subset of CFS, which comprises only a fraction of those enduring the more general symptom of chronic fatigue. In contrast, in Canada, activists around ME have long advocated for a widening of the definition of ME to include a wider range of system disruptions and more leeway in capturing the variation in the grouping of symptoms. The National ME/FM Action Network (Canada) holds a position on the expert medical panel to develop working definitions of ME/CFS (Carruthers et al., 2003: 2011). Known as the "Canadian Criteria," this working definition is an international standard favoured among those having to deal with extreme fatigue and debilitating pain on a daily basis and those wanting to help them.

While refusing the label of disabled and the claim of living with a disability, people with contested illness are estranged from the umbrella disability groups that would be their entry points into the realm of disability. Disability activists and scholars have fought long and hard against medicalizing disability (Stone, 2008). The idea of raising funds for research that would in effect bring a disabling condition further into the arena of biomedicine is anathema to most disability activists. Because of the reliance on individual experience of illness and the contentious nature of the relationship with biomedicine—that of seeking support while challenging the knowledge from which that support is derived—options for contested-illness activists are somewhat restricted. If the bodily sensations people experience as illness do not fit neatly into existing diagnostic categories, then it makes sense to gain legitimacy through revising categories (see Barker, 2005), especially when specific diagnoses are crucial in securing benefits in a system dependent on and deferent to biomedical knowledge. These actions run counter to social justice principles of challenging hegemony and upending oppression which have been the foundation of the disability movement in Canada. As a result, activism around contested illness is marginalized within the disability community (as defined by Prince, 2009). Such activism is perhaps better situated as embodied health movements (Brown, Morello-Frosch, Zavestoski & the Contested Illness Research Group, 2012; Orsini, 2014), which may or may not be allied with wider social justice values and politics (see Moss, forthcoming).

Emplacing veterans

Veterans with disabilities fit social justice politics through their pursuit of important material resources for meeting their needs and in making claims for respect, dignity and valued recognition of their sacrifices and exceptional struggles. They also raise issues of unfairness and inequality of treatment by government officials through mobilizing collective identities via advocacy organizations and tactics such as rights-based strategic litigation. The federal government department of Veterans Affairs Canada (VAC) has long maintained relationships with such veterans' organizations as the Royal Canadian Legion, National Council of Veteran Associations, the Army, Navy and Air Force Veterans in Canada, Canadian Association of Veterans in United Nations Peacekeeping, and the Canadian Peacekeeping Veterans Association.

Veterans' affairs policy is a field of intense symbolism, profound emotional aspects, and nationalist identifiers. Not for the first time in Canada's history though increasingly notable in recent years, veteran activism has become visibly assertive and vocally contentious (Moss & Prince, 2014). Struggles take place over: the legitimacy of post-traumatic stress disorder (PTSD) as a medical condition; the stigmatization of soldiers and veterans with mental health symptoms; and the administration of benefits and services to veterans and their families. At the core of this controversy is the contested idea of a social covenant or sacred obligation between Canadian veterans and the Canadian state, a historically grounded and politically distinctive set of relationships sited in commitments, rights and obligations (Prince & Moss, 2015).

Today, veteran activism confronts the dominant cultural trope and official political rhetoric of supporting our troops, remembering those who have fallen, and acknowledging our collective debt to those who have made this sacrifice. Various veteran groups have emerged in the last decade, representing new platforms for mounting challenges as well as for seeking accommodations with the federal government. This activism, especially by disabled veterans, is presenting alternative images and circulating critical knowledge and different ways of thinking about the life experiences and treatment of veterans by the Canadian state.

With increased politicization of veteran policies and veterans affairs generally, the style of activism and choice of advocacy techniques by certain veteran organizations has become contentious. A former chief of the defence staff in Canada has warned that militant advocacy by veteran groups has taken an ominous political tone which could result in the loss of broad public support (Manson, 2014: A11). In contrast to mainstream moderate veteran organizations, Paul Manson points to "the appearance of several veterans' advocacy groups that comprise little more than a website and a handful of officers, with few members in the traditional sense. Small as they are, these have dominated the headlines by virtue of a non-traditional, militant approach in support of veterans' causes, notably in the form of aggressive and vitriolic attacks on the federal government, the Prime Minister, Veterans Affairs Minister...and his bureaucrats" (A11). According to the former chief of the defence staff, "the veterans' cause must transcend party politics and campaign issues. Mainstream veterans firmly believe that political gamesmanship is not the answer" (A11).

Manson's remarks illustrate that tensions emerge around organizing dissent by and on behalf of disabled veterans, antagonism between what he positions as the moderates and militants. More fundamentally, his appraisal expresses a view of veterans' issues as above the particularities of democratic politics, as more properly located in the national interest and general good of the country. Expressed by an elite insider, this is the hegemonic view of the military and of how veterans ought to conduct themselves. Within this frame, many tactics and methods for mobilizing interests, by definition, are deemed to be aggressive and dubious and thus highly questionable. It is a discursive attempt at disciplining veterans as activists, at regulating the sites, sounds and objects of veteran advocacy.

Nonetheless, veteran activists and veteran advocacy groups, many associated with Canada's military involvement in Afghanistan, are mobilizing in numerous sites, such as courtrooms, review tribunals, social media postings, Parliament Hill demonstrations and parliamentary committee hearings, press conferences and journalistic reports, and protests on or around Remembrance Day. These sites are where the master frame of the military collides with contending views articulated by veteran activists and their families. Politics at play entail far more than electoral campaigns and political parties. They mobilize identities and counter-narratives that are the representative of interests and expression of conceptions of community, citizenship, and justice and injustice.

Despite a diminishing veterans population overall, the visibility of veterans' issues and veterans' disability politics has been on the rise. This politicization stems from frustrations of veterans with government restraints of programs and a gap between the rhetoric of grateful support and a reality of a begrudging bureaucracy. The growing visibility of veteran disability politics is both virtual and physical in character through more overt and assertive action online as well as on the ground. It is also cultural in that veterans' political activism unsettles benign assumptions in the general public about the provision of timely medical treatment and adequate financial compensation for disabled veterans and shifts traditional images of veterans, rooted in the First and Second World Wars, to more contemporary figures of dissenting bodies, the marginalized soldiers with operational stress injuries and psychological trauma.

Challenging compulsory heroism

While disability activism can be informed generally with ideas about equality and inclusion, it is not necessarily informed by social justice.

The "overcomer"—the person who succeeds against all odds—has become a persistent disability narrative with endless iterations, from the blind man who scales mountaintops, to the smiling young girl in a wheelchair who inspires with her never-say-never attitude. The response of the disability community to this discursive framing of disability is divided. While disability scholars have long critiqued "supercrip" stories (Clare, 1999; Hevey, 1992; Titchkosky, 2007), many disability-related organizations depend upon such "success" stories to raise funds and promote awareness.

Whether or not aligned with the aims of social justice, overcoming narratives make heroism *compulsory* (DeVolder, 2013), an extension of Rich's (1994) compulsory heterosexuality and McRuer's (2006) compulsory able-bodiedness. *Compulsory heroism* can be defined as both an effect and a strategy of normalization that has become the only acceptable subject position available to persons with disabilities. Emphasis on the compulsory nature of normalization shifts attention away from individuals who depart from the norm (the "abnormal") toward the normative violence of enforced sameness. A large part of the identity, body and interpersonal work of disability involves the ongoing management and negotiation of compulsory heroism. Individual responses to powerful narratives policing disability (its boundaries and criteria for social acceptability) are neither static nor homogeneous; individuals navigate compulsory heroism in various changing, ambiguous and often conflicting ways (Berger, 2008; Peers, 2009; Chrisman, 2011).

Heroism can be considered to be compulsory in two respects. First, because nobody really aspires to being socially cast as abnormal (McRuer, 2006), persons with disabilities are in effect coerced into normality via the illusion of choice. Not being a hero is impossible for the very practice of engaging in everyday life enacts the person with a disability as a hero. Second, attributions of heroism are unavoidable for "the heroic mantle cannot be refused; heroism is bestowed regardless of protests to the contrary" (DeVolder, 2013: 748).

Yet it is not simply a matter of grappling with the discursive constructions circulating in media, institutions and lay parlance. Persons with a disability are tasked with managing compulsory heroism in everyday encounters where heroic effort is expected and the badge of heroism is liberally bestowed. Goupil (1997: n.p.) describes an incident when, while out with friends in a bar, a total stranger asked to shake her hand and launched into what she calls "the standard I-really-admire-you-people speech,"

> My first reactions to the man's comments were embarrassment and anger. Embarrassment because he singled me out in a public place to congratulate me for doing something that would be ordinary if someone else did it. But since I have a disability I must be "strong and brave." Then came the anger because he just didn't get it. He was saying, "What a shame," as if physical perfection is the only thing worth a damn. Finally, after my initial rush of feelings, I felt sorry for the man. To him I really was a hero. He imagined that if he were in my situation, he just wouldn't be able to go on.

The work of negotiating compulsory heroism also involves the imperative to always be positive, something Ehrenreich (2009) refers to as "mandatory optimism." There is the expectation to always be cheerful, to never complain, to disregard any negative emotion (read as self-pity), and to refuse to give in. While keeping positive may be a helpful, and perhaps effective, personal strategy for managing difficult life situations, the harsh effects of mandatory optimism need to be acknowledged: feelings, needs and responses are invalidated; individual difference is refused; and attention is directed toward disciplining the individual (undoubtedly making friends, family and professionals more comfortable), rather than towards any necessary social change. Clearly, "No amount of smiling at a flight of stairs has ever made it turn into a ramp" (Young, 2014).

Compulsory heroism is a tough nut to crack. Many disability organizations and audiences are attached to these tales of triumph over adversity: They are feel-good stories, positioned as antidotes to all the bad-news ones (DeVolder, 2013). They raise a lot of money for worthy causes. They sell books, increase the viewership of television talk shows, and validate the hard work of rehabilitation professionals. However, overcoming stories are not uniquely or even fundamentally disability stories—they are redemption stories (see Gilmore, 2010). And, central to these redemption stories, ironically, disability serves as both the exemplar and the exception. It is only in confrontation with the exception that compulsory heroism finally begins to show its cracks. The unruly body, that body that despite all our best efforts refuses normalization, stubbornly proclaims that there are some things that simply cannot be overcome. Faced with the unruly body, compulsory heroism reveals itself in all its mythic, normalizing violence.

Politicizing parents

Parents of children with disabilities may not identify as social justice activists, but their experiences position them as advocates for their sons and daughters. Late 20th century political changes, including access to education, deinstitutionalization and recognition of the right to be free from discrimination, grew out of the first wave of the parents' movement, initiated by parents of persons with developmental disabilities and now termed the Community Living Movement. Today, parents continue to navigate medicalized understandings of disability in search of citizenship for their children who remain under the gaze of doctors, educators and case managers. Measured against developmental norms and gate-keeping criteria, at birth or early in life, parents are convinced to adopt identities for their children outside the norm, thus accepting existing boundaries of power (Fitch, 2002). "It's a girl!" raises the spectre of determination and prescription. With the announcement "He has Down syndrome!" expectations are amplified; a child is labelled with a deemed difference that "assumes a binary opposition between the categories of normal and disabled and thus has the broadest of social implications" (Landsman, 2005: 126).

Parents seek to occupy positions of alliance with their children and, with a child's labelling, they enter into particular relationships, practices, systems and discourses (McLaughlin & Goodley, 2008). Medicine locates disability in deviant anatomies. Disability activists in contrast link disability to social influences, thereby implying that disability is not found in individual bodies, but in the organization of social relations that produces systemic barriers to participation and citizenship (Hughes, 2009). Relocating disability in a social context has allowed the disability movement to shift narratives about disability away from the individual in need of fixing towards forces of discrimination resulting in social and economic deprivation, marginalization and normative violence.

Parents themselves are positioned within competing narratives that focus on the burden of disability which maintains normalizing practices with regard to the child's bodily deviance. Whether or not parents accept a disability label along with its rigid trajectory, embrace non-normative qualities or reassess so-called normal itself may be tied to influences that are contradictory, often stemming from the very systems that produce barriers and limit citizenship. Caught between differing concepts of disability, parents recognize societal prejudice as their children's greatest obstacle while simultaneously holding faith that a child can be changed before a society can (Landsman, 2005).

Three interlinked narratives assist in framing the politicization of parents of persons with disabilities. The linear narrative, associated with medicalized understandings of disability, espouses science as the key to human improvement and aims for certainty in diagnosis which is experienced by parents as restrictive and blocks development of alternative thinking (Fisher & Goodley, 2007). Parents access services to address their children's deficits, and as they experience their children's progress, they also face their children's failure to reach normative targets. Parents, however, may resist normalizing discourses that pathologize their children through narratives that locate disability within "complex social interactions and practices" (71). Definitions of disability and success are open to contestation, thus allowing parents to challenge what constitutes normal with the effect of seeing disability outside a pathological lens. Though this narrative of challenge seems to combat normalization by permitting the exercise of agency by parents, there remains a linear master storyline, often featuring the solitary battling mother overcoming adversity. In contrast to the linear narrative and the narrative of challenge, the philosophy of present and becoming can liberate parents from the need to fight for the future. A focus on the present alongside the recognition that the reality of disability is a process permits parents to interpret uncertainty as opportunity, focus on well-being and realize that the future cannot always be controlled. Recognizing the costs of difference that disability imposes and gradually understanding that the supposed certainty that naming brings is illusory, parents mobilize the range of discourses available to them depending on what is useful politically in time and place.

Parenting literature, parent networking and advocacy training may assist parents to strategically mobilize particular understandings of disability. To secure services, parents use medicalized understandings of disability to engage with healthcare providers, educators and legal systems. Parenting literature encourages parents to take an active role in the identification of disability by providing information and terminology that allows them to challenge professionals and service systems (Ong-Dean, 2005). Support groups serve as nodes in parenting networks and can be effective sites for political organizing. Peers play a role in developing group identity and promoting activism through the reconfiguration of the social relations of disability in ways that challenge normalizing forces of segregation (Singer et al., 1999; Taylor, Buunk & Aspinwall, 1990). Advocacy training is increasingly displacing the parent training conducted under the watchful, collective eye of helping professionals. Examples include the Canadian Inclusive Lives Learning Initiative or Partners in Policymaking which explore history, human rights, policy and practices (Barton, 2011; Partners in Policymaking, n.d.). Yet, even with these resources, parents struggle with their multiple identities arising out of a politicization characterized by informed pragmatism that constantly shifts in search of social justice.

Uneven Sitings of Dissenting Bodies

These vignettes reveal several characteristics about disability politics and the disability movement in Canada. The central role of biomedical knowledge and power relations is clearly apparent in all four vignettes. Conventional paradigms of the human body, of medical research and diagnostic practices shape the meaning and image of disability as a knowable deficit, a personal tragedy and a burden to be overcome with or without public support and services. Consequently, many individuals with disabilities experience a mismatch between their lived circumstances and the classifications of medicine, the military or mass media. The results for many individuals and families are stigma, discrimination, frustration and despair, and multiple forms of exclusion.

Challenging prevailing beliefs about human bodies, deviance and difference figures as a major type of resistance and strategy of dissent by disability activists and movement organizations. In this activism and advocacy, the role of medical science as a knowledge system has a contradictory place for disability politics. Medical understandings of bodies and minds can trap people into narratives and material practices that depict them as abnormal, cowardly, defective or faking a condition. Yet, as the vignettes indicate, individuals use the same medicalized understandings to secure such public services as teaching assistants, therapies, counselling, income benefits or student grants.

The placing of specific strategies within disability activism into a wider disability movement and social justice politics widely varies. As we argue, the politics of contested illness occupies a marginalized place on the terrain of the disability community more generally, as does the politics of compulsory heroism (though both can be linked to rehabilitation and therapy aspects of the disability service sector). Activism by disabled veterans and parents of children with disabilities represents older forms of collective action in Canada, more congruent with the material practices of social movements. Advocacy by veterans after the First World War and Second World War laid the foundation for a number of key disability service organizations, although contemporary veterans' advocacy groups are often distinct from mainstream disability movement organizations. The parents' movement around children with intellectual or developmental disabilities, which emerged in the 1950s and 1960s, continues to play a main role in the disability movement, joined in more recent decades by numerous organizations of people with disabilities.

The uneven siting of the dissenting bodies of persons with disabilities makes for a jagged politics. Competing objectives clash with bodily difference. But, as we have shown, this variation need not deter disability activists from seeking to organize around social justice. Although prickly, disability politics can be a model for the wider social justice movement by reproducing what the disability movement does really well: holding a productive tension between individual bodies and their governing structures while enfolding multiple organizing strategies for its manifold ends.

FROM RESISTING POLICE RAIDS TO CHARTER RIGHTS
Queer and AIDS Organizing in the 1980s

Gary Kinsman

Introduction: Of Disjunctures and Remembering

> *Anger, excitement, and a surging sense of power fuelled our steps as we moved south on Yonge Street, sweeping aside queerbashers and police alike.... It was Feb. 6, 1981. I was among three thousand gay men and lesbians and our supporters taking over Toronto's main street. We were expressing our outrage at the arrest the previous night of close to three hundred men on "bawdy-house" charges following raids on four gay baths.... The demonstration was an unprecedented show of strength—a real high for me. The cops were disoriented and the city was turned on its ear.*[53]

I wrote this in 1986. Contrast this account with current Pride Day parades in the larger urban centres in "Canada"[54] where you not only find police providing "security" for the event but also in a major reversal you have large police contingents, often with police vehicles, *in* the parade (Gentile & Kinsman, 2015; Bain, forthcoming; Burgess, forthcoming). In 2010 these very same police forces engaged in large-scale mass arrests at the global justice protests against the G20 in Toronto, including the mistreatment of queer, trans and gender queer people who were arrested (Keaney, 2011), and continue to engage in arrests and violence against people of colour, Indigenous people, sex workers, street youth, trans* (Tompkins, 2014) people, poor and

53 See Kinsman, 1996: 1. The 1996 text is the same as the 1987 first edition. Sections in italics in this chapter are my memory reflections.

54 In my work I trouble "Canada" and recognize I am writing on Indigenous land. Settler activists need to be committed to actively support Indigenous struggles, decolonization and fighting racialization. See Depelteau & Giroux, 2015 and Morgensen, 2011.

homeless people and others—many of whom are queer.[55] This sets up an important disjuncture between my social experiences of queer resistance in the 1980s and what exists today.

The question I ask is how did resistance to police repression, the moral-conservative right-wing linked to neoliberalism, state sexual censorship, and the impact of the AIDS crisis come to be replaced, for so many, by same-sex marriage as the end game of our struggles in the historical present? How did the current "movement" develop an aim which often seems to be a white middle-class respectability, support for neoliberal capitalism and an affirmation that "we" are just like heterosexuals aside from the gender of those we have sex with and love? What can we learn from how this was put in place and at the same time resisted in the 1980s?

Ways of accounting for this transformation are "homonormativity" and "homonationalism." Lisa Duggan popularized homonormativity as a way of describing the accommodation of layers of queer people with neoliberalism (Duggan, 2003) through new forms of "normalization," and Jasbir Puar uses "homonationalism" (Puar, 2007; Dryden & Lenon, 2015) to describe the identification of white middle-class queers with Western states as the defenders of their rights. While these terms are very suggestive, they need more social and historical grounding in the social relations of class, racialization and gender struggles so they are more useful for activists. In part I attempt to do this for the 1980s.

This is an investigation of how queer organizing was transformed from a counter-hegemonic movement to become—with contradictions and tensions—part of a broader neoliberal hegemony. I am now much less enthusiastic than I was when I wrote "Managing AIDS Organizing" (Kinsman, 1997) about Gramsci's critical analysis

55 I use queer to firstly reclaim it from being a term of abuse used against us. Secondly, I use it as a broader term than homosexual, lesbian, gay, bisexual that can potentially include all those who live even partially in rupture with institutionalized heterosexuality and the two-gender binary "system." But it is also a project, and can also be used to marginalize lesbians and trans* people. Thirdly, I use it in queering and denormalizing what is taken for granted. Finally, I do not use it to displace class struggle as has often taken place in queer theory. Instead, I use it in a more queer Marxist sense. On this see Kinsman, 1996 and Kinsman & Gentile, 2010.

of hegemony, where hegemony is the active construction of relations of ruling combining consent and force. As Richard Day has pointed out there are major statist tendencies in Gramsci's work.[56] But at the same time critical analysis of hegemony usefully directs our attention to the balance of social forces as a continuous social, historical accomplishment. It can assist in opening this set of relations up for critical investigation in explicating how associations between neoliberalism and queers were put in place. Or how the world we won—in major ways—is not the world we were fighting for.

This chapter builds on my initial work on the 1970s and is the second instalment of this story (Kinsman, forthcoming). It is part of my work on the making of the contemporary "neoliberal queer," excavating the social and historical basis for the accommodation of layers of queer communities with capitalist, racialized and patriarchal social relations in the historical present. This includes attempts to "privatize" and institutionalize our sexualities and relationships as well as constructing our "citizenship" (Evans, 1993) claims in more limited "rights" and commercialized terms that developed and spread in the 1980s[57] (Hennessy, 2000; Duggan, 2003; Sycamore, 2004; Sears, 2005; Floyd, 2009; Drucker, 2011; and Conrad, 2014). How did a movement that still had a progressive, and at times a radical character, throughout much of the 1980s, become a class project for integrating some white gay men (and smaller numbers of lesbians) into capitalist social relations?

This investigation is partly based on memory work (Haug, 1992; Frankenburg, 1993) given I was actively involved in queer and AIDS organizing in the 1980s. These memories are placed in the context of archival and other historical research to put my experiences in a broader social context. Four key features of what took place in the

56 See Day, 2005. At the same time this does not mean that I subscribe to all the analysis that Day develops. Unlike Day I continue to hold onto a revolutionary, socially transformative perspective.

57 By the 1980s I am referring to the period from about 1980 to 1990-91. This is not an attempt to do a more general history of queer movements in this period but is instead excavating some of the social roots of resistance to and accommodations with emerging forms of neoliberalism during these years. For work on the history of queer movements during this period see M. Smith, 1999; Ross, 1995; and Warner, 2002.

1980s are examined—police repression; moral conservatism and neoliberalism; the AIDS crisis; and the Charter and equality rights. Although this is the focus here, far more than this was going on during these years which I will explore in future writing.

This is also not the sad story of the inevitable long march towards the neoliberal queer but also records resistance to this during these years. There were always alternatives and things could have been otherwise. I write in opposition to the social organization of forgetting which neoliberal capitalism is based on through the resistance of remembering our past struggles (Kinsman & Gentile, 2010: 21-22; 37-38).

It should already be clear that any narrow analysis that only addresses "sexuality" or "queerness" is inadequate for this project of political and historical recovery. As the perspective developed by Himani Bannerji (1995) points out, sexuality is both autonomous and specific but also is always mediated and mutually constructed through relations of class, racialization, gender, ability, age and other social relations. Narrow notions of "queer" politics that do not grasp this mutually constructed character lead to the construction of false universals that violently abstract away from relations of class, race, gender and other forms of oppression to place the concerns of white middle-class queer men at the centre of "queer" politics.

This transformation of queer organizing and community formation takes place as a series of shifts over several decades and is multi-layered. This is why it was often hard to see where this process was going. Our struggles won very real victories, especially in relation to human and formal rights, against the right-wing and the police. But the "rights" victories "we" won helped some far more than others. This is especially the case regarding formal rights. There was often a double-sided character to these victories with differential class, race, gender, age and ability impacts. This began to open up space for the emergence of a particular white, middle-class queer class project which was put forward as a universal strategy for "our" communities and rights.

The initial emergence of the "pink market" as some capitalists marketed their commodities to queers combined with the advertising by some gay business interests of gays as a growing market, which starts in the second half of the 1970s (Kinsman, forthcoming) and expands in the 1980s with broader community formation. Only some are included within this "market"; others are partially included, while others are excluded. There are class, race, gender, age, ability and other grounds of exclusion while white, middle-class adult men are included. This leads to consumer-based "citizenship" claims, which have a middle-class, white and often "male" character. This leads to new forms of regulatory regimes in queer community formation. This helps to create part of the basis for the emergence of a non-moral conservative form of neoliberalism within and outside queer community formation interested in the further development of this "market." In response to the white hegemony which is buttressed through this "pink market" community construction, we also see the self-organization of queers of colour and two-spirit people in response to racism in this community formation and heterosexism and anti-trans practices within communities of colour and among Indigenous people (Silvera, 1991, 1996; Warner, 2002: 317-29). This becomes a form of resistance to aspects of the emergence of neoliberalism within queer community formation.

Before proceeding, it is necessary to have some analysis of neoliberalism that is grounded in class and social struggles.[58] In the 1960s and early 1970s, there was a global wave of class and social insurgency, which the feminist and gay revolts were part of, that called capitalist profitability and social relations into question. In response to this wave of struggles, "Keynesianism" (or social programs and a limited "welfare state") was now seen in capitalist and many state circles as giving too much income and social power to workers and poor people. Neoliberalism begins to emerge as a distinct capitalist perspective in the mid- to later 1970s out of social struggles and the articulation into a distinct project of a number of existing currents of "economic" and moral conservatism. Neoliberalism as a longer-term transformative project set itself the task of restoring profitability and capitalist relations through undermining this composition of class and social struggles coming out of the '60s and early '70s. This brutal class project was to be accomplished through dismantling social programs,

58 I use a wider autonomist Marxist notion of class and class struggle. On this see Kinsman, 2005: 41-50; Cleaver, 2000; and Dyer-Witheford, 1999.

targeting the social wage, and attacking workers and the poor around the world. Despite weakening aspects of state formation regarding social program funding, there was an intensification of disciplinary forms of state formation including campaigns against unions, against people living in poverty, "law and order" campaigns, and the tightening up of borders against poor people of colour from the Global South. Neoliberalism also laid the basis for new waves of capitalist globalization through "free trade" and other regional and international agreements like the Free Trade Agreement with the US in 1988 and NAFTA in 1994 (Dyer-Witheford, 1999; Cleaver, 2000; McNally, 2006). The impact of these neoliberal measures developed unevenly, depending in part on the level of resistance they faced.

Throughout most of the early 1980s, neoliberalism exhibited a moral conservative tendency; its focus on disciplining workers and the poor often included attacks on feminism and gay and lesbian liberation in order to defend the heterosexual and patriarchal family coded as white and middle-class (Gordon & Hunter, 1979). The anti-gay/anti-lesbian/anti-feminist "Moral Majority" in the United States crystallized differently in the Canadian context where there was a weaker fundamentalist Protestant movement. Major mobilizations were organized by the feminist movement, gay and lesbian groups, and sometimes the unions against moral conservatism. These mobilizations combined with popular educational work began to turn the tide against anti-feminist/anti-gay moral conservatism by the later 1980s but it is still very much alive and able to be mobilized against queers, feminists and others.

The Police, Criminalization and Dialogue Committees

The first area I explore is struggles over sexual policing. This includes the police raids on gay baths and bars and the mass resistance to this in the early 1980s. This crucial terrain of struggle continues from the 1970s. The sex police using the 1969 reform strategy clamped down on gay visibility in "public" as it emerged more fully in the 1970s through movement organizing and initial community formation (Kinsman, 1996: 338-45; Kinsman & Gentile, 2010: 302-35). The police started to more systematically use the bawdy-house laws (which cover places resorted to for "acts of indecency") including in the Truxx bar raid in Montreal in 1977 and in the raid on the Barracks bath house in Toronto in 1978. In Toronto the Right to Privacy Committee (RTPC) is formed as the defence organization for those arrested (McCaskell, 1988; Nash, 2014). This also highlights the importance of bars and baths as sites of resistance to police repression.

In 1981 in the resistance to the raids in Toronto—that I started this chapter with—large numbers of gay men and supporters responded in a series of demonstrations involving thousands of people. More than 1,000 people attended the main RTPC organizing meeting after the major raids and hundreds of people were actively involved in organizing. Important alliances were built with the Black and South Asian communities who were also facing police repression and links were also built with the feminist and union movements. This magnified the power of the gay-centred resistance to the bath raids (Kinsman, 2006: 139-44).

The RTPC was initiated with a rather liberal notion of the right to privacy that can easily be accommodated with neoliberal approaches and the widening of the 1969/Wolfenden public/private regulatory approach (Kinsman, 2013). However, as the RTPC developed, especially in the context of the mass resistance to the 1981 raids, a more socially transformative approach that moved far beyond liberal approaches was articulated. Developed in particular by George Smith, this approach focused on the social practices people engaged in in the construction of relations of privacy which could take place in state-defined "public" places like parks and washrooms, and certainly in bathhouses, potentially involving more than two people (G. Smith, 1983; Hooper, 2014; Picher, 2015). While this started within the state-defined public/private distinction it also actively subverted it. It was able to be used to extend the space in which consensual sex between men could take place without police intervention, establishing a certain queer right to the world. This worked against the liberal limitations of the more mainstream right to privacy approaches. However, after the mass mobilizations died down the liberal form of right to privacy used to privatize our sexualities was reasserted.

As a result of this mass defence effort where most men are acquitted of their charges there was a shift in policing from large-scale raids, which provoked a mass response, to more individual and less collective arrests for sex in parks and bathrooms including in Orillia and in St. Catharines (G. Smith, 1985). The RTPC formed Gay Courtwatch to provide assistance to those arrested in these circumstances (Findlay, 1984). At the same time there was escalating Canada Customs censorship of gay and lesbian sexual materials especially at Little Sisters in Vancouver and Glad Day in Toronto (Kinsman, 1996: 345-47; Burtch, Pescitelli & Haskell, 2015: 147-50). Same-gender erotic materials were designated more "obscene" and "indecent" than similar heterosexual materials.

The RTPC called for an inquiry into the organization of the police raids. At first there was some talk of organizing our own people's inquiry, but this was swept aside when the City appointed Toronto lawyer Arnold Bruner to conduct an officially mandated inquiry (Bruner, 1981). The Bruner report both reflected the gains of the struggle against the police, including characterizing the gay community as a "legitimate" community, but also argued centrally for the need for dialogue between the police and the gay community. This assumed that the problem with the police was not the criminal code and police organization but the ignorance and lack of education of individual police officers. This profoundly misunderstood the social power relations involved. The problem was not bad communication but criminalization (Kinsman, 1996: 342-43; G. Smith, 1988; G. Smith, 2006). The RTPC and others pointed out the problem was that dialogue committees could become vehicles for involving community representatives in policing people in our communities.

The formation of police/gay dialogue committees was one of the fronts around which initial neoliberal relations were organized. These dialogue committees, which were formed in a number of centres including Ottawa, provided openings for "community policing" to extend surveillance within and practices of collaboration within gay community formation (Kinsman, 2015). Educational work with the Ottawa police through such a committee did not prevent the police from continuing to engage in racist practices towards people of colour in that city (Kinsman, 1996: 343).

A much earlier dialogue committee formed in Vancouver in 1975 involved collaboration with the police against "public sex" and sex workers (Ross & Sullivan, 2012; Kinsman, forthcoming). Gordon Price, a gay man, helped to form Concerned Residents of the West End (CROWE) in 1980 initiating a successful campaign to purge sex workers from the West End. Their more vigilante-oriented wing called "Shame the Johns" attempted to drive sex workers out of the area, and according to Price significant numbers of gay men were involved in this group (Fairclough, 1985: 100; Ross & Sullivan, 2012: 617 note 3). Their central concerns were property values and maintaining the gentrified character of the neighbourhood. This came to be tied into real estate values and the "respectability" of the neighbourhood in what can be described as the residential aspects of class which tied a layer of gay men into capitalist property relations. As Ross and Sullivan describe it:

> ...white, upwardly mobile gay West Enders sought respectability through access to privatized domesticity and consumption, and the simultaneous expansion of gay public culture through institution building and residential stability in a gentrifying neighbourhood. Concomitantly, on-street sex workers who called the West End home, and who shared gay men's desire for community development, belonging, and freedom from police prosecution and state interference, became caricatured as noisy, truculent, and dirty violators of community values (Ross & Sullivan, 2012: 606).

In organizing as "respectable" gay men who owned property they set themselves against sex workers, men who engaged in sex outside, and also poor and homeless people on the streets. This residential organization of class would later also be mobilized against sex workers and poor and homeless people in Toronto and other centres. This became an important trend leading towards the emergence of the "neoliberal queer" in the later 1980s and 1990s.

The mass resistance to sexual policing in the early 1980s led to an explosion of visible gay community formation. This created a new basis for class (and racialized and gender) formation. A new white and often "male" middle-class layer began to emerge that was now very "out," unlike in the past when given a very different class organization of "homosexuality" they had to be "covert" to maintain their privileged social positions (Kinsman, 1996: 161-65; Kinsman &

Gentile, 2010: 130-31). Their being "out" was now possible precisely because of these mass struggles and expanded community formation. It was this middle-class layer that was able to achieve the most from the struggles in the streets initiated by working-class and street queer people and activists. This layer began to speak for the "community" since they participated in the languages of ruling and came to stand in an administrative relation to the "community."

In Toronto when there was a mass movement and the RTPC was a mass organization, with hundreds of people involved in its activities, the distinct interests of the bar owners, professionals and managers who were involved and had valuable skills were subordinated to this mass organizing. When this cycle of struggle died down, with fewer people involved, the interests of these strata became more distinct and defining (Kinsman, 2006: 139-44). In the context of the mirage of a classless "community" this stratum began to develop its own class project, although never named as such. An unnamed and one-sided class struggle was initiated within gay community formation.

This struggle for rights as a "legitimate minority" group came to be tied up with an ethnic minority model which was an available means for a community to become a "legitimate" minority group. One of the features of this "model" was its basis in a class hierarchy within the "community" with a middle-class and business layer at the top. This also facilitated class formation within gay communities (Kinsman, 1996: 308-11).

NeoLiberalism: From Moral Conservative to Non-Moral Conservative

The second area I explore is the moral conservative right-wing and its relation to neoliberalism. As mentioned previously the first neoliberalism queer organizing encountered was a moral conservative one which faced major feminist and queer opposition. This included anti-right organizing by Gay Liberation Against the Right Everywhere (GLARE), in which I was actively involved, and Lesbians Against The Right (LAR) in Toronto in the early 1980s. This began to undermine moral conservatism.

The early neoliberal offensive in BC in the early 1980s was tied into moral conservatism with a "restraint" budget and a series of bills attacking union and human rights and social programs. There was massive union and community opposition to this with Operation Solidarity in 1983 which involved tens of thousands of people in protests, including strike actions. However, when the union leadership pulled the plug on the organizing the movement quickly subsided.[59] Along with the attacks on union rights and social programs this offensive included the abolishment of the Human Rights Commission and other regulatory bodies. Lesbians and gays were involved in this organizing but not only around distinct lesbian and gay concerns (Diamond, 1983).

> *I was working on Pink Ink at the time, an attempt to build a progressive Toronto-based gay/lesbian publication that was followed up by Rites magazine which was committed to feminism and social justice—and even we did not fully grasp that these broader neoliberal attacks were also centrally attacks on queer people. This suggested some of the problems with narrow notions of gay and lesbian rights which did not see how this connected to the broader neoliberal assault on working-class and poor people.*

The neoliberal attacks in BC continued with an even more overt moral conservative inflection with the Vander Zalm government attacks on reproductive rights, lesbians and gay men and people living with AIDS/HIV in the late 1980s and early 1990s (*Angles*, 1988-90).

For some, especially white middle-class gay men who were making class gains through neoliberalism, it became increasingly difficult to see the connections between their lives and these struggles. A narrow focus on lesbian and gay rights made it hard to see struggles against social program cutbacks and neoliberal attacks as also queer. At the same time even though a major source of support for rights struggles came from the union movement, often pushed on through the self-organization of queer workers, increasingly the narrow focus on "rights" left support for union struggles and struggles against poverty off the "gay" agenda.

59 See Palmer, 1987, although Palmer adopts an orthodox Trotskyist approach focusing on the crisis of leadership rather than the crisis of self-organization.

The resistance to sexual policing and organizing against neoliberal moral conservatism was significant. At the same time I remember a certain naïve sense that winning against moral conservatism was winning against neoliberalism itself. Victories against moral conservatism, although crucial, were not the same as victories against neoliberalism. In response to social struggles this was not the only neoliberalism to emerge.

By the mid- to later 1980s non-moral conservative forms of neoliberalism based on a limited moral deregulation of queers (Sears, 2005) began to emerge, extending the Wolfenden public/private regulatory approach to allow for a privatized homosexuality and community as well as a "consumer" focused form of "citizenship." In part, this was a response to the level of resistance that moral conservatism faced from feminists, gays and others. It was our mass resistance to police repression and to moral conservative neoliberalism that created the basis for the articulation of a neoliberalism that was not tied to moral conservatism. Of course, this was not what we were organizing for as our victories had unintended consequences. Neoliberalism did not disappear. Instead a new neoliberalism emerged partly based on our struggles but also the emergence of a new "out" white middle-class gay stratum that was based on the expanding "pink market," commodification, dialogue committees with the police, attacks against sex workers, and a particular "community" formation. This new white middle-class stratum becomes invested in neoliberal capitalist relations. Direct state forms of normalization and regulation are lessened and are replaced by market forms of regulation and normalization. As Ross Higgins (2011) points out, forms of homonormalization replaced police repression as a means of regulating queer sexualities.

At the same time there was another obstacle that neoliberal tendencies faced. Lesbian feminism as a current within the lesbian movement and community formation, sometimes participating in organizing with the gay movement, presented an obstacle to emerging trends leading towards neoliberalism in the early 1980s. Lesbian feminist critiques of institutionalized heterosexuality (Bunch, 1975), critiques of legal and human rights strategies, an emphasis on addressing the oppression of women in a broader feminist perspective, a general opposition to commercialization, and a greater sensitivity to dealing with questions of class privilege (Bunch & Myron, 1974) created obstacles in the midst of mainstream gay men's circles that were often more open to neoliberal capitalist influences. These critiques existed despite the problems with the gender essentialism and anti-trans* perspectives that existed among currents within lesbian feminism, as well as an often generalized opposition to most erotic materials influenced by currents within radical feminism (Ross, 1995). In the early 1980s, this left gay men's community formation more open to the incursion of an emerging neoliberalism.

The beginning of what I suggest is the weakening of lesbian feminism after the early 1980s with the dissolution of groups like Lesbians Against the Right in Toronto and other lesbian feminist organizations, and the gradual loosening of connections between many lesbians and feminism as a movement, allowed for the entry of neoliberal capitalist relations more pervasively into lesbian "communities" by the later 1980s. This also opened up more possibility for neoliberal inroads to broader forms of gay and lesbian organizing, including Lesbian and Gay Pride events. At the same time the political distinctiveness and far less commitment to commercialization can still be seen in many of the Dyke marches organized during Pride activities in many centres (Burgess, forthcoming).

AIDS Activism and Managing AIDS Organizing

The third area to be explored is the emergence of AIDS in the early 1980s and the response to it in the gay, lesbian and other communities and from state, professional and pharmaceutical agencies. AIDS both devastates gay and other communities, being used to organize discrimination and stigmatization, but also in the face of state inaction generates community-based AIDS groups drawing on aspects of feminist health activism. This first wave of organizing was indispensable in providing support for people living with AIDS/HIV (PLWA/HIVs), in fighting against discrimination and in doing popular education for safer sex and drug use practices as a community and collective responsibility (Silversides, 2003).

These organizations that initially were able to get only make-work project funding were able to access a federal health funding stream (Kinsman, 1997) and later in many cases provincial funding as well. These groups through an uneven process of state funding and regulation become managed by state and professional relations and transformed into AIDS service organizations (ASOs). These forms of reorganization and management include the need for more professionalized staff, boards of directors, executive directors, incorporation and charitable tax status (Kinsman, 1997). All of these shift groups way from activism and towards top-down forms of organization that replicate the form of organizing in the corporate world (Ng, 1990). Many of these ASOs come to control relatively large blocks of funding that did not exist for groups within gay community formation previously and this came to reorganize "community" relations, privileging those who controlled this funding.[60] This created a layer of middle-class professionals at the top of these groups who are linked to the professional managerial strata emerging more generally in gay/lesbian community formation.

I have some early recollections of these tendencies towards professional class and racialized relations within these state-regulated AIDS groups.

> *I was one of the first three employees of the AIDS Committee of Toronto (ACT) in 1983. I remember being at a meeting of the AIDS Support Group. People went around talking about what they did. Almost everyone mentioned some sort of professional or medical connection aside from two gay waiters. These two waiters never came back as they encountered the class and professional relations developing within ACT. One of the areas I was responsible for was developing liaison work with the local Haitian community. It took me a while to gain the trust of the main organizer in the Haitian group that was protesting the discrimination organized through the blanket prohibition by the Red Cross against Haitians donating blood as a "high risk group." I finally convinced him to come to a meeting of the Board of ACT. Unfortunately many members of the Board (all white) with a medical or professional background*

60 From a personal conversation with Ross Higgins about the situation in Montreal that is relevant to other centres as well. Also see Higgins, 2011.

> *decided to go after this representative for not properly understanding medical and epidemiological discourse. This encounter with racializing class and professional relations was a setback in developing relations of solidarity with the Haitian community in Toronto.*

In the period from 1986-87 a number of Persons With AIDS Coalition groups were set up in Vancouver, Halifax, Toronto and elsewhere as PLWA/HIVs increasingly felt that their needs were not being addressed in the mainstream ASOs whose funding most often focussed on prevention education that did not focus on the needs of PLWA/HIVs. Many felt they were being left to die and not enough was being done around their survival. Some formed their own groups based on the self-organization of PLWA/HIV. The Vancouver Persons With AIDS Coalition initiated the first treatment-based activism in 1986.

A more direct action-based wave of activism, often but not entirely focused on treatment activism formed in 1987-91, inspired by the AIDS Coalition to Unleash Power (ACT UP) in New York City with AIDS ACTION NOW! in Toronto and later ACT UP groups forming in Vancouver, Montreal and Halifax. This current often focused on treatment access for PLWA/HIVs and came to challenge state, drug corporations and professional relations that stood in the way of the survival of PLWA/HIVs. Direct action organizing including die-ins, sit-ins, taking over the streets, getting treatments across borders, effigy burnings, and the taking over of the opening session of the International AIDS conference in Montreal in 1989 won major gains in treatment access and representation for PLWA/HIVs (Kinsman, 2014a; Kinsman, 2014b; AIDS Activist History Project, 2015).

While the ASOs were most often contained by state regulation with the impetus of more direct action-oriented activists, they were sometimes willing to move into opposition to state inaction. In May 1988 at a Canadian AIDS conference in Toronto many people from the Canadian AIDS Society network of ASOs were able to be moved into action against the inaction of the federal Tory government and Health Minister Jake Epp. Many members of ASOs joined with AIDS ACTION NOW! under the theme of "Epp = Death" and burned an effigy of Epp. This action and broader forms of non-cooperation forced state agencies to develop a new strategy of "consultation" and "partnership" in the articulation of a national AIDS strategy. This both opened up some possibilities for AIDS groups and became a more effective means of neoliberal management of ASOs where "consultation" and "partnership" become central tactics for managing AIDS groups (Kinsman, 1997). After this wave of AIDS activism subsided by the mid-1990s, that state management of ASOs became even more effective, but this is a topic for later exploration.

While some groups understood AIDS as a condensation of social relations and therefore the need to address racializing, gender and class relations as central, others dealt with AIDS in a much narrower fashion. There were splits and tensions between grassroots and direct action-oriented organizing and the vertical alliances developing with state agencies, professional experts and later with drug companies. Despite the significance of this wave of vibrant AIDS activism that won important victories for PLWA/HIVs, the management and bureaucratization of mainstream AIDS groups intensified. Often this was tied to the generation of an "expert" stratum within gay/lesbian community formation.

The Charter, Equality Rights and Settler Homonationalism

The last area to be explored is the shift in strategies of Canadian state legal formation with the enactment of the Charter in 1982 and especially the implementation of the equality rights section in 1985. This marked a significant shift in state formation since the constitutionality of laws could now be challenged if they were seen as violating "equality rights." The equality rights section was written in an open-ended fashion but it still took until 1996 for the inclusion of sexual orientation protection to be established in federal human rights legislation following the 1995 Egan and Nesbitt versus Canada decision (Burtch, Pescitelli & Haskell, 2015: 154-56). Social and legal struggles, and the support of the union, feminist and other movements were necessary to establish this. This is often missed in what I characterize as popularized neoliberal queer history which views the equality rights section of the Charter as simply being given to us by the Liberal Party and state agencies to secure our rights.[61] It was of course far more complex than this and while the Charter was eventually used to secure some of our rights it only secured particular forms of formal rights.

Formal rights are general rights of access to rights and benefits abstracted from class and other social relations. They are very important but they do not secure the socially substantive equality that is necessary to exercise these rights as social rights in a deeper sense. They do not directly address the social roots of institutionalized heterosexuality or the two-gender binary "system" (Kinsman, 1996: 359-65; Kinsman & Gentile, 2010: 391-401). The formal character of these rights made it easier for there to be differential class, racialized and gendered impacts in the ability to exercise these "rights," providing one means through which the hegemony of emerging white, middle-class layers began to be established within community formation.

Dean Spade (2011) in *Normal Life*, in his critique of the human rights strategy that is on offer to the trans* movements, points out how this focus on formal human rights misses out on the need to address administrative laws and regulations through which the everyday construction and policing of gender and sexuality is accomplished. This includes social welfare policies, the criminalization of sex work, incarceration practices, and the everyday construction of gender in terms of washrooms and gender documentation. It is these administrative

61 The narrative line of this neoliberal queer history reads as follows: (1) the 1969 reform legalized or decriminalized homosexuality; (2) the equality rights section of the Charter established our rights; and (3) same-sex marriage rights ended discrimination against gays and lesbians and established full equality. There are major problems of substance here but also with viewing all of these rights as coming from above so that our struggles tend to disappear from this history. On some of this see: Kinsman, forthcoming and Dryden and Lenon, 2015. Some elements that are open to this neoliberal queer history reading are present in Tremblay (2015) where there is an emphasis on state and institutional processes in bringing about progress and rights and in the assertion by editor Tremblay that many of the authors in the book adopt a "liberal pluralist approach" and an "institutionalist perspective" (8-10) (as opposed to a social struggle oriented perspective) to analyzing state relations. At the same time other chapters (and even some of the same chapters open to a neoliberal reading) adopt more critical approaches that cut across this neoliberal reading.

procedures that must be addressed to get at the everyday social organization of gender and sexual regulation.

> *I remember a discussion I had with gay activist George Smith in the mid-1980s. He and I were both involved in the Canadian Committee Against Customs Censorship (CCACC), which fought against the sexual censorship that Toronto's Glad Day bookstore and other gay/lesbian bookstores faced. We agreed in the mid-'80s that we wanted to work not so much for human rights but more directly against state regulation including sexual policing and state censorship. We were not that interested in being directly involved in rights struggles—they were often too institutional and removed from everyday experiences of oppression. Instead of formal rights we needed to focus on administrative laws and regulations—including police repression and Customs censorship. These were more socially grounded, embodied and material. There were important insights here and not simply for people's personal political priorities but also in opening up critical social analysis.*

Despite these limitations the use of the Charter and equality rights became *the* central focus for struggle in what increasingly came to be put forward as an almost entirely legal strategy. This builds on and transforms the earlier mid-1970s shift to human rights protection in human rights legislation as the central strategy (Kinsman, forthcoming), but it goes much further than this in focusing almost entirely on legal challenges. This leads not only to a shift away from public actions and movement organizing but also to a very different form of organizing revolving around lawyers and clients. This leads to a lack of accountability and a lack of movement-based decision-making which in part reflects the dissipation of movement-organizing itself. There is also the question of who can pay to fund such legal challenges. While there was sometimes funding available from the Court Challenges Program[62] the ability to pursue cases was geared to those who had access to funding and lawyers. Again the social relations of class and professionalization entered into this process, even though some of these legal challenges also came with important union support.

62 The Court Challenges Program was established to provide some financial support for equality rights Charter cases.

EGALE was formed in 1986 to further this project as a new cross-country organization with a legal strategy focusing on using the Charter to win equality rights (M. Smith, 2015: 48-49). Initially called Equality for Gays and Lesbians Everywhere it now goes just by EGALE. It is an individual member-based organization and is not a local group-based coalition like the cross-country coalitions that existed in the 1970s (M. Smith, 1999: 57-66; Kinsman & Gentile, 2010: 317-24). The first phase of legal struggle was to have sexual orientation protection explicitly included in the equality rights section. This was not achieved until the mid-1990s but it did become a central focus of rights organizing for the second half of the 1980s.

While the equality rights section of the Charter created a more favourable terrain for struggles for formal legal rights it also strengthened the integrative dimensions of these struggles at the expense of the transformative. It opened up possibilities for moving in certain directions—including in relation to spousal and family recognition struggles and later for same sex marriage—but not as much regarding continuing battles against sexual policing and sexual censorship. It came to reconstruct our struggles on a specific legal terrain—within law and legal regulation and within existing social forms (Corrigan & Sayer, 1985; Holloway, 2005). This led to a focus on expanding inclusion within existing rights and benefits and to simply accept existing social forms as what we wanted to be included within.

This reliance on the Charter also promoted identification with Canadian state formation as the road to "our" rights. But this state formation is also a settler colonial state based on racism and the colonization of the Indigenous peoples, including the continuing oppression of two spirit people and Indigenous queer people (Depelteau & Giroux, 2015). This identification with existing Canadian state formation led away from solidarity and support for Indigenous struggles organized in opposition to Canadian state formation. This growing identification with Canadian state formation as the necessary framework for the achievement of lesbian and gay "equality" leads to the development of a form of settler homonationalism within queer community formation which is rarely named as such (Morgensen, 2011; Gentile & Kinsman, 2015). Given that this form of state organization comes to be seen as central to the realization of rights and equality, it produces the mainstream gay/LGBT movements as in opposition to Indigenous struggles for self-determination, for land and against racism and colonialism. This settler homonationalism also operates to relegate Indigenous "rights" to a limited "Canadian" perspective that does not address nation-to-nation relations, or continuing colonialism. This has also operated to limit more broad-based queer settler solidarity with two-spirit and other Indigenous struggles. This obscures the need to put Canadian state formation in question if Indigenous struggles are to be effectively supported. As the acceptance of the Charter as the road to "liberation" has deepened this has made it even harder to challenge this perspective as people have increasingly come to fetishize the Charter itself as responsible for our "rights."

In the context of equality rights, a more than decades-long struggle by the Coalition for Lesbian and Gay Rights in Ontario (CLGRO) achieved success in December 1986 when sexual orientation protection was finally added to Ontario human rights legislation. This was the second major human rights victory following up the much earlier addition of sexual orientation protection to Québec human rights legislation in 1977. This Ontario victory was won in part based on the extensive support won from unions, feminists, human rights groups and other community organizations during the years of this campaign (Kinsman, 1987).

For those who thought that sexual orientation protection was all that was needed it soon became clear that far more was required. While it provided for individuals to take organizations and individuals to the human rights commission if there were grounds for discrimination, it did not provide immediate access to rights or benefits or directly address the underlying social organization of queer oppression. Rather than questioning whether this human rights legal strategy was adequate for achieving social equality, supporters of the Charter-based legal strategy simply extended it in pushing towards spousal and family recognition rights by the late 1980s. One of the first fronts of this struggle was for spousal benefits (Kinsman, 2007: 107-19). While these struggles were very important they also came to be based on the acceptance of the social form of "spouse" and advocated integration into existing spousal relations rather than their transformation.

In this context CLGRO held an important conference on spousal benefits struggles in the summer of 1989. This was intended to provide a movement context for clarifying perspectives for these struggles and to open up discussion on alternatives that did not rely on simply being let into existing forms of spousal benefits where access to benefits depends on who one has a relationship with and the kind of benefit plan they have. This was an attempt to articulate a different position—both attempting to cut across lawyers and their clients making decisions that affected the overall struggle and signalling a certain resistance to neoliberal influences regarding the privatization and regulation of relationships and just being accepted into existing heterosexual-defined arrangements. Other criteria raised were the redistribution of wealth and social justice concerns as well as being able to assign benefits to someone you were not in a relationship with (Wilson, 1989).[63] However, despite these important discussions the "just let us into existing arrangements" approach won out as lawyers and legal cases pursued this approach and alternatives were eclipsed.

While winning spousal and family recognition struggles were important victories, they also tended to assimilate people into the developing neoliberal capitalist relations. This was facilitated by the weakening of the feminist challenge to patriarchal familial and married relations during these years. While there were important reforms of family and marriage laws, patriarchal relations did not disappear and the unequal gendered division of labour in households, unpaid reproductive and domestic labour, and sexual and other forms of violence all continued.

Queer nation activism and class struggle

Before drawing some initial conclusions from this investigation, it is necessary to mention the new wave of queer activism that emerged at the very beginning of the 1990s that had both potentials and

63 See the interview transcripts and other information on the AIDS Activist History Project website at http://www.aidsactivisthistory.ca. Also see http://www.aidsactivisthistory.ca/aahp-blog/gary-kinsman-resisting-state-professional-management-of-aids-organizations-memories-of-aids-organizing-in-canada-1983-1990 and http://www.aidsactivisthistory.ca/aahp-blog/gary-kinsman-direct-action life-memories-of-aids-activism-in-canada-19.

limitations in resisting the emergence of the neoliberal queer. In part arising out of the political space created by direct action AIDS activist groups like ACT UP, and Queer Nation groups that formed in the US, a layer of young queer activists formed Queer Nation groups in Toronto, Halifax, Montreal (in Vancouver it was called Queer Planet) that focused on fighting anti-queer violence and invisibility. Anti-queer violence seemed to be on the rise in the context of AIDS and growing queer visibility. Queer Nation groups were also opposed to queer "assimilation" into heterosexual normality and to some extent commercialism—one of their chants was "we're here, we're queer, and we're not going shopping." While responding to escalating violence against queers they were also responding to the normalization of some white middle-class queers.

These groups engaged in a range of activities, including zaps of heterosexual establishments and "bash back" events against anti-queer violence, and they also organized queer contingents in anti-war demonstrations against the first Iraq war. Although there were important differences, they formulated their politics in a militant anti-homophobic fashion. This focuses on the phobic ideas individual heterosexuals have about queers—and therefore often more on individual psychology and not social relations (Kinsman, 1996: 33). They were therefore unable to make fully visible the class basis of what they were up against in queer community formation with the emerging white and largely "male" middle-class stratum. They were unable to name and analyze this given the lack of class focus in their practice. A possible implicit class critique was not able to be developed into a critical class analysis, and they were unable to make sense of the class struggles (mostly one-sided as mentioned earlier) going on in queer communities. The eclipsing of class struggle in queer activism and theory (Maynard, 1991) directed them away from some of the sources of the neoliberal queer.

The simultaneous emergence of queer theory in the academic world despite its welcome destabilization of heterosexuality on the cultural and discursive terrains also largely displaced class struggles (Hennessy, 2000). Often sexuality was abstracted from class relations, even as questions of racialization and gender were addressed in certain ways but never in relation to their mutual construction through class relations. Activists at the time were therefore not adequately prepared to challenge the significant shifts in class formation taking place around them.

Preliminary Conclusions: Resistance and the Emergence of the Neoliberal Queer

The 1980s started with explosive resistance to the sex police and moral conservatism. This provided important sources of challenge to emerging forms of neoliberalism, including the privatization and institutionalization of our sexualities and relationships and to sexual policing, but these struggles also participated in creating an opening for a new non-moral conservative neoliberalism. There are important forms of organizing in response to AIDS, including direct action-oriented treatment-based activism which wins real gains for PLWA/HIVs in the later 1980s and early 1990s. At the same time ASOs came to be professionalized and regulated by state agencies. In the late 1980s and early 1990s there are new waves of AIDS and Queer Nation activism but they were unable to contest the class basis of the emergence of the neoliberal queer. Ironically out of these mass struggles, and the resulting expansion of community formation, the space was created for a new white middle-class and largely "male" strata to emerge to become the "spokespeople" and "leaders" in the community.

While powerful forms of resistance continued into the early 1990s some of the currents leading towards the generation of the neoliberal queer were becoming clearer. There is a process of class formation and stratification—of the emergence of a queer professional managerial middle class that grows out of resistance to police repression, the expansion of community formation and the development of gay business interests and the "pink market." This is also combined with the emergence of new elites developing through the ASOs and the residential formation of class tied up with practices of gentrification, opposition to sex workers and in support of dialogue with the police. It is these emerging social layers who are often able to take most advantage of the Charter and legal struggles in terms of their social positions and who also intensify the integrative over the transformative aspects of these struggles. The legal struggle becomes more and more one of simply being accepted into existing social forms of family, spouse, and in the 1990s marriage. The reliance on the Charter to secure "rights" also leads to a growing identification with the existing Canadian state as necessary to the securing of these "rights," which generates homonationalism among some queer people. The class project of this layer is to become an openly gay/lesbian part of the broader white middle class and therefore they come to see defence of neo liberal capitalist relations as central to their "gay" project. This is given cover by the "classless" community politics that emerged out of struggles in the 1980s that allow this gay class project to be put forward (always with contestation) as *the* "gay" political project.

At the same time the emergence and consolidation of the neoliberal queer was still in formation in the late 1980s/early 1990s. As we have seen there were still important moments of resistance to it. The further development of the neoliberal queer would take place in the 1990s.

THE POWER OF FOSSIL FUEL DIVESTMENT (AND ITS SECRET)

James Rowe, Jessica Dempsey and Peter Gibbs

The first fossil fuel divestment campaign launched at Swarthmore College in 2010 (Farrell, 2013). Frustrated by failed UN climate negotiations in Copenhagen in 2009, and inspired by the example of the movement against apartheid in South Africa, organizers saw divestment as a tactic that allowed students to engage directly in climate politics by leveraging the financial and political power of universities. Two years later Bill McKibben (2012) popularized the case for fossil fuel divestment in his *Rolling Stone* article that went viral—"Global Warming's Terrifying New Math." Since then campaigns have spread like wildfire. This spread has been facilitated by 350.org, the organization McKibben helped start, particularly their online platform "Go Fossil Free," which provides tools for starting and conducting local campaigns. The fossil fuel divestment movement is now the centre of gravity for student activism on climate change in North America (635 campaigns), Europe (181 campaigns) and Australia and New Zealand (42 campaigns).[64] There are also calls for divestment in India, the Philippines and South Africa. While centred on university campuses, the movement extends to foundations, cities, churches, unions and financial managers. The campaign to divest institutional stockholders of fossil fuel companies has supporters of many political stripes from socialists like Cornel West to liberal billionaires like Tom Steyer, all joined together by growing concern over climate change and the slow pace of governmental action. The basic campaign strategy incubated by students at Swarthmore, popularized by McKibben, and since refined by the movement, is to culturally marginalize the fossil fuel industry, making it harder for it to exert political influence and gum up the gears of needed climate legislation.

Already, in three short years, approximately 2,500 investors representing $2.6 trillion in assets have divested (Arabella, 2015).

64 Campaign information can be found at https://campaigns.gofossilfree.org/.

High-profile institutional investors to divest include the Rockefeller Brothers Fund, Stanford University and the Canadian Medical Association. As Geoffrey Morgan (2013), managing editor of *Alberta Oil Magazine*, recently wrote about the movement: "Energy executives ignore the [divestment] campaign at their own peril; even though [divestment] targets their companies' stock price, its real intention is to erode the hydrocarbon industry's social license to operate."

The fossil fuel industry is one of the wealthiest industries to ever exist, and is a formidable foe. The divestment movement, however, knows a secret. We borrow the furtive language of secrecy from Jeremy Brecher, Tim Costello and Brendan Smith's (2000) book *Globalization From Below*. For Brecher et al., social movements understand that elite power ultimately rests on popular consent. Even the most powerful institutions in the world are ultimately reliant on the collective consent of those subject to the powerful. When consent is withdrawn, the mighty can fall. The revolutionary and constitutive power of people acting in concert is kept hidden (hence, "secret") by a variety of forces including the mass media's focus on political and economic elites as the true masters of the universe. In other words, while the political economic, and cultural common sense of our time reinforces the idea of a disempowered, hapless citizen who is subject to structured laws and policies of captured petro-states, Geoffrey Morgan of *Alberta Oil* reminds us that everyday people ultimately hold the reins.

Brecher et al.'s approach is indebted to the Marxist political philosopher Antonio Gramsci. One of Gramsci's (2000) crucial contributions to social movement theory was his insistence that elite power is maintained not only through coercion, but also through the everyday actions of people that confer consent upon hierarchical social orders, even though they may not benefit from them (see the Introduction to this book). Applying the Gramscian emphasis on consent to fossil fuel divestment helps reveal that the carboniferous capitalism of today, while reinforced by a daunting nexus of corporate and state power, is reproduced daily by the everyday consent of popular publics.[65] This consent manifests itself in consumer decisions, the driving of cars,

65 The term "carboniferous capitalism" belongs to Lewis Mumford, and names the centrality of ancient sunlight, in the form of fossil fuels, for powering industrial capitalism (Mumford, 2010).

voting patterns, hands-off approaches to pension and mutual fund investments, and political quiescence. The molecular reach of the fossil fuel economy, the way it reaches into the smallest nooks and crannies of our lives, is a key reason why addressing climate change has been so challenging to date ("we all use them"; "everyone is to blame"; "we are our own enemy"). How do we break the political deadlock on climate change, an impasse that is reinforced by the everyday reliance on fossil fuels? Answering this question requires attentiveness to not only political ends, like stiff carbon taxes and massive investments in public transit, but particularly to the strategies and narratives required for achieving them. How can we spark a collective withdrawal of consent from carboniferous capitalism, while we all still rely on fossil fuels?

The divestment movement is an effort to do just that, by targeting and vilifying companies that profit from fossil fuel extraction, production and sale, and that actively lobby against government action on climate change. The identification of a climate change enemy, one that masses of people can organize against in shared moral outrage, has been key to the movement's success. We all might rely on fossil fuels for the reproduction of our daily lives, but the vast majority of us do not lobby our governments to slow climate action (Dempsey & Rowe, 2015). Enabling the distinction between an *us* who can withdraw our consent from *them* has been a key innovation of the movement.

While the divestment movement has a tactical target in fossil fuel companies, we argue that divestment is best understood as a counter-hegemonic cultural politics that seeks to transform climate change into a justice issue. Climate change is a problem marked by deeply uneven power relations: an elite few are profiting and a great majority are already weathering the effects. The divestment movement helps clarify that responsibility for climate change is uneven, even if we "all" use fossil fuels, and often benefit from them.

Climate justice is not a new concept, but divestment—at least in the Global North—is a key site where climate justice is being actualized. In the Canadian context, for example, divestment campaigns are facilitating important collective learning about the ongoing legacies of colonialism, and the centrality of a decolonization lens to achieving climate justice. At a recent national gathering hosted by Fossil Free Canada, the links between fossil fuel divestment and Indigenous struggles for control over their traditional territories were consistently highlighted (Lameman et al., 2014).

We live on the west coast of Canada where there is a strong Indigenous nationhood movement. Due to the geopolitical specificity of this region, and national efforts on behalf of organizations like Fossil Free Canada, the settler students we work with on divestment are prioritizing a decolonizing lens in their organizing efforts. The divestment movement is a site where solidarity is being slowly constructed between largely white, middle-class university students and faculty, and affected communities, especially First Nations in Canada. During her keynote address to the Fossil Free Canada convergence in 2014, Crystal Lameman from the Beaver Lake Cree Nation in Alberta told the audience: "Will divestment change everything? No, but combined with such things as Indigenous rights practices, we will make a difference... None of these things alone will stop climate change, but it is a part of the change" (quoted in Mazurek, 2014). Divestment, then, is not simply transforming common sense on climate change, it is also part of changing the common sense vision of environmentalism into one that necessarily—especially in settler colonial contexts like Canada—places colonial pasts and presents at its centre (see Adkin, 2016 in this volume).[66]

We are not claiming that all participants in the multitudinous divestment movement are anti-capitalists and decolonizers (McSorley, 2014). Part of the strength of the movement is that it has collected together a broad assemblage of participants into a dynamic and populist force (Rowe & Carroll, 2015). The common enemy of fossil fuel companies binds this assemblage together in a contingent unity. Divestment has the *potential* to serve as a "gateway campaign" that opens participants up to deeper structural critiques of not only Big Carbon, but capitalism itself. This is especially the case given that student leaders with national divestment organizations in the US

66 While a decolonization lens is less common in the US, the Divestment Student Network (2016)—a national student organization providing leadership and resources to local American campaigns—emphasizes "building alliances with frontline communities, those most impacted by fossil fuel extraction and climate change, as they are the experts in resisting fossil fuels and building a better world."

and Canada have consistently emphasized a climate justice frame, acknowledging that "structural inequalities are perpetuated by the fossil fuel industry and exacerbated by climate change" (Grady-Benson & Sarathy, 2015: 5-6). Yet, the word "potential" matters. As a tactic, divestment could also result in a narrow field of vision: reaffirming a liberal political stance that views climate change as an isolated market failure, one that can be addressed with modest reforms to market society. This view leaves untouched the historical and systemic injustices that climate change is rooted in, and aggravates.

Part of the secret of social movements is that they are never exactly as they appear. Always comprised of diverse participants, and often walking uneasily between liberal, radical and neither-nor politics, movements hold plural possibilities; the direction they take is rarely predetermined. A targeted withdrawal of consent can cascade into more systemic change. It was not telegraphed, for instance, that protests against water privatization in Bolivia during the early 2000s would help launch Evo Morales's MAS party into power in 2006. Consent maintains elite power, and withdrawing that consent has unpredictable outcomes given the plurality of forces that form movements.

Being clear about the power of social movements to withdraw consent, and the profound challenges of wielding this power against one of the wealthiest industries in the world, is politically important. For the movement itself this clarity can inoculate against discouragement during what promises to be a protracted campaign. The average length of successful divestment campaigns targeting South African apartheid on Canadian campuses was five years (Connor et al., 2014). While the fossil fuel campaign is the fastest growing divestment movement in history, current students should not expect full divestment before they graduate (Ansar et al., 2013). And yet, well-designed campaigns can keep generating momentum, giving activists a growing sense of their collective power as student referendums, faculty votes and union resolutions are pursued and won (as consent is slowly withdrawn).

For those in the broader environmental movement, being keyed into the "secret," and the profound challenges of manifesting the collective withdrawal of consent, should caution against quick dismissal of the fast-growing but fledgling campaign. Social movements are not born every day. They hold tremendous power, but rely on a rare confluence of timing, resources, opportunity, leadership, fortune and collective enthusiasm (Brecher et al., 2000).

Understandably, the divestment movement has been pilloried by the fossil fuel industry and its servants in the political class (Cox, 2015). But it has also been subject to sustained critique from the left and liberal wings of the environmental movement. In the remainder of this chapter we unpack representative criticisms of divestment, those of journalist and professor Christian Parenti (from the Left) and Harvard President Drew Faust (from the liberal centre). Instead of casting doubt on divestment, we argue that these criticisms help clarify what the movement gets right. Both the left-wing and liberal critics of divestment, for different reasons, miss the importance of a cultural politics that withdraws mass consent from the fossil fuel economy, while planting seeds for larger struggles against neoliberalism, capitalism and colonization.

Christian Parenti's Challenge from the Left

The key critique of divestment from the Left is articulated by Christian Parenti, whose recent work focuses on the politics of climate change (Parenti, 2012a). Parenti first shared his concerns in a November 2012 op-ed in the *Huffington Post* (Parenti, 2012b). Since then, he has developed his criticisms in the *Nation*, the *New York Times*, and on the radio programs *Democracy Now* and *Against the Grain* (Nathanson, 2012; Parenti, 2013b). We take up Parenti in depth here because (1) he is an influential voice on the American Left and (2) because his critiques of divestment have been circulated in influential venues. Anecdotally, we have had his critiques rehearsed to us by other Left scholars and activists. Parenti's high-profile criticisms give would-be supporters an excuse to dismiss the movement. We want to respond to his criticisms, not only as rebuttal, but because his critique can help us elaborate the power of divestment and help explain its efficacy in the current conjuncture.

Parenti's primary argument is that divestment will be unable to materially injure fossil fuel companies, slow their rate of extraction, and keep unburnable reserves in the ground. Parenti's preferred strategy is to pressure governments into action, since only governments have the coercive power to legislate massive emission reductions: "The only force on earth that can really control Exxon is the U.S. government. Moral outrage and symbolic action—like divestment—won't bring it down" (Parenti, 2012b).

Parenti (2012b) was quite right to question early messaging from 350.org implying that fossil fuel divestment could hurt company returns in the short term. The hydrocarbon industry makes windfall profits from selling fossil fuels, not from selling stock. If the divestment movement's primary goal was to impact immediate returns, then it would indeed be resting on shaky ground. But attacking short-term profits has never been the primary aim of the movement. Since the beginning, McKibben and other divestment organizers have emphasized that the short-term goal is to weaken the industry's social licence by having culturally and morally powerful institutions publicly distance themselves from the new petroleum pariahs. As noted, the strategy is that this cultural marginalization will make it harder for the hydrocarbon industry to exert its political influence, making it easier for governments to take needed action. As McKibben (2012) wrote in his original *Rolling Stone* article, "Movements rarely have predictable outcomes. But any campaign that weakens the fossil-fuel industry's political standing clearly increases the chances of retiring its special breaks."

Parenti (2013b) has questioned the strategy to chisel away at political standing, noting that the hydrocarbon industry is already maligned:

> Big Carbon has already lost its "social license" and with no apparent effect on its real operations. Every year Gallup asks Americans how they feel about 25 leading industries. Every year oil shows up dead last as the most disliked industry in America. Last year it had a 61% disapproval rating.

What Parenti's critique fails to acknowledge, however, is that inert and active disdain have different political effects. What Parenti points to is an inert disdain for fossil fuel companies, which is not the same as withdrawing consent. The divestment movement has likely spread quickly because of simmering popular frustration with the industry.

But moving this private grumbling to collective action required a catalyst. The divestment movement has provided a vehicle for mass disapproval. And if the strategy works, then divestment campaigns *will* materially weaken the fossil fuel industry by moving the low grumble into active withdrawal of consent.

Fossil fuel divestment is not the social movement Parenti would have started. "If we were starting from scratch, I don't really think it's the best" (Nathanson, 2012). His preference would be a movement directly focused on state action. "What we need to revoke," he argued in the *New York Times*, "is Big Carbon's actual, legal license to operate. Government grants that right. And the moral crisis generated by protest must crystallize as state action" (2013b). We agree that legislation is needed to rapidly draw down emissions. But what if Parenti is right about the longer-term goal, but wrong about the short-term strategy for getting there? What if divestment is the right strategy for the current conjuncture? Parenti's alternative vision is of activists pressuring their "universities, churches, and towns, as well as their state and local governments to buy clean power and electric vehicles, retrofit buildings for efficiency, and pressure the federal government to allow the EPA to do its job and enforce the clean air act, very vigorously" (Parenti, 2012). All noble goals, but Parenti's campaign alternative is missing key design elements that help explain why his preferred idea has minimal traction, while divestment is rapidly spreading.

For one, Parenti's more positive campaign lacks a clear binding foe. The divestment movement presents the public with a compelling moral case against a clear enemy: "If it is wrong to wreck the climate, then it is wrong to profit from that wreckage" (McKibben, 2012). Emotions such as anger, hope, efficacy and solidarity facilitate individual actions that make up the collective work of social movements (Ganz, 2011). Strategic goals for social movements need to focus on motivational issues and leverage points (Gibbs & Sinnott, 2014). Sustainable procurement policy, while important, is not sufficiently motivational to inspire the emotional intensity needed to spark a social movement. Nor does pressuring governments for climate action offer a strong enough leverage point to inspire feelings of efficacy. Divestment campaigns target local and relatively accessible institutions that are directly invested in climate wreckage. This allows for activists to feel *proximity* to the fossil fuel pariahs in their own communities, even as corporate offices may be miles away. The divestment strategy also enables targeted local action to articulate with a wider movement to marginalize the fossil fuel industry, and to clear the path towards legislation. Local activists can gain momentum from movement wins like the United Nations Framework Convention on Climate Change's endorsement of divestment, even as they contribute to that momentum with successful student and faculty referenda (Carrington, 2015). Parenti's alternative campaign would theoretically allow for the same felt solidarity between local and more global actions, but without the motivating power of a clear enemy that is accessible at the community level (concretized in institutional investments). Simply put, while state action would be the most efficient path to solving the climate crisis, focusing on it at the outset would be ineffective at catalyzing the social movement needed to force the desired result.

In 2012, when the divestment movement launched, the US Congress's approval rating hit an all-time low of 10% (Edwards-Levy, 2012). There are multiple forces combining to produce popular disapproval of government, including 40 years of neoliberal rule. For Stephen McBride and Heather Whiteside (2011), neoliberalism has played a key role in "delegitimizing and discrediting politics by favouring markets as decision making institutions" (97). Parenti sees divestment as complicit in this drift away from the state:

> I think it's really dangerous to fall into this anti-government sensibility—that Washington is broken, etc., etc. That's exactly what corporate America wants the left to think. Corporate America in the age of neoliberalism wants a left opposition that can't even see or imagine what the state is or could be. And I fear that [divestment] falls into that, potentially (Nathanson, 2012).

While we agree with Parenti's goal of valorizing the state as a central force for climate mitigation (as most divestment activists would), his analysis is out of step with popular ambivalence towards governments that are increasingly captured by elite interests.

In a poll taken shortly after the *Citizens United* decision in the US, which blew open the gates on campaign spending, 82% of voters agreed that Congress should limit the amount of money corporations can spend on elections (Jarvis, 2011). Parenti's preferred strategy of directly targeting the state doesn't adequately address popular worries about corporate control of the political process. Action targeting the state can appear futile when moneyed interests are clearly conditioning political outcomes. By targeting companies, and their institutional investors, divestment addresses a key driver of slow policy progress on climate change: industrial obstruction. This framing does not diminish the importance of state action, but instead emphasizes that prior cultural work is required before states can act with the force they need to draw down emissions. Parenti, along with others who view divestment as "symbolic" (Hulme, 2015), misses the importance of cultural politics, especially at a time when publics are rightfully wary of regulatory capture.

Divestment is only one of many strategies for challenging carboniferous capitalism. It has gained impressive political traction in the three years since it proliferated. But culturally marginalizing one of the wealthiest industries in the history of capitalism requires a wide base of support; this is crucial because we cannot convince the state to keep fossil fuels in the ground with a magic wand. The divestment movement is beginning to build this wide base of support, alongside growing alliances against pipelines and extraction. Given the variety of actors with sometimes competing political orientations that comprise the movement, it is not ideologically pure. But in the following section we draw out some of the radical potential of the campaign to serve as a gateway into deeper structural analyses of colonialism and capitalism. We do so by engaging with another set of critiques of the campaign—those expressed by liberals.

The Liberal Critique

While Parenti criticizes divestment from the Left, the movement is also the target of more centrist or liberal critiques. Harvard President Drew Faust exemplifies liberal concerns with the strategy. Harvard is a site of active divestment campaigning; students have employed strategies and tactics emblematic of the campus divestment movement including a successful student referendum, delivering a 1,300-signature petition from Harvard faculty and alumni, and occupying the office of President Faust demanding divestment on two different occasions. In 2013, Faust penned a letter publicly responding to divestment activists, stating that divestment from fossil fuels is neither "warranted nor wise" (Faust, 2013). She has held fast to that line despite the ongoing pressure; the most recent protest (2015) shut down the building housing Faust's office for an entire week with Cornel West (a Harvard alumnus) joining the protest, saying that Harvard risks being on the wrong side of a "planetary Selma" (Woolf, 2015).

In this final section of our chapter, we address two interlocking arguments against divestment that appear in Faust's letter, but are representative of wider liberal criticisms of the movement. The first concern is that the tactic is too confrontational and should be replaced by more cooperative and pragmatic approaches such as shareholder engagement (see also Bocking, 2014; Hulme, 2015; Krosinsky, 2012). Secondly, liberals like Faust have argued that universities should not use their endowments to take political stands (see also Hall & Charest, 2015). In making this argument, liberal critics have emphasized the supposed neutrality of institutional investments whose sole purpose is to maximize returns, not to forward political agendas.

The liberal critiques of divestment are not limited to the two we draw out here. Indeed there are overlaps between Parenti's criticisms of the ineffectual or symbolic nature of the campaign, and concerns raised by a number of liberal critics (Bocking, 2014; Faust, 2013; Hall & Charest, 2015; Hulme, 2015; Krosinsky, n.d.; Welch, 2014). We draw out the above two points because they help us demonstrate what is politically powerful about a movement that is regularly dismissed for being merely symbolic. In other words, we think these two liberal counter-arguments actually help clarify the power of the divestment strategy, and its radical potential. We also think that these two arguments against divestment will become more central as the financial challenge to the divestment strategy becomes increasingly tenuous.

In her letter, Faust also warns against the economic implications of divestment: "We should also be clear-sighted about the risks that divestment could pose.... Significantly constraining investment options risks significantly constraining investment returns" (Faust, 2012). But recent research undertaken by MSCI, which runs global indices used by thousands of pension and hedge funds, shows that fossil fuel divestment would have theoretically *increased* investor returns from 2010 to 2015 (Collinson, 2015). Moreover, a key economic argument in favour of divestment is that once needed climate legislation is passed, fossil fuel companies will see a major devaluation, resulting in significant losses for shareholders. This is because the current valuation of fossil fuel companies includes reserves that are unburnable if we are to avoid triggering catastrophic climate change (McKibben, 2012). According to the International Energy Agency (2012), at least 60% of known reserves are unburnable (McGlade & Elkins, 2015). When legislation is passed to keep these fossil fuels in the ground, the industry is poised to lose trillions of dollars—what is increasingly being referred to as the "Carbon Bubble" (Leaton, 2011).

If divestment is both morally righteous and financially prudent, then why aren't all institutional investors pursuing it? One reason is that the movement's combativeness contradicts the liberal preference for dialogue among experts as the preferred problem-solving approach. What Naomi Klein (2014) calls the fetish of centrism—"of reasonableness, seriousness, splitting the difference, and generally not getting overly excited about anything"—helps explain resistance among liberals like Faust (22). For Klein,

> [t]his is the habit of thought that truly rules our era, far more among the liberals who concern themselves with matters of climate policy than among conservatives, many of whom simply deny the existence of the crisis. Climate change presents a profound challenge to this cautious centrism because half measures won't cut it.[67]

The existential threat that climate change poses has provided the fossil fuel divestment movement with an unsettling boldness. The confidence with which activists have swaggered into the elite arena of investment

67 Complementing Klein's analysis, Tariq Ali (2015) recently published a book called *The Extreme Centre*. While much media scrum and academic analysis focuses on the extreme Left and Right, Ali argues that the extreme centre—liberals—should receive more attention, because they are now perpetuating and concretizing neoliberal governance, propping up the extreme Right, often under the veil of neutrality, technical efficiency, and even political harmony.

is worrying for stakeholders with a material and cultural attachment to the status quo of liberal capitalism. Divestment refuses the neutrality of institutional investment, seeking to insert moral and ecological considerations into the calculus. It is a slippery slope from criticizing the morality of fossil fuel investments, to challenging the fetishes of impartiality and maximum return that protect investments in general from moral scrutiny and democratic intervention. Divestment prefigures a deeper withdrawal of consent from capitalist relations. We think this is partly why liberals like Faust are unsettled by it, why they find it too divisive.

"Divestment pits concerned citizens and institutions," wrote Faust in her letter to the Harvard community, "against companies that have enormous capacity and responsibility to promote progress toward a more sustainable future" (Faust, 2013). We saw this same sentiment expressed first-hand in a debate on divestment on our campus, when an executive from tar sands giant Suncor explained to students and faculty that climate change demands that we all form a giant peloton to solve it, referring to the energy-saving trick of cyclists riding in a pack. This is an attractive image—that we can all bond together and catch a slipstream towards a fossil-free future. But this vision is rooted in a fantastical reading of political change, one where the different players can find common ground through earnest dialogue (no matter how asymmetrical the power differentials are). The limits of this approach are illustrated by decades of failed climate action—from UN negotiations that consistently acknowledge scientifically determined targets while failing to meet them, to the lifestyle changes emphasized in Al Gore's *An Inconvenient Truth*. The divestment movement, rather, places differentials of interest, benefit and power at the core of the climate change debate. At its best, divestment draws attention to the class relations underpinning the lack of climate action: the fact that while many of us (especially in the Global North) benefit from fossil fuel combustion, *some* benefit more than others and those *some* are at times working very hard to protect their interests. In Canada, for example, oil and gas industry groups actively lobby against climate action, and it is widely known that oil and gas fund the perpetuation of climate doubt (De Souza, 2013; Linnitt, 2012, 2013; Oreskes & Conway, 2011). Divestment, we suggest, signals an environmental politics that is unafraid of referring to *interests* (movement participants may not always use the term "class," but for us class conflict is at the heart of divestment). Thus, divestment is powerful because it counters the "we can all work together" mantra of liberal politics, a mantra that works to obfuscate the operation of power (and its secret: that power relations change swiftly after mass withdrawals of consent).

Divestment is not only too confrontational, say liberals like Faust, but it also threatens the (supposed) neutrality of the University. The University, we are told, is a place to discuss and debate policies, to study them—but it is not a place to take political stands. For Faust,

> we should...be very wary of steps intended to instrumentalize our endowment in ways that would appear to position the University as a political actor rather than an academic institution. Conceiving of the endowment not as an economic resource, but as a tool to inject the University into the political process or as a lever to exert economic pressure for social purposes, can entail serious risks to the independence of the academic enterprise. The endowment is a resource, not an instrument to impel social or political change (2013).

In this quote, Faust perpetuates the notion that status quo social relations are neutral or not political. Her response points to divestment's radical potential, especially how it begins to peel away the notion that investments, and thus money itself, are somehow neutral. In asking for investments to be accountable to something other than profit, divestment activists are reminding everyone how power-laden and often cruel capitalist social relations are. Sound and "rational" investment decisions are not based on how socially useful an enterprise is, or how ecologically regenerative it might be, but rather on how much financial return it will yield. Fossil fuel companies can still generate decent returns, but their business model is in direct opposition to the biophysical livability of our planet. Until the fossil fuel divestment movement arose, financial markets were largely silent on this stunning contradiction.

As former Harvard Undergraduate Council President Tara Raghuveer (2015) wrote in a recent issue of *Time*, Harvard's endowment is not simply a resource; it is a "political tool." Indeed, Raghuveer reports how it was Harvard's response to divestment, particularly claims about the neutrality of its endowment, that led her to become an activist on the issue:

> These meetings showed me a side of Harvard—an institution that I love—that terrified me. Harvard the corporation seemed to represent interests that ran directly counter to those of Harvard the venue for intellectual and social transformation. For the first time, it hit me. On this issue, impartiality was a false posture, and performing it made me complicit in the university's iniquities.

Investments are not neutral, and neither is maintaining the status quo. Harvard has already taken sides by owning shares in companies that threaten the rights of future generations by obstructing strong climate policy. Fossil fuel divestment reflects a division that already exists: multiple generations of human beings yearning for a bright future, up against an industry that wields its power to stall desperately needed government action. Student activists are refusing to let financial returns be the impartial metric that liberals like Faust claim they are.

Both the knee-jerk centrism and the insistence on investor neutrality that have been mobilized by liberal critics like Faust help hide the vast asymmetries of power that mark contemporary capitalism. They also militate against the democratic intervention into financial markets that fossil fuel divestment represents. A claim to "reasonableness" and "seriousness" typically justifies the centrist approach, but divestment puts the lie to this mythology. It is irrational and wild-eyed to assume that the fossil fuel industry will forgo short-term returns (that happen to imperil planetary livability) without collective confrontation. It is also increasingly insane to keep assuming the neutrality of maximum returns, when profits from fossil fuel companies threaten the biophysical preconditions for our species to flourish.

Conclusion

The fossil fuel divestment movement is spreading fast. "No tactic in the climate wars has resonated more powerfully," notes Naomi Klein (2014) in *This Changes Everything* (354). We've argued that this success has much to do with how the campaign transforms climate change into a justice issue. More specifically, a key to the movement's popular traction has been the location of a climate change foe: the fossil fuel industry. The campaign allows activists to target the industry via relatively accessible but culturally powerful institutional investors, like universities, municipalities, churches, charitable trusts and pension funds.

Leftist critics like Christian Parenti worry that "market-based" campaigns like divestment divert needed attention away from the state. For Parenti, the state is the only institution powerful enough to force fossil fuel companies to leave unburnable reserves untouched. We agree, but argue that culturally marginalizing the fossil fuel industry, and thereby diminishing its capacity to obstruct climate legislation, is a necessary precondition for effective state action.

The divestment movement irritates Harvard President Drew Faust's liberal preference for dialogue among experts to solve vexing challenges. But relying on polite dialogue and piecemeal incentives to keep fossil fuel companies from extracting increasingly unburnable reserves is a dream-becoming-nightmare. The polite centrism of liberals like Faust—rooted in the desire to address worldly problems without upending power hierarchies that often generate these problems in the first place—has the practical effect of shrouding the craven self-seeking of fossil fuel companies. Emphasizing the impartiality of investments has the same effect: "nothing to see here but the smooth functioning of the market, innocently generating value-free value." But the value Harvard receives from fossil fuel investments threatens a central precondition for all human value: a livable planet. There is nothing innocent or impartial about privileging returns over the relative hospitality of the Holocene.

As the evidence begins to pile up supporting both the moral and financial case for divestment, the question is now becoming: why not divest? Divestment is ultimately a "pragmatic" and relatively easy democratization of capital. That Faust and other university presidents remain staunchly opposed suggests to us that the campaign has more radical potential than perhaps meets the eye. What worries liberals should excite Leftists; as noted, it is a slippery slope from criticizing the morality of fossil fuel investments to challenging the supposed neutrality of maximum returns more generally.

Already, divestment—at least in Canada—is making connections between settler colonial rule, public institutions and international capital. As Klein (2014) writes in her recent book,

> [C]limate change isn't an "issue" to add to the list of things to worry about, next to health care and taxes. It is a civilizational wake-up call. A powerful message—spoken in the language of fires, floods, droughts, and extinctions—telling us that we need an entirely new economic model and a new way of sharing this planet (25).

Klein's argument that fighting climate change means fighting neoliberalism, capitalism and colonialism has informed the movement, but was also crafted in conversation with divesters, anti-pipeline activists and climate justice organizers (Klein, 2014, 2015).

What could next steps that deepen this already existing intersectional analysis look like? One potential is for fossil fuel divestment campaigns to begin working in alliance with the private prison divestment movement, and the boycott, divest and sanctions (BDS) movement targeting apartheid Israel (Barrows-Friedman, 2015). Forging these solidarities will not be easy, and could fracture the alliances that hold up fossil fuel divestment's big tent. But as one begins to pry open the supposedly neutral world of investment, it only makes sense to continue asking questions about the moral, economic and ecological costs of business as usual. We wonder if the movement might begin to articulate a prefigurative vision of how to more democratically control our collective public wealth like endowments, pensions and sovereign wealth funds: it could be an exciting place to dream about new institutional forms, new systems of decision-making that are not bound to the market form. The ways that systemic challenges like neoliberalism, capitalism and colonialism are being grappled with in the context of the movement, alongside the more immediate challenge of culturally marginalizing one of the most powerful industries in the world, make it a crucial site for engagement and learning as we teeter on the edge of the Holocene.

BLAME CANADA
Environmental Movements, National Media and Canada's Reputation as a Climate Villain[68]

Mark C.J. Stoddart, Jillian Smith and David B. Tindall

In December 2009, politicians, diplomats and social movement activists from around the world gathered in Copenhagen, Denmark for yet another round of international climate change policy negotiations at the Conference of the Parties 15 (COP 15). While government representatives debated what steps to take towards a post-Kyoto agreement on addressing global climate change, activists engaged in an "unprecedented level" of protest in the streets outside the COP negotiations, hoping that the pressure of public opinion might help push the negotiations towards a more productive outcome (Hadden, 2015).

The Copenhagen meetings generated an especially high level of media coverage in Canada, with major dailies including *The Globe and Mail* sending reporters to cover the event (Tegelberg, Yagodin & Russell, 2014). Many of the environmentalists who protested in Copenhagen, as well as environmentally minded audiences watching the COP meetings from around the world, perceived the meetings to be a political failure. These meetings were characterized by a division of political interests that cohered around carbon emission responsibility, on one hand, and vulnerability to climate impacts, on the other

68 This research was supported by the Social Sciences and Humanities Research Council of Canada (SSHRC). The authors would like to thank Jeffrey Broadbent and Philip Leifeld for their feedback throughout the development of this research. The authors would also like to acknowledge the assistance of Noelani Dubeta, Michelle Hay, Emily Maynard, Jackson McLean and Kelly Hunter on this project. This paper utilizes comparative research methods and data collection instruments collaboratively developed by the program on Comparing Climate Change Policy Networks (COMPON; http://www.compon.org) initiated and led by Jeffrey Broadbent, University of Minnesota, with co-principal investigators Dana R. Fisher and Katsumi Matsumoto and funded by the US National Science Foundation (Grant Number BCS-08270069).

(Roberts, 2011). The Copenhagen meetings also highlighted the increasing power of China, India and other rapidly growing economies within climate governance, coupled with the declining influence of the European Union and United States (Roberts, 2011). Blühdorn argues that the Copenhagen meetings reflected an increasing political "normalization of the environmental crisis" that he describes as "the curious simultaneity of an unprecedented recognition of the urgency of radical ecological policy change...and an equally unprecedented unwillingness and inability to perform such change" (Blühdorn, 2011: 36). The Copenhagen COP meetings are, from this perspective, a key example of moving away from the goal of climate change mitigation towards the "governance of unsustainability" (36).

However, the Copenhagen meetings were noteworthy for another reason. At this event, Canada, which was symbolically defined by activists as a singular political entity, was targeted by environmental organizations as a climate change pariah because of the federal government's commitment to the Alberta oil sands and its obstinacy towards a meaningful post-Kyoto agreement. After numerous Fossil of the Year awards, Canada was given a "Lifetime Unachievement" award from the Climate Action Network during the meetings (Hayden, 2014). Defining Canada through a nation-state lens as an environmental villain was a productive strategy for environmental movements. However, by adopting and promoting this nation-state definition of global climate politics, environmental movements risk neglecting important eco-political tensions between the federal government, opposition parties, provincial governments and municipalities. As Paul Nadasdy argues:

> [What] we call "the state," far from being a unified entity capable of coherent action, is in fact an illusion... Rather than viewing the state as a thing, then, we do better to see it as an ideological project, one that confers legitimacy upon the complex constellation of government institutions and processes that have many different (and often contradictory) agendas and interests.... It is therefore more accurate to think of state power itself as emerging from the complexity of state processes...rather than as a quality possessed and wielded by a monolithic state-as-entity (Nadasdy, 2003: 4).

Through our analysis, we will describe some of the limitations of a focus on Canada as an ostensibly unified political actor and offer suggestions that may help inform future social movement efforts to push for pro-environmental social change.

Our analysis focuses on Canadian news coverage of environmental movements in climate policy debate during the period of the Copenhagen meetings. A key thread in social movements scholarship focuses on activists' work to access mass media in order to reach the public, mobilize potential supporters and engage governments and other opponents in public debate (Cammaerts, Mattoni & McCurdy, 2013; Gamson, 2007). Another thread in social movements scholarship focuses on the increasingly transnational character of social movements (Castells, 2004; Smith & Wiest, 2012). We weave these two threads together to examine how environmental movements used the Copenhagen COP meetings as a "critical event" (Ramos, 2008) to target the Canadian government. We analyze national news coverage of climate change from *The Globe and Mail* and the *National Post* from the period leading up to and following the Copenhagen COP meetings (June, 2009; June, 2010). We focus on these outlets because they are the two Canadian daily newspapers that have large-scale national distribution as well as online editions. Specifically, we ask: How did environmental groups use the Copenhagen meetings as a critical event to leverage their entry into national news media as a public space for targeting the Canadian government for its poor environmental performance? Did national news media work as a space for environmental critique during the Copenhagen meetings, or did they instead work primarily to legitimize Canadian fossil fuel interests to Canadian bystander publics? By answering these questions, we gain insight into how environmental movements may more effectively take advantage of international meetings and moments of protest as critical events that can provide increased media visibility.

In their classic work on transnational social movement activism, Keck and Sikkink (1998) describe the "boomerang effect," wherein social movements make use of international political spheres to create pressure on national governments. They define the boomerang effect as follows: "When channels between the state and its domestic actors are blocked, the boomerang pattern of influence characteristic of transnational networks may occur: domestic NGOs bypass their state and directly search out international allies to try to bring pressure on their states from outside" (Keck & Sikkink, 1998: 12). Other scholars have extended this model of the boomerang effect through case studies of local-transnational movement bridging involving anti-sweatshop movements in Mexico and Central America; local women's movements in Serbia, Bosnia-Herzegovina and Kosovo and the international political sphere of the United Nations; and the "ping-pong" effect of gender equality movements that moved back and forth between the European Union and national governments in order to change national policies related to gender equality (Armbruster & Sandoval, 2003; Zippel, 2004; Irvine, 2013). In their original analysis, Keck and Sikkink are primarily concerned with how local movements in the Global South are able to draw on the resources and political power of social movements in the Global North to create international pressure on national governments. As we show, transnational protest also creates valuable space for social movements to publicly target politically powerful G8 member countries, such as Canada, in front of a global audience. We examine how environmental movement attempts to create a boomerang effect through protest at the Copenhagen climate change meetings were translated back to Canadian "bystander publics"—the majority of news audience members without a stake or particular interest in social movement conflicts—through national news coverage (McCarthy & Zald, 1977).

Social Movements and Mass Media

Social movements seek media coverage for several key reasons. Media coverage allows movements to reach potential sympathizers and mobilize new supporters (Andrews & Biggs, 2006). Media coverage also allows movements to engage governments and opponents in public debate (Castells, 2009). Movements rely on media to reach various "bystander publics" who are not necessarily invested in movement goals or will not join in movement activity, but whose opinion may help sway conflict between social movements, governments and opponents (Gamson, 2007). The importance of gaining media access is highlighted by Manuel Castells (2009), who argues that social movement politics has largely become "symbolic politics," where social movement conflict with governments and opponents is necessarily carried out in the media sphere.

Movements and media have been described as having a relationship of "asymmetrical dependence" (Carroll & Ratner, 1999). Social movements depend on media to gain public visibility and convey their claims to bystander publics. At the same time, social movements provide interesting news content to journalists. The relationship is described as asymmetrical, however, because movements rely upon media for coverage to a far greater extent than media rely on movements for content. As a result, social movements often choose protest tactics that fit into dominant media logics that orient around conflict, drama, spectacle and celebrity (Sobieraj, 2011). This comes with a trade-off. Instead of communicating the substance of movement claims to bystander publics, news coverage often makes conflict, spectacle or celebrity involvement the central focus of media coverage of social movements (Smith, McCarthy, McPhail & Augustyn, 2001; Brockington, 2008).

With the shift to digital media and Web 2.0 social media applications, evidence suggests that this traditional asymmetrical relationship is being rebalanced as social movements make use of the "affordances" of the Internet to expand their capacities to produce their own content and communicate directly to supporters and bystanders outside the structures of the mass media (Earl & Kimport, 2011). Nevertheless, most social movements also continue to seek mainstream news media coverage. As Castells notes, though media audiences increasingly get their news through the Internet and social media applications, the news content that is most often circulated continues to come from legacy media outlets (Castells, 2009). Furthermore, coverage in mainstream news outlets is valuable for reaching bystander publics who may lack awareness of social movement-produced content, or lack the motivation to engage with movement-produced web content (Hestres, 2013).

Social movements often build campaigns around "critical events" to gain public visibility (Ramos, 2008). In Canada, a recent example of this is the Idle No More movement, which built on the Conservative government's Bill C-38 as a critical event to link issues of Indigenous sovereignty and the federal government's attempts to weaken Canadian environmental regulations. In this chapter, we examine whether and how environmental movements were able to make use of the Copenhagen Conference of the Parties meetings as an international critical event for gaining access to national news media in order to convey their claims to bystander publics in Canada.

A Note on Method

We conducted keyword searches using the online database Factiva for "climate change" and/or "global warming" between 1997 (when the Kyoto Protocol was negotiated) to 2010 for *The Globe and Mail*, and from Oct. 27, 1988 (its first date of publication) through 2010 for the *National Post*. We also searched "IPCC" and its full name (Intergovernmental Panel on Climate Change). The number of articles containing one or more of the keywords was 15,021. The media data set was cleaned by manually scanning and removing duplicate articles or articles that mentioned the keyword(s) "global warming" and/or "climate change" without providing any substantive information, producing a data set of 8,960 articles. We selected a 20% sample (1,792 articles) for detailed coding and analysis by using a random start and selecting every fifth article. The results presented here are based on the period from June 2009 to June 2010 inclusive, which gives us roughly a one-year period centred on the Copenhagen COP meetings.

We used the tools of network analysis to examine the connections between news outlets and article content. Social network analysis typically focuses on relationships between individuals or organizations (i.e. ties based on communication, collaboration, friendship or conflict), in order to identify which social actors are most central, to examine how groups of actors cluster together, or to assess the density of the network. However, we can also use network analysis to examine connections between social groups (people or organizations) and the cultural frameworks or issue categories that structure media debate. This is a discourse network approach to media analysis, which is valuable because it provides a visual image of multiple connections between cultural discourses and social actors emphasizing complexity and relationality, which may be obscured when data are presented in either a linear, narrative manner, or in a two-dimensional tabular form (Leifeld, 2013).

The visual representations of our data were created using Visone software for social network analysis and visualization (http://visone.info). For the present analysis, we use two-mode network diagrams (Borgatti & Halgin, 2011) that focus on specific organizations as actors who play a central role in articulating cultural discourses about climate change. These organizations are one mode of network data, which are represented by circular nodes in the sociograms.[69] Issue categories are treated as a second mode of network data, represented by square nodes. Node size is weighted to reflect the centrality of nodes in the network (that is, how well-connected the node is to others). Ties between nodes indicate that the issue category is connected to the organizational actor. Tie thickness is weighted to reflect the frequency by which a particular issue category is linked to each organization. We present our results using two-mode network sociograms to examine the clustering of key organizational actors around issue agreement and issue disagreement. We place the analytical focus on environmental organizations and their relationships to other key organizational actors (particularly those from government and industry), which are structured through similar rhetorical positions in either agreement or disagreement on particular climate change discourses. To simplify the structure of the networks and make the diagrams more legible, we have set a threshold whereby organizations must appear in the media archive two or more times in order to be included in the analysis.

With the assistance of NVIVO software for qualitative analysis, we engaged in a deeper analysis of a set of 152 articles published during the period June 2009-June 2010 inclusive, filtered for articles that have a focus on international dimensions of climate change. This layer of analysis allows for a deeper examination of mass-mediated interactions among national politics, transnational climate governance and

69 It is important to note that not all organizational actors can be treated as categorically the same. Some actors, such as those associated with a political party, government, business or non-governmental organization are likely speaking on behalf of the organization. However, other actors, particularly those with university affiliations, are generally providing their own perspective, not that of their organization.

social movement mobilization around the period of the Copenhagen COP meetings.[70]

Environmental Groups and Media Discourse Networks

Our first layer of analysis focuses on discourse networks formed by ties between organizational actors and discourses about climate change. Figure 1 visualizes the network of shared agreement between actors on specific themes. Several environmental organizations are present in national news media during the 2009-10 period. The most central of these are the Pembina Institute, followed by Forest Ethics and Greenpeace Canada. Other visible environmental organizations include the David Suzuki Foundation, Sierra Club of Canada, Greenpeace International, WWF Canada and Climate Action Network Canada. Many of the claims made by environmental organizations during this period focus on negative impacts of the oil and gas industry, the notion that reliance on the oil sands works against progress on climate change, and the need for the Canadian oil industry to address its carbon emissions as part of a response to climate change.

News sources also often use media coverage to voice opposition to climate change discourses. Figure 2 visualizes the climate change *disagreement* network (which shows which groups disagree with each of these statements) for the same period. The most central environmental groups in this figure are the Pembina Institute and Greenpeace Canada. Several environmental organizations cluster together in disagreement with the statement, "the federal government is taking meaningful action on climate change," including Greenpeace Canada, Pembina Institute and World Wildlife Fund (WWF). Similarly, Friends of the Earth Canada appears in opposition to the notion that "Canada is an international leader in climate change action."

70 Our analysis is part of the broader COMPON (Comparing Climate Change Policy Networks) research project (http://www.compon.org). The COMPON project involves case study teams working in 19 societies, including the United States, Mexico, Brazil, Japan, China, Korea, India, Germany, Portugal, the United Kingdom and Sweden, among others. While our results stand on their own, a common set of research protocols was used by all teams to produce results that are comparable across cases (Broadbent et al., 2013).

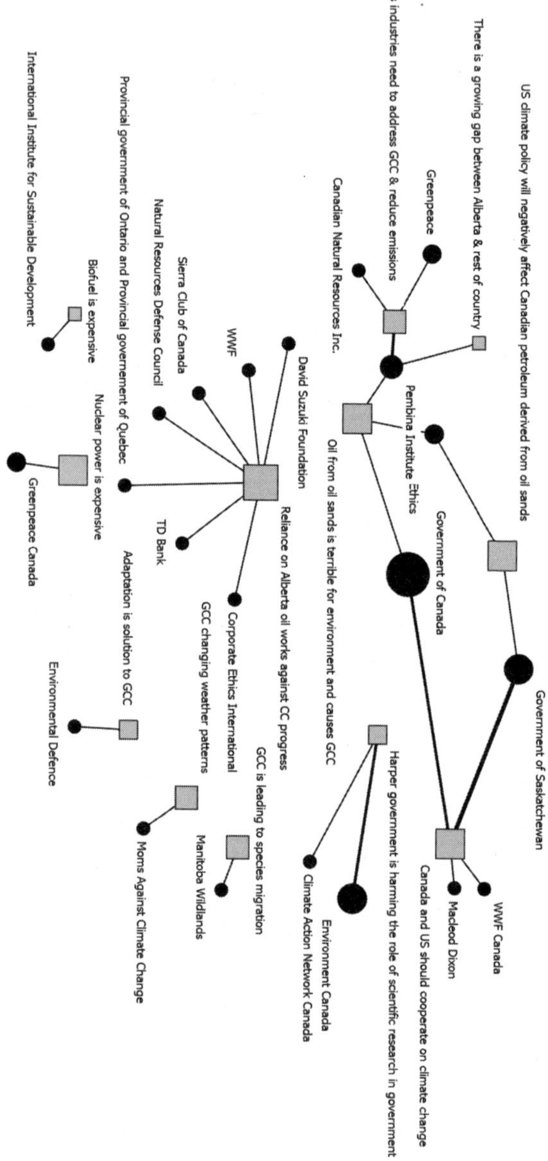

FIGURE 1. Agreement discourse network linking discourses, environmental organizations and other key organizations.

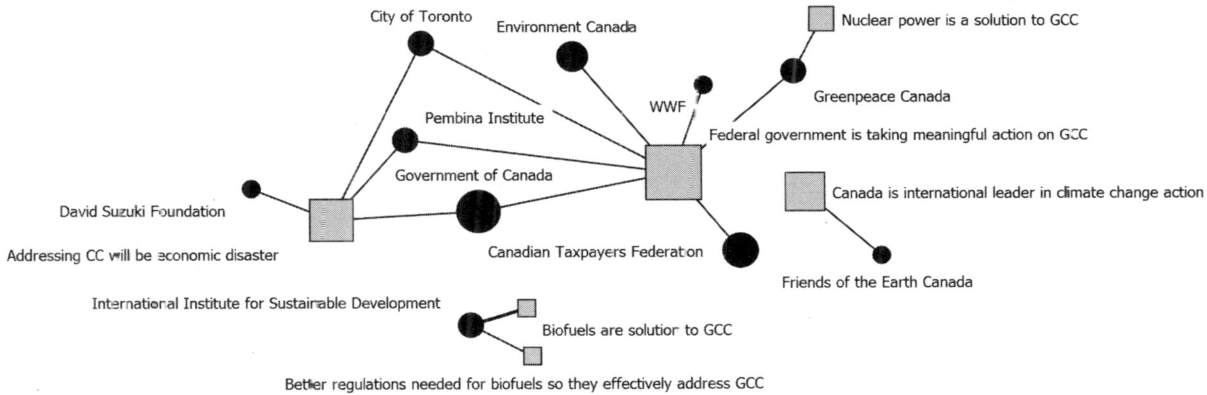

FIGURE 2. Disagreement discourse network linking discourses, environmental organizations and other key organizations.

The other main theme that structures this network is disagreement with the idea that "addressing climate change will be an economic disaster," which is articulated by the David Suzuki Foundation. As in the previous figure, here we see environmental organizations are able to gain entrée to national news media as key organizational actors, and to articulate substantive claims that are critical of the Canadian government performance on climate change.

Canada's Role in International Climate Governance

A prominent discourse in the Canadian national news media is criticism of the Harper government's inaction on climate change, which has earned Canada an internationally recognized negative reputation. IPCC head Rajendra Pachauri, Mexican President Felipe Calderon and UN Secretary-General Ban Ki-moon, among others, have publicly urged the Canadian government to do more on climate action. The Harper government has been vilified in the domestic and international political spheres, and publicly adorned with various anti-environmental "awards," such as the Fossil of the Year in Poland and Fossil of the Day in Copenhagen, 2009. Symbolic acts of public shaming such as these have contributed to Canada's tarnished reputation at home and abroad. Reasons for Canada being targeted include attempting to maintain involvement in the Kyoto Protocol while disregarding its targets (and as of 2011 becoming the first country to formally withdraw its agreement) and not having a regulatory framework in place at the domestic level for GHG emitters. Canada has been labelled an environmental "laggard," stating that it will passively harmonize its reduction strategies with the United States and will not commit to serious action on climate change unless India and China do the same (McCarthy, 2009: A1).

Canada has also been shamed in the international arena because the oil sands' vast emissions are viewed as a significant hindrance in the international quest to reduce GHG emissions. While Canada is defined in the international realm as a nation that is failing to take action on climate change, this masks heterogeneity within Canadian climate politics, where several provinces are embarking on separate paths to address climate change. The Saskatchewan government has demonstrated keen interest in developing carbon capture and storage technology, and is collaborating with Montana in a joint subnational carbon capture project. The Alberta government has also supported carbon storage projects. However, emissions-reduction targets and mitigation tactics vary by province, as premiers have "disparate interests" regarding climate and energy (Alberts, 2010: A5). The Québec government has the most ambitious emissions target of 20% below 1990 levels by 2020, which parallels the EU target (Morgan, 2009: B7). Conversely, Alberta aims to stabilize emissions by 2020 at an estimated 58% higher than 1990 levels. Provincial leaders demonstrate an unwillingness to compensate for other provinces' (particularly Alberta's) increased emissions due to the expansion of the oil sands. At Copenhagen, Ontario and Québec Environment Ministers demonstrated that their position differed from the federal government's position, and that they would not carry higher emission-reduction burdens.

News media framing of Canada's international reputation focused on how Canada's reliance on Alberta oil works against climate change progress, which in turn negatively impacts Canada's international reputation. The primary reason for Canada's vilification at the Copenhagen climate talks was because of the country's reliance on Alberta's oil sands, "the world's most energy-intensive oil production" project (Reguly, 2009: A1). The Harper government was accused by climate scientists, environmental groups and developing nations of favouring the oil sands, and that this distinctive protection worked in contradiction with reducing GHG emissions. Prior to the Copenhagen meetings, Canada was referred to as a "corrupt petro-state," with national news coverage stating that Canada comes to Copenhagen with a "tarred image," as the country is perceived to want to protect the oil sands rather than work to reduce GHG emissions (Reguly & Vanderklippe, 2009: A1). Although the Copenhagen meetings provided Canada an opportunity to redeem itself in the eyes of the international body, because delegates from the country attended the climate talks without a clear plan for climate change action—stating instead that it would wait to see how the US plans to tackle emissions—the

Canadian government was rendered irrelevant in negotiations, and thus, the country's reputation remained unrepaired.

The Copenhagen Meetings as a Critical Event

Though the outcome was disappointing to many, the international climate summit in Copenhagen was initially seen as a pivotal event amidst the climate change crisis. Over 190 countries met in Copenhagen to discuss the parameters for a new, post-Kyoto climate agreement. Countries involved in the Copenhagen Accord, an outcome of the meetings, agreed on the importance of international collaboration and cooperation in tackling climate change, and that global temperatures should not increase by more than two degrees Celsius. IPCC Head Rajendra Pachauri stated that this figure "is not universally accepted," however, and that it may be met with resistance from some nations, such as Canada. He calls for "urgent grassroots action by civil society, business and local governments towards a pattern of sustainable development" ("The UN's Enviro-Activist in-Chief," 2010: A12).

Supporters of the Copenhagen climate summit have deemed the meetings a success because of the creation of the Copenhagen Accord, while critics condemned the climate talks as a predictable failure in creating a binding treaty that could succeed the Kyoto Protocol. Drawing into question the effectiveness of international meetings, the Pew Center on Global Climate Change argued that the chance of countries reaching even a broad political agreement is slim as there is a lot of disagreement among countries (McCarthy, 2009: A1).

The Copenhagen climate talks were critical as they provided a political space to negotiate tensions between developed and developing nations and climate change action. Specifically, the meetings acted as a symbolic sphere used by non-industrialized countries to pressure industrialized countries to reduce emissions and finance mitigation efforts. During the summit, the federal government was accused of diverting attention from Canada's responsibilities in reducing GHG emissions. The Harper government, instead, focused on the responsibilities of developing countries in addressing climate change, disregarding how industrialized countries account for 75% of global GHG emissions (Drexhage, 2009: A19).

Environmental Movement Intervention in Copenhagen

The 2009 Copenhagen climate conference was formally organized for national governments to discuss, and ideally come to an agreement on, ways to address a rapidly changing climate. However, this international meeting of governments was also understood by environmental activists as an opportunity to attract media attention for their own agendas by using the global political arena as a protest venue. As Hadden (2015) notes in her analysis of social movement mobilization at the COP meetings, the Copenhagen meetings saw an "unprecedented" level of social movement mobilization and protest. This included involvement by a broader range of groups and wider range of protest tactics than seen at prior COP meetings. Different segments of protesters aligned around demands for action framed through the language of "scientific urgency" and "climate justice." As Hadden concludes, though the Copenhagen COP meeting may have been politically disappointing, it was a pivotal event with lasting effects in the evolution of the climate change movement.

Environmental movement interventions in Copenhagen were translated in various ways through Canadian national news media. Some activities were planned with the UN's Framework Convention on Climate Change, such as the Young and Future Generations Day. Over 1,000 youths participated in this demonstration by distributing T-shirts at the summit reading "How old will you be in 2050?" in an effort to remind delegates of the impacts of their decisions (or non-decisions) on future generations (Agence France-Presse, 2009: A11). Other events were not organized in collaboration with the UN, such as when approximately 1,500 people took to the streets of Copenhagen to publicly protest the summit.

Conclusion

The COP 15 meetings held in Copenhagen served as a "critical event" for environmental movements to intervene in mass media narratives of international climate change policy-making (Ramos, 2008). Drawing on Keck and Sikkink's (1998) notion of the boomerang effect, the COP 15 protests served as an opportunity for Canadian environmental movements to connect to a transnational episode of social movement protest and draw international public attention to the Canadian government's poor performance on climate change, thereby generating public awareness and political pressure within Canada. Through the news stories produced in the period leading up to and following the meetings, Canadian national news media conveyed claims about Canada's damaged reputation to bystander audiences. The Copenhagen meetings served as a critical event that allowed environmentalists to draw public attention and symbolically shame the Canadian government and fossil fuel interests, and this social movement critique was circulated by national news media to bystander audiences. News coverage also drew attention to tensions between Canada and much of the international community, as well as the sub-national political tensions within Canada. By contrast, there is little evidence in this body of texts that national news media coverage of the Copenhagen meetings played a strong role in legitimizing Canadian fossil fuel interests or doing reputation repair for the Canadian government for bystander publics. As such, environmental movements were able to use the Copenhagen meetings to produce a boomerang effect within the mass media sphere. Further research is needed, however, to assess the impact that this environmental movement and mass media discourse has within Canadian political networks beyond the media sphere.

Our findings are consistent with others who argue that environmental movements-media relationships are moving away from the traditional model of asymmetrical dependence as the media landscape is transformed and reconfigured by the Internet and Web 2.0 applications (Cottle, 2008; Castells, 2009; Lester & Hutchins, 2009). At the same time, it should be noted that the environmental groups that get into the media and are granted "media-derived authority" (Herbst, 2003) to speak about Canada's role in international climate policy debate tend to be the larger, well-established and professionalized organizations, such as the David Suzuki Foundation, Pembina Institute and Greenpeace Canada. This echoes Carroll and Ratner's (1999) original comparative research, which found that Greenpeace was more skilled than smaller, grassroots and radical organizations at managing the asymmetrical dependency between movements and media. Despite significant changes to the media landscape over the past fifteen years, we continue to see that smaller, grassroots, less professionalized or more radical environmental voices are rarely granted the same degree of media-derived authority. The model of asymmetrical dependence continues to hold true for some branches of the environmental movement more than for others.

This has important implications for which discourses are made visible within global climate change debate. As Stevenson and Dryzek (2014) observe in their analysis of the COP 15 meetings, the "empowered space" of climate change decision-making inside the boundaries of the UNFCCC (United Nations Framework Convention on Climate Change) is dominated by "moderate discourses of Mainstream Sustainability, *ecological modernization,* and *climate marketization*" (Stevenson & Dryzek, 2014: 149). While "Green Radicalism" discourses of "*ecofeminism, radical decentralization,* and *new globalism*" circulate in the public space of environmental protest, these largely fail to translate into the empowered space of UNFCCC deliberations and decision-making (132). A parallel pattern is demonstrated by Canadian national media coverage of the COP 15 meetings and protests, which privileges larger, well-established environmental organizations as news sources, who typically give voice to "Mainstream Sustainability" discourses. As such, national news media can regularly incorporate environmental movement actors as key news sources, while simultaneously marginalizing alternative ways of interpreting the eco-politics of climate change.

Research on climate governance tends to treat nations as collective actors with largely unified and coherent political interests within the sphere of international policy-making (Fisher, 2004; Stoett, 2012). In a similar vein, work on climate justice—which focuses on the social justice implications of who is more responsible for producing climate change, and who is most at risk from its impacts—also tends to treats climate justice as an issue involving national level disparities between more and less developed countries (Roberts, 2011; Shue, 2014). Following Nadasdy's (2003) definition of the state as an "ideological project" that is "often contradictory" rather than unified, one of the main implications of our analysis is to destabilize the model of Canada as a singular political actor with homogeneous interests in international climate governance.

The notion of a singular Canada that stands as a climate villain is a productive trope for environmental movements and the media, but it reduces the complexity of divergent interpretations of climate change and policy responses to this problem among federal political parties, provincial governments and municipal governments, and risks drawing attention away from the sub-national spaces that currently show the most promise for addressing climate change within Canada. John Urry and Ulrich Beck, among others, argue for an increasingly cosmopolitan view of climate change, where the focus shifts outwards from the interests of individual nations to a more global view (Beck, 2010; Urry, 2011). Such a perspective is valuable, but would be complemented by a parallel shift in focus inwards towards the eco-politics of climate change at the municipal and provincial levels. We might define this multi-scalar vision of the politics of climate change as "localized cosmopolitanism," which maintains a simultaneous focus on the impacts of and responses to climate change in our communities and around the world.[71] In addition to using the transnational political terrain to draw attention to the Canadian government's poor performance, environmental movements may simultaneously draw greater public attention to sub-national tensions around the eco-politics of climate change by emphasizing discrepancies between climate change leaders and laggards across political scales within Canada.

71 This is a term that emerged from discussions that the first author participated in at the Sustainable Canada Dialogues: St. John's Visioning Workshop (convened by the first author and facilitated by Natalie Richards).

NO ONE IS ILLEGAL

Undoing Borders

Harsha Walia

> Walls turned on their sides are bridges.
> (Graffiti on the US-Mexico border wall)

In 2005, Ali Reza Monemi was detained by immigration enforcement in Vancouver and faced deportation within the week. Members of his family, the International Federation of Iranian Refugees, and No One Is Illegal (NOII) announced an indefinite hunger strike. For four days, in subzero temperatures, over 20 hunger strikers and hundreds of supporters camped outside the immigration offices. Less than twelve hours prior to his scheduled deportation, Ali was granted a stay. During a victory rally, his elderly mother chanted, "Stop the Deportations! No One Is Illegal" (No one Is Illegal-Vancouver, n.d.). The next year, Farah Kulmiyeh Abdil, an HIV-positive Somali refugee living in limbo for sixteen years and under a deportation order, chained himself to the Immigration and Refugee Board headquarters in Montreal. Supported by migrant justice activists, he declared his refusal to be invisible (Solidarity across Borders, 2006). These specific struggles connect to a broader NOII movement that actively confronts borders. Through the individual as well as collective power of defiance, subversion and prefiguration, NOII challenges and counters the hegemony and violence of border controls.

NOII groups were initiated in Canada during heightened racist national hysteria and escalating attacks on immigrant and refugee communities after the incidents of September 11, 2001. The first NOII group formed that year in Montreal. Groups have since formed in Calgary, Halifax, Kingston, London, Toronto, Ottawa, Winnipeg, Vancouver, Victoria and Québec City. NOII is concurrently an ideological framework to counter border violence, and an extended network of grassroots migrant justice groups "rooted in anticolonial, anticapitalist, ecological justice, Indigenous self-determination, anti-occupation and antioppressive communities" (No One is Illegal, 2012).

NOII organizing practices are founded on a commitment to interconnected analysis and a political vision aimed at growing resistance beyond our own organizational boundaries. This means that although migrant justice is our emphasis, NOII groups are more than a single-issue group. NOII groups have been pivotal in contributing to anti-capitalist, Indigenous solidarity, feminist, anti-oppression, Palestinian self-determination and workers movements. Another critical strength of NOII groups is the emphasis on empowering and supporting organizers from immigrant and racialized backgrounds. The personal experience of racialization and colonialism becomes a site for enacting movement leadership. Our lived experiences and political analysis provide a critical foundation to anchor mobilizing efforts and through which to envision the nature of solidarities across communities.

This chapter serves as both an observation of NOII's strongest movement-based practices and an illumination of strategies that are useful for other radical social movements within North America to consider. It is a reflection of NOII's commitment to five key movement-based practices: community organizing and anti-oppressive leadership through direct support work, advocating status for all migrants and prefiguring safe spaces for undocumented migrants, building broad alliances toward a systemic abolition of the security apparatus, the centrality of Indigenous self-determination within anti-colonial migrant justice struggles, and strengthening anti-capitalist resistance. These five forms of praxis provide useful insights for other social movement organizers.

A few acknowledgements about the limits of this chapter are necessary. The radical migrant justice movement includes a diverse range of community groups and campaigns. This chapter is not an analysis of this wide-ranging migrant justice movement. Given the highly decentralized and heterogeneous nature of NOII organizing, this chapter is not intended to supply any kind of definitive history of NOII either. Rather, this chapter revolves around my involvement in the migrant justice movement as a current member of NOII-Vancouver (Indigenous Coast Salish territories) and previous member of NOII-Montreal. The strength of this chapter comes from an analysis based on actual experience and active participation as opposed to an abstract sociological study of the entire movement.

Direct Support Work

Over the past decade, NOII has fought against hundreds of cases of detention and deportation. Direct support work is a daily aspect of NOII's community organizing, and encompasses the practical advocacy needed to defend migrants from detention, deportation, immigration enforcement raids and other forms of control and exploitation. Responding to lived realities, NOII's support work involves drafting legal submissions, coordinating group delegations to immigration offices, providing child care, mobilizing court support, raising funds, hosting press conferences, running errands, organizing public actions and offering emotional support. Many migrants we have supported over the years have been torn from their communities and violently deported; many others have won their fight to stay.

Karla Lottini, a Mexican refugee in Vancouver, recently won her fight to stay based on a campaign by NOII. She spoke to media about the values that motivated how support work was organized for her: "I respect NOII very much—they acted very quickly. They worked fast, and were very organized. It wasn't just a relationship of sending memos or just writing letters. We talked and reviewed our words until midnight some nights. They came and brought me a lot of food. I have two daughters to care for. It goes beyond organization or community work—that's love and it's very human" (Ball, 2012).

Direct support work is based on five tenets that Lottini alludes to. Direct support is premised on the notion that supporting people in fighting for their most basic needs, especially to live in safety, is necessary in advancing the struggle. Second, the practice of anti-oppression encourages people with privilege to take on tangible responsibilities in ensuring a more dignified survival for those without full immigration status. Even though many of us, as racialized immigrants, come with our own histories of border imperialism, we recognize that we must offer support to those migrants who are currently caught within the system's tentacles. The third tenet is to mobilize on the basis of solidarity not charity, which means that support is mobilized alongside rather than on behalf of people. Chris Ramsaroop of Justice for Migrant Workers has often reminded well-intentioned activists who want to work with migrant workers to listen to the workers and their own articulations of their needs and demands (Ramsaroop, 2012).

Direct support work also encourages us to name and confront political systems in order to break through the psychological isolation that is intended to silence, blame, shame and ultimately disempower people. Direct actions such as group delegations or disruptions of bureaucracies are key processes to flip from the internalized logic of being an "ungrateful" or "unworthy" migrant to laying the blame squarely on the system of border controls. Finally, direct support is explicitly political, and part of a process of empowerment, consciousness-raising and movement building. Migrant justice organizer Sarita Ahooja notes the critical difference between social worker or non-governmental organization (NGO) models of service provision and NOII's models, where support work "is done as part of a long-term struggle for a radical restructuring of society" (Maynard, 2010).

A persistent question has been how to keep support work politicized, and avoid its devolution into a form of radical social or paralegal work that offloads responsibility from the welfare state and paid service providers on to volunteer community activists. In my experience, the most powerful forms of support work are those that are part of political campaigns that force the struggles of migrants into the public realm and thus ignite the spirit of resistance rather than replicate a dynamic of charity. In Montreal between 2003 and 2006, self-organized committees of refugees in alliance with NOII activists laid the terrain for monumental victories and provided an inspirational model for the migrant justice movement. The Action Committee of Nonstatus Algerians, the Coalition to Stop the Deportation of Palestinian Refugees and the Pakistani Action Committee Against Racial Profiling all had similar demands to stop the deportations of their members and to regularize their legal status as permanent residents. In Vancouver in 2004, Refugees Against Racial Profiling likewise brought together groups of refugees to collectively organize against deportations.

Emerging from invisibility and breaking the silence, these refugees and nonstatus migrants regularly spoke to media and at community events. They gave voice to the violence of living with precarity and in poverty. These committees utilized a number of strategies and tactics: general assemblies, weekly pickets, mass mobilizations including coordinated national days of action, lobbying, delegations to immigration offices, women- and children-led marches, educational forums, press conferences, occupations, legal advocacy, taking sanctuary in churches in defiance of deportation orders and more.

In an astounding victory, after nine months of meetings, petitions, educational forums, workshops, demonstrations that brought thousands to the streets, delegations to immigration offices, and a family taking sanctuary in a Montreal church, Immigration Canada and Immigration Québec announced the regularization of a large majority of the nonstatus Algerians. This regularization program, however, excluded many, including those who lived outside the province of Québec and those with any criminal record. In a gesture of solidarity that rejected state divisions, many of the nonstatus Algerian activists who qualified for the regularization program continued to mobilize for full regularization alongside those who were still excluded. They campaigned to ensure that those who lived outside the province or had criminal records were not left behind (No one is Illegal-Montréal, 2012).

These collective committees of refugees and nonstatus migrants were path-breaking for several reasons. They brought together migrants who were able to share their collective experience and build strength in numbers to organize against detentions and deportations. Given that the inherent nature of the system serves to individualize one's experiences, the process of coming together is crucial in and of itself. These committees also stressed the necessity of political struggle and furthered a systemic analysis of the violence of border controls, while also fighting to stop individual deportations. As nonstatus Algerian activist Mohamed Cherfi often stated, "We need to be radical. That is the best way we are going to grow and be effective" (Lowry & Nyers, 2003). Finally, these committees were able to build mass mobilizations and disruptive resistances by fostering multiracial and multilingual alliances among diverse migrant communities as well as among labour unions, antiwar groups, anti-capitalists, women's centres, and others.

This powerful organization of those directly impacted working in alliance with migrant justice activists became a primary model that was replicated for several years. Several weaknesses started to become apparent, though. As some people won status, while others were deported or began to feel defeated, the weight of facilitating organization among groups of migrants became tremendous. As someone who was involved in daily support work for the Pakistani Action Committee Against Racial Profiling in Montreal and Refugees Against Racial Profiling in Vancouver, it became evident to me that organizing among people in different phases of the legal process was generally perceived as a burden by those just trying to survive. Furthermore, the more routinely these strategies were used, the more predictable they became to the authorities. Their effectiveness was lost; sanctuary cases dragged on for years, immigration offices shut down to prevent delegations, police were increasingly used to repress and deter.

Political organizing requires us to assess changes in conditions and adapt accordingly. Direct support work should be seen less as a definitive model and more as a system of values to guide how we work alongside those facing deportation. In its most potent form, support work is expressed through the organization and mobilization of thousands of migrants joining forces. But it also takes the form of patiently organizing alongside migrants and offering support—ranging from emotional to legal support—to break isolation and shame, and instead affirm dignity and choice. Since 2006, most of NOII's support work has taken this individualized form. In many cases, public campaigns have developed around these cases of detention or deportation. Stopping one deportation at a time makes a significant difference in people's lives and helps build movement morale.

An example of a public campaign focused on fighting an individual deportation was the struggle to prevent the deportation of Laibar Singh, a paralyzed refugee from India. Between 2007 and 2008, NOII-Vancouver (Indigenous Coast Salish territories) organized intensely including speaking daily on Punjabi radio shows, writing commentaries in multilingual newspapers, building alliances at campus and union meetings, leafleting at gurdwaras to connect with other immigrants, coordinating national days of action, facilitating community meetings and debates, and lobbying. NOII organizers felt that the odds were stacked against us because few people seemed supportive of an irregularly arrived refugee with a permanent disability. Given the campaign's highly polarized nature, a few NOII organizers of colour also received numerous death threats. Yet we persisted—unsure of whether our strategies were helping or hindering and tentative about what to expect, but knowing that community organizing is often messy yet always necessary.

After months of such intense consternation on top of day-to-day mobilizing, we were stunned when 2,000 people, mostly Punjabi elders and aunties, showed up at the Vancouver International Airport to create a blockade preventing the deportation. The entire international terminal was shut down, and dozens of flights were cancelled throughout the day. After hours of thousands of us forming a protective circle around Singh, immigration enforcement backed away. This historic blockade in December 2007 is the only documented time in recent North American history that the violence of deportation has been prevented through the power of a mass mobilization and direct action.

NOII centres direct support work in our mobilizing because it grounds our work in migrant communities. What form it will take—whether launching a large-scale public campaign or helping to fill out paperwork—depends on the specific political context and specific needs of those affected by the systems we are confronting. The greatest value of support work comes from building relationships of respect, trust and accountability.

Status and Access for All

NOII groups across the country have laid the ground for a comprehensive regularization program. We advocate for full regularization, also known as legalization or amnesty, for all undocumented, non-status and temporary migrants. Regularization is an extension of the demand for an end to all detentions and deportations, and means that migrants can live without constant fear. Regularization is a step toward ensuring that bosses can no longer so casually and callously exploit undocumented and migrant labour. Regularization facilitates access to health care, education, child care, social assistance, labour protection, housing, legal aid and antiviolence services. Demanding full regularization is a humanizing force in the face of the state's dehumanizing trend toward criminalization and precarity.

NOII's framework for regularization is drawn from our basic belief that no one person is more deserving of a self-determined life than another person. Because we refuse distinctions and divisions between good/deserving migrants and bad/undeserving ones, our principles for regularization are inclusive. Regularization cannot discriminate or exclude based on race, class, educational background, national origin, faith, gender, mental or physical disability, sexual orientation, medical condition or criminal record. The framework for regularization that NOII advocates for, therefore, is fundamentally equitable in its call for status for *all* those without full immigration status (No One Is Illegal, 2012).

One of the most common retorts to NOII is that we would "let anyone stay, including criminals and rapists." This reveals a form of double racism or double punishment that Steve Cohen of NOII in the United Kingdom describes as "an exercise in imperial arrogance," where the "offending conduct is merely being shipped overseas" (Cohen, 2003). On top of dealing with the injustices of the criminal justice system and prison-industrial complex that oversurveils and overincarcerates racialized communities, particularly Black and Indigenous communities, Black non-citizens are especially targeted further with deportation.

Many labour unions and mainstream immigrant rights groups support the regularization of nonstatus workers employed in certain trade sectors. However, advertently or inadvertently, this reinforces the idea that migrants are only worth their labour. NOII believes that regularization must not be contingent on a person's participation in the labour force, and should not exclude the poor, unwaged, unemployed or disabled. It must also be ongoing, meaning that it does not exclude migrants who have lived in Canada for a short period of time, or temporary workers whose transient status is enforced by the state and an inherent part of their labour exploitation and social stigmatization.

In addition to advocating and popularizing a No One Is Illegal, Status for All People campaign, various NOII groups have worked to actualize and prefigure regularization from the ground up. As NOII-Toronto organizers explain, "We need to take back our community centres, schools, health centres and neighbourhoods by declaring them as sanctuary zones free of immigration controls" (Kamal & Mishra, 2007). This means organizing to create community spaces and neighbourhoods where undocumented migrants can access critical services without the threat of deportation. Such campaigns are prefigurative in their aim to ensure that undocumented migrants, despite lacking full legal immigration status, can have their basic needs met and be supported in creating semiautonomous spaces of safety. Sanctuary zones for nonstatus migrants, also known as solidarity zones, take power away from the state because their very existence represents nonparticipation in and subversion of an exclusionary apartheid system of citizenship.

These campaigns have many iterations: Sanctuary City, Solidarity City, Access without Fear and Don't Ask Don't Tell. Over 30 US municipalities have been pressured to adopt a Don't Ask Don't Tell policy that prohibits municipal employees from asking or sharing information about immigration status when providing city services (Seghetti, Vina & Ester, 2006). In Canada, powerful and effective campaigns to ensure that people accessing city and social services are not discriminated against based on immigration status have been led primarily by NOII in Toronto, the city with the largest number of nonstatus migrants in the country. In 2013, the city of Toronto declared that all city services would be accessible to undocumented migrants and migrant workers. I describe below some of the persistent mobilizing that built toward this historic Sanctuary City victory.

In 2006, after two years of advocating for Don't Ask Don't Tell policies within various municipal and governmental bodies, NOII-Toronto concentrated on building an Education Not Deportation campaign. This was precipitated by the removal of two undocumented children by immigration enforcement officers from a Toronto school. Within a month, the Toronto District School Board was swamped with official submissions from parents, teachers, migrant justice activists and educators (including the largest teachers' union in Ontario) calling on the school board to welcome all students and defend schools from immigration enforcement. Shortly thereafter, the Toronto District School Board passed a Don't Ask Don't Tell policy stipulating that all students under the age of eighteen had a right to access education without the fear of detention or deportation. The campaign then shifted to ensure that every local school was informed about how to meaningfully implement this policy. In 2010, the Toronto District School Board was pressured to provide appropriate training to teachers and administrative staff. Over 500 schools were given educational posters about the policy to ensure that they were truly becoming safe spaces for all elementary and secondary school students (No One Is Illegal-Toronto, 2010).

In a similar vein, the Shelter Sanctuary Status campaign was initiated in 2008 to prevent immigration officers from entering women's shelters in Toronto. For two years, the campaign emphasized outreach to women and trans resource centres. Over 120 groups endorsed the main campaign demand: ensuring that antiviolence services are accessible to undocumented survivors of violence, and barring immigration enforcement from entering or waiting outside these centres. In 2010, the Shelter Sanctuary Status campaign won a significant victory when the Canadian Border Services Agency (CBSA) was pressured to issue a directive that enforcement officers would not enter women's shelters or other spaces for women who are experiencing violence. Nor could the CBSA make inquiries of staff or other shelter residents about the identity and legal status of any nonstatus women seeking these services.

The Education Not Deportation and Shelter Sanctuary Status campaigns are impressive, as they have ensured that some of the most marginalized within our communities can live more freely. Alliances between migrant justice organizers, undocumented migrants, high school and university students, women and trans activists, and neighbourhood associations have led to significant and concrete victories. The victories within schools and women's shelters laid the foundation to force a larger victory with Toronto City Council declaring that all city-operated spaces were accessible to undocumented migrants. These are also struggles to reclaim public space and social services by holding increasingly bureaucratized institutions and service providers accountable to those they are supposed to serve.

More important, these campaigns illustrate how NOII is creating a de facto grassroots regularization program from the ground up. As NOII-Toronto organizer Fariah Chowdhury describes it, "Solidarity City is a way of organizing as well as a goal. It is a way to get access to services for non-status people right now, and to involve people in the control and organization of the places they work, live, and receive education, healthcare, and basic services.... We know that this is only possible when all grassroots movements in the city collaborate, connect, and commit to a politic based on autonomous power that is separate from state power" (Nail, 2010). Beyond just demanding a regularization program from the state, these prefigurative campaigns demonstrate the necessity *and* possibility of movements to organize zones of safety for undocumented migrants beyond the state's authority.

Abolish the Security Apparatus

The post-9/11 era has furthered racist anti-immigrant hysteria through the particular discourse of "national security." This has entrenched state securitization and border militarization in Canada through, for example, the creation of the CBSA, the implementation of a number of antiterror provisions that legalize extensive surveillance and lengthy interrogations, and a multibillion-dollar joint border security plan with the United States that includes biometrics and armed border guards. In an essay on race and national security, Razack draws attention to how race thinking "becomes embedded in law and bureaucracy so that the suspension of rights appears not as a violence but as the law itself" (Razack, 2008). Canada, along with other Western states, has utilized the War on Terror to justify draconian sanctions under the jurisdiction of intelligence services as well as criminal, tax and immigration laws that target Muslim, Arab and South Asian communities.

One such measure within immigration law is a security certificate. Security certificates are prepared by the Canadian Security Intelligence Service (CSIS) and issued by the Government of Canada against noncitizens, including legal permanent residents, who are deemed "inadmissible on grounds of security" and who thereby could "be detained without the issue of a warrant" (No One Is Illegal-Vancouver, n.d.). Under this Kafkaesque law, detainees can be imprisoned indefinitely without any charges ever being laid against them and face possible deportation to torture. In the cases of the men against whom security certificates were issued, secret evidence and vague allegations—including hearsay—were admissible but never revealed to them in an open court of law.

While security certificates were already being used to unjustly detain and deport migrants prior to 9/11, a particularly heightened and demonizing post-9/11 media focus on security-related investigations created the political context for the development of a national campaign in support of security certificate detainees. The five men held on security certificates, also known as the Secret Trial 5, were Mohammad Mahjoub, Mahmoud Jaballah, Mohamed Harkat, Hassan Almrei and Adil Charkaoui. Four of the detainees were held in a maximum security facility notoriously known as Guantanamo North. From 2002 onward, a well-coordinated movement to abolish security certificates and support the detainees emerged in almost every major city across the country. Committees such as the Justice Coalition for Adil Charkaoui, Justice for Mohamed Harkat, and Justice for Mahjoub Network consisting of migrant justice activists, family members, Muslim organizations and antiracists sprang up to support individual detainees while also mobilizing broader public support against security certificates.

There have been significant victories in this campaign. None of the five men have been deported. No new certificate has been issued since the campaign gained national prominence in 2003. Detainees were released, though on stringent conditions, after years of harrowing incarceration. While a limited victory since the legislation was reformed instead of completely scrapped, the post-9/11 security certificate regime was struck down by the Supreme Court of Canada in 2007. Two of the detainees had the cases against them completely quashed in 2009, and Guantanamo North was eventually shut down in 2011.

I remember attending the initial meetings and gatherings in Montreal to denounce Charkaoui's arrest on a security certificate in 2003. The first few rallies brought out only a handful of people, led by Hind Charkaoui, Adil's sister, and Mary Foster, an anti-capitalist and migrant justice activist who would end up being one of the many indefatigable organizers within the campaign. Slowly but surely, over the next six years—and to some degree, continuing today—a national campaign developed to highlight the injustices of security certificates. At the peak of the campaign between 2005 and 2006, critics of security certificates included Human Rights Watch, Amnesty International, three UN committees, politicians from every level of government, the Canadian Bar Association and the International Civil Liberties Monitoring Group.

This growing momentum was possible due to a widespread, multi-pronged grassroots campaign to empower and support detainees and their families to lead this struggle while building as many alliances as possible. This is the principle of uniting all who can be united. Radicals are often skeptical of moving beyond our own ideological and political circles. There is a valid concern about lowest-common-denominator coalition politics, wherein aligning with others who have a more mainstream analysis will necessarily change the message to a minimalist one that everyone can agree to. Effective campaigns, however, do require us to bring in and work alongside those who may not share our systemic analysis.

So how do we build alliances without devolving into a race to the bottom that dilutes our principles? One approach is to build strategic alliances to meet others where they are comfortable, while maintaining the autonomy to shape our own work. In this campaign, instead of a formal coalition, groups are loosely aligned through the overarching framework of End Secret Trials. This creates the momentum for a diversity of strategies that allows groups to contribute what they are best suited for—legal submissions, petitioning, lobbying, educational forums or actions—without having to be responsible for others' tactics or messaging.

Co-optation of the campaign toward mainstream legal reform has not been a significant issue because grassroots migrant justice activists alongside family members of the detainees were able to establish a firm foundation for the anti-security certificates campaign. The sustained consciousness-raising and careful leadership of radicals unexpectedly brought many mainstream allies into the campaign for complete abolition of security certificates, rather than mere legal reform. Under the new reformed legislation, three men continue to have outstanding security certificates. The veneer of fairness exhibited by the new law masks the fact that these Muslim men are still facing possible deportation to torture, are living under draconian conditions of house arrest, and have to defend themselves against vague allegations without being charged. Sophie Harkat, Mohamed's wife, calls this "out with the old, in with the old!" (Harkat, 2011).

Another notable aspect of the campaign has been the emphasis on anti-racism as a key analytic framework through which to oppose security certificates. The main demands of the campaign are the abolition of security certificates, an end to all deportations to torture, and an end to the racist scapegoating of Muslim and Arab communities. This stands in contrast to the dominant discourse in the United States to shut down Guantanamo Bay that stresses the exceptional legal nature of the detentions. As scholar Luke Vervaet asserts, "Even if Guantánamo eventually closes, the problem that Guantánamo symbolizes—the lawlessness, racism and imperialist mentality of the powerful—remains" (Vervaet, 2010). While the particular civil liberties violations of security-related detentions are abhorrent, the suggestion that they are arbitrary or exceptional obscures the fact that they are a deliberate extension of the torture, killings, Islamophobia and colonial crusading that marks the global War on Terror.

The main effectiveness of this campaign, therefore, has been the consistent call for the abolition of security certificates, forwarded through a principled analysis of systemic racism along with widespread education to build support for this position. There is now an extraordinary understanding within much of the broader Left that mere legal reform through "fairer" trials misses the mark. Legal instruments such as security certificates are selectively deployed against certain noncitizen communities caught in the tentacles of the racialized global empire. During the June 2006 Freedom Caravan, when dozens of events were organized leading up to the Supreme Court constitutional challenge to security certificates, there was focused attention on grassroots, radical and anti-racist struggles beyond the courtroom. Matthew Behrens of the Campaign to Stop Secret Trials wrote at the time, "Although the Supreme Court hearings will be a significant moment, they are not the end of the road. Indeed, no matter how the Court rules, spy agency CSIS and the cruel bureaucracy of Canadian Immigration are likely to continue their harassment of immigrant and refugee communities" (Behrens, 2006). The campaign to end secret trials and abolish security certificates has been critical in highlighting the dehumanizing experiences of security certificate detainees as part of a wider struggle to dismantle the racism inherent in state securitization.

Canada Is Illegal

The slogan No One Is Illegal, Canada Is Illegal was popularized at a rally during the 2005 International Indigenous Youth Conference in Vancouver. NOII-Vancouver (Indigenous Coast Salish territories) was involved in supporting this conference by providing logistical assistance, translation and child care. Through this process, we built relationships with the Indigenous youth organizers and shared stories about our homelands, the idea of "belonging" within Canada, and global resistance to imperialism. At the end of the conference, a rally took to the streets, and we suddenly heard the emcee chanting "No One Is Illegal, Canada Is Illegal." Since then, we have been using that slogan as a key framework toward decolonization and our collective liberation.

Within the migrant justice movement, there has been much discussion on how we understand the positioning of migrants of colour within settler colonialism. While I believe that migrants of colour are inevitably implicated in settler colonialism and have a responsibility to ally with Indigenous struggles, I do not believe that migration as a process in and of itself, especially in this late period of capitalist globalization and global neo-colonialism, can inherently be understood as a form of settler colonialism. Settler colonialism is an ideology that seeks to dominate, control and commodify communities and lands, while migration—largely characterized as precarious migration—is an expression of self-determination. Displacement and precarious migration are products of colonialism and capitalism, and it would be a mistake to identify all those who migrate, whether as refugees or immigrant workers, as those seeking to colonize. Andrea Smith (2010) notes that "without a critique of the settler state as simultaneously also white supremacist, all 'settlers' become morally undifferentiated" (77). NOII-Montreal member Jaggi Singh similarly maintains that "settlement is as much an ideology as a practice, and the only way to escape complicity with settlement is active opposition to it. I do organize on the basis of a vision for no borders and free movement. But, I have never heard of an Indigenous theory of decolonization that is about expulsion—expulsion of a corporate mine perhaps—but never of people who migrate to achieve dignity in their lives" (Henaway, 2007).

As a migrant myself, I realize that migrant justice will be short-lived if gained at the expense of Indigenous self-determination. Many other members of NOII are also cautious to not call for a simple unity between migrants of colour and Indigenous communities. Despite the violence of deportation and detention against nonstatus migrants along with the racialization of immigrant communities as eternal outsiders, oversimplifications that suggest our struggles are the same as those of Indigenous peoples are irresponsible. The founding violence of settler colonialism is, by definition, against Indigenous people. We cannot ignore or minimize the reality of genocide of Indigenous peoples and the ongoing erasure of Indigenous sovereignty on these lands. Given the devastating cultural, spiritual, economic, linguistic and political impacts of colonialism on Indigenous nations across Turtle Island, all social and environmental justice movements, including migrant justice movements, must involve nonnative solidarity in the fight against colonization.

Cultivating an ethic of responsibility among migrants of colour toward Indigenous struggles is essential. We have to understand ourselves as those displaced victims of global empire and capitalism who enter into, and hence become complicit in and benefit from, the processes of colonization in North America. This means we have to go beyond a politics of optional alliance. We cannot debate the merits of whether or not to align with Indigenous communities; we are *obligated* to educate ourselves and each other about the histories of the illegal settlement and appropriation of Indigenous lands. NOII members have, for example, consistently translated and included Indigenous communiqués into immigrant community publications, appeared on multilingual radio stations to increase the understanding of Indigenous issues within immigrant communities, hosted discussions within community and faith centres about Indigenous histories, and frequently facilitated the travel of migrant and refugee delegations to Indigenous land reclamations to hear first-hand from Indigenous communities. This awareness leads to the active participation of migrant communities in the struggle for decolonization.

Engaging in decolonization struggles also involves tangible solidarity with Indigenous communities. Since 2003, NOII-Vancouver

(Indigenous Coast Salish territories) has been supporting the Skwelkwek'welt Protection Centre against tourism, mining and real estate development on Secwepemc lands, located in the interior of the province. This has included monthly pickets, public events, court support as well as fundraising to support speaking tours, community land reclamation and language revitalization efforts. NOII was also involved in organizing an historic convergence against the Sun Peaks Resort that brought hundreds of migrant justice activists, Palestinian refugees, environmentalists and anti-capitalists into the community to construct a Secwepemc resistance camp on the land.

Many solidarity activists enter Indigenous communities during moments of crisis—for instance, to support a blockade against development—and exit shortly thereafter. But as feminist writer bell hooks reminds us, "Solidarity is not the same as support. To experience solidarity, we must have a community of interests, shared beliefs and goals around which to unite, to build Sisterhood. Support can be occasional. It can be given and just as easily withdrawn. Solidarity requires sustained, ongoing commitment" (Hooks, 2000). The relationship between Secwepemc land defenders and NOII has continued for ten years, with frequent delegations, meetings, strategizing workshops and a deepening of personal trust and respect. It has been a central experience in informing my own learning about the depth and breadth of resistance and resilience within Indigenous communities—from stewardship of the land to cultural resurgence, from affirming natural laws to learning the centrality of prophecies and ceremonies. Rather than campaign-based or NGO approaches to working with Indigenous communities—approaches that can seem manipulative and goal-oriented—our focus has been on building relationships and trust with no ulterior motive other than learning Indigenous histories, offering support to front-line communities, and sharing visions for our futures.

The Indigenous Defenders of the Land network recently brought together grassroots land defenders from dozens of Indigenous communities across Canada. As part of these historic Defenders of the Land gatherings, NOII groups and a few other allies were invited to participate in and support the network. We worked with other activists to develop a Supporters Declaration, which in part reads:

> As non-Indigenous supporters, we have come from different places and we have come for different reasons. As multiracial settlers, migrants, refugees, and descendants of slaves, we came across many oceans or continents, four hundred years ago or yesterday. Many of us feel deeply attached to places across Turtle Island, but we recognize that our homes are built on the ruins of others. We are on the lands of Indigenous peoples: lands unjustly seized, unsurrendered lands, treaty lands, and urbanized lands (Defenders of the Land, 2008).

This declaration and the process that led to it are significant for two reasons. First, they highlighted that migrant justice activists have been identified by Indigenous communities themselves as having worked on Indigenous solidarity efforts, which usually tend to be dominated by white solidarity activists. Second, they articulated a shift in nonnative solidarity discourse toward understanding the layered, differential dynamics of settlement to include oppressed peoples who are differently complicit in settler colonialism than those with white settler background and privilege.

Steady relationship-building, mutual learning and sharing of experiences, and solidarity delegations to Indigenous communities have led to powerful reciprocities between migrants of colour and Indigenous people. One of my first experiences of the revolutionary possibility of such alliances was at a march in 2003 by the Action Committee for Nonstatus Algerians, where Tyendinaga Mohawk activist Shawn Brant expressed his support for the fight against deportations. Brant, himself imprisoned numerous times for his stand against corporate and colonial development on Indigenous land, stood outside the Citizenship and Immigration offices and welcomed nonstatus Algerians on to Turtle Island. He not only expressed solidarity but also affirmed Indigenous jurisdiction over the land as a direct challenge to the Canadian state's authority to execute deportations. The hairs on my arms again stood up when, years later, I watched Melissa Elliott, the cofounder of Young Onkwehonwe United, give a powerful speech at an NOII rally. She proclaimed to a crowd of thousands of migrants and allies that "the Canadian government has no jurisdiction in our lands to be deporting you people, to be treating you the way that they are, or us the way that they are" (No One Is Illegal-Toronto, 2011).

I have been humbled by the gestures of Indigenous communities to consistently welcome displaced migrants and refugees onto their lands. In 2010, when 492 Tamil refugees aboard the *MV Sun Sea* arrived on the shores of the west coast and faced immediate incarceration, Indigenous elders opened the weekly demonstrations outside the jails by welcoming the refugees. As their contributions toward a national day of action to support the detained Tamil refugees, the Lhe Lin Liyin of the Wet'suwet'en nation hung a banner affirming "We welcome refugees." And as part of this same national day of action, Pierre Beaulieu-Blais, an Indigenous Anishnabe member of NOII-Ottawa, declared, "From one community of resistance to another, we welcome you. As people who have also lost our land and been displaced because of colonialism and racism, we say Open All the Borders! Status for All!" (No One Is Illegal, 2010). Such public affirmations subvert state controls and colonially imposed divisions in profound ways.

In describing Indigenous host laws that are still alive on these lands, Indigenous feminist writer Lee Maracle articulates how Indigenous laws offer a clear counter to colonial immigration laws. She says:

> You [migrants] have a counter-law. It is my law. It is the host law of Indigenous people. Everybody eats, every woman has a right to a house, and everyone has access to the wealth of the land.... As you respect and honour Indigenous sovereignty, you also take on the law and the legal framework of our people here.... We are all here to conjure up a living with each other.... No one is illegal, no one is a bastard child, no one is an illegal alien. We have to get that very clear in our minds, and in our hearts, and in our bodies, and move with it.... So if you support Indigenous sovereignty, you are also supporting No One Is Illegal, there is no disconnect between those two things (Maracle, 2011).

As Maracle suggests, there is nothing contradictory about supporting struggles for migrant justice and Indigenous self-determination; our liberation is interconnected. As migrants of colour, understanding ourselves as complicit within settler colonialism, taking up the responsibility to educate our communities about Indigenous histories on the lands we reside on, and prioritizing active support for Indigenous self-determination are three critical steps in building long-term alliances with Indigenous communities. Simple calls for racial unity between migrants of colour, particularly non-Black immigrant communities, and Indigenous people obscure the matrix of differential racial power within settler colonialism. Through engaged relations based on solidarity and respect, NOII-Vancouver (Indigenous Coast Salish territories) has started to identify and organize as an explicitly *anti-colonial* migrant justice group. This reflects our belief that our visions must steer away from seeking greater recognition from a colonial system and go beyond demanding citizenship rights from a settler state. Slowly, we are negotiating a decolonized path toward relations based on dismantling settler colonialism through the affirmation of Indigenous self-determination and the welcoming of migrants to live in respectful relationship to existing communities and the land.

Anti-Capitalist Resistance

Canada has one of the highest proportions of low-paid workers in the industrialized world (Chow, 2009). Labour precarity under capitalism is most acute for migrant and undocumented workers, and is evident in the state's thrust to expand temporary worker programs. Canada now accepts more migrants under temporary permits than those who can come permanently (Canadian Council for Refugees, n.d.).

Accordingly, NOII groups have been working within the labour movement to link immigrants' rights to workers' rights. In Vancouver, one of the dialogue sessions between union delegates and migrant justice organizations resulted in a set of resolutions that vows to "work to build solidarity between unionized workers, non unionized workers—recognizing that (im)migrant and nonstatus workers often fill non unionized, precarious jobs and that the struggle of (im)migrants encompasses the movement against neoliberal exploitation and against war, occupation, poverty, and displacement" (No One Is Illegal-Vancouver, 2007). Annual May Day (International Workers' Day) marches also provide a critical framework to link workers' struggles and movements against neoliberal capitalism to migrant justice.

The influence of NOII groups within anti-capitalist and anti-authoritarian movements is also noteworthy. In 2000, with her influential piece "Where Was the Color in Seattle?" Elizabeth Martinez sparked conversations within the anti-globalization movement about "summit hopping"—and the privileges associated with it, such as travelling across the continent—as opposed to prioritizing local resistance. Being grounded in local community struggles is critical; however, I believe that as a strategy, mega-mobilizations against the global elite should not be dismissed outright as symbolic rituals of privileged protest. These actions are necessary to assert and be invigorated by our collective power of refusal, to delegitimize and disrupt the institutions of capitalism and imperialism, to increase the social and financial costs for elites at these summits, to strengthen our networks of resistance across often-disparate movements, and to actualize freer social relations through the process of engaging in struggle.

Movements such as NOII, along with Indigenous as well as poor and working-class movements, help bridge anti-capitalist movements with the strength of local resistance. In 2002, the anti-capitalist Take the Capital convergence was announced in Ottawa to oppose a meeting of the G8 leaders taking place in Kananaskis, Alberta. Coordinated through People's Global Action, a decentralized network of anti-capitalist groups across Ontario and Québec, an NOII march endorsed by over a hundred groups was held on the first of these days of action. "No One Is Illegal: A March of 1,000 Flags of Resistance" expressed opposition to racism, imperialism and genocide as well as affirmed solidarity with global self-determination struggles and Indigenous sovereignty. As the notice for the march emphasized, "The new 'war on terror' is really something very old—the continuance of systematic policies of exploitation and dispossession" (No One Is Illegal, 2012).

This march brought together local immigrant community organizations, Palestinian refugee and Latin American diasporic groups working on international solidarity campaigns, and grassroots Indigenous land defenders from the region. It was one of most diverse and genuinely representative anti-capitalist marches that I had witnessed at the time. While the tone of the march did not involve direct action, it expressed solidarity with separate, more confrontational actions.

This marked the first of many similar NOII actions and contingents during anti-capitalist convergences, including against the WTO mini-ministerial meeting in Montreal in 2003, the Security and Prosperity Partnership summit in Montebello in 2007, the 2010 Winter Olympics in Vancouver, and the G20 meetings in Toronto in 2010.

NOII groups in Vancouver and Toronto were involved in cofounding the Olympic Resistance Network in 2008 and Toronto Community Mobilization Network in 2010. These networks organized the cross-country No Olympics on Stolen Native Land campaign and anti-G20 convergence. These convergences had three notable achievements. First, they served to successfully link anti-capitalist movements to community resistance. Beyond articulating an ideological opposition to capitalism, these convergences explicitly named—and did active outreach to—those most impacted by capitalism: migrants, workers, Indigenous and rural communities, poor and homeless people, and diasporic communities from the Global South. This allowed local community groups to see their specific issues mirrored within an anti-capitalist movement. Alliances strengthened between migrant justice, Indigenous, antiwar, queer and trans, environmental, anarchist, labour, disability rights and antipoverty groups. Geographer David Harvey observes that "the unities beginning to emerge around these different vectors of struggle are vital to nurture for within them we can discern the lineaments of an entirely different, non-imperialistic, form of globalization" (Harvey, 2005b: 83). By articulating and enacting a politics that is relevant across communities, while also facilitating an anti-capitalist basis of unity across struggles, we create a potentially potent and revolutionary movement.

Second, both convergences were organized on an anti-capitalist *and* anti-colonial basis. This reflects the oft-repeated call by Indigenous communities that Indigenous self-determination must become more central within social and environmental struggles. Rather than being a single issue within a longer laundry list, the recognition of Indigenous self-determination was the foundation for mobilizing against the Olympics, as No Olympics on Stolen Native Land became the rallying call for the campaign over four years. Indigenous land defenders, especially those from the St'at'imc and Secwepemc communities, and Indigenous people residing in low-income urban neighbourhoods in Vancouver led a groundswell of popular resistance against the Olympics. On the first day of the anti-Olympics convergence, a No One Is Illegal, Canada Is Illegal contingent walked alongside Indigenous elders and land defenders who were leading the march. In Toronto, one of the main days of action against the G20 was called Canada Can't Hide Genocide, an Indigenous-organized day of action. One of the long-term impacts of these mobilizations has been more widespread dialogue among movements at a national level about strengthening an anticolonial politics as well as understanding the connection between capitalism and colonialism, and their impacts, as being mutually reinforcing.

Finally, despite preemptive infiltration of activist groups by state intelligence officers and intimidation of organizers by law enforcement, the anti-Olympics and anti-G20 convergences saw an escalation in confrontational tactics. Leadership of racialized, queer, disabled and poor people's movements during these convergences is evidence of the commitment and courage of marginalized communities to participate in militant social struggle. Some of those who risked arrest and faced charges lacked full citizenship status. Like the Undocumented and Unafraid actions and DREAM activists in the United States, they exhibited moral fortitude despite risking possible deportation. Several NOII members faced lengthy trials on trumped-up, politically motivated charges for being so-called ringleaders in anti-G20 mobilizing.

Activists Clare O'Connor and Kalin Stacey write that the challenge of revolutionary organizing is "to build a base capable of not only appealing to constituted power but of displacing it" (O'Connor & Stacey, 2012). Migrant justice organizers, some without full immigration status, remain on the front lines daily, affirming our visions of and organizing toward a world free of border controls and state violence, where people have the right to stay, freedom to move, and right to return; where liberated communities have control over their own lands, lives and labour, and where each of us is able to self-determine and express our dreams and desires free of the coercive, oppressive, exploitative relations of capitalism and colonialism.

ON SOLIDARITY AND COUNTER-HEGEMONY

The philosophers have only interpreted the world,
in various ways; the point is to change it.
—KARL MARX

INTERNATIONALIZING THE STRUGGLE
From Slogans to Class Politics

Sam Gindin

In apportioning blame for the labour movement's precipitous decline in the developed world, a special responsibility is placed on the capitalism-on-geographic-steroids that we dub "globalization"—a capitalism that has come to "nestle everywhere, settle everywhere, establish connexions everywhere" (Marx & Engels, 1998: 4). Not to be undone, governments (not least governments supported by the labour movement) justify the erosion of social standards, even as technology and profits advance and the concentration of wealth accelerates, by appealing to the mantra "globalization made us do it."

The argument is straightforward. If corporations are free to move, then workers, unions and even worker-friendly governments are pressured to compete to retain or attract investment and the jobs and tax revenue such investment brings. The social impact that follows is profound. It not only directly undermines the living standards of working people but also, by way of the implications of the competitive restructuring of the economy, affects the internal cohesion of the working class and consequently its capacity to act as a countervailing social force. The spread of value chains, the accelerated growth in precarious work (an aspect of increased inequalities within the working class), the breakup of communities with a previous solidaristic culture, the perpetual insecurity—all this contributes to undermining the development of workers into an effective collectivity standing against capital.

One counter-response has been to match the advanced internationalization of capital with a parallel internationalization of working-class solidarity. In one particular form, it looks to extend domestic collective bargaining across borders and on occasion—here too mimicking corporations—to cross-border union mergers. A different reaction, prevalent in the social justice movements, looks to a universalism focused on minimum standards to protect all workers. Abroad, it attacks multinational corporations and their suppliers in the Global South that have particularly bad working conditions and pay. At home, it argues for "open borders" that treat all workers the same independent of their home country. And to enforce standards that competing states would otherwise sacrifice to attract capital, this orientation turns for enforcement to international "para-state" institutions like the United Nations, International Labour Organization and World Bank.

Such responses, however well-meaning and morally attractive, have had limited salience. That alone may of course simply reflect how difficult it is to deal with the complexities of globalization. The argument made here, however, is that this goes beyond "complexities"; these kinds of reactions cannot, by their very nature, succeed. They ultimately only offer slogans—and often empty or even dangerous slogans at that. In the sections that follow I elaborate this criticism and root its misguided internationalism in a misunderstanding of the nature of the weakness of labour in the Global "North" and a failure to properly grasp the continuing centrality, even under globalization, of nation-states. I conclude with a discussion of what a more grounded and promising working-class internationalism—a true international solidarity—might entail.

International Unionism?

It's hardly surprising that nation-based unions, confronting multinational corporations, would be attracted to a strategy pointing towards cross-border collective bargaining. Yet once we turn to the daunting practical barriers involved, this is no longer self-evident. In fact it appears otherworldly to expect unions that have been so unable to develop solidarity at home to have the will and capacity to do so internationally. If unions haven't been able to organize precarious workers at home; if cross-union city-wide cooperation to organize fast food workers (and other workers not directly vulnerable to jobs leaving the country) has been so rare; if there is so little solidarity between auto and steel workers, private and public sector workers, or workers in Alberta and Ontario—where then are the grounds for raising the banner of international solidarity across the vaster distances of geography, culture, legal frameworks and economic differences?

The main issue here is in fact not so much that of overcoming the barriers to cooperating across borders but the *kind* of unions undertaking this task. Globalization has undoubtedly had a negative impact on unions in the developed countries, but why were they so unable to block or at least limit globalization as it unfolded? And even if there were originally mixed feelings about globalization's implications (some workers expected to gain as exporters or consumers), why, as the costs became clearer, was labour so unable to mobilize for the reversal of globalization or at least place significant limits on its further development? Why, in key sectors like auto—where the US and (Canadian) industries were not so much "hollowed out" as *restructured* through the shift of assembly plants, outsourced components and an influx of foreign investment to rural areas and the American South—were unions so incapable of unionizing these facilities? Furthermore, globalization included its own contradictions. Value chains, for example, leave corporations extremely susceptible to costly interruptions in one link in the chain. Why then have there been so few examples of the labour movement taking advantage of such corporate vulnerabilities?

The point is that while globalization certainly aggravated labour's weakness, the labour movement has had long-standing and serious internal problems *globalization apart*. In the US, by the end of the 1940s communists were being marginalized and unions faced the aggressions of a state solidifying the domestic conditions for US capital moving outward. In that context, unions accepted an economistic productivism rooted in sharing the pie rather than challenging control over production and investment. This accommodation to capitalism, along with the diffusion of US unionism abroad, was a crucial condition for—and not just the outcome of—furthering the American empire and the making of a global capitalism. Even as workers retained their economic militancy through the 1960s, their limited political orientation and the legalistic capacities that increasingly replaced workplace and community organizing soon left unions on the sidelines in terms of the large questions of their times.

The real dilemma facing unions as globalization threatened labour and social standards was therefore not primarily a matter of how to extend their geographic space, but of whether they could escape their deep-seated sectionalism. That is, whether they could move beyond their focus on particular group interests and the development of essentially private welfare states towards a class-based political unionism. Ironically, at the very time in the 1970s that the limits of American unionism were becoming more evident, a push was emerging among some labour leaders and academics to "develop structures with which they could mirror the reach of the MNC's, with which they could eventually engage in transnational collective bargaining" (Munck, 2002: 145).[72] This tended to set aside the deeper challenges the movement faced. International solidarity was the slogan, but the underlying thrust was essentially the internationalization of business unionism.

This process did sometimes include genuine solidaristic intentions, but the primary message in mobilizing workers to this cause was the instrumental goal of raising wages elsewhere so as to save jobs at home. At home, this reinforced the sectionalism of unions in a way that a broader political perspective might have countered. Overseas, this focus on supporting higher wages in sectors that were generally already relatively highly paid by local standards (e.g. the Mexican auto industry) risked further isolating these workers from other workers—a highly problematic process when the real need was for strengthening the domestic class solidarity essential to the politics of economic development. Especially in the 1970s, when liberation movements were being crushed or integrated, this economistic "internationalism" fit all too comfortably with the imperial project of depoliticizing class relations and establishing the favourable conditions abroad for the making of a global capitalism.

A related observation might be made about the more recent interest in cross-border union mergers. Such mergers might of course be positive in particular circumstances. But to workers asking how their union is responding to incessant attacks, posing the answer in terms of organizational size and resources diverts attention from looking inward to the failures of unions structures and strategies. Bureaucratic reorganization becomes the fix, not issues of union democracy, activating existing members, organizing new members, or building the class across unions and in the community.

72 An especially influential book in this regard was Charles Levinson's book on international trade unionism (1972).

This is as well the lesson in the experience of the international confederations of trade unions which go back to Marx and his involvement in the formation of the International Workingmen's Association (The First International) in 1864. These attempts have floundered on sectarian debates and jurisdictional divisions, but the larger problem is that their relevance is conditional on the existence of coherent working classes within each national space that have a unifying vision of a working-class movement with the ideological, institutional and strategic capacity to act independent of capital and capitalist states. Without that, as Dan Gallin, longtime head of the International Union of Food Workers warned in a recent speech, "you can have international trade union organizations, even large ones, but you cannot have international policies that show the way forward, nor can you have international action that is more than a feeble defensive reflex" (Gallin, 2015).[73]

Universal Rights?

A different approach to defending and raising standards in the face of globalization looked to universalizing basic standards in pay and workplace rights, an obviously admirable goal. This contributed to exposing the conditions in the foreign operations of "our" corporations and introduced a good many young people to social and union activism. But though the sentiment is noble, the politics are naïve. The focus on victims and guilt obscures the structural dimensions of these conditions and the depth of the solutions consequently needed. Focusing on bad capitalists implies there are good capitalists and ignores the steamroller of corporations responding to the ever intensifying competitive pressures of the overall system. And winning more humane standards without those affected having the organization to enforce them inevitably leads to limited and vulnerable gains.

An associated example that parallels the seduction of international unions being the pinnacle of solidarity is the notion that

73 For a short overview of the minefield of international union restructuring see Rudolf Traub-Merz and Jürgen Eckl, International Trade Union Movement: Mergers and Contradictions, Briefing Papers, No. 1, Friedrich Ebert Stiftung, 2007. Can be retrieved at http://www.library.fes.de/pdf-files/iez/04589.pdf.

open borders—the right to move anywhere and achieve equal citizenship—is the moral pinnacle of universal rights. Here too, however high-minded the intentions, practical considerations bring daunting tensions. Though US- or Canadian-born workers might be won over to a relatively more humanitarian immigration and refugee policy, the complete end of borders is a de facto non-starter. This is so especially when the erosion of the welfare state has created a meaner sense of basic rights even among its own citizens. In the absence of structures and policies to deal with worker insecurities, and with open-ended migration amounting to or being perceived as increasing the reserve army of the unemployed to the end of weakening domestic labour standards, the call for open borders can only lead to a backlash.

More significant, however, it is not at all clear how progressive this goal of open borders actually is. This is perhaps most evident when proponents argue that if corporations should be free to move and obtain equal treatment within states, so should individuals. Though such liberal rights should certainly not be written off, they should give us pause. Looked at from a class perspective, it raises a number of questions that tend to qualify even the moral rightness of open doors. Isn't the real issue that of collective development in the South, not confronting individuals with unpalatable choices that include allowing some of them to escape to the North? Given who is most capable of moving, might not an acceleration of individual mobility mean a costly brain drain from the South to the North, an implicit transfer of previous social investments? Would movement to the North by those most able and determined to do so mean, as Judy Hellman (1994) has argued in the case of Mexico, a loss to the South of potential leaders fighting for domestic change?

Turning to the enforcement concerns of the universalization of standards, since this is rooted in the workers themselves not being able to do so, it raises the question of the role of states. The understanding that globalization has bypassed states implies the need for some supranational agency to take on the enforcement role, and this shifts attention to what have been seen as the emerging "international para-states" mentioned earlier (UN, ILO, World Bank). But these international institutions hardly stand above states. They are creatures of nation-states and whatever autonomy they have is limited by those constituent states and the power balance within them. It has been nation-states that organized and established the framework of free trade agreements, endorsed the free flow of capital, enshrined equal treatment for foreign capital, etc.[74] As with international trade union solidarity, universal standards can only be achieved through struggles affecting the balance of social forces where power matters most: at the level of the nation-state.

The Bypassing of States?

It may be counterintuitive that in a discussion of working-class *internationalism* we place so much emphasis on the centrality of *nation* states as the critical site of struggle. After all, doesn't the internationalization of the space of accumulation contradict the territorially bounded space of nation-states and relegate nation-states to secondary importance?

To begin with, the significance of the nation-state doesn't lie in "logical" arguments derived from economic structures but in three historical realities. First, nation-states were and remain fundamental to the making of global capitalism. States are not powerless victims of globalization, but as Leo Panitch (1994) has emphasized, its actual *authors*. With globalization, corporations have not bypassed states but have come to depend on *many* states (and the American state above all) for establishing and reproducing the conditions for a global capitalism (Panitch & Gindin, 2012). Second, the relative weights of collective bargaining and state action in determining the conditions of working people has shifted in recent decades towards the impact of states: e.g. freer trade, the erosion of social programs and austerity, privatizations of public assets, tax policy, attacks on the institution of trade unionism. Third, the development of workers into a social

74 In the case of NAFTA, for example, the pressures for this agreement didn't come from an external international body, and though businesses in each of the countries had lobbied for formalizing freer trade, the actual mobilization for NAFTA was led by the Canadian and Mexican states who were looking to guarantee their access to American investment and markets in the context of rumbles of American protectionism.

force with the power to address their needs is shaped domestically, within and against their nation-states.

The contradiction between internationalized capital and nation-states played itself out in the first half of the 20th century in the form of two world wars and a global depression that dramatically interrupted international trade and capital flows. As World War II came to an end, it seemed to many that an international capitalism was actually impossible precisely because there was no international state or state-like institution with the capacity to support the international property rights such a capitalism required. Later, as globalization in fact proceeded, this was mistakenly understood as marginalizing states.

It was the American state that squared the circle and established the conditions for making a global capitalism not only possible, but able to expand to previously unimaginable scales. For American elites, recent history had made it clear that the expanded reproduction of domestic capital depended on an open global order. And of even greater importance, the history of the American state and especially the experiences and institutional changes from the Great Depression on, had created the actual capacities within the American state (and American capital) for carrying this through.

Key to the uneven historical process that followed was the post-war waning of former empires and the gradual integration of the former imperial powers into an American-led informal global empire. This led, over a longer period, to the more complex integration of key economies and states of the Global South. What emerged was an empire of sovereign states, with each state being internationalized in the sense of taking responsibility for the reproduction of global capital *within their borders* and agreeing to *international rules that framed a liberal global capitalism* (Poulantzas, 1974: 73; Panitch & Gindin, 2012: 4, 8).

Tensions between states of course continued and states still competed for investment, export markets and jobs. But against those who still looked to the politicization of competition and inter-imperial rivalry, that competition was now generally channelled into a liberal framework in which foreign capital was increasingly treated as no different from domestic capital. Corporations could be attracted through more favourable taxation and "competitive" labour markets, but not by imposing tariffs or conditions on them. International agreements institutionalized those rules.

The neoliberal response to the crisis of the '70s, unlike that of the 1930s, did not lead to an interruption in the globalization process but in fact accelerated it. Neoliberalism was integral to this. Under the leadership of the American state, competitive tensions shifted from inter-state rivalries to class conflicts and discipline *within* each state. The profound effect was to further disorganize working classes that were already stumbling. At the same time, the extent to which inter-imperial rivalry was no longer a substantive factor was made clear when, in the midst of the Great Financial Crisis of the new millennium, the commitment to avoid protectionism was made and kept by virtually all states.

As states competed to make their own territories most competitive and supported the restructuring of international accumulation, generally at the cost of working-class standards, this raised the stakes for working-class internationalism. But, to re-emphasize an insistent theme in this chapter, only classes that developed a degree of unity and coherence within their own social formation, rooted in their history, culture and struggles against employers and their own state, could significantly contribute to that internationalism.

Competitiveness: Goal or Constraint?

No issue is more important to workers than to earn a livelihood through employment. And no solidarity is possible, national or international, if workers are in an endless competition with other workers for those jobs. Competition serves as a faceless constraint on working-class expectations and possibilities and thereby on building the working class as a social force. Neoliberal globalization in particular boxed workers into buying their jobs through restraint or concessions. Though many unionized workers in the Global North at first resisted these pressures, the concern to hang on to the very gains achieved through previous decades made them more amenable to some concessions to preserve the bulk of those past gains even if this undermined other workers.

American pulp-fiction writer Don Westlake (1997) satirically captured this fractious desperation. It begins with a now common event: a lower-level American manager in his late 40s is laid off from a pulp mill that is moving to Brazil and confronts the possibility that he may never again get a comparable job. Anxious about what he'll be up against as he re-enters the labour market, he puts an ad in local papers for a fictitious job based on his own particular strengths. Responses flow in and he carefully narrows them down to the six competitors he might face if a real job came up. He contemplates his situation: "...If I were to kill a thousand stockholders and get away with it clean, what would I gain?... If I were to kill seven chief executives, each of whom had ordered the firing of at least two thousand good workers in healthy industries, what would I get out of it?... Nothing." He concludes that "the CEOs and the stockholders who put them there are the enemy, but they are not the problem. They are society's problem, but not my personal problem.... These six résumés. These are my personal problem" (51-52). Reluctantly, he concludes that to adequately support his family again he must, literally, be ready to "kill for a job." He must get rid of the senders of those six résumés.

Heavy-handed as the black humour might be, it captures the reality that if we can't cope with competitiveness ideologically and practically, we can neither build the class at home nor act as internationalists. In the private sector, competitiveness translates into dependency on the survival of the employer; in the public sector it demands, in the context of a capitalist society, a growing private sector to finance social programs. In both cases, class solidarity tends to give way to identification with individual employers or the strength of domestic capital.

Competitiveness, it is important to soberly stress, is not just an ideological weapon used against workers; it is a real-world constraint. But there is the greatest difference between acknowledging a constraint that workers must deal with, as opposed to raising it to the status of a goal by way of the oxymoron of "progressive competitiveness." As a goal, the underlying principle of competitiveness—that access to jobs for some essentially comes at the expense of others—is morally indefensible. And at best, it promises permanent insecurity since even "winning" is an inherently temporary and fragile circumstance.[75]

Pursuing competitiveness is ultimately destructive to building any kind of independent political capacity because the alliances it invites are with "our employers" (whether home or foreign-based), while the enemy it identifies is other workers and other nations. There is in this regard also a class asymmetry in the implications of competition. For capital, competition may destroy particular competitors but as other more effective capitalists replace them, this process may strengthen capital as a class. For workers, competition undermines their primary vehicle for self-defence—their solidarity—and so weakens them as a class.

It is equally important to stress that to reject competitiveness is not to reject being "productive," but to distinguish between being productive for capital, and developing workers' individual and collective capacities to democratically address their needs. The issue therefore is how to cope with this constraint as part of also struggling to stretch it, limit it, and eventually eradicate its dominance over working-class lives. On the terrain of competitiveness, the removal of tools and equipment from a community may be rational; on the terrain of democratic capacities this robs workers and their communities of their productive potentials. Competitiveness directs training towards teaching workers to adapt to technology; the focus on democratic capacities looks to workers controlling that technology. Competitiveness hoards knowledge; a focus on collective capacities looks to generalize and therefore democratize knowledge.

The problem, in other words, is not the competitive résumés of other workers, bad corporate apples, nor a disembodied, stateless globalization. Rather it is *a system that gives capital the unilateral freedom to restructure production across firms, sectors and borders.* Today, challenging this system especially demands removing the power of finance to impose capitalist discipline—i.e. it points to converting

75 General Motors workers in the US began to accept concessions at the end of the 1970s in order to save jobs, and in each subsequent round the union claimed a successful trade of minor concessions for "job security." At the beginning of that period, GM counted some 450,000 hourly jobs in the US; today it counts some 65,000, a decline of 85%.

finance into a public utility. Limiting capital's freedom to cross borders at will inherently involves a degree of "protectionism," risking a tendency to national chauvinism. It is therefore crucial, as Greg Albo (1997) has insisted, to place this response in the context of attempts to create and protect national spaces for democratic experimentation in alternative ways to organize our lives. What workers are "protecting" themselves from is not other societies (whose popular forces also need to develop such spaces) but capital's unilateral right to decide the allocation of resources, goods, investment and labour. What is being rejected isn't integration into an international economy, but an integration which negates what workers are struggling to build within each of their national spaces.

The Rise of the South: Foundation for a New Internationalism?

The rise of the Global South raised international competition in both the North and the South to merciless new levels. That rise was, for most Marxists, unexpected. In the decades after World War II it had been a staple of Marxist development theory that the dynamics of capitalism and imperialism condemned the Global South to "underdevelopment." Yet taken as a whole the Global South is today a manufacturing powerhouse. While at the end of the 1960s the G7, the most developed capitalist countries, accounted for over 70% of global value-added manufacturing, the manufacturing explosion in the Global South has reduced that to under 50% today (Ferrarini & Hummels, 2014).[76] And currently the 20 fastest growing countries are *all* in the Global South; none of the G7 countries are on that list (Robinson, 2015).

The dramatic transformation of the role of the Global South within capitalism and in particular the doubling of the global proletariat might suggest a broadening basis for a new internationalism. But this change has also multiplied the barriers to realizing that goal.

76 These numbers are very much affected by the emergence of China but they reflect the broader entry into and growth of key countries of the Global South (e.g. Korea, Brazil, India, Turkey, Mexico, Philippines, Taiwan, Indonesia, etc.).

Five specific factors are notable. First, in spite of the advances in the Global South, a global hierarchy in production persists. The highest tech goods and services are still concentrated in the G7, the wage differential between the North and South remains disconcertingly large, and even the "success stories" in the Global South have been concentrated in a few states and regions. It is, as noted earlier, difficult enough to build solidarity in a relatively homogeneous historical space; this is dramatically magnified at the extremely uneven global level.

Second, the integration of the Global South came with the defeat of the former liberation movements. These movements had represented some hope internationally for a broader human liberation and had been the focus of much solidarity work. The depoliticization of struggles in the South, as capitalism came to be the only de facto option, removed an inspiration for international unity. There were of course some counter-examples. Chavez and Morales called for a 21st century international socialism and brought a number of other small countries into the regional cooperative project of ALBA (the Bolivarian Alliance for the Peoples of Our America). But the countries involved represented a fraction of Latin America's population—never mind that of the world as a whole—and in spite of the attempt to set up a regional trade structure, their exports—largely commodities—remained overwhelmingly dependent on the Global North.[77] What has been more instructive has been the political fight taken on *within* these and other Latin American countries against neoliberalism, which brings us back to the national foundations of international struggles.

The interaction of globalization's uneven development with its escalating competition is a third factor. Rather than the spread of proletarianization building on the commonalities of workers, the integration of regions like Asia via the orientation to exporting manufactured goods—as opposed, for example, to a rise in domestic income and the development of internal markets alongside planned trade—pitted workers against each other politically. In the case of free trade, though there was at first some unity around opposition to it as workers worried about the impact on jobs and sovereignty, the South's

77 In the case of Venezuela, 90% of its exports are oil or refined oil products and of the top five destinations for Venezuela's total exports none are in ALBA. Of Bolivia's exports, only 2.4% go to member countries of ALBA.

dependency on markets abroad came to translate the North's opposition into a threat to the South's development. Critiques of free trade from key countries like Brazil and India turned more on removing specific barriers to their interests—essentially a reinforcement of freer trade—than on reversing free trade.

This is directly related to a fourth factor: the Global South emerged in the context of a specifically neoliberal globalization. The aggravation of inequalities within states was hardly conducive to creating a social base, inside unions or out, for the spread of equality across states. This gets us to our final factor: globalization's creation of "third worlds within the first world." As global restructuring pushed immigrants into the Global North, this directly posed the internationalist question within each society. Would the labour movement succumb to a nationalism that blurred class lines and identified these émigrés from the Global South as an undesirable "other," or could the labour movement—as part of its renewal—lead the fight for seeing these immigrants in solidaristic and internationalist terms, as members of their class whose economic, social and political rights must be actively defended?

National Struggles, Internationalist Sensibilities

The central argument of this chapter is that internationalism begins with struggles at home. It must, however, be added that for those whose "home" is in transition, this emphasis has its ambiguities. In the case of migrants, does it represent the home to which they go for work or the place they return to? For migrants and immigrants, does it reference a forsaken historic home with all its roots, or a new home? Such complexities need to be incorporated into our analyses, but they do not negate the point that the struggles of working people and the classes built alongside these struggles must be rooted within particular states. The ambiguities of "home" are a crucial part of that process.

Without strong labour movements within states, calls for internationalism and universal rights will remain at the level of rhetoric and/or posturing. If labour hasn't developed a coherent class culture and capacity to effectively challenge neoliberal individualism and inequality at home, it will hardly have the will or embody the capacity to effect a new internationalism. If it can't retain and build on the welfare state to defend principles of basic social, material and political rights across the nation, labour can hardly be expected to seriously take on the fight for the equality issues surrounding new immigrants. If unions are making concessions in the vain hope of gaining jobs, they are effectively undermining workers elsewhere; only in resisting the lowering of expectations at home can workers create the space for workers in other countries to struggle and make gains.

And it is—not exclusively, but generally—only through struggles in their workplaces, communities and within their own states that the kind of solidaristic culture can emerge that might translate into a solidaristic internationalism. Without such a cultural transformation, it is hard to contemplate the kind of international commitments that are necessary. If, for example, we believe that the environmental crisis imposes limits on the growth of global consumption of individual goods, this has two implications: a shift in values towards collective goods and especially services, and an acceptance that the poorer countries of the globe have a greater moral claim to the world's limited resources. The latter means transferring to the Global South technologies we already have and a significant redistribution of global wealth in their direction. Moreover, such cultural sentiments are of course only the beginning. To actually implement such a radical solidarity is impossible without controlling production and the state.

This is not to say that specific acts of international solidarity must wait for the renewal of national labour movements. Internationalist traditions of the past which, on an ad hoc basis, opposed imperial interventions and supported especially significant strikes and struggles abroad should of course be maintained and expanded. This is not just a matter of respect for the sovereignty and humanity of others but also of keeping progressive experiments and developments elsewhere alive.

In regard to such promising experiments that periodically surface, the bias to cheerlead what we cannot yet ourselves do has its own problems. To take these experiments seriously—as opposed to using them to stimulate shallow hopes and then at the first signs of "betrayal" jump to the next model—would mean actually learning from them. That is, in addition to supporting these emerging attempts at social transformation, having the humility not to judge them from afar and according to ahistoric standards, but to analyze what they teach us about the barriers to radical change and the depth of organizing needed to overcome those evolving barriers.

Similarly, to be conscious of the limits of institutionalized internationalism or open doors is not to reject a host of less ambitious, practical and even prosaic steps that can be systematically addressed. Adequate comparative information on international working conditions, on corporate performance and strategies, and on industrial and public sector restructuring remain to be collected. Unions that have gone through internal battles on gender and race issues can pass on their experience and innovations to those just starting such fights. Developing documentation in a particular sector (like auto or hospital care) on best practices by specific job, and sharing this information internationally, can contribute towards ratcheting standards up rather than seeing them steadily decline. Passing on the computerized health and safety information banks that have been developed in the North to workers in the South can—because health and safety is inevitably an issue that depends on local intervention—support the development of strong local bases of struggle. If this comes with international training support for organizing shop floor battles around health and safety, all the better (as long, of course, as such education-training in fact identifies the problems as class issues, not "technical problems"—something that is all too often not the perspective transmitted).

It may also be that while a generalized international plane is too broad and vague a space for concrete struggles given the fact of unevenness and deep differences in context, regional cooperation might be more effective in practical terms and might also constructively build towards something larger. The International Union of Food Workers, for example, has been able to wage effective solidarity and corporate campaigns within Asia. In the two most regionally integrated areas of the world—the European Union and the Canada-US-Mexico nexus—the conspicuous difference in the original responses to deeper integration was the extent to which in Europe, unions along with social movements and much of the Left looked with some enthusiasm to a "social Europe" while on this continent popular forces led an impressive opposition to deeper integration. What however can we say now, in light of the consequent reality of greater integration, about a progressive new regional working-class internationalism?

The optimism of a new Europe, based on either the promises of greater social protection as part of European integration or a two-stage theory (internationalization first, building a "social Europe" second), was stunningly naïve. The imbalance of power within each country was only partly due to the lack of international links across unions; the more fundamental problem was—as I raised more generally above—the weak organization and mobilization within each country. European integration was primarily a neoliberal project to make Europe more competitive internationally, with the weaker social programs and greater labour "flexibility" of the US an admired target. This meant not only a predictable retreat from the promise of raising Europe's standards, but a profound weakening of unions on the way to integration that would have long-term consequences. If there is to be a redirection of Europe, hope springs not from Europe's new layer of bureaucrats but, as we see in Greece, from struggles rooted at the national level that then spread to other countries and eventually add up to a truly "new Europe."

On this continent, Arregui and Roman (2013) have made a brave attempt to raise possibilities for building on the international links formed in the joint oppositions to free trade and the material-institutional integration of the three countries. As Arregui and Roman emphasize, this is not only a matter of deep economic integration, but of the potential solidarity based on Mexican workers that straddle these countries, and the existence of ostensibly international unions. To this might be added the potentials to run joint cross-country organizing campaigns in sectors like auto, making it clear that runaway plants won't escape unionization, or joining in living income campaigns to ratchet wages up rather than competitively ratchet them down (Gindin, 2004).

Yet it is not at all clear that the mobility of Mexican workers makes them potential bearers of a new internationalism rather than displaced workers with a tenuous relationship to both Mexico and the working class in Canada or the US. Nor is there a substantive basis for seeing the "Internationals" as being so in more than name only. The

Internationals have essentially been American unions with Canadian branches and the extent of their de facto internationalism was always very limited. Moreover, key Canadian sections of these unions (like the paper workers and autoworkers) have over the years chosen to break away. This was not just a matter of abstract nationalism but of the conservative turn of the American parents in the neoliberal era and the increased weight of the state in determining working-class lives—both of which weakened the significance of cross-border bargaining and solidarity relative to building class alliances to engage the state. Here too, regional potentials await national renewals.

For Canadians, such an emphasis on the national does of course raise the obvious question, much in the back of activists' minds but rarely openly discussed, of how far—given the integration of our economy, military and state with the US—Canadian workers can in fact go if change is not also occurring in the US? There is no easy answer to this. Our integrated relationship to the US demands strategies that move us to reduce that dependency. And as those in the Waffle who called for an independent socialist Canada in the 1970s understood, Canadian business will hardly be a nationalist ally in any such conflict.[78] If anything, Corporate Canada would be the main antagonists to any such considerations. And so, though we could not complete any radical transformation without parallel rebellions elsewhere, above all in the US, we cannot wait for a "simultaneous" revolution to occur across states. There is no choice but to start where we are. "It is altogether self-evident," Marx noted in 1875, "that to be able to fight at all, the working class must organize itself at home *as a class* and that its own country is the immediate arena of its struggle" (Marx, 1962: 27).[79]

78 The Waffle, otherwise known as the Movement for an Independent Socialist Canada, was a radical wing of the NDP that emerged in the late 1960s and, after intense debate within the NDP, formed its own short-lived political party in the mid-70s.

79 This restated Marx and Engel's earlier emphasis in the *Communist Manifesto* that "the proletariat of each country must, of course, first of all settle matters with its own bourgeoisie" (Marx & Engels, 1962: 11).

Conclusion

The nation-centric emphasis here may leave internationalists uncomfortable because it seems to leave too much room for the residues of the "nationalism" that progressives are so wary of. This is indeed a danger, but it is an unavoidable one that we must learn to navigate. The risk of nationalism is that in obscuring class and fetishizing the nation it conceals the power of private capital over our lives and turns workers against marginalized sections of the class. But the only antidote to this kind of nationalism (which we rightly fear) and the only foundation for building towards the internationalist principles (which we aspire to) is to begin with and sustain the class perspective that separates us from national and international capital and engage in the struggle within each nation-state, always with "internationalist sensibilities." To do otherwise leaves us with abstract slogans and a politics that, because of its tendency to practical irrelevance, unwittingly opens the door wider for precisely the kind of nationalism we abhor.

This cannot, I would insist in conclusion, happen without an organized socialist presence. Absent such a Left, with its universalist principles and strategic grasp of capitalism, class and the capitalist state, the renewal of the labour movement seems virtually impossible. And it is only such a renewal that can create the kind of working class with the capacities and sensibilities to play a central role in the creation of a true internationalism.

DOES DIRECT ACTION GET THE GOODS?

The Possibilities and Limits of Solidarity Networks

Matthew Corbeil and Jordan House

A young worker calmly enters his former employer's office with a letter in hand. He is here to confront his old boss, the owner of an underground temp agency, about $230 missing from his last paycheque. Normally, this worker would be alone. He has no fixed workplace, no fixed co-workers, no fixed payday and, most importantly, no union. But today is different. Behind him is group of 25 supporters, members of the Toronto Industrial Workers of the World Solidarity Committee. The worker reads a letter listing his demands aloud to his boss, who looks on with incredulity as the supporters stand by silent but firm. The letter concludes with a vague threat: "If these demands are not met within five days, we will take further action."

In recent years such scenes have become more common as solidarity networks and other organizations employing direct action casework have mushroomed throughout urban centres in North America and Europe. As the problem of precarity persists and even broadens, and as unions continue to struggle to take on the challenges of organizing workplaces outside their traditional strongholds, many workers are left with little choice but to use new and creative solutions simply to ensure a modicum of dignity and decency on the job. Solidarity networks, small "workers' and tenants' mutual support organizations that fight for specific demands using collective direct action," are one such solution (Cold & Barnacle, 2011: 1).

In this chapter, we explore the origins of these burgeoning organizations and evaluate their possibilities and limits. To do so, we consider two sets of interrelated questions. First, we ask what explains the emergence of solidarity networks as a particular form of working-class organization and resistance? What do organizers find attractive about the model? What do they hope to achieve in forming solidarity networks? Second, we examine the model's efficacy. Here, our goal is to assess the extent to which solidarity networks offer effective lessons to the labour movement in its ongoing quest for renewal. Before we tackle these questions we situate our work within the broader field of "labour movement renewal" and then describe how solidarity networks operate. Ultimately, we argue, solidarity networks have only limited potential in themselves. But the principles that underpin them—their explicit commitments to militancy, rank-and-file participation and class analysis and their ability to act as spaces of experimentation and learning—are the essential components of a revitalized, transformative labour movement.

Labour Movement Renewal?

By now, the story of the rise of neoliberalism and the "reassertion of ruling-class hegemony" is well known (Harvey, 2005a). The so-called "postwar compromise," which was premised on labour conceding control over the productive process in exchange for a limited set of workplace-based collective-bargaining rights and a larger share of the economic pie, is a thing of the past (Panitch & Swartz, 2003; Palmer, 1992; Workman, 2009). If unions could once count on continual improvements in wages and other benefits, they now struggle simply to stay afloat. Although Canadian unions have not suffered to the same extent as their American counterparts, declining levels of private-sector union density, stagnating real wages, increasing violations of collective bargaining rights and a decreasing strike propensity all point to a difficult truth: Canadian unions are at their lowest ebb since anytime in the postwar period (Camfield, 2011; Jackson, 2010; Workman, 2009).

To counter this trend, a growing body of research has arisen in both academic and activist circles. The study of labour movement renewal is dedicated to parsing out and assessing some of the strategic and tactical innovations that unions have undertaken in their efforts to reaffirm their relevance in an increasingly hostile world. In the Canadian context, Pradeep Kumar and Christopher Schenk's (2006) edited volume *Paths to Union Renewal: Canadian Experiences* is one of the most exhaustive of such accounts. In a series of theoretically informed case studies, this volume focuses on the ways in which unions have been "reassessing their strategies, organizational structures, and methods and approaches to more effectively organize the unorganized and provide better services to their members" (15). Questions of increasing membership to reflect Canada's diverse population, forging stronger links with "community groups," improving internal communications and building more membership-driven, participatory structures figure prominently in this and other similar works.

But if many of these efforts have met with success, there is at least one challenge that even renewed trade unions have been hard-pressed to solve. Crucially, to date the traditional union model has had little success in incorporating the growing numbers of precarious workers into their structures. There are many reasons for this, but perhaps the most important is the way in which Canada's system of "industrial pluralism" privileges union representation for certain types of workers, namely "a relatively settled, semi-skilled male worker within a large industrial corporation," while excluding others (Fudge & Tucker, 2001: 280). The legally certified collective bargaining model is simply not feasible for most precarious workers who find themselves in irregular and insecure forms of employment.

But even so, precarious workers have not been the mere passive victims of circumstance. This is why many scholars are not only looking to unions, but also to "new forms of worker organization" for inspiration when it comes to labour movement renewal (Ness, 2014). While, to be sure, trade unions remain the largest and most well-resourced social movement in Canada, there are a host of new challenges that they are struggling to overcome. For this reason, it is crucial to look to the innovative actions that workers outside the traditional realm of labour activism are taking and to consider what kinds of lessons they may offer. It is in this vein that we assess the possibilities and limits of solidarity networks.

What Are Solidarity Networks?

Before assessing the possibilities and limits of solidarity networks, we first need to clarify what they are. To that end, in this section we focus mainly on the Seattle Solidarity Network and the Toronto IWW Solidarity Committee to look at two relatively simple questions: How are solidarity networks organized and how do they operate?[80]

Solidarity networks rely exclusively on one strategy, what we call "direct action casework" (see Shantz, 2010: 72). This type of action is straightforward: Solidarity networks fight single-issue campaigns with clearly identifiable goals using collective direct action, rather than the legal system, to achieve them. Solidarity networks are not the only organizations to use direct action casework, but they are the only organizations whose sole function is such work.

Solidarity networks have a rather distinct organizational model. Membership is open to any worker or tenant and there is no dues-paying structure. Because of this, actual membership can be difficult to define with precision. However, in general it is clear that there are "layers" of participation even if there is a considerable degree of fluidity between them. The organizational model of solidarity networks is not set by strict policy, but is rather a question of personal commitment. At the centre are what we call "core organizers." Core organizers make up only a minority of all network participants, but they perform the bulk of its activities. They serve both executive and administrative functions. In terms of the former, core organizers are responsible for making all decisions regarding the overall direction of the network. For instance, it is at their discretion to determine the scope of the network's central focus. Will the network put its efforts to addressing a wide range of issues both in workplaces and neighbourhoods, or will it focus on one particular area of concern? For example, the Seattle Solidarity Network takes on both worker and tenant problems, while the Toronto IWW Solidarity Committee focuses its efforts mostly on wage theft. Other executive-type functions include attending regular strategy meetings, designing the network's outreach posters and deciding whether or not the network should take on a given case

80 We have derived our knowledge about solidarity networks, including their organizational model, their tactical repertoire and so on, not only from SeaSol's published material (Cold & Barnacle, 2011; LibCom, n.d.; SeaSol Organizer, n.d.), but also from our personal experiences as network organizers in Toronto. Thus, many of our assessments stem from participant observation.

Core organizers are also responsible for a number of day-to-day administrative tasks that contribute to the network's smooth operation. Among the most important of these is managing the network's telephone, its main point of contact with potential cases. Both the Seattle Solidarity Network and the Toronto Solidarity Committee have adopted a rotating model in this regard. At a given point, each organizer is responsible for holding on to the telephone, handling incoming calls and reporting telephone activity back to the larger group. Apart from this, administrative tasks include building and maintaining the network's contact list, updating its website with news of recent cases and victories, reposting torn-down posters and so on.

Solidarity networks consist of a second layer of membership whose participation is much more limited than that of core organizers, but is nonetheless vital to the network's operation: supporters. Indeed, without supporters there would be no "network" to speak of. Supporters are those people that core organizers can call upon once the network has officially launched a case. They do not attend strategy sessions, nor do they perform any administrative tasks. Instead, supporters agree to participate in network actions when the time comes. Because solidarity networks often work with people in precarious circumstances, a greater number of "bodies" to pressure a bad boss or landlord can be crucial. It is more likely that a bad boss will take a demand seriously when it is backed up by 25 people than if it were only backed up by three or four.

An illustration of a campaign can help to clarify how solidarity networks function. Networks solicit "cases" through the use of posters offering workers assistance in dealing with "bad bosses."[81] To attract attention, these posters emphasize concrete problems, like wage theft or unpaid overtime. Once a worker contacts the network, each campaign follows a similar pattern. The first step is for organizers to meet the affected worker in person. Here the goal is to get a sense of the worker's problem and his/her interest in engaging in direct

81 Posters may also offer assistance in fighting "bad landlords," but for the sake of simplicity, in this illustration we focus on a "bad boss" campaign. For an example of the Seattle Solidarity Network's posters see: http://seattlesolidarity.net/index.php?option=com_content&view=article&id=18&Itemid=29.

action. From there, the network holds a meeting, without the affected worker,[82] to decide whether or not to take the case. The most important criterion in this regard is "winnability." Organizers evaluate whether or not the network has the necessary resources to "hurt" the bad boss to the point where he or she will give in to the demand. If this is so, the network officially launches the campaign and invites the affected worker to a strategizing session. At this session, the network and the affected worker collaborate to establish a clear set of demands, identify potential choke points to leverage the bad boss and work out a plan of action (Cold & Barnacle, 2011).

Because each campaign is context-specific and strategy is based on a reading of the employer's vulnerabilities, solidarity networks are able to employ a diverse range of tactics in those instances where further action is required. However, the guiding principle behind every campaign is escalation. That is, each action should be progressively more painful to the boss than the one that preceded it. As Cold and Barnacle put it, "Our campaign strategy is based on the basic insight that the boss or landlord doesn't cave in as a result of what we just did to them—*they cave in as a result of their fear of what we're going to do next*" (2011, emphasis added). For instance, if the bad boss were the owner of a sandwich shop, a campaign may move from a "phone zap," in which members overload the restaurant's telephone line with calls insisting the demand be met, to a "soft picket" in which members gently encourage potential customers to eat elsewhere (perhaps even handing out a competitor's coupons), to a "hard picket" in which members make efforts to block entrance to the shop. Once the boss has given in to the network's demands, the campaign ceases.

In a sense, organizers consider solidarity networks to be microcosms of the kind of self-directed workers' organizations necessary for building a social movement against capitalism. Organizers emphasize the liberating potential of direct participation in struggle.

82 If the worker were to attend, it would be difficult to turn the case down, even if the network did not have the capacity to win. In those instances when the Toronto IWW Solidarity Committee feels it cannot take on a case, it refers the affected worker to the Toronto Workers Action Centre, a community union that also has an anti-wage theft campaign, one that relies much more on the legal framework.

The guiding principle is simple: those affected by a problem are best suited to resolving it. Taking part in efforts to address immediate concerns is the basis of movement building and politicization. Cold and Barnacle (2011) note: "We want all our actions to build people's experience, confidence, knowledge, and radicalization. We want to take action in an empowering manner, avoiding the disempowerment that comes from relying on bureaucrats, social workers, politicians, lawyers, and other 'experts'" (15).

To summarize, the solidarity network model is both an organizationally and strategically distinct form of workers' organization. Unlike legally certified trade unions, and a growing number of workers' centres, solidarity networks do not rely on permanent, full-time paid staff. Membership is voluntary rather than a function of employment in a given workplace. There are no dues in the strict sense of the term, but organizers will only take a case if the affected worker agrees to participate in all phases of the campaign from the initial strategizing session to direct confrontation with the boss. In placing the affected worker at the centre of the campaign, organizers look to overcome what they consider the demobilizing and disempowering character of mainstream unionism, which tends to rely on bureaucratic proceduralism rather than worker self-activity (Wells, 1995). An additional purpose is to train affected workers to think like activists and to build their political capacities. By encouraging active participation, then, solidarity networks look to offer affected workers not only an immediate redress to their grievance, but also a crash course in class politics.

The Origins of Solidarity Networks

In this section, we explain the emergence of solidarity networks as a new form of social movement organization. We identify two main factors. First, we look at how certain activist communities made strategic reorientations in their political work. Second, we describe the political-economic context in which this work has become increasingly relevant.

The Seattle Solidarity Network (SeaSol), the first, largest and most successful of the networks, was founded in 2007. The founding members of SeaSol were members of the Industrial Workers of the World

(IWW), a small radical labour union, who were looking for a concrete way of expressing their politics. According to SeaSol founders, the Seattle branch of the IWW was "too small and lacking in resources to attempt to organize any workplaces" (LibCom, n.d.: 32). Seeking inspiration, activists turned to the history of the direct-action campaigns of the Ontario Coalition Against Poverty (OCAP), as well as union flying squads—groups of union workers who, with or without the support of union officialdom, mobilized members to bulk up picket lines, attend or organize demonstrations, or engage in other actions in support of striking workers (see Shantz, 2010). More than any other organization, OCAP pioneered direct-action casework in the 1990s. Scholar-activist Jeff Shantz describes OCAP's tactics:

> OCAP brings large numbers of members and allies directly to the offending agency, landlord or workplace and insist[s] on staying until [it gets] what [it] came for. If no settlement is forthcoming [it raises] the costs of offending agencies to the point where it is no longer worthwhile for them to act in an oppressive way (Shantz, 2000: 4).

Throughout the 1990s and early 2000s, OCAP took on a number of cases in which it supported immigrants facing deportation, workers fired without cause and tenants fighting their landlords for routine repairs. These campaigns were notable for their militancy and their creative direct-action tactics. For example, in 2003 OCAP took on a reinstatement campaign on behalf of a group of unfairly dismissed workers from Toronto's Metropolitan Hotel. Throughout the two-year campaign OCAP organized a "Rank and File Hotel Workers Committee" autonomous from HERE, the union officially representing the workers, and organized community pickets of the hotel (Shantz, 2009). In another case in 2004, OCAP delivered a bucket of raw sewage to the offices of the Toronto Community Housing Corporation to protest the Corporation's refusal to repair a bathroom of a tenant that had sewage leaking into it. The bathroom was repaired that afternoon (OCAP, 2004).

SeaSol gathered the disparate elements of these campaigns and synthesized them into a coherent and easily replicable process. In doing so, SeaSol has been remarkably successful. The organization has won dozens of fights ranging from $500 in stolen wages to over

$50,000 of repairs and renovations from one of Seattle's largest residential landlords. It has also successfully fought off a lawsuit; won $22,000 in back pay for a fired secretary; ousted an abusive property manager, while recovering stolen security deposits; and organized a multi-worker strike to combat tip theft and reinstate fired workers (Seattle Solidarity Network, 2009; 2014). Owing to such an impressive track record, solidarity networks have since emerged in numerous cities across North America and Europe, including Portland, Toronto, Hamilton, Kitchener-Waterloo, Victoria and Bristol, among others.

SeaSol organizers have located their turn to direct-action casework in the growing sense of futility that came with their previous political interventions. More specifically, organizers were looking to move away from what they considered the aimless ritualism of much of the anti-globalization and anti-Iraq War movements. Protests and demonstrations, teach-ins, graffiti and culture-jamming, though well-intentioned, seemed to have no real purpose. As one SeaSol organizer has explained:

> All over the U.S., in fact the Anarchist organizations I had worked with could be summed up in one word—they were aimless. They had vague objectives. They had no discernible, immediate goals. Actually, if you asked most of them what they were doing, I'm not sure you could get a straight answer (SeaSol Organizer, n.d.: 26).

This seeming lack of purpose was compounded by an utter sense of defeat, as movement-building produced few tangible results. The same SeaSol organizer noted:

> For those of us who have poured our hearts into a lot of "symbolic" anarchist projects—a lot of anti-police brutality work, anti-war organizing, anti-G8 campaigns, and so on—for those of us who have spent time around these campaigns, we have felt extremely demoralized. We have felt this way because despite all the sacrifice, we never won anything. The campaigns never seemed to end after the enemy conceded something; instead they always seemed to stop when people just became exhausted (SeaSol Organizer, n.d.: 26).

In contrast to, say, antiwar organizing, single-issue direct-action casework campaigns—with their emphasis on small, concrete, winnable fights—offer organizers a realistic opportunity to effectively express their politics. Solidarity network campaigns are not merely symbolic gestures. They have a direct bearing on working people's lives. Success is not only achievable, it is visible.

Another important element in explaining the emergence of solidarity networks is the current political-economic climate. The neoliberal class offensive has not only left unions on the defensive, it has also fundamentally remade workplaces and patterns of employment. Levels of precarious employment—employment that is "either insecure and/or low paid"—are on the rise across North America (Jackson, 2010: 35). Indeed, one recent study of the Toronto-Hamilton metropolitan area found that 40% of workers were in insecure employment (Hennessy et al., 2013: 15). These patterns have mirrored both the entry of more women into the labour force and the general growth in service sector employment, where both wages and union coverage have traditionally been low.

Owing to their insecurity, precarious workers are vulnerable to a host of employer malpractices. Wage theft is one such problem, and as many studies have shown, things are only getting worse (Bobo, 2008; Bernhardt et al., 2008). For instance, in their report entitled "Broken Laws, Unprotected Workers," Annette Bernhardt and her colleagues surveyed 4,387 low-wage workers in three US cities and found that "fully 26% of workers in [their] sample were paid less than the legally required minimum wage in the previous week" (2). What is more, they argue, these "violations were not trivial in magnitude: 60% of workers were underpaid by more than $1 per hour" (ibid.: 2). To make things worse, while legal redress is available, enforcement mechanisms are often weak or non-existent. Indeed, a recent *Toronto Star* investigation into the Ontario Ministry of Labour's regulation of wage theft revealed that in 2013-14 "63% of all orders to pay issued to employers by the Ministry of Labour went uncollected" (Mojtehedzadeh, 2015).

In this context, solidarity networks have emerged as an effective vehicle for addressing some of the most pressing concerns that working people now face. As bosses continue to violate employment standards, and as governments continue to do little about it, solidarity networks are in some instances the only option that working people have.

Possibilities and Limits

We are now in a position to assess the possibilities and limits of solidarity networks as agents of labour movement renewal. The solidarity network model has much to offer. Indeed, the core principles that make solidarity networks what they are—their commitments to militancy, active participation and class politics—are integral elements of any revitalized labour movement. At the same time, however, we also need to recognize the challenges that solidarity networks face in scaling up their work, and the risks they face in maintaining a balanced vision of their purposes and objectives.

The principal institutions of the North American labour movement, that is legally certified trade unions, are at an impasse. The form of unionism that took hold in the mid-20th century, a period of intense industrial expansion and economic growth, is less suited for today's altered political-economic context. Not only do fewer and fewer workers find themselves in those industrial sectors, like manufacturing and resource extraction, where North American unionism has traditionally been strongest, but also the state and employing class have made it abundantly clear that they are no longer interested in upholding their end of the bargain. The neoliberal class offensive and its accompanying attacks on the social rights and institutions of the postwar era signal the need to radically rethink labour movement strategies. So long as the labour movement remains wedded to these institutions, it will be unable to make the necessary adjustments to reinvent itself.

This is why solidarity networks are so exciting. Network organizers harbour no illusions about the continuing viability of the postwar compromise. Their strategies and tactics reflect their recognition that the state's minimal labour and employment standards offer insufficient mechanisms to uphold the rights and advance the interests of growing numbers of working people. Instead of relying on increasingly diluted state agencies for protection and redress, organizers insist on taking matters into their own hands.

In assessments of what the labour movement now needs, there have been calls for more militancy (Burns, 2011; Camfield, 2011), greater rank-and-file participation (McAlevey, 2014) and a return to a class analysis (Fletcher & Gapasin, 2009; Gindin, 2012). Crucially, solidarity networks embody all of these principles at their very core. Indeed, because they reject the legal system as a matter of course, reflecting their emphasis on class antagonisms, solidarity networks cannot function, let alone win, without militant collective action.

Winning a case, however, is not the only thing that matters. Capacity building is equally important. This is why organizers insist that affected workers participate from start to finish. Rather than acting as a "servicing agency," organizers consider their work to be a kind of "propaganda of the deed." Each campaign is a learning process, one that entails much more than uncovering the potential power of collective action. A campaign is a real-life training ground that allows workers to develop their skills as militants and activists. In taking an active role in redressing their immediate grievances, affected workers have an opportunity to think strategically, to learn and share new ideas about resistance and to build their self-confidence and sense of self-worth in the face of their employers and landlords. Thus, the promise of solidarity networks is not principally in their ability to hold miscreant bosses and landlords to account for violations of the law. Rather, it is more in their ability to serve as small spaces for experimentation and learning, for rebuilding the collective capacities of working-class militants.

This is a point that cannot be overlooked. The most important historical period in North American labour history, the upheavals of the 1930s and 1940s, limited as their outcomes came to be, were not the spontaneous eruption of an unorganized mass of suddenly class-conscious workers. As Dan La Botz (2010) has made clear, an experienced, organized and strategically minded *labour-Left* was an integral element of this juncture:

> The great strikes of 1934 in San Francisco, Toledo, and Minneapolis, the sit-down strikes of 1936-1938 in rubber and auto, and the entire labor rebellion of that period were led on the ground by and large by labor leftists, Communists, Socialists, Trotskyists and others. The revolutionary left provided not only strategic leadership for the large scale struggles, but also the local militants who had established relationships in workplaces and communities.

Militants need time and effort to hone their skills. Solidarity networks can do their small part in reviving these capacities, so many of which have been lost under neoliberalism.

But even if solidarity networks offer some promise, in isolation they are not enough to reverse the fortunes of the labour movement more broadly. Not only do they face significant barriers in terms of "scaling up" their work, but their method of operation risks reproducing some of the limitations of the very model of unionism network organizers look to overcome.

As things stand now, solidarity networks lack the necessary resources to tackle systematically the most pressing issues confronting the working class as a whole. Simply put, the scale of the problem is much too large to address on a case-by-case basis. If, as Bernhardt and her colleagues have shown, more than a quarter of low-wage American workers are routinely paid less than the legal minimum wage, these violations and others like them are best conceived as a structural issue. Structural problems require structural fixes. To be sure, a solidarity network campaign is an effective method for retaining an individual worker's stolen wages or repairing an individual tenant's mouldy bathroom, but these campaigns in themselves do not directly address the underlying conditions that allow, or even encourage, employers to steal wages or landlords to ignore building codes in the first place.

Having a small resource base carries with it other important implications. These require network organizers to remain vigilant and cognizant of their long-term strategy. To be sure, there is some irony in this regard. Small, radical labour organizations are simply not used to winning under neoliberalism, but the solidarity network model allows for a steady flow of continual success. Yet for every stolen paycheque reclaimed, there are hundreds of others just like it, and the conditions of labour market precarity remain firmly entrenched. Winning, therefore, is a risk in itself. As the number of successful cases begins to pile up, and as organizers begin to think only in terms of their track record, they lose sight of what we argue solidarity networks should really be about: spaces of experimentation and learning to develop, if only in a limited fashion, the skills and capacities of working-class militants.

This is important not only because solidarity networks are too small to address structural problems. More fundamentally, in losing sight of long-term strategy and focusing only on winning, network organizers run the risk of reproducing many of the limitations of mainstream unionism of which they are so critical. If organizers are not vigilant, solidarity networks may develop their own forms of sectionalism and conservatism. To the extent that winning campaigns becomes the ultimate objective, network organizers risk reducing their organizations to militant service providers for a small number of working people. And this form of narrow instrumentalism is exactly the model of unionism organizers hope to overcome. Organizers, therefore, must always maintain a balanced vision of their organizations and their goals. They must continually reflect on their work and consider the extent to which campaigns are contributing to the longer-term goals of rebuilding working-class capacities.

In sum, while solidarity networks have much to offer in terms of labour movement renewal, they are not free of certain risks. On one hand, they contain, on a small scale, the seeds of what the labour movement needs. They harbour no illusions about the continuing viability of increasingly fragile institutions, and instead are committed to militant collective action in defence of the working class as a whole. At the same time, however, networks remain far too small to change the conditions that make their work necessary, and if organizers are not vigilant, they risk losing sight of the bigger strategic picture.

Conclusion

The anemic response of progressive forces to the "Great Recession" that began in 2008 demonstrated again the need for labour movement renewal. At a moment when neoliberalism could not have been more vulnerable, when it seemed there might be an alternative after all, it was working people that were put on the defensive yet again. Indeed, the endless rounds of austerity that have occurred in the post-crisis aftermath have only deepened working people's woes. If they did not cause the crisis, they are surely being made to pay for it.

Working people's only hope in stemming the onslaught that is post-crisis neoliberal capitalism is a renewed audacity. As inequalities in wealth and decision-making power continue to tilt in favour of established elites, militant and disruptive collective action is not simply a matter of good strategy; it is a moral imperative. Solidarity networks can do their part in reviving collective capacities to make a better world possible.

SOLIDARITY WITH WHOM?
Occupy Wall Street and Responsibility to the Other(s)[83]

Michael Bueckert

Over the past decade, anti-capitalist social movements have increasingly chosen to reject institutions, leaders and representation in favour of "horizontal" tactics and processes of organization, such as consensus-based decision-making. Intending to prefigure the world in radically democratic ways, these tactics have been tremendously popular, especially among anarchists, yet they have also been subject to considerable critique from other scholars and activists on the Left who see them as inherently limited in their capacities for effective organization.

> For the moment, the survival of the new social movements—the occupiers, the *indignados,* the small European anti-capitalist parties and the Arab new left—demands that they sink deeper roots in mass resistance to the global economic catastrophe, which in turn presupposes—let's be honest—that the current temper for "horizontality" can eventually accommodate enough disciplined "verticality" to debate and enact organizing strategies (Davis, 2011: 5).

Such statements are seen by proponents of horizontality as indicative of a "dismissive attitude" among the Old Left towards the new forms of organizing (Featherstone, 2012: 215), and as such there exists a noticeable sense of mutual condescension between the so-called "horizontals" and "verticals." While on the surface this debate tends to revolve around assertions of effectiveness or strategy, there is an underlying conflict between implicit yet distinct notions of solidarity; that is, over what it means to be responsible to the other.

This chapter examines the role of organizational structures in mediating anti-capitalist solidarity in the Occupy movement, teasing out the different practices of solidarity implied in competing organizational forms. While horizontalism is predicated on a notion of

83 I would like to thank Janet Siltanen and Heather Whiteside for their comments on an earlier version of this chapter

solidarity rooted in respect for the individual autonomy of the other, contradictions emerged in practice, most significantly when the horizontalist emphasis on participation prevented solidarity from being extended to those unable to participate. This chapter argues that the experience of Occupy reveals the limits to the horizontalist practice of solidarity, and points to the necessity of formal structures of leadership and representation. Although such forms are indeed vertical, they allow for practices of solidarity which are actually more inclusive, and are therefore necessary for prefiguring a desired, post-capitalist future.

Horizontal Solidarities

It is widely acknowledged that the initial popularity of the Occupy movement can be attributed in part to its adoption of horizontal forms of organization, including its emphases on consensus, inclusivity and leaderlessness (see Dean, 2012b: 52-53; Graeber, 2013). These practices had already been widespread within the anti/alter globalization movement a decade earlier, and have been explored theoretically by several key anarchist thinkers (see Graeber, 2002; Day, 2004; Maeckelbergh, 2011).[84] Strictly anti-hierarchical and non-coercive in intent, horizontality reflects an understanding of solidarity that first and foremost privileges the autonomy of the individual against conformity and the centralization of power.

Horizontality is therefore understood as operating according to logics of organization which are fundamentally different from the dominant practices of the Left. Day (2004) has formulated this as a "logic of affinity," which is counterposed to a Gramscian "logic of hegemony." Rather than seeking to achieve hegemony by seizing the "constituted" power of the state and other institutions, new social movements privilege "'social' revolutions based on the construction of affinities (constituent power)" (738). This involves disengaging from the state and creating alternative forms of social organization "with

84 In this chapter I will primarily draw upon these authors to discuss horizontalism. It should be noted, however, that similar themes are discussed in the work of Zibechi (2010), Sitrin (2012) and Holloway (2002), usually in the context of Latin American social movements in Chiapas and Argentina, and using the comparable term *horizontalidad*. Sometimes the connection is made explicitly between Occupy and these movements "from below" (Sitrin, 2011; Solnit, 2011).

the end of creating not a new knowable totality (counter-hegemony), but of enabling experiments and the emergence of new forms of subjectivity" (740).

In a similar fashion, horizontality also reflects a logic of prefiguration, which is understood as the "creation of alternatives in the here and now" (Maeckelbergh, 2011: 3). In this way, *process* is of central importance; if processes do not reflect the principles of the desired future, social movements may become what they are fighting against (8). Rejecting the notion that their emphasis on process is somehow opposed to strategy, horizontalists argue that prefiguration *is* strategy:

> Prefiguration is a practice that assumes the ends and the means to be inextricably linked, where the means are the result of past ends and result in future ends, and therefore prefiguration rejects a focus on either means or ends to the exclusion of the other (8).

It is because of this connection between means and ends that if you want to create a radically democratic society, you cannot use hierarchical or authoritarian mechanisms to do so (Day, 2007; Maeckelbergh, 2011).

Two specific practices of prefiguration are relevant here. First, there are direct action tactics, the "physical intervention against state power in a form that itself prefigures an alternative" (Graeber, 2002: 62; Day, 2004: 731-32). This involves the creation of "experiments," ranging from Independent Media Centres (IMCs) as community-based alternatives to corporate media (Day, 2004: 731), to large-scale mobilizations of non-violent civil disobedience (Graeber, 2002: 66). Another prefigurative practice is consensus-based decision-making—itself sometimes understood as a direct action tactic—which is central to the horizontalist goal of reinventing "viable models" of decentralized direct democracy (71).

Prefigurative practices therefore tend to be viewed as opposed, rather than complementary, to efforts to appeal to the state for demands.[85] Day (2004) characterizes such efforts as a "politics of

85 This is not a monolithic view, but it is common in the literature. For anarchist-leaning authors in favour of some limited engagement with the state, seeing the state as a multiplicity of practices and forms, see Martin & Pierce (2013) and McGuirk & O'Neill (2012). The relationship between prefiguration and formal structures will be discussed further below.

demand," in which politics are oriented to state power in order to achieve "irradiation effects"—a term which is never adequately defined, but seems to refer to more universal consequences of political agitation. Not only is this kind of engagement with the state inevitably corrosive,[86] but it perpetuates "structures of domination" (733-34). Conversely, a "politics of the act" gives up on looking to the state for emancipation, "inventing a response that precludes the necessity of the demand and thereby breaks out of the loop of the endless perpetuation of desire for emancipation" (734). As Graeber suggests, "by actively delegitimating the structure, we are in a position, perhaps as a side effect of our actions, to create the forms that will actually be of the most benefit to ordinary people" (quoted in Wolfe, 2012).

Looking closer, it is possible to identify a "horizontal" approach to solidarity, in which respecting the autonomy and diversity of the individual other is central. This is perhaps most easily recognizable in the emphasis on consensus, which is celebrated for its capacity for inclusion of diverse perspectives in decision-making, and for its anti-coercive principles:

> [Consensus-based processes] allow initiatives to rise from below and attain *maximum effective solidarity*, without stifling dissenting voices, creating leadership positions or compelling anyone to do anything which they have not freely agreed to do (Graeber, 2002: 71, emphasis added).

The need for inclusion of a "radical diversity of perspectives" (Graeber, 2013: 203) reflects a strong concern for individuality, and any sign of infringement upon this diversity is interpreted as coercion. For this reason, there is skepticism towards closure and unity; the goal of consensus is to maintain a "permanently open process," so that movements can be open to "many possible future needs/goals"

86 As Maeckelbergh (2011) argues, "appealing to the state for reform would be anything but strategic when the goal is to decentralize power" (16). David Graeber has outlined a similar position: "The moment you engage with a system, you're not only legitimating it, you're delegitimating yourself, because your own internal politics become warped. Even accepting money has pernicious effects. But the moment you're interfacing with vertically organized structures of power, which are ultimately based on coercion, it poisons everything" (quoted in Wolfe, 2012).

(Maeckelbergh, 2011: 12). Consensus is lauded because it forecloses the possibility of favouring any one perspective at the expense of another; since anyone can veto a proposal, for any proposal to be passed it must be "acceptable to everyone—or at least, not highly objectionable to anyone" (Graeber, 2002: 71). There is a conviction that "no one should be forced to go along with a decision to which they did not assent" (Graeber, 2013: 211), that activists should not be "reduced to an element of someone else's paradigm" (Day, 2007). From this standpoint of individual autonomy, leadership and representation can only be authoritarian (Day, 2007), unity can only be subordination (Maeckelbergh, 2011: 11). Indeed, this conviction is so strong that even the act of persuasion is suspect.[87]

Occupy and the Limits of Horizontality

Despite enthusiastic assertions by anarchists that horizontal practices directly contributed to Occupy's "success" (Graeber, 2013; Solnit, 2011),[88] some participants and observers of the movement have noted important limitations to horizontality in practice and in theory.

In particular, many of these critiques suggest that Occupy suffered from what the New York art collective *Not An Alternative* (2010) has termed "participationism"; that is, by idealizing participation and

87 For example, see the following statements: consensus requires "the ability to listen well enough to understand perspectives that are fundamentally different from one's own, and then try to find pragmatic common ground *without attempting to convert one's interlocutors completely to one's own perspective*" (Graeber, 2013: 202-03, emphasis added). Dialogue must "respect the particularity of one's interlocutors," as many radical activists "don't want to be reduced to an element of someone else's paradigm" (Day, 2007). It is preferable to engage in direct action tactics, creating spaces "where we can live in the kinds of worlds we want to live in, here and now," rather than to "die trying to convince someone else to let us live / live like us, later on, somewhere else" (Day, 2007). These statements do not rule out persuasion altogether, but they privilege the autonomy of individual perspectives to the point that they treat them as almost fixed, and this discourages attempts to challenge existing viewpoints through persuasion.

88 Success, of course, is different from popularity. See the contrast between Dean's (2012b) statement that anarchism was a major element in reigniting an anti-capitalist movement (55), and Solnit's (2011) claim that the movement is "already winning" (149).

consensus, Occupy actually obscured and reproduced the operations of power that it intended to dismantle.

First, although leaderlessness was intended to make decision-making as horizontal as possible, and therefore free from domination by any individuals, in the absence of formal leadership informal hierarchies emerged which were unacknowledged (Dean, 2012b; Smith & Glidden, 2012; Amirault, 2014). This is reminiscent of what Jo Freeman referred to as the "tyranny of structurelessness" in the context of feminist organizing,[89] but it also reflects the specific "relational dynamics" related to the tactic of occupation (Smith & Glidden, 2012: 289): activists who were able to remain on site for longer periods of time inevitably "claimed a higher status in group decision-making" to which others deferred (289). Since decisions were based on consensus among all present, this basic inequality of participation reproduced itself: the timing and locations of General Assemblies (GAs) were determined by the minority capable of being present, and meetings were both very frequent and seemingly "endless," which made it difficult if not impossible for the least privileged to participate (289-90; Kaufman, 2011: 49). The informal leadership which emerged, in turn, "could not be acknowledged or held accountable as leaders" (Dean, 2012b: 54), leading to a degree of paranoia and suspicion (Dean, 2012b: 54; 2012a: 227-28); as one participant-observer noticed, problems of transparency were evident when key decisions about strategy were—perhaps justifiably—being made in secret and outside of the GA, and there were also rumours of "backroom dealings with various NGOs and unions" (Gessan, Taylor & Resnick, 2011: 54).

Second, whereas Occupy tried to bring together both inclusion and consensus, Dean (2012b) has argued that there is a fundamental "incompatibility" between them (54); you cannot fully include a radical diversity of perspectives into a movement *and* require them all to agree. By celebrating inclusion and "post-partisanship," Occupy actually contributed to the "repression of political differences" (54), which made strategy difficult: "basic issues of what the movement

89 This is somewhat ironic, given that the "consensus process" is sometimes upheld as a response and solution to Freeman's critiques of how cliques and tacit leaders emerge in the absence of structures (see Graeber, 2013: 221; Kaufman, 2011: 47).

opposed remained unanswered, precisely because posing them would rupture the consensus Occupy wanted to build" (54). This refusal to define common goals and demands from the outset, which would certainly have excluded certain viewpoints, led to practical setbacks as the movement would spend time on building consensus with those who did not share "the same strategic orientations or goals, only to see decisions blocked in the end" (Smith & Glidden, 2012: 290). Consistent failures to be sufficiently inclusive of all perspectives led to an "obsession" over process at the expense of action (Dean, 2012b: 54; 2012a), detracting from movement building and reflecting an "avoidance of a larger discussion of goals and strategies" (Smith & Glidden, 2012: 290).

Apart from these operational and strategic issues, Amirault (2014) argues that the emphases on participation and consensus also tended to reproduce relations of hierarchy and privilege, since Occupy's "adherence to a procedural democracy treats all persons as equals thereby disguising deep structures of oppression (i.e. colonization, racism, sexism) that prevent traditionally marginalized groups from fully participating in the consensus processes to begin with" (135). Furthermore, the requirement for General Assemblies to reach consensus meant in practice that voices from marginalized groups were silenced, and demands for the recognition of forms of oppression such as racism, sexism and colonialism were ignored or faced hostility on the grounds that those activists were "dividing the movement" (137).

By emphasizing the primacy of consensus-based politics, Dean (2012a) argues that activists in Occupy held to a fantasy of "multiplicity without antagonism, of difference without division" (228). Such a fantasy denies the reality that "politics is necessarily divisive" (Dean, 2009: 13), and anti-capitalist politics especially so, for it politicizes and mobilizes around an economic division—something that Occupy itself did through its declaration that "We are the 99%" (Dean, 2012b: 56; 2012a: 218). And so even as Occupy based its identity upon a certain exclusion, its internal politics proceeded as if division need not take place. For example, when Graeber (2013) argues that consensus is representative of an approach to politics as "problem solving," rather than "as a struggle between fixed interests" (Graeber, 2013: 205), the implication would seem to be that antagonistic interests are merely differences of opinion which can be overcome through "reasonableness" and "genuine deliberation" (202). While these are certainly positive traits in political debate, they are not sufficient for coming to consensus on issues where incompatible interests are at stake. Moreover, an emphasis on inclusivity downplays the violence inherent in any act of decision-making, which is precisely the exclusion of other possibilities and futures, so that "part of the challenge of politics is taking responsibility for such exclusion" (Dean, 2009: 13). And indeed, whereas consensus-based politics "proceed as if all political ideas are equal" (Dean, 2013a: 27), the egalitarian spirit behind Occupy clearly privileged certain political ideas over others. And rightly so; some futures are truly undesirable and deserve to be excluded.

The above arguments are indications that horizontal practices cannot entirely achieve what they claim: the rejection of formal leadership leaves the movement open to the tyranny of informal hierarchies, and celebrations of consensus and inclusion conceal rather than address underlying divisions and conflicting interests. These are practical limitations that weaken the organizational capacity of the movement, which is why Smith & Glidden (2012) have argued for the need to create "more effective structures for collective decision-making and accountability" (293). Although largely sympathetic to horizontalist arguments, they suggest modifications which would add a degree of "verticality": for example, they note that participatory democracy "does not require consensus-based models" but can include various voting-based formulas (291). Similarly, despite being in favour of the decentralization of power so that individuals can participate and develop their skills, they also note that strongly anti-hierarchical positions can prevent those "with particular skills from contributing their leadership to the struggle"; therefore, it is better to identify and acknowledge leadership "while also constantly scrutinizing the operation of power within the movement" (291).

Graeber (2013), for his part, recognizes and has responded to some of these issues, albeit unconvincingly. He acknowledges the risk of informal leadership, but argues for tweaks to the consensus process—rotation of facilitators, transparency and so forth—rather than imposing a formal leadership structure, arguing that all evidence suggests that formality does not lead to accountability (221-23). Graeber argues that a radical diversity of perspectives should not be seen as a weakness but a strength, for it provides for the ability to see problems differently, and come up with "creative" solutions (203). As for the horror of endless meetings, he offers that meetings can be made more enjoyable, and that strict time limits should be posed on deliberation (226-27). In each case, the problems with consensus are treated as either fixable through the application of creativity and dedication, or as unavoidable and regrettable aspects that are tied to the unquestionable good of participatory democracy, and therefore must be tolerated.

Horizontal Solidarity with Whom?

Setting aside the practical weaknesses of the Occupy movement, it is worth questioning whether the conception of solidarity as implied in practices of horizontalism is even desirable. As argued above, the horizontal approach to solidarity privileges respect for the autonomy of the individual other. However, this commitment to individualism is at odds with the essentially *collective* nature of the Occupy movement, which brought diverse existing movements under a common name: "because of Occupy, we now appear to *ourselves as us*—we say 'we,' even as we argue over who we are and what we want" (Dean, 2012b: 59, emphasis in original).[90]

This is an important point to note, for if the horizontalism of the "anarchist moment" contributed to exciting and attracting individuals into the collective subject known as Occupy, its "basic tenets undermined large-scale collective organization" (Dean, 2012b: 55). That is to say, Occupy's horizontal practices made it impossible for its diverse constitutive elements to act in a collective manner. This is perhaps most visible in the difficulty that General Assemblies had in reaching consensus on even basic operational matters—laundry, for example (see Gessen, 2011)—let alone defining long-term goals

90 This somewhat contradicts Day's (2004) claims that a "key value" of prefigurative social experiments is that "they consciously defy the logic of hegemony by warding off the appearance of overarching centres of power/signification that would place themselves above the constituent groups"; that they resist any general equivalent "within yet above" these networks (732). It would appear that Occupy served as precisely such an equivalent, for how else can we make sense of Occupy Oakland and Occupy Ottawa?

and strategy. This is not a question of whether horizontality can be "scaled up," *per se*, for it is a matter of debate whether it even worked at the level of occupation.

This dysfunctionality between constitutive elements of Occupy is also visible when looking at the relationships between on-site participants and others who were sympathetic and potentially identifying themselves under the banner of the movement. Organized labour is one such constituency which lent support to the movement, but was kept at a distance in an effort to maintain autonomy and avoid co-optation; as Saval (2011) notes, Occupy treated labour as "as a source of bodies and money, a mere service that tends to be thanked and repudiated in the same breath" (112). The message to unions was that they "are welcome to assist the occupations, but they shouldn't expect any help in return" (112). Without any sense of obligation to the other, Saval warned that Occupy was "in danger of evacuating the concept" of solidarity (112).

A more fundamental contradiction is inherent in the slogan "We Are the 99%": on one hand, this slogan was taken up by the popular tumblr (web blog) of the same name, where people from all over the United States posted photos of themselves along with personal testimonies of their financial hardship. In this act, individuals identified themselves with the movement and gave their experience of suffering a collective meaning. As Roth (2011) correctly points out, this public expression revealed that Occupy's constituency was far more inclusive than "hippies" and "anarchists" (25). On the other hand, and despite the anti-representation stance of the horizontals:

> Occupy Wall Street is not *actually* the movement of 99% of the population of the United States (or the world) against the top 1%. It is a movement mobilizing itself around an occupied Wall Street *in the name of* the 99% (Dean, 2012a: 229, emphasis in the original).

The contradiction is that Occupy was simultaneously a collective subject so inclusive that almost anyone could identify with it, and also a physical occupation by a self-appointed minority. The question that immediately arises is what obligation, if any, did on-site participants have to others who identified with the message but who were excluded from participating? If the priority of individual autonomy requires that "no one can or should speak for another person" (Dean, 2012a: 225), then how can solidarity be extended to those who are not present to speak?

Once again, this speaks to the problems of participationism, or participation as an ideal (Not An Alternative, 2010). Although assumed to be more democratic, decision-making based on participation is inherently exclusionary towards those who are not capable of participating, whether as a result of physical ability, the requirements of child care, or simply a lack of available time. Without formal mechanisms of representation to include the interests of those absent, the result is that only the interests of those present count. Another problem with participation is that "it stands for activity for its own sake...individuals just 'participate,' stop by, say something, do their thing, and move on" (Dean, 2012c). While this appears to offer a great degree of freedom to individuals, such a voluntaristic and contingent connection to the movement offers little in terms of responsibility or obligation, and therefore is a weak basis for organizing as a collectivity.

Other Prefigurations

If solidarity can be thought of in broad terms as responsibility to the other (see Dean, 1995), then proponents of horizontality argue in effect that this responsibility requires that relationships are as voluntary and inclusive as possible; responsibility involves acknowledging the autonomy of every individual, acting together in a spirit of consensus and non-coercion, and respect for the particular and contingent. The experiences of Occupy, however, suggest that these horizontal practices of solidarity have practical limitations that prevent this responsibility from being fully enacted. Further, their very desirability is in question, as the privileging of individual autonomy means that any collective demands or desires are subordinated to the particularity and diversity of individual needs and preferences. An anti-capitalist politics, then, that is capable of organizing and maintaining collective action, must resist this interpretation of solidarity; being responsible to the other will require "vertical and diagonal components in addition to horizontal ones" (Dean, 2012a: 238). In other words, for solidarity to be meaningful, it must be mediated through structures capable of facilitating long-term commitment, mutual obligation and accountability to the other—and this is impossible unless those structures have some degree of verticality, such as forms of leadership or representation.

In fact, it is possible to interpret formal structures and representation as actually *strengthening* solidarity, both internally and externally. First, there are solidarity relationships internal to the organizational form, among participants. On one hand, vertical structures can mediate these relationships in a way that ensures that decision-making can function without repressing division, and that leaders are recognized and subject to accountability. More broadly, formal organizations can be one aspect of what Sears (2014) called an "infrastructure of dissent," defined as the "means through which activists develop political communities capable of learning, communicating and mobilizing together" (2). In this way, organizational infrastructure can build and sustain long-term commitment among participants to each other, by fostering "sustained relationships and sustained political dialogue" (Schein, 2011: 116), and providing a coherence that comes with being centred around unifying demands (Gindin, 2012: 38). Furthermore, by building the capacity of members "to participate and thereby develop their overall political and administrative capacities," formal organizations can facilitate the development of human capacities necessary to act collectively (Panitch, 2008: 199).

Second, vertical structures are capable of expressing a responsibility to an "external" other, outside of the organization; this involves political intervention on another's behalf. Whereas proponents of horizontalism argue that one can not speak on behalf of anyone else, and argue against making demands on the state to achieve "irradiation effects," a representational politics can help to achieve systemic gains that would benefit others, including those who are not present and not participating. This external other can take different forms; on the Left, labour-affiliated parties identify with and ostensibly fight for the interests of the working class, even though the great majority of that class does not participate nor necessarily support the party, and Occupy itself references the more inclusive yet ambiguous "99%."

But whereas labour-affiliated parties ostensibly express solidarity with the external other by raising minimum wages or improving working standards, Occupy has failed to show any responsibility or obligation to its external other, even as it receives its legitimacy by occupying in its name. If the only thing that Occupy can offer those outside of the encampments is to "spread a certain notion of direct democracy" (David Graeber, quoted in Wolfe, 2012), an invitation to create their own encampments, then it is only really expressing solidarity with those capable of participating. Alternatively, vertical structures can be built in a way that represents the interests of an external other, thus taking the barriers to participation seriously.

To the extent that formal and vertical organizational structures build the relationships and capacities necessary for a post-capitalist future, they fulfill roles which can be thought of in terms of prefiguration. However, there is clearly a contestation here over the meaning of prefigurative politics. Attempts by socialists to adopt the term, for instance when Carroll (2006) interprets counter-hegemonic struggles as prefigurative, tend to be rejected by anarchists who see the presence of verticality as fundamentally opposed to the spirit of prefiguration. In response to Carroll, Day (2007) argued that if you want "non-authoritarian diversity" you cannot "'prefigure it' by using 'leadership' to force people into a 'strategically coherent form.' You have to actually live and organize in a non-authoritarian way, here and now." However, there are several reasons to be skeptical about such claims that verticality undermines the prefiguration of a desired democratic future. First, there is an assumption of a direct line between tactics in the present and the desired future, so that formalized hierarchies of leadership *now* predetermine authoritarianism *later*. This is both simplistic and deterministic, denying the possibility of multiple futures as a result of any particular practice or social form. Second, it allows for no substantive differentiation between leadership and authoritarianism, a profound conflation that can only obscure the analysis of any situation, and rigged to prevent any appraisal of verticality. Third, such claims involve a narrowing of the concept of prefiguration, which itself has no "pre-given content"—whether or not a political practice can be identified as prefigurative is therefore "a matter of context, situated judgment and experimentation" (Siltanen, Klodawsky & Andrew, 2015: 276).[91]

All of this suggests that there is nothing about prefigurative politics that automatically excludes the use of vertical structures in creating a better world; in fact, there are indications that they might be more desirable, if not necessary. After all, if the horizontal processes of Occupy are prefiguring the future, is that future even desirable, given its limitations as discussed above? This is particularly questionable when it comes to the exclusivity of Occupy's participationism: if the majority of working people do not have the freedom to participate in these projects, is this not prefiguring an unequal world? The fact is that the present context of capitalism creates real barriers to participation, which proponents of horizontality do not address—this is not just a matter of subjectivity, but the unfortunate reality of market imperatives and financial obligations which allow most people little time to engage in meetings or occupations. Above all, it is not obvious that horizontalism is even appropriate for anti-capitalist politics, given that it has been uncritically adopted from the organizing tactics of second-wave feminism (see Gibson-Graham, 2006: xxiii-xxiv), a move dependent on the major assumption that capitalism has a logic similar to patriarchy, and that it can be combatted as such. If, however, economic exploitation operates in a manner quite differently from systems of oppression based on sex and gender, then it is unlikely that the same organizing tactics will apply to both.[92] For these

91 Further on this point, Siltanen et al. (2015) argue that "prefiguration can be used strategically within the relational dynamics of a more formalized organization—both as an end in itself, and as 'outside' ballast to enable engagements with the political mainstream" (276). This points to the potential complementarity of prefiguration and formal institutions, but also with representation (leadership) on behalf of an external other, and making demands on the state. Indeed, in their case study prefigurative politics is practised by an organization that is "positioned 'inside' and 'outside' the local state" (276).

92 This is a debate that goes beyond the scope of this chapter. For an extended critique of how capitalism is reconceptualized in certain horizontalist literature, and especially of the notion of "economic difference," see Bueckert (2013). I will just raise the point that horizontalist economic politics, whether direct action tactics or "post-capitalist" community economies (Gibson-Graham, 2006) which involve the creation of experiments "here and now," are inherently participationist; rather than seeking systemic changes to working conditions across economic sectors and industries (as the labour movement does), they rely on the initiative (and freedom) of each individual (or community) to improve their own conditions through experimentation. Once again, the unfreedom of the majority of working people to engage in such experiments is not acknowledged.

reasons, verticality might actually be a requirement for prefiguring a desired future, not an impediment.

Without verticality, anti-capitalist solidarity only obliges the individual to themself. Without means of negotiating political divisions, prioritizing what is common over what is individual, or expressing a substantive commitment to those who would be the "99%," Occupy collapsed into the individualism that it first appeared to challenge. Unless movements like Occupy can incorporate vertical structures capable of fostering collectivity, they can only let down many of those who found their politics so resonant, so promising in the first place—those who hoped Occupy might serve a common purpose, and not just the individual desires of those in Zuccotti Park.

SYNERGY BETWEEN FEMINISM AND THE LEFT

Two Moments in the Genealogy of Feminism as a Political Movement

Jacinthe Michaud

Introduction: What It Means to Be Engaged in More than One Political World

There is a persistent narrative surrounding the circumstances of the emergence of contemporary feminism which suggests that, at the turn of the 1970s, the renewal of the women's movement was associated with the influence of other political actors such as the civil rights movement, the student movement, the working-class movement, the anti-poverty movement and the nationalist movement.[93] These movements have, the narrative continues, influenced the political awakening of many women who, having explored the limits of mixed-gender organizations or perhaps were fed up with the hostility of male comrades, decided to build a movement of their own. Yet, as a political movement, feminism did not really need a push to emerge onto the political/public scene as a number of feminist activists were already there, building an autonomous/separate movement. The women's/feminist movement is after all the creation of several categories of women coming from a variety of activist positions and is not derived directly from—although it is transformed by—other political movements (Winter, 2000: 107). Still, a significant number of women activists have crossed the frontiers, in and out of feminism, bringing feminist theories and principles within mixed-gender organizations as well as the spirit of social and political struggles within feminist collectives.

Building an autonomous feminist collective and being at the same time active within a leftist group is defined by Italian feminists as

93 Parts of this chapter come from a book in preparation which is a comparative study of Québécois and Italian feminisms from the end of 1960s until the mid-1980s. I would like to thank Meg Luxton for her challenging comments and careful editing of this text.

"double activism,"[94] creating some sort of synergy between feminism and other political movements. This chapter intends to revisit two historical moments where such synergy was particularly noticeable in Québec. The first moment unfolded during the 1960s and the 1970s when many feminist activists were moving in and out of the Left and the New Left in particular: female students, while leaving the student movement—or young women activists quitting extra-parliamentary Left groups—gave us more than just the impression that the "women's question" was impossible to address within these movements. They quit New Left organizations because the pressure they felt from feminism challenged them about their loyalties and their political motivations in regard to this emerging political context (Trimberger, 1979: 433). The second moment happened during the spring of 2012 when major student associations provoked a long and enduring strike within colleges and universities which evolved later on into a mass popular movement that lasted several months (Poirier St-Pierre & Ethier, 2013). Their primary goal was to counter the Québec government policy to increase university tuition fees by $1,625 over a period of five years, which represented an increase of 75%. The student movement presented an inclusive platform of demands inspired by subaltern and anti-oppression groups, including anarcho-feminist groups and radical feminist collectives that contributed to the success of the student mobilization.

The first section of this chapter presents feminist and other political actors at the centre of these two historical moments. The second section highlights the specific feminist consciousness of those who were crossing the frontiers of movements. Such political consciousness is unique among activists who are moving in and out of mixed-gender

94 This concept describes the simultaneous involvement of women within political organizations (often the Communist Party) and autonomous feminist collectives. Laura Lilli and Chiara Valentini (1979) present double activism as a political engagement specific to a historic period of the Italian political life but also as one that has the potential to go beyond that period. Lilli and Valentini use the word "schizophrenia" to characterize feminist activists who were both members of the Italian Communist Party (PCI) and of autonomous feminist collectives. Their choice of the term suggests that one's own consciousness is split and torn apart; that there is a risk of exhausting the double activist's political will regardless of the level of enthusiasm she puts into her political involvement.

groups and who are also racialized or coming from the LGBTQ communities; in other words, those who have the practice of being engaged within two (or multiple) worlds while not feeling fully whole in any of them.

Feminist Desires to Change the Meaning of Doing Political Struggle

"Should women's questions have priority over class struggle" was the main problem early feminist collectives struggled with. In 1971, a small women's group carrying an undetermined name "Un groupe de femmes de Montréal" [A Montréal women's group] published the *Manifeste des femmes québécoises* [Manifesto of Québécois women]. One of the main concerns expressed in the document was the presence of women within mixed-gender groups. The manifesto was published in the particular context of the judicial history of Québec as the Montréal criminal court had just begun to prosecute members of the Front de libération du Québec (FLQ) [Québec Liberation Front] for terrorism during what was known as the "Crise d'octobre" [October Crisis]. The "Manifeste" set the tone for a feminist materialist analysis of women's condition, pointing to a double oppression, capitalist and patriarchal, and demanded an organizational strategy to construct a feminist analysis to oppose Marxist schemes (Un groupe de femmes, 1971).

The *Manifeste des femmes québécoises* was written by a short-lived collective but was nonetheless the first document to proclaim the autonomy of feminism in relation to the Québécois Left. Later that year, the Front de libération des femmes du Québec (FLFQ) emerged onto the political scene. This collective was structured in small cells whose activities were conducted independently and run almost secretively from one another. Each one of these cells demanded enormous amounts of energy but counted on the participation of ordinary women who came from working-class Montréal neighbourhoods. Right from the beginning, members of the FLFQ were determined to conduct their struggles from an autonomous feminist perspective (Péloquin, 2007: 248). Members of the collective were regular readers of the Québécois journal *Parti pris* (1963-68)[95] but most importantly, they studied contemporary publications like the special issue on feminism by the French journal *Partisans* and other major texts that came from France, the US and many other European countries (O'Leary & Toupin, 1982: 40-41). These texts were discussed collectively; the tension of the usual divide between the necessity to remain engaged in social economic struggles—which implied remaining connected with mixed-gender groups using both the class struggles and the nationalist terms of reference—intermingled constantly with the desire to explore women's issues autonomously, especially the theoretical exploration of the conditions within which women lived their sexuality. There was no consensus within the FLFQ concerning the extent of its connection with other groups as the collective attempted to keep its activities outside the direct control of the male-dominated Left. The collective was always the site of large influxes of new members who were fascinated by the possibility of acting on urgent issues like abortion. The dissolution of the FLFQ in late 1971 was ultimately caused by the difficulty of maintaining unity and cohesion amid so many ideas and demands. Immediately after the dissolution of the FLFQ, two ex-members of the group decided to create the Centre des femmes (CdF) in January 1972. The connection with the extreme-Left became more explicit although the CdF still proclaimed the fundamental necessity to build an autonomous women's movement.

In their respective ways women activists in early feminist collectives, like the FLFQ and the CdF, were engaged in a sort of double activism which took several forms with overlapping allegiances. Indeed, being an active member of a union or being a community organizer within a popular group within a working-class neighbourhood was not the same as being a woman activist in the extreme-Left groups like En lutte! (1972-82) or the LCMLC-PCO (1975-83).[96] The fact is that the particularity and the experience of being a double activist

95 *Parti pris* was devoted to revolutionary socialism and anti colonialism and supported the independence of Québec. According to Malcolm Reid, the history of revolutionary writings began with the first issue of *Parti pris* in 1963 (Reid, 2009 [1972]: 33).

96 In 1979, the Ligue communiste marxiste-léniniste du Canada (LCMLC) became the Parti communiste ouvrier (PCO) [WCP in its English version].

involved in mixed-gender organizations have never been fully explored in Québécois feminist literature (Kruzynski, 2005), albeit a significant number of feminists continue to share their loyalties to both feminism and the Left. Reading feminist journals and other archival documents from the 1970s, anxieties vis-à-vis external interference are palpable, coupled with the fear that the collective's priorities could be decided elsewhere and brought in through the presence of women who get their orders from Marxist-Leninist leaders. Suspicions and accusations of infiltrations by women members of the extreme-Left were numerous and many feminists thought that their group's autonomy was threatened and their consciousness contaminated by a masculine system of thought. In 1982, two round tables organized with former members of the FLFQ and the CdF provided details of how these collectives experienced the political climate back then. Some of the participants recalled intense pressures coming from women known to be members of extreme-Left organizations, who were making the usual criticisms of dividing the working class and therefore, of not being true feminists. Women who were not members of the extreme-Left felt they were losing control of their structures because of these intense pressures coming from outside the collectives they were determined to run autonomously. There was an acute sense that too much time was lost trying to justify feminism by using the same terms of reference of the extreme-Left and answering women's needs from a political terrain that was not their own (O'Leary & Toupin, 1982/1983).

Indeed, the period was marked by hostile attempts to take over the political leadership of grassroots organizations, feminist collectives included. As far as women's groups were concerned, these attempts did not succeed entirely and the women activists never abandoned the desire to build a genuine autonomous feminist movement free of any political interference (O'Leary & Toupin, 1982/1983, 338; Péloquin, 2005: 247-48). There are of course other reasons why FLFQ and CdF disappeared so suddenly after having enjoyed so much popularity, surprising everyone, including their own members. The desire to be the feminist avant-garde with the capacity to provide a genuine Québécois feminist theory on women's oppression clashed with the impossibility of answering all questions and requests coming from all regions outside Montréal. By the time protagonists met again for the round tables, women members of the extreme-Left had massively exited En lutte! and the PCO; many of them were ready to admit that their previous attacks on the idea of an autonomous feminism were wrong but justified nonetheless their persistent desires for unity of voices and unity of action.

Many aspects of the student strike in 2012 share similarities with the 1970s. The specific interaction of/intersection between two powerful political actors—women and youth—characterized the anti-authoritarian spirit and created "places where collisions often occur."[97] This type of interaction/intersection between women and youth cemented a specific type of historical moment provoked by a multiplicity of movements demanding the end to exploitation in ways that are not solely cast in economic terms. In the media, the student strike was sometimes referred as the "Printemps Québécois" [Québécois Spring]; on other occasions, and not without ambiguity, it was called the "Printemps érable" [Maple Spring] in order to connect with the "Arab Spring" that had taken place in North African countries, namely Egypt, Tunisia and Libya in 2011 (Tremblay-Pépin, 2013: 14; Clain, 2013: 405) but generally the strike was referred to as the "Printemps étudiant" [Student Spring].[98] The red square, a small piece of felt, was the visual symbol that the protesters and those who were supportive of their cause proudly attached to their clothes. This symbol was immediately reproduced and diffused in a multiplicity of ways through visual arts and other means of cultural productions throughout the strike and after (Bonenfant et al., 2013). The red square was also the most reviled symbol by those—the Liberal Party of Québec (PLQ), the police and most of the media—who attempted to discredit the student

97 See, Ruth B. Phillips, 2011, p. 173.

98 The three most mediatized student associations are the Association pour une solidarité syndicale étudiante (ASSÉ), the Fédération étudiante universitaire du Québec (FEUQ) and the Fédération étudiante collégiale du Québec (FECQ). The ASSÉ is the most combative and was founded during the American Summit in 2001 in Québec City. The two other associations, the FEUQ and the FECQ, have a strategy of conciliation and of negotiation with the government but during most of the strike of 2012 the three associations maintained a united front despite the government strategy to break their ranks. For a description of major student associations in Québec, see Bonenfant et al. (2013: xxv).

movement as well as their supporters. It served as the pretext for the police to "politically streamline" the protesters during the months that followed the mass popular mobilization that accompanied the strike (Dupuis-Déri & L'Écuyer, 2013: 329-30).

The 2012 student strike was not a spontaneous movement emerging out of nowhere. Two years before, in the winter of 2010, the Association pour une solidarité étudiante (ASSÉ), the most combative student association, began networking and establishing strategic links of solidarity with the Coalition de la main rouge [Coalition of the Red Hand] a large solidarity coalition composed of several hundred popular groups created to fight the commodification and the privatization of public services (Laflamme, 2013: 262; Clain, 2013; Martin, 2013: 433). The ASSÉ carefully planned in detail all phases of the mobilization to come (Poirier St-Pierre & Ethier, 2013). In December 2011, it created the Coalition pour une solidarité syndicale étudiante (CLASSE) especially for the strike, in order to attract independent student associations and to build the largest coalition possible. The CLASSE dominated the entire movement with anarchist-unionist principles and direct action strategies (Laflamme, 2013: 262; Bellemare-Caron, 2013; Martin, 2013: 422; 433). More than any other coalition of student associations, the CLASSE was able to present a comprehensive critical analysis that consistently connected the increase of tuition fees with the deterioration of post-secondary education, the badly managed financing of universities forced to compete within the international scene, the commodification and commercialization of knowledge, the privatization and disappearance of public services, the degradation of the environment and so forth (Poirier St-Pierre and Ethier, 2013; Clain, 2013: 403-04). Its ultimate goal was to make post-secondary education free, although the CLASSE strategically agreed to reduce its demands to a simple freeze on university tuitions in order to maintain unity with the two other student associations, the FECQ and the FEUQ.

The ASSÉ/CLASSE was not only remarkable for being combative and politically astute in its capacity to channel or focus students' anger. Its strength lay in its ability to coalesce; to create a political platform that included all sorts of subaltern subjectivities as well as political movements such as feminism, LGBTQ politics, Indigenous people, activists for social housing and so forth. It is within that context that feminist members of CLASSE proposed to debate the "Déclaration sur la hausse des frais de scolarité" [Declaration on the university tuition fees increase] written by the Comité de coordination de l'Institut Simone de Beauvoir [Simone de Beauvoir Institute Coordination Committee] at Concordia University, which was made public in February 2012. The document denounced the sexist nature of the tuition increase based on the discrepancy of incomes between women and men, the discriminatory effect on single mothers and the negative impact such a policy would have on student diversity on university campuses (Institut Simone de Beauvoir, 2013: 33-40). Normally, such a feminist analysis of the strike contained in the "Déclaration" should have found space for debate within the CLASSE but this did not happen. Thus, in February 2012, all members of the Committee decided to leave the CLASSE and join the women's collective affiliated with the Grève générale illimitée (GGI) at the Université du Québec à Montréal (UQAM) (Delvaux et al., 2013: 142). Many women activists remained with the CLASSE but the reasons for the Committee leaving the coalition were multiple: the recurrent attitude of certain male activists in the Left echoed criticisms made during the previous student strike in 2005. In other countries where similar anti-authoritarian coalitions exist, similar criticisms underline recurrent male hostility towards feminist analysis, harassment of women who want to organize in separate meeting spaces, the hierarchical and sexual division of labour, misogynist attitudes and even cases of sexual aggressions (Mensah, 2005; Beauzamy, 2005; Fillieule et al., 2007; Blais, 2008; Fillieule & Roux, 2009; Galerand, 2009; Lagalisse, 2011; Reynolds, 2013; Roy-Blais, 2013; Landry, 2013; Tremblay-Fournier, 2013; Delvaux et al., 2013; Ancelovici & Roy-Allard, 2013).[99] By claiming inclusivity, ASSÉ/CLASSE seemed to have exposed itself to criticisms more than any other student associations.

Some questions remain nonetheless. Did the declaration of openness to all subaltern subjectivities signal a significant change in leftist

99 The ASSÉ/CLASSE was apparently the student association that received most criticism for sexism and of racism, its inclusive platform being its strength as much as its weakness (Tremblay-Fournier, 2013: 85; Ancelovici & Dupuis-Déri, 2013: 28; Ancelovici & Roy-Allard, 2003: 111).

politics? Had feminist consciousness succeeded in forcing a shift in the original discursive paradigm or were we simply witnessing an attempt of political recuperation? The turn of the 21st century witnessed a diversity of feminist collectives evolving on the margins of the institutionalized women's movement, claiming their right to organize in a non-mixed environment while conducting some of their actions in synergy with mixed-gender and pro-feminist organizations (Breton et al., 2012; Leblanc, 2013). The time of the witch hunts against autonomous feminist collectives was over but, looking closely at the genealogy of events, the student strike—as well as other solidarity coalitions created before—while being truly inclusive in organizing a series of events, still encountered many difficulties in going beyond a declaration of principles coupled with resistance to using feminist theorizations produced by the women's movement (Roux et al., 2005; Falquet, 2005: 19; Michaud, 2010; Jacquemart, 2013; Surprenant & Bigaouette, 2013). By trying to (re)define the terms of the struggle, many feminist activists discovered that they were placed in the same subaltern position they were hoping to fight with the help of the organization and/or the coalition itself; they discovered that, when men declared their solidarity with women's issues, they tended to limit the space taken by feminist analysis within the movement and to control the use of its terms of reference (Falquet, 2005; Fillieule et al., 2007: 10; Jacquemart, 2013). Activists' lives, their gender, their race, their class, their sexuality and their trajectory, in and outside political activities that bring them together, differed and their goals within a larger coalition are not always entirely compatible with the dominant political discourse, especially if defined in generic and neutral terms. The following section looks at issues of loyalties and consciousness as well as the problem of space for the expression of diversities within coalitions.

Crossing Frontiers of Movements: Allegiances, Loyalties and Erasures of Struggles

During the 1970s, the synergy between feminism and the extreme-Left highlighted tensions and divergences within early feminist collectives over how feminists should respond to the diktat of the Left: Either rejecting male politics or embracing the opportunity to connect with struggles conducted by leftist organizations. Many feminists who rejected being members of mixed-gender organizations wanted to develop an autonomous women's movement not only free from external interference but completely separated from any kind of political movements dominated by masculine thought. Feminists interested in working with men's organizations did not hesitate to insist that feminism *was* a political movement—something that the vast majority of their male counterparts always refused to admit—but they were also convinced that their discourses, their practices and modes of organizing contributed to enlarging the sphere of traditional politics through the democratization of public/political practices. They recognized the urgency of participating in social struggles but they also felt the pressure coming from autonomous feminism coupled with certain alienation in the mixed organizations. They often felt divided between two worlds that were very far apart. For these activists, evolving as feminists within spaces that denied their subjectivity and expressed doubts about their loyalty, the challenge was to refuse the split of their political consciousness. This meant becoming political subjects according to their own rules, accepting their own gaze on their own action: both against and beyond the gaze of others (be they male comrades or feminist allies). They could at least claim their autonomy of speech and their autonomy of action in whatever terrain they chose to speak or act.

In the 1970s, there were two dimensions to the meaning of autonomy which intervened simultaneously in the construction of a political subject from the position of the lives of double activists: (1) the autonomy within and outside male defined organizations—the party, the extra-parliamentary Left, the unions—against masculine interventions in women's structures and/or committees women worked to create; and, (2) the autonomy that connected affirmatively and defensively activists with other feminists; affirmatively because it created conditions of solidarity among women and defensively because the affirmation of their autonomy, in and outside feminist collectives, became the means by which they could defend themselves against attacks concerning their loyalties and against the temptation of separation from the rest of society.

The tension brought by double activism in the lives of those who experienced it as well as those who witnessed it within feminist collectives did not fade away with the decline of mass mobilizations in the '80s. The phenomenon continues to raise questions about how feminist activists are involved in political parties and unions. Furthermore, the multifaceted dimensions of double activism have appeared in other mixed-gender groups organizing, for instance, around gay and lesbian sexual practices and political visibility. For lesbians involved in mixed homosexual groups, the difficulty was to find their expression within the women's movement as well. Within feminism, if the profile of a double activist is one of a heterosexual woman suspected of a false consciousness and of living with divided loyalty, the profile of a lesbian double activist is more likely one who tries to conciliate a dual subjectivity: one in a mixed-gender homosexual group and the other in a feminist collective. In all cases, neither the gay collective nor the feminist collective were able to give her the space she required.

Then, there was also the invisibility of racialized groups of people within the Left as much as within the women's movement: Indigenous, immigrants and racialized women. In early Québécois political anti-colonialist and socialist publications (Austin, 2007; Mills, 2010), the notion of race was often used as an element of comparison; the condition of African-Americans in the US was used to illustrate Québec national oppression. It was also used within feminism as a means of comparing oppressions that implicitly revealed its own process of racialization. In doing so, feminist activists hinted at—although not explicitly and perhaps not knowingly—Fanon's exposure of Black consciousness when he stated that "Les nègres sont comparison" [The Negro is comparison] (Fanon, 1952: 170-71), by which he meant that Black men [sic] always want to compare themselves to someone of higher social status, always wondering if the other is better or worse than they are. Fanon's thinking indirectly provides some clues as to the reasons why African-Americans were the most likely chosen group some feminists used to describe the oppression of women in Québec and elsewhere among feminists of the Western world. One of these clues points to the fascination many had for the US, which appeared to deal with a brand of diversity/discrimination that placed race at the core of liberation discourse, including feminist discourses.

However, Fanon's approach to comparison has nothing to do with what feminists of the 1970s in the West were actually doing when they compared women's condition to that of African-Americans. Yet only male voices that came from the Black movement fascinated Western Europeans and Québécois feminists. Their focus was directed at addressing the commonality of race oppression with White female oppression. Little or no attention was given to African-American feminist theories as well as to the feminist theories developed by other racialized categories of women such as Chicanas and Indigenous women, which were also circulating during the same period (Hull, Scott & Smith, 1982; Ship, 1991; Smith, 2005). Race was the terrain for comparison and opened the space for connection, but in this process, race became an appendix of gender just as class analysis uses gender as an extension of its own revolutionary project without integrating it. By making such a comparison, feminist activists found a solid ground on which to demand autonomy for their organizations, leaving behind what is absent from the comparison, namely subaltern feminist critiques of mainstream feminism. Feminism in the 1970s needed to remove the notion of race from the notion of "woman" before reintroducing the latter into the movement. The most important task of the moment was to build solidarity without the threat of divisiveness sometimes caused by the call of racism.

Anti-racist movements, with their critique of whiteness, represented the most fundamental challenge to come for political movements, feminism included. If the presence of young queer is more noticeable within the horizon of creating sustainable coalitions in Québec (Breton et al., 2012)—although LGBT and queer issues are still marginalized during public events (Roux et al., 2005: 6)—the almost complete absence of racialized people and their organizations persists. If during the 2012 student strike a feminist analysis of the tuition increase was proposed but not debated, thus not included, the coalition remained silent on the impact the increase would have on women and men students of colour and foreign students (Cyr et al., 2013; Ancelovici & Roy-Allard, 2013: 112). It is outside the proposed analysis by major student associations—and most importantly the CLASSE—that one finds a discursive connection between the government's plans to increase tuition with the economic development of the Québec north named the Plan Nord [North Plan]. In April 2012, a group of Innu women, following the arrest of members of their communities for blocking the main road near Sept-Iles, decided to march 1,000 kilometres, from the Basse Côte Nord [lower northern coast] to Montréal. There, they joined the student protest in front of the Salon des Congrès and disrupted Premier Jean Charest's speech on the development of the Québécois North. The students protested the increase of tuition fees—discursively within the context of globalization, competition among universities and the commercialization of knowledge—while the Innu women denounced the direct connection of the same increase of university tuitions with the development of the North without consulting Indigenous communities whose ways of lives are being destroyed. There was at the end some sort of connection between the two struggles as the presence of Indigenous women forced the student movement, concretely even if temporarily, to connect with a subaltern subjectivity that is most often ignored by other political movements (Duhaime et al., 2013: 493-94; Delvaux et al., 2013: 147). Despite its inclusiveness and desire for intersectionality with gender, race and sexuality, the CLASSE did not really succeed in uprooting the masculine vision of class from its dominant historical position (Laflamme, 2013; Martin, 2013: 446).

Conclusion

There are some similarities between these two moments, in particular the feminists' desire to preserve at all cost—then and now—spaces of autonomy in the face of resistance, even open male hostility vis-à-vis feminist principles and analysis. The fact that many political groups proclaim themselves to be inclusive of women's issues—or other issues carried by subaltern groups—does not guarantee the elimination of exclusionary practices aimed at controlling feminism and the space it takes within mixed-gender coalitions, nor does it guarantee the safety and comfort of individual women participating in those groups. There is however a noticeable difference between the two historical moments. In the 1970s, extreme-Left groups attempted to control autonomous feminist collectives, trying to determine which ones were truly feminists and devoted to working-class women. In 2012 it was the turn of feminist activists who were attempting to transform the meaning of the struggle within organizations and coalitions they were involved in. As a certain dualism persists between two types of socially and politically constructed terrains—the terrain of women's organizing and the terrain delimited by public/political spheres—the formation of the feminist political consciousness specific to those who are crossing the borders between movements is a feminist issue as well as a terrain of struggle and as such it should be included in feminist scholarly research. Activists' itineraries and political consciousness are no longer linear nor split as in the 1970s but shaped by political protests created around temporary coalitions composed of female and male activists. Some of these activists are racialized or queer or characterized as neutral female or male actors, all subjected to internal power relations within fragmented coalitions of anti-authoritarian activists and anti-capitalist groups in which several regroupings of feminist queers, feminist radicals and anarcho-feminists participate (Breton et al., 2012; Fiore, 2014). Thus, if there is no real rupture or interruption that irremediably separated these two historical moments, there is at least one thing that needs to be reckoned with for present and future coalitions: the persistent attitude of those who are accustomed to being at the centre of political struggles. If feminism, Indigenous politics and LGBTQ politics are to be included—whose subjectivities usually come in from the margins—then the transformation of coalitions' core discourse needs to go much deeper than simply adding demands.

BIBLIOGRAPHY

Abbot, N. (2009). ME/CFS Research: What do Patients Want? Why isn't it Happening? *Royal Society of Medicine*. Retrieved Aug. 13, 2015 from http://www.meresearch.org.uk/information/publications/what-do-patients-want/.

Adam, B.D. (1978). *The Survival of Domination*. New York: Elsevier/Greenwood.

Adam, B.D. (1993). Post-Marxism and the New Social Movements. *Canadian Review of Sociology and Anthropology*, 30(3), 316-36.

Adam, B.D. (2001). Globalization and the Mobilization of Gay and Lesbian Communities. In Hamel, P., Lustiger-Thaler, H., Pieterse, J.N. & Roseneil, S. (eds.), *Globalization and Social Movements*. New York: St Martin's/Palgrave.

Adam, B.D. (2002). Theorizing the Globalization of Gay and Lesbian Movements. *Research in Political Sociology*, 10, 123-37.

Adam, B.D. (2005). Domination, Resistance, and Subjectivity. In Romero, M. & Margolis, E. (eds.), *The Blackwell Companion to Social Inequalities* (pp. 100-14). Malden, MA: Blackwell.

Adese, J. (2015). Behaving Unexpectedly in Expected Places: First Nation Artists and the Embodiment of Visual Sovereignty. In Coburn, E. (ed.), *More Will Sing Their Way to Freedom: Indigenous Resistance and Resurgence* (pp. 129-49). Winnipeg: Fernwood.

Adkin, L. (1992). Counter-Hegemony and Environmental Politics in Canada. In Carroll, W. (ed.), *Organizing Dissent: Contemporary Social Movements in Theory and Practice* (pp. 135-56). Toronto: Garamond Press.

Adkin, L. (1998). Ecological Politics in Canada: Elements of a Strategy of Collective Action. In Keil, R., Bell, D., Penz, P. & Fawcett, L. (eds.), *Political Ecology: Global and Local* (pp. 292-324). London & New York. Routledge.

Adkin, L. (2003). Ecology, Political Economy, and Social Transformation. In Clement, W. & Vosko, L. (eds.), *Changing Canada: Political Economy as Transformation* (pp. 393-421). Montreal & Kingston: McGill-Queen's University Press.

Adkin, L. (2014). Environmental Movement in Canada. In Doyle, T. & MacGregor, S. (eds.), *Environmental Movements Around the World: Shades of Green in Politics and Culture* (pp. 131-62). Vol. 1. Santa Barbara, CA: ABC-CLIO, LLC.

Adkin, L. (ed.). (2009). *Environmental Conflict and Democracy in Canada*. Vancouver: UBC Press.

Adkin, L. & Courteau, B. (Forthcoming). "All Against the Haul": The Long Road to the Athabasca Tar Sands. In Adkin, L. (ed.), *First World Petro-Politics: The Political Ecology and Governance of Alberta*. Toronto: University of Toronto Press.

Adorno, T. (1973). *Negative Dialectics*. London: Routledge.

Agartan, T., Choi, W.Y. & Huynh, T. (2011). The Transformation of the Capitalist World: 1750-1850. In Martin, W.G. (ed.), *Making Waves: Worldwide Social Movements, 1750-2005* (pp. 168-80). London: Paradigm Publishers.

Agence France-Presse. (2009). Younger Delegates Issue Reminder to Anyone Who Will Still Be Alive in 2050. *National Post*, Dec. 11, p. A11.

AIDS Activist History Project. (2015). Retrieved Aug. 24, 2015 from http://www.aidsactivisthistory.ca/.

Alberts, S. (2010, Feb. 19). Premiers Seek Exemption from U.S. Green Tariffs. *National Post*, p. A5.

Albo, G. & Fanelli, C. (2014). *Austerity Against Democracy: An Authoritarian Phase of Neoliberalism?* Toronto: Socialist Project. Retrieved Aug. 10, 2015 from http://www.socialistproject.ca/documents/AusterityAgainstDemocracy.pdf.

Albo, G. (1994). Competitive Austerity and Capitalist Employment Policy. *Socialist Register*, 30.

Albo, G. (1997). A World Market of Opportunities? Capitalist Obstacles and Left Economic Policies. In Panitch, L. (ed.), *Socialist Register 1997*. London: Merlin Press.

Alfred, T. (1999). *Peace, Power, Righteousness*. Don Mills, ON: Oxford University Press.

Alfred, T. (2009a). Colonialism and State Dependency. *Journal of Aboriginal Health*. 5(1), 42-60.

Alfred, T. (2009b). *Wasáse: Indigenous Pathways of Action and Freedom*. Toronto: University of Toronto.

Ali, T. (2015). *The Extreme Centre: A Warning*. London: Verso Books.

Alinsky, S. (1971). *Rules for Radicals*. New York: Random House.

Altamirano-Jiminez, I. (2013). *Indigenous Encounters with Neoliberalism: Place, Women, and the Environment in Canada and Mexico*. Vancouver: UBC Press.

Altvater, E. (2006). The Social and Natural Environment of Fossil Capitalism. In Panitch, L. & Leys, C. (eds.), *Coming to Terms with Nature: Socialist Register 2007*. London: The Merlin Press.

Ambler, S. (2013). *Invisible Women: A Call to Action. A Report on Missing and Murdered Indigenous Women in Canada*. Speaker of the House of Commons. <acatcanada.org/downloadXC2-411-2-1-1-eng.pdf.

Amin, A. & Thrift, A. (2002). *Cities: Reimagining the Urban*. Cambridge: Polity.

Amirault, J.R. (2014). Lessons of Occupy: Towards a Consequential Socialist Politics for the 99 Percent. *Socialist Studies*, 10(1), 133-51.

Ancelovici, M. & Dupuis-Déri, F. (2013). Retour sur le Printemps érable. In Ancelovoci, M. & Francis Dupuis, D. (eds.), *Un Printemps Rouge et Noir : Regards Croisés sur la Grève étudiante de 2012* (pp. 7-33). Montréal: Les éditions écosociété.

Ancelovici, M. & Roy-Allard, M. (2013). La Démocratie Directe en Mouvement : Structures et Rapports de Pouvoir au Sein de la Classe. In Ancelovoci, M. & Dupuis-Déri, F. (eds.), *Un Printemps Rouge et Noir: Regards Croisés sur la Grève étudiante de 2012*, (pp. 87-114). Montréal: Les éditions écosociété.

Anderson, P. (1998). *The Origins of Postmodernity*. London: Verso.

Andrews, K.T. & Biggs, M. (2006). The Dynamics of Protest Diffusion: Movement Organizations, Social Networks, and News Media in the 1960 Sit-ins. *American Sociological Review*, 71(5), 752-77.

Ansar, A., Caldecott, B. & Tilbury, J. (2013). Stranded Assets and the Fossil Fuel Divestment Campaign: What does Divestment Mean for the Valuation of Fossil Fuel Assets? *Smith School of Enterprise and the Environment*. Retrieved Aug. 23, 2015 from http://www.smithschool.ox.ac.uk/research-programmes/stranded-assets/SAP-divestment-report-final.pdf.

Appudurai, A. (1996). *Modernity at Large: Cultural Dimensions of Globalization*. Minneapolis: University of Minnesota Press.

APTN. (2013). Journey of Nishiuu Walkers Names Now Etched into the History of this Country. Retrieved March 26, 2015 from http://aptn.ca/news/2013/03/26/journey-of-nishiyuu-walkers-names-now-etched-into-history-of-this-country/.

Arabella Advisors. (2015, Sept. 15). Measuring the Growth of the Global Fossil Fuel Divestment Movement. Retrieved from http://www.arabellaadvisors.com/wp-content/uploads/2015/09/Measuring-the-Growth-of-the-Divestment-Movement.pdf.

Archibugi, D. & Held, D. (eds.). (1995). *Cosmopolitan Democracy: An Agenda for a New World Order*. Cambridge: Polity.

Arendt, H. (1958). *The Human Condition*. Chicago: University of Chicago Press.

Aristotle. (1963). *Ethics*. Translated and edited by Thomson, J.A.K. London: Penguin.

Aristotle. (1996). *The Politics* and *The Constitution of Athens*. Everson, S. (ed.). Cambridge: Cambridge University Press.

Armbruster-Sandoval, R. (2003). Globalization and Transnational Labor Organizing: The Honduran Maquiladora Industry and the Kimi Campaign. *Social Science History*, 27(4), 551-76.

Armstrong, E.A. & Bernstein, M. (2008). Culture, Power, and Institutions: A Multi-Institutional Politics Approach to Social Movement. *Sociological Theory*, 26(1), 74-99.

Aronowitz, S. (2003). *How Class Works*. New Haven: Yale University Press.

Arquette, M., Cole, M. & the Akwesasne Task Force on the Environment. (2004). Restoring our relationships for the future. In Blaser, M. et al. (eds.), *In the Way of Development: Indigenous Peoples, Life Projects, and Globalization* (pp. 332-50). London: Zed Books.

Arregui, E.V. & Roman, R. (2013). *Continental Crucible: Big Business, Workers and Unions in the Transformation of North America*. Halifax: Fernwood.

Arrighi, G., Hopkins, T.K. & Wallerstein, I. (1989). *Antisystemic Movements*. London: Verso.

Arrighi, G. (1994). *The Long Twentieth Century*. London: Verso.

Association Pour une Solidarité Syndicale étudiante. (2014). *Statuts et Règlements de l'Association Pour une Solidarité Syndicale Étudiante*. Montréal: Association Pour une Solidarité Syndicale étudiante. Retreived Aug. 20, 2015 from http://www.asse-solidarite.qc.ca/wp-content/uploads/2014/09/statuts-et-reglements-derniere-mise-a-jour-avril-2014.pdf.

Atleo, C. (Kam'ayaam/Chachim'multhnii). (2015). Aboriginal Economic Development and Living Nuu-chah-nulth-aht. In Coburn, E. (ed.), *More Will Sing Their Way to Freedom: Indigenous Resistance and Resurgence* (pp. 150-66). Winnipeg: Fernwood.

Atleo, C. (Kam'ayaam/Chachim'multhnii). (n.d.). *From Indigenous Nationhood to Neoliberal Aboriginal Economic Development: Charting the Evolution of Indigenous-Settler Relations in Canada*. University of Victoria: Canadian Social Economy Hub.

Atleo, E.R. (Umeek). (2004). *Tsawalk: A Nuu-chah-Nulth Worldview*. Vancouver: University of British Columbia.

Atleo, E.R. (Umeek). (2011). *Principles of Tsawalk: An Indigenous Approach to Global Crisis*. Vancouver: University of British Columbia.

Austin, D. (2007). All Roads Led to Montreal: Black Power, the Caribbean, and the Black Radical Tradition in Canada. *Journal of African History*, 92(4), 516-39.

Bain, B. (forthcoming). Fire, Passion and Politics: The Creation of Blockorama as Black Queer Diasporic Space in the Toronto Pride Festivities. In Gentile, P., Kinsman, G. & Rankin, P. (eds.), *Activating Resistance: Remembering Sex/Gender Struggles*. Vancouver: UBC Press.

Bakker, I. & Gill, S. (eds.). (2003). *Power, Production and Social Reproduction*. New York: Palgrave Macmillan.

Bakker, K. (2005). Katrina: The Public Transcript of "Disaster." *Environment & Planning D: Society and Space*, 23, 795-802.

Ball, D. (2012, Apr. 9). Mexican Journalist Karla Ramírez Wins Battle against Deportation. *Vancouver Observer*. Retrieved Oct. 31, 2012 from http://www.vancouverobserver.com/politics/2012/04/09/mexican-journalist-karla-ram%C3%ADrez-wins-battle-against-deportation-others-face.

Bannerji, H. (1995). *Thinking Through: Essays on Feminism, Marxism and Anti-Racism*. Toronto: Women's Press.

Banting, K. & Myles, J. (eds.). (2013). *Inequality and the Fading of Redistributive Politics*. Vancouver: UBC Press.

Barker, C., Cox, L., Krinsky, J. & Nilsen, A.G. (eds.). (2013) *Marxism and Social Movements*. Leiden: Brill.

Barker, C. (2013). Class Struggle and Social Movements. In Barker, C., Cox, L., Krinsky, J. & Nilsen, A.G. (eds.), *Marxism and Social Movements* (pp. 41-62). Leiden: Brill.

Barker, K.K. (2005). *The fibromyalgia story: Medical Authority and Women's Worlds of Pain*. Philadelphia: Temple University Press.

Barrows-Friedman, N. (2015, Apr. 22). Wesleyan Students Demand Divestment from Prisons, Fossil Fuels, and Israeli Occupation. *Electronic Intifada*. Retrieved Aug. 23, 2015 from http://www.electronicintifada.net/blogs/nora-barrows-friedman/wesleyan-students-demand-divestment-prisons-fossil-fuels-and-israeli.

Barry, A., Osborne, T. & Rose, N. (1996). *Foucault and Political Reason*. Chicago: University of Chicago Press.

Bartelson, J. (1995). *A Genealogy of Sovereignty*. Cambridge: Cambridge University Press.

Bartelson, J. (2001). *The Critique of the State*. Cambridge: Cambridge University Press.

Bartholomew, A. & Mayer, M. (1992). Nomads of the Present: Mellucci's Contribution to "New Social Movement" Theory. *Theory, Culture & Society*, 9(4), 141-59.

Barton, A. (2011, Dec. 18). B.C. Program Offers Independence to People with Intellectual Disabilities. *The Globe and Mail*. Vancouver. Retrieved Mar. 13, 2015 from http://www.theglobeandmail.com/life/health-and-fitness/bc-program-offers-independence-to-people-with-intellectual-disabilities/article4247784/.

Batellier, P. & Sauvé, L. (2009/10). La Mobilisation des Citoyens Autour du Gaz de Schiste au Québec: Les Leçons à Tirer. *Gestion*. 36, 49-58.

Bauman, Z. (2000). *Liquid Modernity*. London: Polity.

Beaumont, M. & Dart, G. (eds.) (2010). *Restless Cities*. London: Verso.

Beauzamy, B. (2005). Quel est le coût de l'Intégration des Mouvements Féministes à la Sphère Altermondialiste? *Anthropologie et Sociétés*, 29(3), 59-76.

Beck, U. (1992). *Risk Society*. London: Sage.

Beck, U. (2010). Climate for Change, or How to Create a Green Modernity? *Theory, Culture & Society*, 27(2-3), 254-66.

Bégin-Caouette, O. & Jones, G. (2014). Student Organizations in Canada and Quebec's "Maple Spring." *Studies in Higher Education*, 39(3), 412-25.

Behrens, M. (2006). Get on Board: Freedom Caravan and Camp Hope. *Homes Not Bombs*. Retrieved Sept. 20, 2012 from http://www.homesnotbombs.ca/caravan.htm.

Bélanger, P. (1984). *Le Mouvement Etudiant Québecois : Son Passé, Ses Revendications et Ses Luttes (1960-1983)*. Montréal: Association nationale des étudiants et étudiantes du Québec.

Bellemare-Caron, R. (2013). Les Anarchistes et le Mouvement étudiant. In Bellemare-Caron, R., Breton, É., Cyr, M.A., Dupuis-Déri, F. & Kruzynski, A. (eds.), *Nous Sommes Ingouvernables : Les Anarchistes Aujourd'Hui* (pp. 95-117). Montréal: Lux Éditeur.

Benford, R. & Snow, D. (2000). Framing Processes and Social Movements: An Overview and Assessment. *Annual Review of Sociology*, 26, 611-39.

Benhabib, S. (1990). Afterword: Communicative Ethics and Contemporary Controversies in Practical Philosophy. In Benhabib, S. & Dallmayr F.R. (eds.), *The Communicative Ethics Controversy* (pp. 330-69). Cambridge: MIT Press.

Berger, R.J. (2008). Disability and the Dedicated Wheelchair Athlete: Beyond the "Supercrip" Critique. *Journal of Contemporary Ethnography*, 37(6), 647-78. Beverly Hills: Sage.

Bernhardt, A. et al. (2008). *Broken Laws, Unprotected Workers*. Retrieved Jan. 8, 2016 from http://www.nelp.org/content/uploads/2015/03/BrokenLawsReport2009.pdf?nocdn=1.

Blackstock, C. (2003). First Nations Child and Family Services: Restoring Peace and Harmony in First Nations Communities. In Kufeldt, K. & McKenzie, B. (eds.), *Child Welfare: Connecting Research Policy and Practice* (pp. 331-42). Waterloo: Wilfrid Laurier University Press.

Blais, M. (2008). Féministes Radicales et Hommes Proféministes: l'Alliance Piégée. In Dupuis-Déri, F. (ed.), *Québec en Mouvements: Idées et Pratiques Militantes Contemporaines* (pp. 147-75). Montréal: Lux Éditeur.

Bloom, J. & Martin, Jr., W.E. (2013). *Black Against Empire: The History and Politics of the Black Panther Party*. Berkeley: UC Press.

Blühdorn, I. (2011). The Politics of Unsustainability: COP15, Post-Ecologism, and the Ecological Paradox. *Organization & Environment*, 24(1), 34-53.

Bobo, K. (2008). *Wage Theft in America*. New York: The New Press.

Bocking, S. (2014, Aug. 21). Why Divestment Won't Succeed. *Alternatives Journal*. Retrieved Aug. 23, 2015 from http://www.alternativesjournal.ca/community/blogs/ecologic/why-divestment-wont-succeed.

Bocock, R. (1986). *Hegemony*. London & New York: Ellis Horwood & Tavistock Publication.

Boggs, C. (1976). *Gramsci's Marxism*. London: Pluto

Bonenfant, M., Glinoer, A. & Lapointe, M-E. (2013). *Le Printemps Québécois: Une Anthologie*. Montréal: Écosociété.

Borgatti, S.P. & Halgin, D.S. (2011). Analyzing Affiliation Networks. In Scott, J. & Carrington, P.J. (eds.), *The Sage Handbook of Social Network Analysis* (pp. 417-33). London: Sage.

Bowles, S. & Gintis, H. (1987). *Democracy and Capitalism*. New York: Basic.

Braidotti, R. (2011). *Nomadic Theory: The Portable Rosi Braidotti*. New York: Columbia University Press.

Braun, B. (2002). *The Intemperate Rainforest: Nature, Culture, and Power on Canada's West Coast*. Minneapolis: University of Minnesota Press.

Brecher, J., Costello, T. & Smith, B. (2000). *Globalization from Below: The Power of Solidarity*. Cambridge: South End Press.

Breines, W. (1989). *Community and Organization in the New Left, 1962-1968: The Great Refusal*. New Brunswick: Rutgers University Press.

Brennan, J. (2015). *Ascent of Giants: NAFTA, Corporate Power and the Growing Income Gap* (p. 63). Ottawa: Canadian Centre for Policy Alternatives.

Breton, É., Jeppesen, S., Kruzynski, A. and Sarrasin, R. (2012). Feminisms at the Heart of Contemporary Anarchism in Québec: Grassroots Practices on Intersectionality. *Canadian Women's Studies/les Cahiers de la femme*, 29(3), 147-59.

Broadbent Institute. (2014). *Haves and Have-Nots* (p. 16). Ottawa: Broadbent Institute.

Brockington, D. (2008). Powerful Environmentalisms: Conservation, Celebrity and Capitalism. *Media, Culture & Society*, 30(4), 551-68.

Brody, H. (2001). *The Other Side of Eden: Hunters, Farmers and the Shaping of the World*. Vancouver: Douglas & McIntyre.

Brown, P., Morello-Frosch, R., Zavestoski, & the Contested Illness Research Group. (2012). *Contested Illnesses: Citizens, Science, and Health Social Movements*. Berkeley: University of California Press.

Bruff, I. (2014). The Rise of Authoritarian Neoliberalism. *Rethinking Marxism*, (26), 113-29.

Brugmann, J. (2009). *Welcome to the Urban Revolution: How Cities Are Changing the World*. Toronto: Viking Canada.

Brulle, R. (2014). Environmentalism in the United States. In Doyle, T. & MacGregor, S. (eds.), *Environmental Movements Around the World: Shades of Green in Politics and Culture* (pp. 163-94). Vol. 1. Santa Barbara: ABC-CLIO, LLC.

Bruner, A. (1981). Out of the Closet: Study of Relations between the Homosexual Community and the Police. In *Report to Mayor Arthur Eggleton and the Council of the City of Toronto*, Sept. 24.

Buechler, S.M. (2008). *Critical Sociology*. Boulder: Paradigm Publishers.

Buechler, S.M. (2000). *Social Movements in Advanced Capitalism*. New York: Oxford University Press.

Buechler, S. M. (2002). Toward a Structural Approach to Social Movements. *Sociological Views on Political Participation in the 21st Century*, (10), 1-45.

Buechler, S.M. (2011). *Understanding Social Movements*. Boulder: Paradigm Publishers.

Bueckert, M. (2013). *Reification and Alternatives to Development*. Unpublished Master's thesis. Ottawa: Carleton University.

Building Relationships and Community in an IWW workplace Committee. (2012). Retrieved Aug. 20, 2015 from http://recomposition.info/2012/10/11/building-relationships-and-community-in-an-iww-workplace-committee/.

Bunch, C. and Myron, N. (eds.). (1974). *Class and Feminism, A Collection of Essays from The Furies*. Baltimore: Diana Press.

Bunch, C. (1975). Not For Lesbians Only... *Quest*, 2(2), 50-56.

Burgess. A. (forthcoming). The Multiple Emergences of the Toronto Dyke March. In Gentile, P., Kinsman, G. & Rankin, P. (eds.), *Activating Resistance: Remembering Sex/Gender Struggles*. Vancouver: UBC Press.

Burns, J. (2011). *Reviving the Strike: How Working People can Regain Power and Transform America*. Brookyln: Ig Publishing.

Burtch, B., Pescitelli, A. & Haskell, R. (2015). LGBTQ Movements in Western Canada: British Columbia. In Tremblay, M. (ed.), *Queer Mobilizations, Social Movement Activism and Canadian Public Policy* (pp. 142-62). Vancouver: UBC Press.

Butler, J. (1997). Merely Cultural. *Social Text*, 5(3/4), 265-77.

Butler, J., Laclau, E. & Zizek, S. (2000). *Contingency, Hegemony, Universality: Contemporary Dialogues on the Left*. London: Verso.

Byrne, J., Toly, N. & Glover, L. (2011). *Transforming Power: Energy, Environment, and Society in Conflict*. Piscataway: Transaction Publishers.

Camfield, D. (2011). *Canadian Labour in Crisis: Reinventing the Workers' Movement*. Winnipeg: Fernwood.

Cammaerts, B., Mattoni, A. & McCurdy, P. (eds.). (2013). *Mediation and Protest Movements*. Bristol, UK: Intellect.

Campaign 2000. (2015). *Child Poverty 25 Years On: We Can Fix This*. Toronto: Family Service Toronto.

Campbell, D. & Dillon, M. (eds.). (1993). *The Political Subject of Violence*. Manchester: Manchester University Press.

Canadian Council for Refugees. (n.d.). Migrant Workers: Canada's Disposable Workforce. Retrieved Sept. 12, 2012 from http://ccrweb.ca/en/migrant-workers.

Cardinal, H. (1969). *The Unjust Society: The Tragedy of Canada's Indians*. Edmonton: M.G. Hurtig.

Carr, K. (1999, Nov. 17). Identity Politics: A Politics of Defeat. *Green Left Weekly*. Retrieved Aug. 21, 2015 from http://www.greenleft.org.au/.

Carrington, D. (2015, Mar. 15). Climate Change: UN Backs Fossil Fuel Divestment Campaign. *The Guardian*. Retrieved Aug. 23, 2015 from http://www.theguardian.com/environment/2015/mar/15/climate-change-un-backs-divestment-campaign-paris-summit-fossil-fuels.

Carroll, W.K. (1997). *Organizing Dissent: Contemporary Social Movements in Theory and Practice* (2nd ed). Toronto: Garamond Press.

Carroll, W.K. (2006). Hegemony, Counter-Hegemony, Anti-Hegemony. *Socialist Studies*, 2(2), 9-43.

Carroll, W.K. (2010). Crisis, Movements, Counter-Hegemony: In Search of the New. *Interface* 2(2), 168-98.

Carroll, W.K. (2015a). Modes of Cognitive Praxis in Transnational Alternative Policy Groups. *Globalizations* 12, 710-27.

Carroll, W.K. (2015b). What Radical Means in the 21st Century: Robust Radicalism. *Review of Radical Political Economics* 47, 663-68.

Carroll, W.K. (2016). *Expose, Oppose, Propose: Alternative Policy Groups and the Struggle for Global Justice*. London & Halifax: Zed Books & Fernwood.

Carroll, W.K. & Huxtable, D. (2014). Building Capacity for Alternative Knowledge: The Canadian Centre for Policy Alternatives. *Canadian Review of Social Policy* 70, 93-111.

Carroll, W.K. & Ratner, R.S. (1989). Social Democracy, Neo-Conservatism and Hegemonic Crisis in British Columbia. *Critical Sociology*, 16(1), 29-53.

Carroll, W.K. & Ratner, R.S. (1994). Between Leninism and Radical Pluralism: Gramscian Reflections on Counter-Hegemony and the New Social Movements. *Critical Sociology,* 20(2), 3-26.

Carroll, W.K. & Ratner, R.S. (1995). Old Unions and New Social Movements. *Labour/Le Travail* (35), 195-221.

Carroll, W.K. & Ratner, R.S. (1996). Framing and Cross-Movement Networking in Contemporary Social Movements. *The Sociological Quarterly,* (37), 601-25.

Carroll, W.K. & Ratner, R.S. (1999). Media Strategies and Political Projects: A Comparative Study of Social Movements. *Canadian Journal of Sociology,* 24(1), 1-34.

Carroll, W.K. & Ratner, R.S. (2001). Sustaining Oppositional Culture in "Post-Socialist" Times: A Comparative Study of Three Social Movement Organizations. *Sociology,* 35, 605-29.

Carroll, W.K. & Ratner, R.S. (2010) Social Movements and Counter-Hegemony: Lessons from the Field. *New Proposals,* 4(1), 7-22.

Carroll, W.K. & Shaw, M. (2001) Consolidating a Neoliberal Policy Bloc in Canada, 19761996. *Canadian Public Policy,* 27(2), 123.

Carruthers, B.M. et al. (2003). Myalgic Encephalomyelitis/Chronic Fatigue Syndrome: Clinical Working Case Definition, Diagnostic and Treatment Protocols. *Journal of Chronic Fatigue Syndrome,* 11(1), 7-97.

Carruthers, B.M. et al. (2011). Myalgic Encephalomyelitis: International Consensus Criteria. *Journal of Internal Medicine,* 270, 327-38.

Castells, M. (1996). *The Rise of the Network Society.* Oxford: Blackwell.

Castells, M. (2004). *The Power of Identity* (2nd ed.). Malden: Blackwell.

Castells, M. (2009). *Communication Power.* Oxford: Oxford University Press.

Castells, M. (2012). *Networks of Outrage and Hope.* Malden: Polity.

Chase-Dunn, C. (2010). Globalization from Below: Toward a Democratic Global Commonwealth. *Journal of Globalization Studies,* 1(1), 46-57.

Choonara, E. & Prasad, Y. (2014). What's Wrong with Privilege Theory? *International Socialism,* 2, 142.

Chote, R. (2013). Letter from Robert Chote to the Prime Minister's Office for Budget Responsibility. Retrieved Mar. 8, 2015 from http://budgetresponsibility.org.uk/letter-from-robert-chote-to-the-prime-minister/.

Choudry, A., Hanley, J. & Shragge, E. (eds.). (2012). *Organize! Building from the Local for Global Justice.* Toronto: Between the Lines.

Chow, O. (2009). Crooked Consultants, Temporary Foreign Workers. Retrieved July 12, 2012 from http://www.oliviachow.ca/2009/11/olivia-chow-moves-concurrence-motion-on-immigration-consultants-and-temporary-foreign-workers/.

Chrisman, W.L. (2011). A Reflection on Inspiration: A Recuperative Call for Emotion in Disability Studies. *Journal of Literary & Cultural Disability Studies*, 5(2), 173-84.

Clain, O. (2013). Présentation : Carrés Rouges. Éléments de Sociographie du Mouvement de 2012. *Recherches Sociographiques*, LIV(3), 399-417.

Clare, E. (1999). *Exile and Pride: Disability, Queerness and Liberation.* Cambridge: South End Press.

Cleaver, H. (2000). *Reading Capital Politically.* Oakland: AK Press/ Antithesis.

Coates, T. (2014). The Smartest Nerd in the Room. *The Atlantic.* Retrieved Aug. 21, 2015 from http://www.theatlantic.com/.

Coburn, E. (2011). Resisting Neoliberal Capitalism: Insights from Political Economy. In McBride, S. & Teeple, G. (eds.), *Relations of Global Power: Neoliberal Order and Disorder* (pp. 194-256). Toronto: University of Toronto Press.

Cohen, J. & Arato, A. (1992). *Civil Society and Political Theory.* Cambridge, MA: MIT Press.

Cohen, J.L. (1985). Strategy or Identity: New Theoretical Paradigms and Contemporary Social Movements. *Social Research,* 52(4), 663-716.

Cohen, S. (2003). *No One Is Illegal: Immigration Control and Asylum.* London: Trentham Books.

Cold, B. & Barnacle, T. (2011). Build Your Own Solidarity Network. Retrieved Aug. 18, 2015 from http://libcom.org/library/you-say-you-want-to-build-solidarity-network.

Combahee River Collective. (1977). A Black Feminist Statement. In Guy-Sheftall, B. (ed.), (1995), *Words of Fire: An Anthology of African-American Feminist Thought.* New York: New Press.

Connor, A., Powell, A., Marr, J. & Morrison, M. (2014). *The Tipping Point: Determining Factors for Divestment on Canadian Campuses.* Available from James Rowe at jkrowe@uvic.ca.

Conrad, C. (ed.). (2014). *Against Equality, Queer Revolution Not Mere Inclusion.* Oakland: AK Press.

Conway, J. (2004). *Identity, Place, Knowledge: Social Movements Contesting Globalization.* Halifax: Fernwood.

Corntassel, J. (2012). Re-Envisioning Resurgence: Indigenous Pathways to Decolonization and Sustainable Self-determination. *Decolonization: Indigeneity, Education and Society.* 1(1), 86-101.

Corrigan, P. & Sayer, D. (1985). *The Great Arch: English State Formation as Cultural Revolution.* Oxford: Basil Blackwell.

Coté, C. (2010). *Spirits of our Whaling Ancestors: Revitalizing Makah & Nuu-chah-nulth Traditions.* Seattle: University of Washington Press.

Cottle, S. (2008). Reporting Demonstrations: The Changing Media Politics of Dissent. *Media, Culture & Society, 30*(6), 853-72.

Coulthard, G. (2013). Placing #Idle No More in Context. *The Tyee.* Retrieved Aug. 24, 2015 from http://thetyee.ca/Opinion/2013/01/04/IdleNoMore-Historical-Context/.

Coulthard, G. (2014a). From Wards of the State to Subjects of Recognition?: Marx, Indigenous Peoples, and the Politics of Dispossession in Denendeh. In Simpson, A. & Smith Durham, A. (eds.), *Theorizing Native Studies*. Durham: Duke University Press.

Coulthard, G. (2014b). *Red Skin, White Masks: Rejecting the Colonial Politics of Recognition.* Minneapolis: University of Minnesota Press.

Cox, E. (2015). Liberal Heavy Hitters Trade the Public Interest for the Oil Interest. *Ricochet*, Feb. 4. Retrieved Aug. 23, 2015 from http://www.ricochet.media/en/323/liberal-heavy-hitters-trade-the-public-interest-for-the-oil-interest.

Cox, L. & Nilsen, A.G. (2014). *We Make Our Own History.* London: Pluto Press.

Cox, L. (2011). Building Counter Culture: The Radical Praxis of Social Movement Milieux. Retrieved Aug. 22, 2015 from http://into-ebooks.com.

Cox, R. (1987). *Production, Power and World Order.* New York: Columbia University Press.

Cremin, C. (2015). *Totaled: Salvaging the Future for the Wreckage of Capitalism.* London: Pluto Press.

Crick, B. (2005). *In Defence of Politics* (5th ed.). London: Continuum.

Cronon, W. (1991). *Nature's Metropolis: Chicago and the Great West.* New York: W.W. Norton.

Cronon, W. (ed.). (1996). *Uncommon Ground: Rethinking the Human Place in Nature.* New York: W.W. Norton.

Crook, S. (1991). *Modernism, Radicalism and Its Aftermath.* London: Routledge.

Crozier, M., Huntington, S.P. & Watanuki, J. (1975). *The Crisis of Democracy.* New York: NYU Press.

Cruikshank, B. (1999). *The Will to Empower: Democratic Citizens and Other Subjects.* Ithaca: Cornell University Press.

Cuthand, D. (2015, May 6). Bill C-51 has Potential to Scoop up Aboriginal Rights Activists. *CBC News.*

Cyr, G., Dumaine, P., Larochelle, M-É. & Vallée, M. (2013). P!nk Bloc, Stratégies Subversives en Temps de Grève. In Surprenant, M-È. & Biguaouette, M. (eds.). *Les Femmes Changent la Lutte au Cœur du Printemps Québécois* (pp. 131-40) Montréal: remue-ménage.

D'Arcy, S. (2013). *Languages of the Unheard: Why Militant Protest is Good for Democracy*. Toronto: Between the Lines.

D'Arcy, S. (2014). Two Models of Anti-racist Struggle: Allyship and Self-Emancipation. *The Public Autonomy Project*. Retrieved Aug. 21, 2015, from http://publicautonomy.org/.

Da Silva-Powell, E. (2014). Average Unionized Skilled Trades Wages in Western Canada. Retrieved July 29, 2014 from http://talentegg.ca/incubator/2013/03/12/western-canadas-salaries-skilled-trades/#sthash.qoprbChC.dpuf.

Dafnos, T. (2014). *Negotiating Colonial Encounters: (Un) Mapping the Contemporary Policing of Indigenous Protests in Canada*. Unpublished dissertation. Department of Sociology: York University.

Dalby, S. (2002). *Environmental Security*. Minneapolis: University of Minnesota Press.

David Harvey, D. (2003). The "New" Imperialism: Accumulation by Dispossession. In Panitch, L. & Leyes, C. (eds.), *The New Imperial Challenge* (83). London: Merlin Press.

Davidson, M. (2008). *Concerto for the Left Hand: Disability and the Defamiliar Body*. Ann Arbor: University of Michigan Press.

Davis, M. (2006). *Planet of Slums*. London: Verso.

Davis, M. (2011). Spring Confronts Winter. *New Left Review*, 72, 5-15.

Day, R.J.F. (2004). From Hegemony to Affinity: The Political Logic of the Newest Social Movements. *Cultural Studies*, 18(5), 716-48.

Day, R.J.F. (2007). Walking Away From Failure: A Response to AK Thompson (And Others). *Upping the Anti*, 4. [Electronic version: unpaginated] Retrieved July 21, 2015 from http://uppingtheanti.org/journal/article/04-walking-away-from-failure/.

Day, R.J.F. (2005). *Gramsci Is Dead: Anarchist Currents in the Newest Social Movements*. Toronto: Between the Lines.

De Lint, W. & Hall, A. (2009). *Intelligent Control: Developments in Public Order Policing in Canada*. Toronto: University of Toronto Press.

De Souza, M. (2013, Apr. 10). Stephen Harper's "Omnibus" Strategy to Overhaul Green Laws was Proposed by Oil Industry, Says Records. *Canada.com*. Retrieved Aug. 23, 2015, from www.o.canada.com.news/national/blog-stephen-harpers-omnibus-strategy-to-overhaul-green-laws-was-proposed-by-oil-industry-says-records.

De Young, R. & Princen, T. (eds.). (2012). *The Localization Reader: Adapting to the Coming Downshift*. Cambridge: MIT Press.

Dean, J. (1995). Reflective Solidarity. *Constellations*, 2(1), 114-40.

Dean, J. (2009). *Democracy and Other Neoliberal Fantasies: Communicative Capitalism and Left Politics*. Durham: Duke University Press.

Dean, J. (2012a). *The Communist Horizon*. New York: Verso.

Dean, J. (2012b). Occupy Wall Street: After the Anarchist Moment. In Panitch, L., Albo, G. & Chibber, V. (eds.), *Socialist Register 2013: The Question of Strategy* (pp. 52-62). Pontypool: Merlin Press.

Dean, J. (2012a, Jan. 4). Arena: Occupy Wall Street—Conversation with Marco DeSeriis and Jodi Dean [Web log post]. Retrieved Aug. 23, 2015 from www.jdeanicite.typepad.com/i_cite/2012/01/occupy-wall-street-arena.html.

Dean, J. (2013b). Division and Desire: Jodi Dean Discusses The Communist Horizon with Joseph G. Ramsey. *Socialism and Democracy*, 27(2), 23-41.

Dean, J. (2013c, May 28). Party in the USA: Optimism of the Will [Web log post]. Retrieved Aug. 23, 2015 from http://www.jdeanicite.typepad.com/i_cite/2013/05/party-in-the-us-optimism-of-the-will.html.

Dean, J. (2014). Communicative Capitalism and Class Struggle. *Sphere: Journal for Digital Culture*, 1, 1-16.

Dean, M. (2010). *Governmentality: Power and Rule in Modern Society* (2nd ed.). London: Sage.

deBoer, F. (2014). Those Other Men, Those Other White People. *Fredrik deBoer.* Retrieved Aug. 21, 2015 from http://fredrikdeboer.com/.

Defenders of the Land (2008, Nov. 12-14). Declaration of Non-Indigenous Support for Defenders of the Land. Retrieved Sept. 11, 2011 from http://www.defendersoftheland.org/supporters.

Deleuze, G. & Guatarri, F. (1987). *A Thousand Plateaus*. Minneapolis: University of Minnesota Press.

Della Porta, D. & Reiter, H. (1998). *Policing Protest: The Control of Mass Demonstrations in Western Democracies*. Minneapolis: University of Minnesota Press.

Della Porta, D. (2009). Social Movements. *The SAGE Handbook of European Studies* (pp. 365-84). London: Sage.

Delvaux, M., Desrosiers, G., Galerand, E. & L'écuyer, V. (2014). Militantes féministes grévistes. Du comité femmes de l'ASSÉ au comité femmes GGI de l'UQAM. In Ancelovici, M. & Dupuis-Déri, F. (eds.), *Un Printemps Rouge et Noir. Regards Croisés sur la Grève étudiante de 2012* (pp. 115-249). Montréal: Écosociété.

Demas, Doreen. (1993). Triple Jeopardy: Native Women with Disabilities. *Canadian Woman Studies*. 13, 4.

Dempsey, J. & Rowe, J. (2015, Feb. 2). Is Petro-Divestment too Divisive? *The Tyee*. Retrieved Aug. 25, 2015 from http://www.thetyee.ca/Opinion/2015/02/02/Divisive-Petro-Divestment.

Depelteau, J. & Giroux, D. (2015). LGBTQ Issues as Indigenous Politics: Two Spirit Mobilization in Canada. In Tremblay, M. (ed.), *Queer Mobilizations, Social Movement Activism and Canadian Public Policy*, (pp. 64-81). Vancouver: UBC Press.

Derrida, J. (1994). *Specters of Marx: The State of the Debt, the Work of Mourning, and the New International*. New York: Routledge.

DeVolder, B. (2013). Overcoming the Overcoming Story: A Case of "Compulsory Heroism." *Feminist Media Studies*, 13(4), 746-54.

Diamond, S. (1983). Lesbians Against the B.C. Budget. *Pink Ink*, (Toronto), 1(4), 9-10.

Diani, M. (2003). Networks and Social Movements: A Research Programme. In Diani, M. & McAdam, D. (eds.), *Social Movements and Networks* (pp. 299-319). Oxford: Oxford University Press.

Divest Student Network. (2016). Fossil Fuel Divestment Student Network Principles. Retrieved Jan. 25, 2015 from http://www.studentsdivest.org/.

Dixon, C. (2014). *Another Politics*. Oakland: University of California Press.

Doetsch-Kidder, S. (2012). *Social Change and Intersectional Activism*. New York: Palgrave Macmillan.

Douglas, D. & Coburn, E. (2015). Who Will Hear?: Aboriginal Persons with Disabilities. In Coburn, E. (ed.), *More Will Sing Their Way to Freedom: Indigenous Resistance and Resurgence*. Winnipeg: Fernwood.

Drexhage, J. (2009, Nov. 19). How Canada Can Restore Its International Reputation. *The Globe and Mail*, p. A19.

Driskell, Q.L. et al. (eds.). (2011). *Queer Indigenous Studies: Critical Interventions in Theory, Politics and Literature*. Tucson: University of Arizona Press.

Drucker, P. (2011). Towards a Queer Marxism. *Against The Current*, 151 (Mar.-Apr. 2011).

Dryden, O.H. & Lenon, S. (eds.). (2015). *Dismantling Queer Inclusion, Canadian Homonationalism and the Politics of Belonging*. Vancouver: UBC Press.

Duggan, L. (2003). *The Twilight of Equality? Neoliberalism, Cultural Politics and the Attack on Democracy*. Boston: Beacon.

Duhaime, G. et al. (2013). Le développement du nord et le destin du Québec. *Recherches sociographiques*, LIV (3) 477-511.

Dupuis-Déri, F. & L'Écuyer, D.L. (2013). Printemps de la Matraque: Répression et Autorépression. In Ancolovici, M. & Dupuis-Déri, F. (eds.), *Un Printemps Rouge et Noir: Regards Croisés sur la Grève étudiante de 2012* (pp. 327-54). Montréal: Les éditions écosociété.

Dupuy, J.P. (2012). *L'Avenir de l'économie*. Paris: Flammarion.

Dyer-Witheford, N. (1999). *Cyber-Marx, Circuits and Cycles of Struggle in High Technology Marxism*. Chicago: University of Illinois Press.

Earl, J. & Kimport, K. (2011). *Digitally Enabled Social Change: Activism in the Internet Age*. Cambridge: MIT Press.

Eckersley, R. (2004). Ecocentric Discourses: Problems and Prospects for Nature Advocacy. *Tamkang Review*, 34(3-4), 155-86.

Edwards-Levy, A. (2012, Aug. 14). Congress Approval Rating Hits All-time Low in Gallup Poll. *Huffington Post*. Retrieved Aug. 23, 2015 from http://www.huffingtonpost.com/2012/08/14/congress-approval-rating-all-time-low-gallup-poll_n_1777207.html.

Ehrenreich, B. (2009). *Bright-Sided: How Positive Thinking is Undermining America*. New York: Metropolitan Books.

Ellner, S. (2012). The Distinguishing Features of Latin America's New Left in Power. *Latin American Perspectives*, 39(1), 96-114.

Ely, J. (1993). Post-Fordism Restructuring in Germany: What Role for the New Social Movements. *New Political Science*, 25, 145-73.

Emsley, C. (1999). A Typology of Nineteenth-Century Police. *Crime, Histoire & Sociétés/Crime, History & Societies*, 3(1), 29-44.

Epstein, B. (1990). Rethinking Social Movement Theory. *Socialist Review*, 20(1), 35-65.

Eribon, D. (2004). *Insult and the Making of the Gay Self*. Durham: Duke University Press.

Ernie, G. and Fournier, S. (1998). *Stolen from Our Embrace: The Abduction of First Nations Children and the Restoration of Aboriginal Communities*. Vancouver: Douglas & McIntyre.

Eschle, C. (2001). *Global Democracy, Social Movements, and Feminism*. Boulder: Westview Press.

Evans, D. (1993). *Sexual Citizenship: The Material Construction of Sexualities*. London: Routledge.

Eyerman, R. & Jamison, A. (1991). *Social Movements: A Cognitive Approach*. Cambridge: Polity Press.

Fairclough, T.J. (1985). *The Gay Community of Vancouver's West End: The Geography of a Modern Urban Phenomenon*. Unpublished Master's thesis. Dept. of Geography: University of British Columbia.

Falquet, J. (2005). Trois Questions aux Mouvements Sociaux "Progressites. " Apports de la Théorie Féministe à l'analyse des Mouvements Sociaux. *Nouvelles Questions féministes*, 24(3), 18-35.

Fanon, F. (1952). *Peau Noire, Masques Blancs*. Paris: Seuil.

Fanon, F. (1967). *Black Skin, White Masks*. New York: Grove Press.

Farrell, B. (2013, Aug. 30). Fossil Fuel Divestment Continues to Grow: A Conversation with Student Organizer Kate Aronoff. *Waging Nonviolence*. Retrieved from http://wagingnonviolence.org/2013/08/fossil-fuel-divestment-continues-to-grow-a-conversation-with-student-organizer-kate-aronoff/.

Faust, D. (2013, Oct. 3). Fossil Fuel Divestment Statement. *Harvard University*. Retrieved Aug. 23, 2015 from http://www.harvard.edu/president/fossil-fuels.

Featherstone, D. (2012). *Solidarity: Hidden Histories and Geographies of Internationalism*. New York: Zed Books.

Felkerson, J. (2011). $29,000,000,000,000: A Detailed Look at the Fed's Bailout by Funding Facility and Recipient. In *Levy Economics Institute Working Paper*, 698.

Ferguson, S. (2008). Canadian Contributions to Social Reproduction Feminism, Race and Embodied Labor. *Race, Gender & Class*. 15(1-2), 42-57.

Ferguson, S. & McNally, D. (2014). Precarious Migrants: Gender, Race, and the Social Reproduction of a Global Working Class. *Socialist Register 2015* (pp. 1-23). London: Merlin Press.

Ferrarini, B. & Hummels, D. (eds.). (2014). *Asia and Global Production Networks: Implications for Trade, Incomes and Economic Vulnerability*. Cheltenham: Edward Elgar.

Fillieule, O. & Roux, P. (eds.). (2009). *Le Sexe du Militantisme*. Paris: Presse de Science Po.

Fillieule, O., Mathieu, L. & Roux, P. (2007). Introduction. *Politix*. 2(78). 7-12.

Findlay, D. (1984). Courtwatch. *Pink Ink*, (Toronto), Dec./Jan. p. 35.

Fiore, G. (2014). L'anacha-féminisme. *Possibles*. 38(1), 71-78.

Fisher, D.R. (2004). *National Governance and the Global Climate Change Regime*. Lanham: Rowman & Littlefield.

Fisher, M. (2013). Exit from the Vampire Castle. *The North Star*. Retrieved Aug. 21, 2014 from http://www.thenorthstar.info/.

Fisher, P. & Goodley, D. (2007). The Linear Medical Model of Disability: Mothers of Disabled Babies Resist with Counter-Narratives. *Sociology of Health & Illness*, 29(1), 66-81.

Fiske, J. (1989). *Understanding Popular Culture*. Boston: Unwin Hyman.

Fitch, E.F. (2002). Disability and Inclusion: From Labeling Deviance to Social Valuing. *Educational Theory*, 52(4), 463-77.

Fletcher, B. & Gapasin, F. (2008). *Solidarity Divided: The Crisis in Organized Labor and a New Path for Social Justice*. Berkeley: University of California Press.

Floyd, K. (2009). *The Reification of Desire: Toward a Queer Marxism.* Minneapolis: University of Minnesota Press.

Foucault, M. (1980). *Power/Knowledge.* New York: Pantheon.

Foucault, M. (1982). The Subject and Power. In Dreyfus, H.L. & Rabinow, P. (eds.), *Michel Foucault: Beyond Structuralism and Hermeneutics.* Chicago: University of Chicago Press.

Foucault, M. (1984). The Order of Discourse. In Shapiro, M. (ed.), *Language and Politics.* New York: NYU Press.

Frankenburg, R. (1993). *White Women, Race Matter: The Social Construction of Whiteness.* Minneapolis: University of Minnesota Press.

Fraser, N. (1990). Rethinking the Public Sphere. *Social Text*, 25/26, 56-80.

Fraser, N. (1997). *Justice Interruptus.* New York: Routledge.

Fraser, N. (2013). *Fortunes of Feminism.* New York: Verso.

Fudge, J. & Tucker, E. (2001). *Labour Before the Law: The Regulation of Workers' Collective Action in Canada, 1900-1948.* Toronto: Oxford University Press.

Fukuda, K. et al. (1994). Chronic Fatigue Syndrome: A Comprehensive Approach to Its Definition and Study. *Annals of Internal Medicine*, 121, 953-59.

Galerand, E. (2009). Contradiction de Sexe et de Classe: la Marche Mondiale des Femmes de 2000. In Fillieule, O. & Roux, P. (eds.), *Le Sexe du Militantisme* (pp. 225-41). Paris: Presse de Science Po.

Gallin, D. (2015). Workers of All Lands Unite? Reflections on Working Class Nationalism and Internationalism. Presented at University of Nottingham, March 7.

Gamson, W.A. (2007). Bystanders, Public Opinion, and the Media. In Snow, D.A., Soule, S.A. & Kriesi, H. (eds.), *The Blackwell Companion to Social Movements* (pp. 242-61). Oxford: Blackwell.

Ganz, M. (2011). Public Narrative, Collective Action, and Power. *From Inertia to Public Action*, 273.

Genc, E. (2015). Meet the Women of the HDP: Gender, Resistance and Radical Democracy. *The Bullet*, 1133. Retrieved June 24, 2015 from http:*//www.socialistproject.ca/bullet/1133.php.*

Gentile, P. and Kinsman, G. (2015). National Security and Homonationalism: The QuAIA Wars and the Making of the Neo-Liberal Queer. In Dryden, O.H. & Lenon, S. (eds.), *Dismantling Queer Inclusion, Canadian Homonationalism and the Politics of Belonging.* Vancouver: UBC Press.

George, M. & Posluns, M. (1974). *The Fourth World: An Indian Reality.* New York: The Free Press.

Gessan, K., Taylor, A. & Resnick, S. (2011). Scenes From an Occupation. In Blumenkranz, C. et al. (eds.), *Occupy!: Scenes from Occupied America* (pp. 51-54). New York: Verso.

Gessen, K. (2011). Laundry Day. In Blumenkranz, C. et al. (eds.), *Occupy!: Scenes from Occupied America* (pp. 195-221). New York: Verso.

Gibbs, P. & Sinnott, S. (2014). *Organizing: People, Power, Change.* Available from Peter Gibbs at peterrgibbs@gmail.com.

Gibson-Graham, J.K. (2006). *A Post-Capitalist Politics.* Minneapolis: University of Minnesota Press.

Giddens, A. (1991). *Modernity and Self-Identity.* Palo Alto: Stanford University Press.

Gill, S. (1990). *American Hegemony and the Trilateral Commission.* Cambridge: Cambridge University Press.

Gill, S. & Cutler, A.C. (eds.). (2014). *New Constitutionalism and World Order.* Cambridge: Cambridge University Press.

Gillham, P.F. (2011). Securitizing America: Strategic Incapacitation and the Policing of Protest Since the 11 September 2001 Terrorist Attacks. *Sociology Compass*, 5, 636-52.

Gilmore, L. (2010). American Neoconfessional: Memoir, Self-Help, and Redemption on Oprah's Couch. *Biography*, 33(4), 657-81.

Gindin, S. (2012). Rethinking Unions, Registering Socialism. In Panitch, L., Albo, G. & Chibber, V. (eds.), *Socialist Register 2013: The Question of Strategy* (pp. 26-51). Pontypool: Merlin.

Gindin, S. (1998). Socialism with Sober Senses: Developing Workers' Capacities. In Panitch, L. & Leys, C. (eds.), *Socialist Register*, 34 (pp. 75-101). Pontypool: Merlin.

Gindin, S. (2004). The Auto Industry: Concretizing Working Class Struggles—Internationalism Beyond Slogans, *Socialist Project.*

Gitlin, T. (2013). Occupy's Predicament. *British Journal of Sociology*, 64(1), 3-25.

Goldenberg, S. (2014, Sept. 22). Heirs to Rockefeller Oil Fortune Divest from Fossil Fuels Over Climate Change. *The Guardian.* Retrieved Aug. 23, 2015 from http://www.theguardian.com/environment/ 2014/sep/22/ rockefeller-heirs-divest-fossil-fuels-climate-change.

Gonzalez, G. (2005). Urban Sprawl, Global Warming and the Limits of Ecological Modernisation. *Environmental Politics,* 14(3), 344-62.

Goodman, J. & Salleh, A. (2013). The Green Economy: Class Hegemony and Counter-Hegemony. *Globalizations,* 10(3), 411-24.

Gordon, L. & Hunter, A. (1979). *Sex, Family and the New Right: Anti-Feminism as a Political Force.* Somerville: New England Free Press.

Gordon, T. (2013). Canadian Capitalism and the Dispossession of Indigenous Peoples. *New Socialist*. Retrieved Aug. 23, 2015 from http://newsocialist.org/714-canadian-capitalism-and-the-dispossession-of-indigenous-peoples.

Goupil, T. (1997). The Trouble with Heroism. *From the Mouth Magazine*, 42. Retrieved Feb. 13, 2015 from http://www.mouthmag.com/heroes.htm.

Grady-Benson, J. & Sarathy, B. (2015). Fossil Fuel Divestment in US Higher Education: Student-Led Organising for Climate Justice. *Local Environment: The International Journal of Justice and Sustainability*, 1-21.

Graeber, D. (2002). The New Anarchists. *New Left Review*, 13, 61-73.

Graeber, D. (2013). *The Democracy Project: A History, a Crisis, a Movement*. New York: Penguin.

Gramsci, A. (1971). *The Prison Notebooks of Antonio Gramsci*. New York: International.

Gramsci, A. (1977). *Selections from Political Writings, 1910-1920*. Hoare, Q. (ed.). London: Lawrence & Wishart.

Gramsci, A. (2000). *The Antonio Gramsci Reader: Selected Writings 1916-1935*. Forgacs, D. (ed.). New York: NYU Press.

Green, J. (ed.). (2007). *Making Space for Indigenous Feminism*. Winnipeg: Fernwood.

Greenhouse, S. (2013, Jan. 13). Productivity Climbs, But Wages Stagnate. *New York Times*.

Greenwald, A.G. (2012). There is Nothing so Theoretical as a Good Method. *Perspectives on Psychological Science*, 7(2), 99-108.

Gunderson, C. (2015). Review Essay: Marxism and Social Movements, Social Movements in Latin America, Neoliberalism and Popular Resistance. *Social Movement Studies*, 14(2), 242-49.

Gutstein, D. (2014). *Harperism*. Toronto: Lorimer.

Habermas, J. (1987). *The Theory of Communicative Action* (Vol. 2). Boston: Beacon.

Habermas, J. (1989). *The Structural Transformation of the Public Sphere*. Cambridge: MIT.

Hadden, J. (2015). *Networks in Contention: The Divisive Politics of Climate Change*. New York: Cambridge University Press.

Hall, M. & Charest, J. (2015, Feb. 2). Fossil Fuels Divestment Movement: Good Intention, Bad Idea. *The Globe and Mail*. Retrieved Aug. 23, 2015 from http://www.theglobeandmail.com/globe-debate/fossil-fuels-divestment-movement-good-intention-bad-idea/article22743277/?service=mobile.

Hall, S. (1985). Signification, Representation, Ideology: Althusser and the Post-structuralist Debates. *Critical Studies in Mass Communication*, 2(2), 91-114.

Hall, T.D. & Fenelon, J. (2005). Indigenous Peoples and Hegemonic Change: Threats to Sovereignty. In Friedman, J. & Chase-Dunn, C. (eds.), *Hegemonic Declines* (pp. 25-205). Boulder: Paradigm Publishers.

Hamel, P. & Mahue, L. (2004). Beyond New Social Movements: Social Conflicts and Institutions. In Nash, K. & Scott, A. (eds.), *Blackwell Companion to Political Sociology* (pp. 261-70). Oxford: Blackwell.

Harada, M. et al. (2005). Follow up Study of Mercury Pollution in Indigenous Tribe Reservations in the Province of Ontario, Canada, 1975-2002. *Bulletin of Environmental Contamination and Toxicology*, 74(4), 689-697.

Haraway, D. (1991). *Simians, Cyborgs, and Women: The Reinvention of Nature*. New York: Routledge.

Harden, J.D. (2013). *Quiet No More: New Political Activism in Canada and Around the Globe*. Toronto: Lorimer.

Hardt, M. & Negri, A. (2000). *Empire*. Cambridge: Harvard University Press.

Hardt, M. & Negri, A. (2004). *Multitude: War and Democracy in the Age of Empire*. New York: Penguin.

Hardt, M. & Negri, A. (2009). *Commonwealth*. Cambridge: Harvard University Press.

Harkat, S. (2011, Jan. 11). Fighting for Mohamed Harkat. *Rabble*. Retrieved Sept. 30, 2012 from http://rabble.ca/news/2011/01/fighting-mohamed-harkat.

Harnecker, M. (2014). *A Decentralised Participatory Planning Proposal*. Paper presented at the International Scientific Academic Meeting on Methodology and Experiences in Socio-environmental Participatory Processes, Cuenca University, Nov. 13-15.

Harrison, D. (2009). Modern Enclosure: Salmon Aquaculture and First Nations Resistance in British Columbia. In Adkin, L. (ed.), *Environmental Conflict and Democracy in Canada* (pp. 51-68). Vancouver: UBC Press.

Harvey, D. (1999). Considerations on the Environment of Justice. In Low, N. (ed.), *Global Ethics and Environment* (pp. 109-30). London & New York: Routledge.

Harvey, D. (2005a). *A Brief History of Neoliberalism*. New York: Oxford University Press.

Harvey, D. (2005b). *The New Imperialism*. New York: Oxford University Press.

Haug, F. (1992). *Beyond Female Masochism: Memory Work and Politics*. London: Verso.

Hayden, A. (2014). Enough of that Already: Sufficiency-based Challenges to High-Carbon Consumption in Canada. *Environmental Politics*, 23(1), 97-114.

Hegel, G.W.F. (1991). *Elements of the Philosophy of Right*. Edited by A.W. Wood, and Translated by Nisbet, H.B. Cambridge: Cambridge University Press.

Held, D. (1995). *Democracy and the Global Order: From the Modern State to Cosmopolitan Governance*. Cambridge: Polity.

Held, D. (2010). *Cosmopolitanism: Ideals and Realities*. Cambridge: Polity.

Held, D. & McGrew, A. (eds.). (2003). *The Global Transformations Reader: An Introduction to the Globalization Debate* (2nd ed.). Cambridge: Polity Press.

Hellman, J. (1994). *Mexican Lives*. New York: The New Press.

Henaway, M. et al. (2007, Oct. 22). Organizing for Migrant Justice and Self-Determination. Retrieved Sept. 23, 2012 from http://www.leftturn.org/organizing-migrant-justice-and-self-determination.

Henderson, J.S.Y. (2015). The Split Head Resistance: Using Imperial Law to Contradict Colonial Law for Aboriginal Justice. In Coburn, E. (ed.), *More Will Sing Their Way to Freedom: Indigenous Resistance and Resurgence*)pp. 50-66(. Halifax: Fernwood.

Henley, J. (2015, June 17). Making Us Poorer Won't Save Greece: How Pension Crisis Is Hurting Its People. *Guardian*.

Hennessy, R. (2000). *Profit and Pleasure: Sexual Identities in Late Capitalism*. New York: Routledge.

Hennessy, T., Tiessen, K. & Yalnizyan, A. (2013). *Making Every Job a Good Job*. Toronto: Canadian Centre for Policy Alternatives.

Herbst, S. (2003). Political Authority in a Mediated Age. *Theory and Society*, 32, 481-503.

Hern, M. (2010). *Common Ground in a Liquid City: Essays in Defense of an Urban Future*. Edinburgh: AK Press.

Hestres, L.E. (2013). Preaching to the Choir: Internet-Mediated Advocacy, Issue Public Mobilization, and Climate Change. *New Media & Society*, 16(2), 323-39.

Hetland, G. & Goodwin, J. (2013). The Strange Dissappearance of Capitalism from Social Movement Studies. In Barker, C., Cox, L., Krinsky, J. & Nilsen, A.G. (eds.), *Marxism and Social Movements* (pp. 83-102). Leiden: Brill.

Hevey, D. (1992). *The Creatures Time Forgot: Photography and Disability Imagery*. New York: Routledge.

Heynen, N., McCarthy, J., Prudham, S. & Robbins, P. (eds.). (2007). *Neoliberal Environments: False Promises and Unnatural Consequences*. London & New York: Routledge.

Higgins, R. (2011). La Regulation Sociale de l'Homosexualite: De la Repression Policiere a la Normalization. In Corriveau, P. & Daust, V. (eds.), *La Regulation Sociale des Minorities Sexuelles: L'inequietude de la Difference* (pp. 67-102). Québec: Presses de l'Universite du Québec.

Hill, G. (2010). *500 Years of Indigenous Resistance*. Oakland: PM Press.

Holloway, J. (2002). *Change the World Without Taking Power*. New York: Pluto Press.

Holloway, J. (2005). *Change the World Without Taking Power: The Meaning of Revolution Today* (2nd ed.). London: Pluto Press.

Holloway, J. (2010). *Crack Capitalism*. London: Pluto Press.

Holmes, G.P. et al. (1988). Chronic Fatigue Syndrome: A Working Case Definition. *Annals of Internal Medicine*, 108, 387-89.

Hooks, B. (2000). *Feminist Theory: From Margin to Center*. London: Pluto Press.

Hooper, T. (2014). More than Two Is a Crowd: Mononormativity and Gross Indecency in the Criminal Code, 1981-1982. *Journal of Canadian Studies*, 48(1), 53-81.

Horguelin, C. (2010). Postface. Front de Libération du Québec. *Manifeste d'Octobre 1970* (pp. 27-40). Montréal: Lux.

Hughes, B. (2009). Disability Activisms: Social Model Stalwarts and Biological Citizens. *Disability & Society*, 24(6), 677-88.

Hull, G.T., Bell Scott, P. & Smith, P. (eds.). (1982). *All the Women Are White, All the Blacks Are Men, But Some of Us Are Brave*. New York: The Feminist Press.

Hulme, M. (2015, Apr. 17). Why Fossil Fuel Divestment Is a Misguided Tactic. *The Guardian*. Retrieved Aug. 23, 2015 from http://www.theguardian.com/environment/2015/apr/17/why-fossil-fuel-divestment-is-a-misguided-tactic.

ILO. (2015). *World Employment and Social Outlook*. Geneva: International Labour Organization.

Indian Country Media Today. (2014, Jan. 7). More Than 4000 Indigenous Children Died in Canada's Residential Schools: Commission. Retrieved Aug. 23, 2015 from http://indiancountrytodaymedianetwork.com/2014/01/07/more-4000-indigenous-children-died-canadas-residential-schools-commission-153011.

Indigenous Nationhood Movement. (2015). Retrieved Aug. 23, 2015 from https://www.facebook.com/IndigenousNationhoodMovement/.

Ingalsbee, T. (1994). Resource and Action Mobilization Theories: The New Social Psychological Research Agenda. *Berkeley Journal of Sociology*, 38, 139-55.

Ingram, J. (2013). *Radical Cosmopolitics: The Ethics and Politics of Democratic Universalism*. New York: Columbia University Press.

Inman, P. (2011, Mar. 1). Bank of England Governor Blames Spending Cuts on Bank Bailouts, *Guardian*.

Institut Simone de Beauvoir. (2013). Déclaration Sur la Hausse des Droits de Scolarité au Québec et son Impact sur les Femmes. In Bouchard, G. & Namaste, V. (spokepersons). Surprenant, M.-È. & Biguaouette, M. (eds.), *Les Femmes Changent la Lutte au Cœur du printemps québécois* (pp. 33-40). Montréal: remue-ménage.

Institute of Medicine. (2015). *Beyond Myalgic Encephalomyelitis/Chronic Fatigue Syndrome: Redefining an Illness*. Washington: The National Academies Press.

International Energy Agency. (2012). *World Energy Outlook 2012*. Retrieved Aug. 23, 2015 from http://www.iea.org/ publications/freepublications/publication/English.pdf>.

Irvine, J.A. (2013). Leveraging change. *International Feminist Journal of Politics,* 15(1), 20-38.

Isin, E.F. (2002). *Being Political: Genealogies of Citizenship*. Minneapolis: University of Minnesota Press.

Isin, E.F. (ed.). (2000). *Democracy, Citizenship and the Global City*. London: Routledge.

Jackson, A. (2010). *Work and Labour in Canada*. Toronto: Canadian Scholars' Press.

Jacquemart, A. (2013). L'Engagement Féministe Des Hommes, Entre Contestation et Reproduction du Genre, *Cahiers du genre*, 2(55), 49-63.

James, P. & Steger, M. (2014). A Genealogy of "Globalization": The Career of a Concept. *Globalizations*, 11(4), 417-34.

Jarvis, B. (2011, Jan. 21). Citizens United? *Yes! Magazine*. Retrieved Aug. 23, 2015 from http://www.yesmagazine.org/blogs/brooke-jarvis/citizens-united.

Jasper, J. (2010). *Social Movement Theory Today*. Sociology Compass, 4(11), 965-76.

Jenkins, J.C. (1983). Resource Mobilization Theory and the Study of Social Movements. *Annual Review of Sociology*, 9, 527-53.

Jones, J.C. (2014). Bad-faith Justice: Ethics of the Call-out. *Paperhouse*. Retrieved Aug. 21, 2015 from http://sarahditum.com/.

Joseph, J. (2002). *Hegemony: A Realist Analysis*. London: Routledge.

Justice, D.H. (2010). Notes Toward a Theory of Anomaly. *GLQ: A Journal of Lesbian and Gay Studies*, 16(1-2), 207-42.

Kaku, M. (1994). *Hyperspace: A Scientific Odyssey Through Parallel Universes, Time Warps, and the Tenth Dimension*. New York: Oxford University Press.

Kamal, F. & Mishra, M. (2007, May 6). Regularisation from the Ground Up: The Don't Ask Don't Tell Campaign. Retrieved Sept. 30, 2012 from http://noii-van.resist.ca/?p=149.

Kauffman, C. (1990). The Anti-Politics of Identity. *Socialist Review,* 20(1).

Kaufman, C. (1994). Postmodernism and Praxis. *Socialist Review,* 24(3), 57-80.

Kaufman, L.A. (2011). The Theology of Consensus. In Blumenkranz, C. et al. (eds.), *Occupy!: Scenes from Occupied America* (pp. 46-49). New York: Verso.

Keane, J. (2003). *Global Civil Society?* Cambridge: Cambridge University Press.

Keaney, S. (2011). Women Resist, Police Repress, Gendered Police Violence at the Toronto G20. In Malleson, T. & Wachsmuth, D. (eds.), *Whose Streets? The Toronto G20 Summit and the Challenges of Summit Protest* (pp. 115-24). Toronto: Between the Lines.

Keck, M.E. & Sikkink, K. (1998). *Activists Beyond Borders: Advocacy Networks in International Politics.* Ithaca: Cornell University Press.

Khan, A. (2014). Toxicity: The True Story of Mainstream Feminism's Violent Gatekeepers. *Black Girl Dangerous.* Retrieved Aug. 21, 2015 from http://www.blackgirldangerous.org/.

King, H. (2015). The Problem with "Indigenous Peoples": Re-considering International Indigenous Rights Activism. In Coburn, E. (ed.), *More Will Sing Their Way to Freedom: Indigenous Resistance and Resurgence* (pp. 167-83). Winnipeg: Fernwood.

Kingwell, M. (2008). *Concrete Reveries: Consciousness and the City.* Toronto: Penguin.

Kinsman, G. (forthcoming). Queer Resistance and Regulation in the 1970s: From Liberation to Rights. In Gentile, P., Kinsman, G. & Rankin, P. (eds.), *Activating Resistance: Remembering Sex/Gender Struggles.* Vancouver: UBC Press.

Kinsman, G. (1987). Bill 7 A Human Rights Victory in Ontario, Affecting the Future of our Movement. *Rites,* 3(8), 5.

Kinsman, G. (1996). *The Regulation of Desire: Homo and Hetero Sexualities.* Montreal: Black Rose.

Kinsman, G. (1997). Managing AIDS Organizing: Consultation, Partnership, and Responsibility as Strategies of Regulation. In William, C. (ed.), *Organizing Dissent: Contemporary Social Movements in Theory and Practice* (2nd ed.), (pp. 213-39). Toronto: Garamond.

Kinsman, G. (2005). The Politics of Revolution: Learning from Autonomist Marxism. *Upping the Anti,* 1(1), 41-50.

Kinsman, G. (2006). Mapping Social Relations of Struggle: Activism, Ethnography, Social Organization. In Frampton, C. et al. (eds.), *Sociology for Changing the World* (pp. 133-56). Halifax: Fernwood.

Kinsman, G. (2013). Wolfenden in Canada: Within and Beyond Official Discourse in Law Reform Struggles. In Lennox, C. & Waites, M. (eds.), *Human Rights, Sexual Orientation and Gender Identity in the Commonwealth: Struggles for Decriminalization and Change* (pp. 183-205). London: School of Advanced Study, University of London.

Kinsman, G. (2014a). Direct Action = Life: Memories of AIDS Activism in Canada, 1987-1993. Retrieved Aug. 24, 2015 from http://www.aidsactivisthistory.ca/aahp-blog/gary-kinsman-direct-action-life-memories-of-aids-activism-in-canada-19.

Kinsman, G. (2014b). Resisting State and Professional Management of AIDS Organizations, Memories of AIDS Organizing in Canada, 1983-1990. Retrieved Aug. 24, 2015 from http://www.aidsactivisthistory.ca/aahp-blog/gary-kinsman-resisting-state-professional-management-of-aids-organizations-memories-of-aids-organizing-in-canada-1983-1990.

Kinsman, G. (2015). Troubling Policing and Community Policing. *Radical Noise*. Retrieved Aug. 24, 2015 from http://radicalnoise.ca/2015/02/04/troubling-policing-and-community-policing/.

Kinsman, G. & Gentile, P. (2010). *The Canadian War on Queers, National Security as Sexual Regulation*. Vancouver: UBC Press.

Kinsman, G. (2007). Constructing Sexual Problems, These Things May Lead to the Tragedy of Our Species. In Samuelson, L. & Antony, W. (eds.), *Power and Resistance: Critical Thinking About Canadian Social Issues* (pp. 96-134). Halifax: Fernwood.

Klandermans, B. (2013). The Dynamics of Demand. In Stelkelenburg J., Roggeband, C. & Klandermans, B. (eds.), *The Future of Social Movement Research* (pp. 3-16). Minneapolis: University of Minnesota Press.

Klein, N. (2008). *The Shock Doctrine*. Toronto: Vintage Canada.

Klein, N. (2014). *This Changes Everything*. New York: Simon & Schuster.

Klein, N. (2015, Feb. 11). Naomi Klein on the Power of Fossil Fuel Divestment. *Grist.org*. Retrieved Aug. 23, 2015 from http://www.grist.org/climate-energy/naomi-klein-on-the-power-of-fossil-fuel-divestment/.

Kleiss, K. (2014). Most Low-Wage Alberta Workers are Women, Reports Show. *Edmonton Journal*. Retrieved Aug. 18, 2015. From http://www.edmontonjournal.com/Most+wage+Alberta+workers+women+reports+show/10165344/story.html.

Knoke, D. & Yang, S. (2008). *Social Network Analysis* (2nd ed.). Los Angeles: Sage.

Knox, P.L & Taylor, P.J. (eds.). (1995). *World Cities in a World-System*. Cambridge: Cambridge University Press.

Konopacki, M. & Ness, I. (2015). *Solidarity Unionism: Rebuilding the Labor Movement from Below* (2nd ed.). Oakland: PM Press.

Korpi, W. (2006). Power Resources and Employer-Centered Approaches in Explanations of Welfare States and Varieties of Capitalism: Protagonists, Consenters, and Antagonists. *World Politics*, 58(02), 167-206.

Krosinsky, C. (2012, Nov. 27). Why the "Do the Math" Tour Doesn't Add up. *GreenBiz.com*. Retrieved Aug. 23, 2015 from http://www.greenbiz.com/blog/2012/11/19/do-math-tour-doesnt-add-up.

Krosinsky, C. (n.d.). Invest not Divest. *About.com*. Retrieved July 10, 2015 from http://www.socialinvesting.about.com/od/Sustainable-Investing/fl/Do-Not-Divest-Sustainability-through-Ownership.htm.

Kruzynski, A. (2005). Trajectoires de Militantes Dans un Quartier Ouvrier de Montréal: Tente ans de Changement-s. *Nouvelles Questions Féministes*, 4(3), 86-104.

Kulchyski, P. (1988). A Considerable Unrest: F.O. Loft and the League of Indians. *Native Studies Review*, 4(1-2), 95-117.

Kumar, P. & Schenk, C. (eds.). (2006): *Paths to Union Renewal: Canadian Experiences*.

La Botz, D. (2010). What Happened to the American Working Class? *New Politics*. Retrieved Jan. 8, 2016 from http://newpol.org/content/what-happened-american-working-class.

Laclau, E. & Mouffe, C. (1985). *Hegemony and Socialist Strategy: Toward a Radical Democratic Politics*. London: Verso.

Lacoursière, B. (2007). *Le Mouvement étudiant au Québec de 1983 à 2006*. Montréal: Sabotart Édition.

LaDuke, W. (1999). *All Our Relations*. Cambridge: South End Press.

Laflamme, V. (2013). L'Apport des Mouvements Sociaux au Printemps érable: l'Expérience de la Coalition 'Main Rouge.' In Surprenant, M.-È. & Bigaouette, M. (eds.). *Les Femmes Changent la Lutte: au Cœur du Printemps Québécois* (pp. 261-72). Montréal: remue-ménage.

Lafrance, X. (2014). Social Movements and Self-Transformation. In Collectif D.N. (ed.), *This Is Fucking Class War: Voices from the 2012 Québec Student Strike* (pp. 61-71). Montréal: Collectif Dix.

Lagalisse, E.M. (2011) Marginalizing Magdalena: Intersections of Gender and the Secular in Anarchoindigenist Solidarity Activism. *Signs: Journal of Women in Culture and Society*, 36(3), 653-78.

Lameman, C., Milton-Lightening, H., Thomas-Muller, C. & Smith, D. (2014, Nov.). Fossil Fuel Divestment as a Solidarity Tactic. Panel presented at the Go Fossil Free Convergence, Montreal, QC.

Landry, I. (2013). Les Mimes du Comité Femmes GGI, Histoire d'une Action à Contre-sens de l'Humour Sexiste. In Surprenant, M.-È. & Biguaouette, M. (eds.). *Les Femmes Changent la Lutte au Cœur du Printemps Québécois* (pp. 59-71). Montréal: remue-ménage.

Landsman, G.H. (2005). Mothers and Models of Disability. *Journal of Medical Humanities, 26(2/3)*, 121-39.

Langille, D. (1987). The Business Council on National Issues and the Canadian State. *Studies in Political Economy*, 24, 41-85.

Langman, L. (2013). Occupy: A New Social Movement. *Current Sociology*, 61(4), 510-24.

LaRocque, E. (2010). *When the Other Is Me: Native Resistance Discourse 1850-1990*. Winnipeg: University of Manitoba Press.

LaRocque, E. (1996). The Colonization of a Native Woman Scholar. In Miller, C. & Chuchyrk, P. (eds.), *Women of the First Nations: Power, Wisdom and Strength* (p. 9). Winnipeg: University of Manitoba Press.

LaRocque, E. (2015). Resist No Longer: Reflections on Resistance Writing and Teaching. In Coburn, E. (ed.), *More Will Sing Their Way to Freedom: Indigenous Resistance and Resurgence* (pp. 5-23). Winnipeg: Fernwood.

Leaton, J. (2011). Unburnable Carbon: Are the World's Financial Markets Carrying a Carbon Bubble? *Carbon Tracker*. Retrieved Aug. 23, 2015 from http://www.carbontracker.org/wp-content/uploads/2014/09/Unburnable-Carbon-Full-rev2-1.pdf.

Leblanc, J. (2013). Contre le Patriarcat, Je Résiste et Je Me Bats! In Bellemare-Caron, É. et al. (eds.), *Nous Sommes Ingouvernables: Les Anarchistes Aujourd'hui* (pp. 241-54). Montreal: Lux Éditeur.

Lebowitz, M. (2003). *Beyond Capital* (2nd ed.). New York: Palgrave Macmillan.

Leduc, A. (2010). *Centrale Syndicale étudiante: L'Idéologie Syndicale au Sein du Mouvement étudiant Québécois des Années 1960*. Unpublished Master's thesis. Université du Québec à Montréal.

Lefebvre, H. (2003). *The Urban Revolution*. Minneapolis: University of Minnesota Press.

LeGates, R.T. & Stout, F. (eds.). (2016). *The City Reader*. New York: Routledge.

Leifeld, P. (2013). Reconceptualizing Major Policy Change in the Advocacy Coalition Framework: A Discourse Network Analysis of German Pension Politics. *The Policy Studies Journal*, 41(1), 169-98.

Lenin, V.I. (1914). The Right of Nations to Self-Determination. *Marxists internet archive*. Retrieved May 26, 2015 from https://www.marxists.org/archive/lenin/works/1914/self-det/index.htm.

Lerner, B. (2014). *10:04*. Toronto: McLelland & Stewart.

Lerner, S. (2012). *Sacrifice Zones: The Front Lines of Toxic Chemical Exposure in the United States*. Boston: MIT Press.

Levinson, C. (1972). *International Trade Unionism*. London: Allen & Unwin.

Leys, C. (2001). *Market-Driven Politics (Neoliberal Democracy and the Public Interest)*. London & New York: Verso.

LibCom. (n.d.). Interview With SeaSol. In *Seattle Solidarity Networks: Examples and Ideas of Direct Action* (pp. 31-37).

Ligue des Droits et Libertés (Québec). (2015). *Manifestions et Repressions*. Montréal: juin. Retrieved Aug. 18, 2015 from http://liguedesdroits.ca/wp-content/fichiers/rapport_manifestations_repressions_ldl.pdf.

Lilli, L. & Valentini, C. (1979). *Care Compagne: Il femminismo nel PCI e Nelle Organizzazioni di Massa*. Rome: Editore Riuniti.

Linnitt, C. (2012, Dec. 4). Polaris Institute Documents Harper Government Entanglement With Tar Sands Lobby. *Desmog Blog*. Retrieved Aug. 23, 2015, from http://www.desmogblog.com/2012/12/04/big-oil-s-oily-grasp-polaris-institute-documents-government-entanglement-tar-sands-lobby.

Linnitt, C. (2013, Nov. 11). Oil and Gas Industry Resists New Emissions Standards, Calls Oilsands Opposition "Ideological," Documents Reveal. *Desmog Blog*. Retrieved Aug. 23, 2015 from http://www.desmog.ca/2013/11/11/objection-oil-sands-ideological-says-industry-resisting-new-emissions-standards.

Lowry, M. & Nyers, P. (2003) No One Is Illegal: The Fight for Refugee and Migrant Rights in Canada *Refuge: Canada's Periodical on Refugees*, 3, 66-72.

Luxemburg, R. (1919). Order Prevails in Berlin. *Marxists Internet Archive*. Retrieved Aug. 21, 2015 from http://www.marxists.org/.

MacLeod, R.C. (1976). The North West Mounted Police and Law Enforcement, 1873-1905. Toronto: University of Toronto Press.

Maeckelbergh, M. (2011). Doing Is Believing: Prefiguration as Strategic Practice in the Alterglobalization Movement. *Social Movement Studies*, 10(1), 1-20.

Magnusson, W. & Walker, R. (1988). De-Centring the State: Political Theory and Canadian Political Economy. *Studies in Political Economy*, 26, 37-71.

Magnusson, W. (2000). Hyperspace: A Political Ontology of the Global City. In Ericson, R. & Stehr, N. (eds.), *Governing Modern Societies* (pp. 80-104). Toronto: University of Toronto Press.

Magnusson, W. (2011). *Politics of Urbanism: Seeing Like a City*. London: Routledge.

Magnusson, W. (2015). *Local Self-Government and the Right to the City*. Kingston & Montreal: McGill-Queen's University Press.

Magnusson, W. & Shaw, K. (eds.). (2003). *A Political Space: Reading the Global Through Clayoquot Sound*. Minneapolis: University of Minnesota Press.

Maier, C. (ed.). (1987). *Changing Boundaries of the Political.* Cambridge: Cambridge University Press.

Manson, P. (2014, Sept. 5). Veterans Should Transcend this Battle. *The Globe and Mail*, p. A11.

Mao, T. (1967). Analysis of the Classes in Chinese Society. In *Selected Works of Mao Tse-Tung* (pp. 13-21).Vol 1. Peking: Foreign Languages Press.

Maracle, L. (2011). Lee Maracle Speaking at May Day Assembly 2011. Video. Retrieved Sept. 30, 2012 from https://www.youtube.com/watch?v=FNK3KDfMrRc&list=PL966D86F55E443E2A&index=1.

Marquis, G. (1997). The "Irish Model" and Nineteenth Century Canadian Policing. *Journal of Imperial and Commonwealth History,* 25(2), 193-218.

Marquis, G. (2005). Policing Two Imperial Frontiers: The Royal Irish Constabulary and the North-West Mounted Police. In Knafla, L. & and Swainger, J. (eds.), *Laws and Societies in the Canadian Prairie West, 1670-1940* (pp. 198-223). Vancouver: UBC Press.

Marsan, B. (2005). Pourquoi le Syndicalisme étudiant. In Association Pour une Solidarité Syndicale étudiante (ed.), *Recueil de Textes Sur l'Histoire du Mouvement étudiant Québécois* (pp. 48-71). Montréal: Association pour une solidarité syndicale étudiante.

Marshall, K. (2010). Employment Patterns of Post-Secondary Students. *Perspectives on Labour and Income*, 11(9), 6-16.

Martin, D.G. & Pierce, J. (2013). Reconceptualizing Resistance: Residuals of the State and Democratic Radical Pluralism. *Antipode*, 45(1), 61-79.

Martin, É. (2013). Le Printemps Contre l'Hégémonie. La Mobilisation étudiante de 2012 et le Blocage Institutionnel de la Société Québécoise. *Recherches sociographiques*, LIV(3), 419-50.

Martin, W.G. (2008b). Introduction: The Search for Antisystemic Movements. In Martin, W.G. (ed.), *Making Waves: Worldwide Social Movements, 1750-2005* (pp. 1-9). London: Paradigm Publishers.

Martin, W.G. (2008a). Conclusion: World Movement Waves and World Transformation. In Martin, W.G. (ed.), *Making Waves: Worldwide Social Movements, 1750-2005* (pp. 168-80). London: Paradigm Publishers.

Martineau, J. (2015). Rhythms of Change: Mobilizing Decolonial Consciousness, Indigenous Resurgence and the Idle No More Movement. In Coburn, E. (ed.), *More Will Sing Their Way to Freedom: Indigenous Resistance and Resurgence* (pp. 229-54). Winnipeg: Fernwood.

Martin-Hill, D. (2004). Resistance, Determination, and Perseverance of the Lubicon Cree Women. In Blaser, M., Feit, H. & McRae, G. (eds.), *In the Way of Development: Indigenous Peoples, Life Projects and Globalization* (pp. 313-30). London: Zed Books; Ottawa: International Development Research Centre.

Marx, G.T. & McAdam, D. (1994). *Collective Behavior and Social Movements*. Englewod Cliffs: Prentice-Hall.

Marx, K. (1844). Toward a Critique of *Hegel's Philosophy of Right: Introduction*. In Simon, L.H. (ed.), Marx, K. (1994). *Selected Writings* (pp. 27-39). Indianapolis: Hackett.

Marx, K. (1857). Economic Manuscripts: Grundrisse—Introduction. Retrieved June 22, 2015 from https://www.marxists.org/archive/marx/works/1857/grundrisse/ch01.htm.

Marx, K. (1875). Critique of the Gotha Programme. In Marx, K. & Engels, F. (1962) *Selected Works*, Vol 2. Moscow: Foreign Languages Publishing House.

Marx, K. (1976). *Capital*, Vol. 1. Harmondsworth: Penguin.

Marx, K. (1977). *Selected Writings*. McLellan, D. (ed.). Oxford: Oxford University Press.

Marx, K. (1977). *Capital*, Vol. 1. New York: Vintage Books.

Marx, K. & Engels, F. (1998). *The Communist Manifesto*. London: Merlin.

Masquelier, C. (2013). Critical Theory and Contemporary Social Movements. *European Journal of Social Theory*, 16(4), 395-412.

Mayer, M. (1991). Social Movement Research in the United States: A European Perspective. *International Journal of Politics, Culture and Society*, 4(4), 459-80.

Maynard, R. (2010, Nov. 1). Dignity and Solidarity: Community Support Work and Movement Building. *Briarpatch*. Retrieved Sept. 30, 2012 from http://briarpatchmagazine.com/articles/view/dignity-and-solidarity.

Maynard, S. (1991). When Queer Is Not Enough. *Fuse*, Fall, 14-18.

Mazurek, W. (2014, Nov. 13). McGill and Concordia Host the First Fossil Free Canada Climate Convergence. *The McGill Daily*. Retrieved Aug. 23, 2015 from http://www.mcgilldaily.com/2014/11/concordia-hosts-first-fossil-free-canada-climate-convergence.

Mbembe, A. (2006). Nécropolitique. *Raisons politiques: Etudes de pensée politique*, 21.

McAdam, D., McCarthy, J.D. & Zald, M.N. (eds.). (1996). *Comparative Perspectives on Social Movements*. Cambridge: Cambridge University Press.

McAdam, D., Tarrow, S.G. & Tilly, C. (2001). *Dynamics of Contention*. Cambridge: Cambridge University Press.

McAdam, D. (1982). *Political Process and the Development of Black Insurgency, 1930-1970*. Chicago: University of Chicago Press.

McAdam, D., McCarthy, J.D. & Zald, M.N. (1988). Social Movements. In Smelser, N. (ed.), *Handbook of Sociology*. Newbury Park: Sage.

McAlevey, J. (2014). *Raising Expectations (and Raising Hell): My Decade Fighting for the Labor Movement.* New York: Verso.

McBride, S. & Whiteside, H. (2011). *Private Affluence, Public Austerity.* Winnipeg: Fernwood.

McCarthy, J.D. & Zald, M. (1977). Resource Mobilization and Social Movements: A Partial Theory. *American Journal of Sociology,* 82(6), 1212-41.

McCarthy, S. (2009, Dec. 2). World Awash in Half-Promises as Emissions Cuts Fall Short. *The Globe and Mail,* p. A1.

McCaskell, T. (1988). The Bath Raids and Gay Politics. In Cunningham, F. et al. (eds.), *Social Movements/Social Change: The Politics and Practice of Organizing* (pp. 169-98). Toronto: Between the Lines/Socialist Studies.

McGlade, C. & Ekins, P. (2015). The Geographical Distribution of Fossil Fuels Unused When Limiting Global Warming to 2°C. *Nature,* 517, 187-90.

McGuirk, P. & O'Neill, P. (2012). Critical Geographies with the State: The Problem of Social Vulnerability and the Politics of Engaged Research. *Antipode,* 44(4), 1374-94.

McIntosh, P. (1988). White Privilege and Male Privilege: A Personal Account of Coming to See Correspondences through Work in Women's Studies. *Working Paper 189.* Wellesley: Wellesley College Center for Research on Women.

McKegney, S. (2014). *Masculindians: Conversations about Indigenous Manhood.* Winnipeg: University of Manitoba Press.

McKibben, B. (2012, July 19). Global Warming's Terrifying New Math. *Rolling Stone.* Retrieved Aug. 23, 2015 from http://www.rollingstone.com/politics/news/global-warmings-terrifying-new-math-20120719.

McLaughlin, J. & Goodley, D. (2008). Seeking and Rejecting Certainty: Exposing the Sophisticated Lifeworlds of Parents of Disabled Babies. *Sociology,* 42(2), 317-35.

McLuhan, M. (1964). *Understanding Media: The Extensions of Man.* New York: Signet.

McNally, D. (2006). *Another World Is Possible: Globalization and Anti-Capitalism* (2nd ed.). Winnipeg: ARP Books.

McNally, D. (2011a). *Global Slump: The Economics and Politics of Crisis and Resistance.* Oakland: PM Press.

McNally, D. (2011b). Mubarak's Folly: The Rising of Egypt's Workers. Retrieved Feb. 11, 2015 from http://davidmcnally.org/?p=354.

McNally, D. (2011c). Slump, Austerity, and Resistance. *Socialist Register 2012: The Crisis and the Left* (pp. 36-63). London: Merlin Press.

McRuer, R. (2006). *Crip Theory: Cultural Signs of Queerness and Disability*. New York: NYU Press.

McSorley, T. (2014, Jan. 6). Tarsands Divestment and Its Discontents. *Briarpatch*. Retrieved Aug. 23, 2015 from http://www.briarpatchmagazine.com/articles/view/tarsands-divestment-and-its-discontents.

Melucci, A. (1989). *Nomads of the Present: Social Movements and Individual Needs in Contemporary Society*. Philadelphia: Temple University Press.

Melucci, A. (1992). Liberation or Meaning? Social Movements, Culture and Democracy. *Development and Change*, 23(3), 43-77.

Melucci, A. (1994). Paradoxes of Post-Industrial Democracy: Everyday Life and Social Movements. *Berkeley Journal of Sociology*, 38, 185-92.

Melucci, A. (1996). *Challenging Codes: Collective Action in the Information Age*. Cambridge: Cambridge University Press.

Mensah, M.N. (2005). Le comité 'Femmes en Grève': Entrevue avec Isabelle, Françoise et Anne. *Nouvelles pratiques sociales*, 18(1), 9-17.

Merrifield, A. (2013). *The Politics of the Encounter: Urban Theory and Protest under Planetary Urbanization*. Athens: University of Georgia Press.

Métis Nation of Ontario. (2015). Louis Riel. *Métis Nation of Ontario*. Retrieved Aug. 23, 2015 from www.metisnation.org/culture--heritage/louis-riel.

Meyer, D.S. & Tarrow, S.G. (1998). *The Social Movement Society*. Lanham: Lowman & Littlefield.

Meyer, D.S. & Minkoff, D.C. (2004). Conceptualizing Political Opportunity. *Social Forces*, 82(4), 1457-92.

Meyer, D.S. (2004). Protest and Political Process. In Nash, K. & Scott, A. (eds.), *Blackwell Companion to Political Sociology*. Oxford: Blackwell.

Michaud, J. (2010). La Reconnaissance des Apports Théoriques du Féminisme Dans la Presse Alternative de Gauche: le cas du *Temps Fou*. *Politique et Sociétés*, 29(2), 29-45.

Mills, C.W. (1959). *The Sociological Imagination*. New York: Oxford University Press.

Mills, S. (2010). *The Empire Within: Postcolonial Thought and Political Activism in the Sixties Montreal*. Montreal & Kingston: McGill-Queen's University Press.

Mitchell, T. (2009). Carbon Democracy. *Economy and Society*, 38, 399-432.

Mitchell, T. (2011). *Carbon Democracy: Political Power in the Age of Oil*. London: Verso.

Mojtehedzadeh, S. (2015, June 30). Wage Theft Puts Woman at Rock Bottom—and She's not Alone. *Toronto Star.*

Mol, A. (2002). *The Body Multiple: Ontology in Medical Practice.* Durham: Duke University Press.

Monaghan, A. (2014, Nov. 14). UK Companies at Their Most Profitable Since 1998. *The Guardian.*

Monkman, K. (n.d.). Group of Seven Inches: Summary. Retrieved Aug. 23, 2015 from http://urbannation.com/films.php?film=group-of-seven-inches.

Moody, K. (1997). *Workers in a Lean World: Unions in the International Economy.* London: Verso.

More Canadian Workers Are Living Paycheque to Paycheque, Saving Less: Survey. (2015, Sept. 10). *Canadian Press.*

Morgan, G. (2009, Dec. 7). Bizarro World: Taxes to Subsidize Pollution Elsewhere. *The Globe and Mail,* p. B7.

Morgan, G. (2013, Dec. 4). The Energy Industry Ignores the Fossil Fuel Divestiture Movement at Its Own Peril. *Alberta Oil.* Retrieved Aug. 23, 2015 from http://www.albertaoilmagazine.com/ 2013/12/universities-divest-fossil-fuel-holdings/.

Morgan, R. (1970). Goodbye to All That. In Baxandall, R. & Gordon, L. (eds.), (2000), *Dear Sisters: Dispatches from the Women's Liberation Movement.* New York: Basic Books.

Morgensen, S.L. (2011). *Spaces Between Us: Queer Settler Colonialism and Indigenous Decolonization.* Minneapolis: University of Minnesota.

Morrow, R. (2013). Defending Habermas Against Eurocentrism: Latin America and Mignola's Decolonial Challenge. In Bailey, T. (ed.), *Deprovincializing Habermas* (pp. 117-36). London: Routledge.

Moss, P. (forthcoming). Perching as a Strategy for Seeking Legitimacy for Broken Embodiments: Embracing Biomedical Claims for M.E. In Orsini, M. & Kelly, C. (eds.), *Mobilizing Metaphor: Art, Culture and Disability Activism in Canada.* Vancouver: UBC Press.

Moss, P. & Teghtsoonian, K. (2008). Power and Illness: Authority, Bodies, and Context. In Moss, P. & Teghtsoonian, K. (eds.), *Contesting Illness: Processes and Practices* (pp. 3-27). Toronto: University of Toronto Press.

Mouffe, C. (1988). Hegemony and New Political Subjects: Toward a New Concept of Democracy. In Nelson, C. & Grossberg, L. (eds.), *Marxism and the Interpretation of Culture* (pp. 89-104). Urbana-Champaign: University of Illinois Press.

Mouffe, C. (1993). *The Return of the Political.* London: Verso.

Mouffe, C. (2000). *The Democratic Paradox.* London: Verso.

Mouffe, C. (2005). *On the Political.* New York: Routledge.

Moysan-Lapointe, H. (2005). L'ASSÉ Depuis sa Création. In Association Pour une Solidarité Syndicale étudiante (ed.), *Recueil de Textes sur l'Histoire du Mouvement étudiant Québécois* (pp. 102-07). Montréal: Association pour une solidarité syndicale étudiante. http://www.asse-solidarite.qc.ca/wp-content/uploads/2013/02/histoire-du-mouvement-etudiant-hiver-2005.pdf.

Muhr, T. (2013). *Counter-Globalization and Socialism in the 21st Century*. London: Routledge.

Mumford, L. (1961). *The City in History*. New York: Harcourt Brace.

Mumford, L. (2010). *Technics and Civilization*. Chicago: University of Chicago Press.

Munck, R. (2002). *Globalization and Labour: The New "Great Transformation."* London & New York: Zed Books.

Nadasdy, P. (2003). *Hunters and Bureaucrats: Power, Knowledge, and Aboriginal-State Relations in the Southwest Yukon*. Vancouver, BC: UBC Press.

Nail, T. (2010). Building Sanctuary City: NOII-Toronto on Non-Status Migrant Justice Organizing. *Upping the Anti*, 11. Retrieved Sept. 30, 2012 from http://uppingtheanti.org/journal/article/11-noii-sanctuary-city/.

Nash, C.J. (2014). Consuming Sexual Liberation: Gay Business, Politics, and Toronto's Barracks Bathhouse Raids. *Journal of Canadian Studies*. 48(2), 82-105.

Nathanson, R. (2012, Dec. 5). Doing the Math Better: A Talk with Christian Parenti. *The Nation*. Retrieved Aug. 23, 2015 from www.thenation.com/blog/171597/doing-math-better-talk-christian-parenti.

Nature Québec et STOP. (2010). Mémoire Présenté au Bureau d'Audiences Publiques sur l'Environnement (BAPE) : Développement Durable de l'Industrie des Gaz de Schiste au Québec. Retrieved Aug. 16, 2015 from http://www.bape.gouv.qc.ca/sections/mandats/Gaz_de_schiste/documents/DM166.pdf.

Ness, I. (ed.). (2014). *New Forms of Worker Organization:* The Syndicalist and Autonomist Restoration of Class-Struggle Unionism. Oakland: PM Press.

Neumann, R. (2005). *Making Political Ecology*. London: Hodder Arnold.

Newell, P. & Paterson, M. (2010). *Climate Capitalism: Global Warming and the Transformation of the Global Economy*. Cambridge: Cambridge University Press.

Newman, P.C. (2004). *Company of Adventurers: How the Hudson's Bay Empire Determined the Destiny of a Continent*. Toronto: Penguin.

Ng, R. (1996). *The Politics of Community Services, Immigrant Women, Class, and State*. Halifax: Fernwood.

Nilsen, A.G. & Cox, L. (2013). What Would a Marxist Theory of Social Movements Look Like? In Barker, C., Cox, L., Krinsky, J. & Nilsen, A.G. (eds.), *Marxism and Social Movements* (pp. 63-81). Leiden: Brill.

Nimtz, A. (2002). The Eurocentric Marx and Engels and Other Related Myths. In Bartolovich, C. & Lazarus, N. (eds.), *Marxism, Modernity and Postcolonial Studies* (pp. 65-80). Cambridge: Cambridge University Press.

No One Is Illegal—Ottawa. (2002, June 12). Character and Tone of March. Retrieved June 4, 2012 from http://www.ainfos.ca/02/jun/ainfos00212.html.

No One Is Illegal. (n.d.). Principles for Regularization. Retrieved Sept. 30, 2012 from http://noii-van.resist.ca/?page_id=89.

No One Is Illegal. (2011, Apr. 11). Lee Maracle Speaking at May Day Assembly. Retrieved Sept. 13, 2012 from https://www.youtube.com/watch?v=FNK3KDfMrRc&list=PL966D86F55E443E2A&index=1.

No One Is Illegal. (2012, Apr. 12). Important NOII Announcement about Future Communications. Retrieved Oct. 31, 2012 from https://noii-van.resist.ca/?p=4805.

No One Is Illegal—Montreal. (2003, Sept. 22). 10 Days of Picket: Justice for Montreal's Non-Status Algerians. Retrieved Sept. 30, 2012 from http://update.ocap.ca/node/646 .

No One Is Illegal—Ottawa. (2010, Aug. 3). No One Is Illegal Ottawa Says Let Them Stay. Retrieved Sept. 13, 2012 from http://noii-ottawa.blogspot.ca/2010/08/no-one-is-illegal-noii-ottawa-says-let.html.

No One Is Illegal—Toronto. (2010, Nov. 11). Toronto Schools a Little More Welcoming for Undocumented Students. Retrieved Sept. 25, 2012 from http://toronto.nooneisillegal.org/node/497.

No One Is Illegal—Toronto. (2011, May 8). May Day 2011 March for Status for All. Retrieved Sept. 13, 2012 from http://www.youtube.com/watch?v=RKR1atTluCw.

No One Is Illegal—Vancouver. (n.d.). What Are Security Certificates? Retrieved Sept. 12, 2012 from http://noii-van.resist.ca/?page_id=90.

No One Is Illegal—Vancouver (2007, June 13). Labour Resolutions to Uphold Dignity of (Im)migrant Workers. Retrieved July 21, 2012 from http://noii-van.resist.ca/?page_id=90.

No One Is Illegal—Vancouver. (2005, Jan. 11). Victory for Ali Reza Monemi. Retrieved Oct. 31, 2012 from https://noii-van.resist.ca/?p=409.

Normandeau, A. & *Leighton,* B. (1990). *A Vision of the Future of Policing in Canada: Police-Challenge 2000.* In Solicitor General's Office of Canada (p. 30).

Not An Alternative. (2010). Curatorial Statement for Re: Group: Beyond Models of Consensus. Exhibit at Eyebeam Art & Technology Center in New York, June-August 2010. Retrieved Aug. 23, 2015 from www.en.flossmanuals.net/collaborative futures/ch011_limits-of-participation/.

Nuu-chah-nulth Tribal Council and Natural Resources Defense Council. (2001). *Restoring First Nations to the Land: Lessons from Clayoquot Sound*. Port Alberni.

O'Connor, C. & Stacey, K. (2012, Sept. 1). Defunding the Public Interest. *Briarpatch*. Retrieved Sept. 22, 2012 from https://briarpatchmagazine.com/articles/view/defunding-the-public-interest.

O'Leary, K. (2009, Feb. 16). Interview. *CBC Radio One*.

O'Leary, V. & Toupin, L. (1982/1983). Québécoises Deboutte! Vol. 1 & 2. Montréal: Éditions du remue-ménage.

OCAP. (2004). Managers of Slum Housing Finally Get Fixed [blog post]. Retrieved from http://update.ocap.ca/node/572.

Offe, C. (1985). New Social Movements: Challenging the Boundaries of Institutional Politics. *Social Research*, 817-68.

Omi, M. & Winant, H. (1994). *Racial Formation in the United States* (2nd ed.). New York: Routledge.

Ong-Dean, C. (2005). Reconsidering the Social Location of the Medical Model: An Examination of Disability in Parenting Literature. *Journal of Medical Humanities*, 26(2/3), 141-58.

Opp, K.D. (2009). *Theories of Political Protest and Social Movements*. London: Routledge.

Oreskes, N. & Conway, E. (2011). *Merchants of Doubt: How a Handful of Scientists Obscured the Truth on Issues from Tobacco Smoke to Global Warming*. New York: Bloomsbury Press.

Organization for Economic Cooperation and Development. (2015). *Global Economic Outlook*. Paris: OECD.

Orsini, M. (2014). Health Social Movements: The Next Wave in Contentious Politics? In Smith, M. (ed.), *Group Politics and Social Movements in Canada* (pp. 333-55). Toronto: University of Toronto Press.

Oxfam. (2015). *Wealth: Having It All and Wanting More*. London: Oxfam.

Palmer, B.D. (1987). *Solidarity: The Rise and Fall of an Opposition in British Columbia*. Vancouver: New Star Books.

Palmer, B.D. (1992). *Working-Class Experience: Rethinking the History of Canadian Labour, 1800-1991*. Toronto: McClelland & Stewart.

Panitch, L. & Swartz, D. (2003). *From Consent to Coercion: The Assault on Trade Union Freedoms* (3rd ed.). Aurora: Garamond Press.

Panitch, L. & Gindin, S. (2012). *The Making of Global Capitalism: The Political Economy of American Empire*. London: Verso.

Panitch, L. (1994). Globalization and the State. In Panitch L. & Miliband, R. (eds.), *Socialist Register*. London: Merlin.

Panitch, L. (2008). *Renewing Socialism: Transforming Democracy, Strategy and Imagination*. Pontypool: Merlin Press.

Parenti, C. (2012). *Tropic of Chaos*. New York: Nation Books.

Parenti, C. (2012, Nov. 29). Problems with the Math: Is 350's Carbon Divestment Campaign Complete? *Huffington Post*. Retrieved Aug. 23, 2015 from www.huffingtonpost.com/christian-parenti/carbon-divestment-_b_2213124.html.

Parenti, C. (2013, Jan. 27). A Worthy Goal, but a Suspect Method. *New York Times*. Retrieved Aug. 23, 2015 from www.nytimes.com/roomfordebate/2013/01/27/is-divestment-an-effective-means-of-protest/a-worthy-goal-but-a-suspect-method.

Parenti, C. (2015). Why NYU Should Divest. *NYU Divest*. Retrieved Aug. 23, 2015 from http://www.nyu-divest.squarespace.com/#endorsements-section.

Parker, S. (2004). *Urban Theory and the Urban Experience: Encountering the City*. London: Routledge.

Parkinson, D. (2013, Jan. 17). Canada's Cash Hoard Not the Work of Misers. *The Globe and Mail*.

Parkinson, D. (2015, May 30). Oil Shock Sends Economy Reeling. *The Globe and Mail*.

Partners in Policymaking [PIP]. (n.d.). Minneapolis: Minnesota Governor's Council on Developmental Disabilities. Retrieved Jul. 13, 2015 from http://www.partnersinpolicymaking.com/.

Patton, P. (1988). Marxism and Beyond: Strategies of Reterritorialization. In Nelson, C. & Grossberg, L (eds.), *Marxism and the Interpretation of Culture*. Urbana: University of Illinois Press.

Paulson, H.M. (2010). *On the Brink: Inside the Race to Stop the Collapse of the Global Financial System*. New York: Business Plus.

Peers, D. (2009). (Dis)empowering Paralympic Histories: Absent Athletes and Disabling Discourses. *Disability and Society*, 24(5), 653-65.

Peet, R. & Watts, M. (eds.). (2004). *Liberation Ecologies: Environment, Development, Social Movements* (2nd ed.). New York: Routledge.

Péloquin, M. (2007). *En Prison Pour la Cause des Femmes: la Conquête du Banc des Jurés*. Montréal: Éditions du remue-ménage.

Peluso, N. & Watts, M. (eds.). (2001). *Violent Environments*. Ithaca: Cornell University Press.

Penn Medicine. (2015). Sharp, Sustained Increases in Suicides Closely Shadowed Austerity Events in Greece, Penn Study Finds. *Perelman School of Medicine*, Feb. 3. Peterborough: Broadview Press.

Peters, E. & Andersen, C. (2013). *Indigenous in the City: Contemporary Identities and Cultural Innovation*. Vancouver: UBC Press.

Phillips, R.B. (2011). APEC at the Museum of Anthropology: The Politics of Site and the Poetics of Sight Bite. In Cronin, J.K. & Robertson, K. (eds.), *Imagining Resistance: Visual Culture and Activism in Canada* (pp. 171-91). Waterloo: Wilfrid Laurier Press.

Picher, F. (2015). Coming Clean About Operation Soap: The 1981 Bathhouse Raids. Retrieved June 29, 2015 from http://activehistory.ca/2015/06/coming-clean-about-operation-soap-the-1981-toronto-bathhouse-raids/.

Piketty, T. (2014). *Capital in the Twenty-First Century*. Trans. by Goldhammer, A. Cambridge: The Belknap Press of Harvard University Press.

Poirier St-Pierre, R. & Ethier, P. (2013). *De l'école à la Rue*. Montréal: les éditions écosociété.

Polanyi, K. (1957). *The Great Transformation*. Boston: Beacon.

Poulantzas, N. (1974). *Classes in Contemporary Capitalism*. London: New Left Books.

Prince, M.J. (2009). *Absent citizens: Disability Politics and Policy in Canada*. Toronto: University of Toronto Press.

Prince, M.J. & Moss, P. (2015). Under Siege: Canadian Veterans, Veterans Affairs and the Harper Legacy. In Stoney, C. &. Doern, G.B. (eds.), *How Ottawa Spends: 2015-2016*. Montreal & Kingston: McGill-Queen's University Press.

Puar, J. (2007). *Terrorist Assemblages: Homonationalism in Queer Times*. Durham: Duke University Press.

Public Interest Alberta (PIA). (2014). 2014 Statistics of Low-Wage Workers in Alberta. Media release. Retrieved Sept. 3, 2014 from http://pialberta.org/sites/default/files/Documents/2014%20Alberta%20Low%20Wage%20Fact%20Sheet%20-%20Calgary.pdf.

Raghuveer, T. (2015). Former Undergraduate Council President: What Happened Behind Divest Harvard Closed Doors. Retrieved Aug. 23, 2015 from http://time.com/3825978/divest-harvard-closed-doors/.

Ramos, H. & Rodgers, K. (2015). *Protest and Politics: The Promise of Social Movement Societies*. Vancouver: UBC Press.

Ramos, H. (2008). Opportunity for Whom? Political Opportunity and Critical Events in Canadian Aboriginal Mobilization, 1951-2000. *Social Forces*, 87(2), 795-823.

Ramsaroop, C. (2008, May 1). Canada: Justice for Migrant Workers: Why We Will March. *Bullet*. Retrieved Oct. 31, 2012 from http://www.socialistproject.ca/bullet/bullet103.html.

Rancière, J. (1995). *On the Shores of Politics*. London: Verso.

Rancière, J. (1998). *Disagreement: Politics and Philosophy*. Minneapolis: University of Minnesota Press.

Rancière, J. (2006). *Hatred of Democracy*. London: Verso.

Raphael, D. & Bryant, T. (2014, Nov. 24). Income Inequality Is a Deadly Problem. *Toronto Star*

Razack, S.H. (2008). *Casting Out: The Eviction of Muslims from Western Law and Politics*. Toronto: University of Toronto Press.

RCMP. (2014). Criminal Threats to the Canadian Petroleum Industry. *Critical Infrastructure Intelligence*. Retrieved Aug. 9, 2015 from http://www.statewatch.org/news/2015/feb/can-2014-01-24-rcmp-anti-petroleum-activists-report.pdf.

Reed, A. (2001). *Class Notes: Posing as Politics and Other Thoughts on the American Scene*. New York: The New Press.

Reguly, E. (2009, Dec. 16). With the World Watching, Canada Draws Line in the Oil Sands. *The Globe and Mail*, p. A1.

Reguly, E. & Vanderklippe, N. (2009, Dec. 7). The World Is Coming to Copenhagen but Canada Is Coming with a Tarred Image. *The Globe and Mail*, p. A1.

Reid, M. (2009) [1972]. *Notre Parti est Pris: un Jeune Reporter Chez les écrivains Révolutionnaires du Québec 1963-1970*. Québec: Presses de l'Université Laval.

Reinhart, C.M. & Rogoff, K. (2009). *This Time Is Different: Eight Centuries of Financial Folly*. Princeton: Princeton University Press.

Bédard, R.E.M. (2008). Keepers of the Water: Nishnaabe-Kwewag Speaking for the Water. In Simpson, L.(ed.). *Lighting the Eighth Fire: The Liberation, Resurgence and Protection of Indigenous Nations*. Winnipeg: ARP Books.

Rénique, G. (2009). Latin America: The New Neoliberalism and Popular Mobilization. *Socialism and Democracy*, 23(3), 1-26.

Reynolds, J. (2013). Le Grève étudiante: une Prise de Conscience Féministe. In Surprenant, M.-È. & Biguaouette, M. (eds.). *Les Femmes Changent la Lutte au Cœur du Printemps Québécois* (pp. 41-51). Montréal: remue-ménage.

Rich, A. (1994). Compulsory Heterosexuality and Lesbian Existence. In *Blood, Bread and Poetry* (pp. 23-75). New York: Norton Paperback.

Robbins, P. (2004). *Political Ecology: A Critical Introduction*. Oxford: Blackwell Publishing.

Roberts, J.T. (2011). Multipolarity and the New World (dis)Order: US Hegemonic Decline and the Fragmentation of the Global Climate Regime. *Global Environmental Change*, 21(3), 776-84.

Robinson, S. (2015). The Twenty Fastest Growing Countries This Year. *Bloomberg*. Retrieved Aug. 20, 2015 from http://www.bloomberg.com/news/articles/2015-02-25/the-20-fastest-growing-economies-this-year.

Rocheleau, D., Thomas-Slayter, B. & Wangari, E. (eds.). (2013). *Feminist Political Ecology: Global Issues and Local Experience* (2nd ed.). New York: Routledge.

Roets, G. & Braidotti, R. (2010). Theorizing the Unity of Bodies and Minds: Nomadology and Subjectivity in Disability Studies. In Goodley, D., Hughes, B. & Davis, L. (eds.), *Disability and Social Theory: New Developments and Directions* (pp. 161-76). London: Palgrave Macmillan.

Rose, N. (1999). *Powers of Freedom: Reframing Political Thought.* Cambridge: Cambridge University Press.

Ross, B. & Sullivan, R. (2012). Tracing Lines of Horizontal Hostility: How Sex Workers and Gay Liberation Activists Battled for Space, Voice, and Belonging in Vancouver, 1975-1985. *Sexualities,* 5(5-6), 604-21.

Ross, B. (1995). *The House that Jill Built: A Lesbian Nation in Formation.* Toronto: University of Toronto Press.

Roth, M. (2011). Letters of Resignation from the American Dream. In Blumenkranz, C. et al. (eds.), *Occupy!: Scenes from Occupied America* (pp.23-9). New York: Verso.

Rousseau, J.-J. (1983). *On the Social Contract, Discourse on the Origin of Inequality, Discourse on Political Economy.* Indianapolis: Hackett.

Roux, P., Perrin, C., Pannatier, G. & Cossy, V. (2005). Le Militantisme n'échappe Pas au Patriarcat. *Nouvelles Questions Féministes,* 24(3), 4-16.

Rowbotham, S., (1981). The Women's Movement and Organizing for Socialism. In Rowbotham, S. Segal, L. & Wainwright, H. (eds.), *Beyond the Fragments: Feminism and the Making of Socialism.* Boston: Alyson.

Rowe, J. & Carroll, M. (2014). Reform or Radicalism. *New Political Science,* 36(2), 149-71.

Rowe, J. & Carroll, M. (2015). What the Left Can Learn from Occupy Wall Street's Swift Rise and Current Impasse. *Studies in Political Economy,* 96, 145-65.

Roy-Blais, C. (2013). Le Prise de Parole des Militantes Féministes au Sein du Mouvement étudiant: un Impératif. In Surprenant, M.-È. & Biguaouette, M. (eds.). *Les Femmes Changent la Lutte au Cœur du Printemps Québécois* (pp. 53-58). Montréal: remue-ménage.

Rubin, J. (2009). *Why Your World Is About To Get A Whole Lot Smaller (Oil and the End of Globalization).* Toronto: Random House.

Russell, E. (2011). Occupy Bailout. Canadian Banks Got Billions in Help. *Rabble.ca.* Retrieved Nov. 15, 2015 from http://rabble.ca/columnists/2011/11/bailed-out-any-other-name-canadian-banks-got-plenty-help.

Sachs, W. (1999). Sustainable Development and the Crisis of Nature: On the Political Anatomy of an Oxymoron. In Fischer, F. & Hajer, M. (eds.), *Living with Nature: Environmental Politics as Cultural Discourse* (pp. 23-41). Oxford: Oxford University Press.

Sadowski, R. (2011). A Cash Buildup and Business Investment. Federal Reserve Bank of Cleveland. Retrieved Aug. 24, 2015 from http://www.clevelandfed.org.

Saez, E. & Zucman, G. (2014). Wealth Inequality in the United States Since 1913. *NBER Working Paper Series*, n. 20625. Cambridge: National Bureau for Economic Research,

Salazer, D.J. & Alper, D.K. (2000). *Forging Truces in the War on the Woods: Sustaining the Forests of the Pacific Coasts.* Vancouver: UBC Press.

Sale, K. (1972). *SDS: The Rise and Development of the Students for a Democratic Society.* New York: Random House.

Sassen, S. (1996). *Losing Control? Sovereignty in an Age of Globalization.* New York: Columbia University Press.

Sassen, S. (1998). *Globalization and Its Discontents: Essays on the Mobility of People and Money.* New York: New Press.

Sassen, S. (2007). *A Sociology of Globalization.* New York: W.W. Norton & Co.

Sassen, S. (2014). *Expulsions: Brutality and Complexity in the Global Economy.* Cambridge, MA: The Belknap Press of Harvard University Press.

Saunders, D. (2010). *Arrival City: The Final Migration and the Next World.* Toronto: A.A. Knopf.

Saval, N. (2011). Labor, Again. In Blumenkranz, C. et al. (eds.), *Occupy!: Scenes from Occupied America* (pp. 110-15). New York: Verso.

Savard, A. & Tremblay-Cléroux, M.-È. (2013). L'ASSÉ, la Démocratie Directe et la Gauche Radicale. In Association Pour une Solidarité Syndicale (ed.), *Cahier de mémoires. Congrès d'orientation 2013* (pp. 129-40). Montréal: Association pour une solidarité syndicale étudiante.

Sawyer, S. (2004). *Crude Chronicles: Indigenous Politics, Multinational Oil, and Neoliberalism in Ecuador.* Durham: Duke University Press.

Scheer, H. (1994). *A Solar Manifesto.* London: James & James Ltd.

Schein, R. (2011). Free Transit and Social Movement Infrastructure: Assessing the Political Potential of Toronto's Nascent Free Transit Campaign. *Alternate Routes: A Journal of Critical Social Research*, 22, 115-22.

Schifferes, S. (2010, Apr. 23). UK Economy Faces Decade of Pain. *BBC News.*

Schwartz, N.D. (2013, Mar. 3). Recovery in U.S. Is Lifting Profits, but Not Adding Jobs. *New York Times.*

Sears, A. (2005). Queer Anti-Capitalism: What's Left of Lesbian and Gay Liberation? *Science & Society,* 69(1), 92-112.

Sears, A. (2014). *The Next New Left: A History of the Future*. Winnipeg: Fernwood.

SeaSol Organizer. (n.d.). Why You Should Start a Solidarity Network. In *Seattle Solidarity Network, Solidarity Networks: Examples and Ideas of Direct Action* (pp. 26-30).

Seattle Solidarity Network. (2014). Sterling Manor Tenants Win Massive Repairs from Landlords [blog post]. Retrieved Aug. 19, 2015 from http://seasol.net/index.php?option=com_content&view=article&id=111:sterling-manor-tenants-win-massive-repairs-from-landlords&catid=1:recent.

Seattle Solidarity Network. (2009). Unpaid Wages Battle Underway in Pioneer Square [blog post]. Retrieved Aug. 19, 2015 from http://www.seattlesolidarity.net/index.php?option=com_content&task=view&id=44.

Seattle Solidarity Network. (n.d.) *Solidarity Networks: Examples and ideas of direct action*. [Edmonton]: Thought Crime Ink.

Seghetti, L.M., Vina, S.R. & Ester, K. (2006, Aug. 14). Enforcing Immigration Law: The Role of State and Local Law Enforcement. *Immigration Law Publisher*. Retrieved Sept. 12, 2012 from http://www.ilw.com/immigrationdaily/news/2006,0912-crs.pdf.

Seymour, R. (2014). *Against Austerity*. London: Pluto Press.

Shantz, J. (2002). Fighting to Win: The Ontario Coalition against Poverty. *Capital & Class*, 26(3), 1-8.

Shantz, J. (2009). Anarchy in the Unions: Contemporary Anarchists at Work. *Working USA*, 12(3), 371-85.

Shantz, J. (2010). *Constructive Anarchy: Building Infrastructures of Resistance*. Surrey: Ashgate Publishing.

Shantz, J. (2011). *Active Anarchy: Political Practice in Contemporary Movements*. Plymouth: Lexington Books.

Sharzer, G. (2012). *No Local: Why Small-Scale Alternatives Won't Change the World*. Winchester: Zero Books.

Shaw, M. (2000). *Theory of the Global State: Globality as Unfinished Revolution*. Cambridge: Cambridge University Press.

Ship, S.J. (1991). Au-Delà de la Solidarité Féminine. *Revue Québécoise de Science Politique*, 19, 5-36.

Shragge, E. (2013). *Activism and Social Change: Lessons for Community Organizing* (2nd ed.). Toronto: University of Toronto Press.

Shue, H. (2014). *Climate Justice: Vulnerability and Protection*. Oxford: Oxford University Press.

Siltanen, J., Klodawsky, F. & Andrew, C. (2015). This Is How I Want to Live My Life: An Experiment in Prefigurative Feminist Organizing for a More Equitable and Inclusive City. *Antipode*, 47(1), 260-79.

Silvera, M. (1996). Man Royals and Sodomites. In Vicinus, M. (ed.), *Lesbian Subjects: A Feminist Studies Reader* (pp. 167-77). Bloomington: Indiana University Press.

Silvera, M. (ed.). (1991). *Piece of my heart: A Lesbian of Colour Anthology*. Toronto: Sister Vision.

Silversides, A. (2003). *AIDS Activist, Michael Lynch and the Politics of Community*. Toronto: Between the Lines.

Simpson, A. (2014). *Mohawk Interruptus: Political Life Across the Borders of Settler States*. Durham: Duke University Press.

Simpson, L. (2013). Fish Broth and Fasting. Retrieved Jan. 16, 2014 from http://dividednomore.ca/2013/01/16/fish-broth-fasting/.

Sinclair, T.J. (ed.). (2004). *Global Governance*. Vol 4. Critical Concepts in Political Science. London: Routledge.

Singer, G.H.S. et al. (1999). A Multi-Site Evaluation of Parent to Parent Programs for Parents of Children with Disabilities. *Journal of Early Intervention, 22(3)*, 217-29.

Sitrin, M. (2011). One No. In Blumenkranz, C. et al. (eds.), *Occupy! : Scenes from Occupied America* (pp. 7-11). New York, Verso.

Sitrin, M. (2012). *Everyday Revolutions: Horizontalism and Autonomy in Argentina*. New York: Zed Books.

Skinner, Q. (1978). *The Foundations of Modern Political Thought*. Cambridge: Cambridge University Press.

Skocpol, T. (1979). *States and Social Revolutions*. New York: Cambridge University Press.

Slack, Jennifer. (1996). The Theory and Method of Articulation in Cultural Studies. In Morley, D. & Chen, K.H. (eds.), *Stuart Hall: Critical Dialogues in Cultural Studies* (pp. 112-27). New York: Routledge.

Smith, A. (2005). *Conquest: Sexual violence and American Indian Genocide*. Cambridge: South End Press.

Smith, A. (2010). Indigeneity, Settler Colonialism, White Supremacy. *Global Dialogue*, 12(2).

Smith, A. (2013). Unsettling the Privilege of Self-Reflexivity. In Winddance Twine, F. & Gardener, B. (eds.). (2013). *Geographies of Privilege*. New York: Routledge.

Smith, G. (1985). Policing Sex in St. Catharines. *Action!* (*Publication of the Right to Privacy Committee*), Feb.1-2.

Smith, G. (1988). Policing the Gay Community: An Inquiry into Textually-Mediated Social Relations. *International Journal of the Sociology of Law*, 16, 163-83.

Smith, G. (1993). In Defence of Privacy, Or Bluntly Put, No More Shit. *Action! (A Publication of the Right to Privacy Committee)*, 3(3,1), 1-3.

Smith, G. (2006). Political Activist as Ethnographer. In Frampton, C., Kinsman, G., Thompson, A.K. & Tilleczek, K. (eds.), *Sociology for Changing the World, Social Movements/Social Research* (pp. 44-70). Halifax: Fernwood.

Smith, J. & Glidden, B. (2012). Occupy Pittsburgh and the Challenges of Participatory Democracy. *Social Movement Studies*, 11(3-4), 288-94.

Smith, J. & Wiest, D. (2012). *Social Movements in the World-System*. New York: Russell Sage.

Smith, J., McCarthy, J.D., McPhail, C. & Augustyn, B. (2001). From Protest to Agenda Building: Description Bias in Media Coverage of Protest Events in Washington, D.C. *Social Forces*, 79(4), 1397-1423.

Smith, M. (2015). LGBTQ Activism: The Pan-Canadian Political Space. In Tremblay, M. (ed.), *Queer Mobilizations, Social Movement Activism and Canadian Public Policy* (pp. 48-49). Vancouver: UBC Press.

Smith, M. (ed.). (2014). *Group Politics and Social Movements in Canada* (2nd ed.). Toronto: University of Toronto Press.

Smith, M. (1999). *Lesbian and Gay Rights in Canada: Social Movements and Equality Seeking, 1971-1995*. Toronto: University of Toronto Press.

Snow, D.A., Rockford, E.B., Worden, S.K. & Benford, R.D. (1986). Frame Alignment Process, Micromobilization and Movement Participation. *American Sociological Review*, 51, 464-81.

Snow, D., Benford, R., McCammon, L.H. & Fitzgerald, S. (2014). The Emergence, Development, and Future of the Framing Perspective: 25+ Years since Frame Alignment. *Mobilization: An International Quarterly*, 19(1), 23-46.

Snow, D.A. & Benford, R.D. (1992). Master Frames and Cycles of Protest. In Morris, A.D. & Muller, C.M. (eds.), *Frontiers in Social Movement Theory*. New Haven: Yale University Press.

Sobieraj, S. (2011). *Soundbitten: The Perils of Media-Centred Political Activism*. New York: NYU Press.

Solidarity Across Borders. (2006, July 12). Surprise Direct Action Report. Retrieved Oct. 31, 2012 from https://masses.tao.ca/pipermail/act-mtl/2006-July/002724.html.

Solnit, R. (2011). Throwing Out the Master's Tools and Building a Better House. In Blumenkranz, C. et al. (eds.), *Occupy!: Scenes from Occupied America* (pp. 146-56). New York, Verso.

Spade, D. (2011). *Normal Life: Administrative Violence, Critical Trans Politics and the Limits of Law*. Boston: South End Press.

Staggenborg, S. (2012). *Social Movements* (2nd ed.). Toronto: Oxford University Press.

Stallings, A.M. (2012). Online Bullying: A New and Ugly Sport for Liberal Commenters. *The Guardian: Comment Is Free.* Retrieved Aug. 21, 2015, from http://www.theguardian.com/commentisfree/.

Stanfield, C. (2014). From Passive Support to Active Engagement. *Canadian Association of Petroleum Producers.* Retrieved Aug. 23, 2015 from www.capp.ca/publications-and-statistics/context-magazine/active-engagement-feature.

Stekelenburg, J.V. & Boekkooi, M. (2013). Mobilizing for Change in a Changing Society. In Stekelenburg, J.V., Roggeband, C. & Klandermans, B. (eds.), *The Future of Social Movement Research* (pp. 217-34). Minneapolis: University of Minnesota Press.

Stendie, L. & Adkin, L. (forthcoming). In the Path of the Pipeline: Environmental Citizenship, Aboriginal Rights, and the Northern Gateway Pipeline Review. In Adkin, L. (ed.), *First World Petro-Politics: The Political Ecology and Governance of Alberta.* University of Toronto Press.

Stevenson, H. & Dryzek, J.S. (2014). *Democratizing Global Climate Governance.* Cambridge: Cambridge University Press.

Steward, G. (2014). Oilsands Wages Driving Push for Temporary Foreign Workers. *The Toronto Star.* Retrieved June 23, 2014 from http://www.thestar.com/opinion/commentary/2014/06/23/oilsands_wages_driving_push_for_temporary_foreign_workers.html.

Stoett, P.J. (2012). *Global Ecopolitics.* Toronto: University of Toronto Press.

Stone, S. (2008). Resisting an Illness Label: Disability, Impairment, and Illness. In Moss, P. & Teghtsoonian, K. (eds.), *Contesting Illness: Processes and Practices* (pp. 201-17). Toronto: University of Toronto Press.

Surprenant, M.-È. & Biguaouette, M. (eds.). (2013). *Les Femmes Changent la Lutte au Cœur du Printemps Québécois.* Montréal: Éditions du Remue-Ménage.

Suzack, C. et al. (eds.). (2010). *Indigenous Women and Feminism: Politics, Activism, Culture.* Vancouver: UBC Press.

Swidler, A. (2001). *Talk of Love.* Chicago: University of Chicago Press.

Sycamore, M.D. (ed.). (2004). *That's Revolting: Queer Strategies for Resisting Assimilation.* Brooklyn: Soft Skull Press.

Tarrow, S. (1994). *Power in Movement: Social Movements, Collective Action and Politics.* Cambridge: Cambridge University Press.

Taylor, K.Y. (2015, Jan. 13). The Rise of the #Black Lives Matter Movement, *Socialist Worker.* Retrieved Aug. 25, 2015 from http://socialistworker.org/2015/01/13/the-rise-of-blacklivesmatter

Taylor, S.E., Buunk, B.P. & Aspinwall, L.G. (1990). Social Comparison, Stress, and Coping. *Personality and Social Psychology Bulletin*, 12(1), 74-89.

Teeple, G. (1995). *Globalization and the Decline of Social Reform*. Toronto: Garamond.

Tegelberg, M., Yagodin, D. & Russell, A. (2014). #Climatenews: Summit Journalism and Digital Networks. In Crow, D.A. & Boykoff, M.T. (eds.), *Culture, Politics and Climate Change* (pp. 63-82). London: Routledge.

Tetzlaff, D. (1991). Divide and Conquer: Popular Culture and Social Control in Late Capitalism. *Media, Culture and Society*, 13, 9-33.

The Future of Capitalism. (2009, Mar. 8), *Financial Times*.

The Council of Canadian Academies. (2014). *Policing Canada in the 21st Century: New Policing for New Challenges: The Expert Panel on the Future of Canadian Policing Models*. Retrieved May 13, 2015 from http://www.scienceadvice.ca/uploads/eng/assessments%20and%20publications%20and%20news%20releases/policing/policing_fullreporten.pdf.

The UN's Enviro-Activist in-Chief. (2010, Feb. 2). *National Post*, p. A12.

Theurillat-Cloutier, A., Leduc, A. & Lacoursière, B. (2014). Les Racines Historiques du Printemps érable. In Ancelovici, M. & Dupuis-Déri, F. (eds.), *Un Printemps Rouge et Noir. Regards Croisés sur la Grève étudiante de 2012* (pp. 37-58). Montréal: Écosociété.

Thomas, P.D. (2013). Hegemony, Passive Revolution and the Modern Prince. *Thesis Eleven*, 117(1), 20-39.

Thomas, P.D. (2010). *The Gramscian Moment*. Chicago: Haymarket Books.

Thompson, E.P. (1968). *The Making of the English Working Class*. Harmondsworth: Penguin.

Thompson, S. (2015, Jan. 12). Is it Time to Stop Ignoring the Fossil Fuel Divestment Campaign? *Alberta Oil*. Retrieved Aug. 23, 2015 from http://www.albertaoilmagazine.com/2015/01/tipping-point.

Tilly, C. & Tarrow, S.G. (2007). *Contentious Politics*. Boulder: Paradigm.

Tilly, C. (1978). *From Mobilization to Revolution*. Reading: Addison-Wesley.

Tilly, C. (1985). War Making and State Making as Organized Crime. In Evans, P., Rueschemeyer, D. & Skocpol, T. (eds.), *Bringing the State Back In*. Cambridge: Cambridge University Press.

Tilly, C. (1992). *Coercion, Capital and European States AD 990-1992*. Cambridge: Blackwell.

Tilly, C. (2006). *Regimes and Repertoires*. Chicago: University of Chicago Press.

Titchkosky, T. (2007). *Reading and Writing Disability Differently: The Textured Life of Embodiment.* Toronto: University of Toronto Press.

Tompkins, A. (2014). Asterisk. *TSQ: Transgender Studies Quarterly.* 1(1-2), 26-27.

Touraine, A., Wieviorka, M. & Dubet, F. (1987). *The Workers' Movement.* New York: Cambridge University Press.

Touraine, A. (1971). The Post-Industrial Society. New York: Random House.

Touraine, A. (1981). *The Voice and the Eye: An Analysis of Social Movements.* Cambridge: Cambridge University Press.

Touraine, A. (1995). *Critique of Modernity.* Oxford: Basil Blackwell.

Touraine, A. (2014). *After the Crisis.* Cambridge: Polity Press.

Traub-Merz, R. & Eckl, J. (2007). International Trade Union Movement: Mergers and Contradictions, Briefing Papers No. 1, *Friedrich Ebert Stiftung.* Retrieved Aug. 22, 2015 from http://library.fes.de/pdf-files/iez/04589.pdf.

Tremblay, M. (ed.). (2015). *Queer Mobilizations, Social Movement Activism and Canadian Public Policy.* Vancouver: UBC Press.

Tremblay, F.C. (2013). La Grève étudiante Pour les Nulles qui Paie le Prix des Résistances au Capitalisme Néolibérales? In Surprenant, M.-È. & Biguaouette, M. (eds.), *Les Femmes Changent la Lutte au Cœur du Printemps Québécois* (pp. 73-89). Montréal: Éditions Remue-ménage.

Tremblay-Pépin, S. (2013). Éducation et Néo-Libéralisme: le Décor du Printemps 2012. In Poirier, R., St-Pierre & Ethier, P. *De l'Ecole à la Rue: Dans les Coulisses de la Grève étudiante* (pp. 13-20). Montréal: Les editions écosociété.

Trimberger, E.K. (1979). Women in the Old and New Left: the Evolution of a Politics of Personal Life. *Feminist Studies*, 5(3), 431-50.

Truth and Reconciliation Committee of Canada. (2015). Honouring the Truth, Reconciling for the Future. Retrieved Aug. 24, 2015, from http://www.trc.ca.

Turk, A.T. (1982). *Political Criminality: The Defiance and Defense of Authority.* London: Sage.

Un groupe de femmes de Montréal. (1971). *Manifeste des Femmes Québécoises.* Montréal: l'étincelle.

Université de Montréal. (2014). Opinion Poll: Canada's Climate Change Consensus Confronts Keystone. *Nouvelles.* Retrieved Nov. 20, 2014 from http://www.nouvelles.umontreal.ca/udem-news/news/20141120-opinion-poll-canadas-climate-change-consensus-confronts-keystone.html.

Urry, J. (2011). *Climate Change and Society.* Cambridge: Polity.

Vahabzadeh, P. (2003). *Articulated Experiences: Toward a Radical Phenomenology of Contemporary Social Movements*. Albany: State University of New York Press.

Vervaet, L. (2010). The Violence of Incarceration: A Response from Mainland Europe. *Race and Class*, 51(4), 31.

Vincent, A. (1987). *Theories of the State*. Oxford: Basil Blackwell.

Voices. (2015). *Dismantling Democracy*. Retrieved Feb. 21, 2016 from http://voices-voix.ca/sites/voices-voix.ca/files/dismantlingdemocracy_voicesvoix.pdf.

Vulliamy, E. (2015). The Rebellion in Baltimore is an Uprising Against Austerity, says Top US Academic. *The Guardian*. Retreived May 2, 2015 from http://www.theguardian.com/us-news/2015/may/02/baltimore-rebellion-is-uprising-against-austerity-freddie-gray.

Walker, R.B.J. (1988). *One World, Many Worlds: Struggles for a Just World Peace*. Boulder: Lynne Rienner.

Walker, R.B.J. (1993). *Inside/Outside: International Relations as Political Theory*. Cambridge: Cambridge University Press.

Walker, R.B.J. (2010). *After the Globe, Before the World*. London: Routledge.

Walter, M. & Andersen, C. (2013). *Indigenous Statistics: A Quantitative Research Methodology*. Walnut Creek: Left Coast Press.

Wapner, M. (1989). What's Left: Marx, Foucault and Contemporary Problems of Social Change. *Praxis International*, 9(1-2), 88-111.

Warner, T. (2002). *Never Going Back: A History of Queer Activism in Canada*. Toronto: University of Toronto Press.

Waters, S. (2008). Situating Movements Historically: May 1968, Alain Touraine, and New Social Movement Theory. *Mobilization*, 13(1), 63-82.

Watkins, M. (ed.). (1977). *Dene Nation: The Colony Within*. Toronto: University of Toronto Press.

Watts, M. & Bohle, H. (1993). The Space of Vulnerability: The Causal Structure of Hunger and Famine. *Progress in Human Geography*. 17(1), 43-67.

Weber, M. (1949) [1904]. Objectivity in Social Science and Social Policy. In Shils, E.A. & Finch, H.A. (eds.), *The Methodology of the Social Sciences*. New York: The Free Press.

Weeks, J. (1981). *Sex, Politics and Society*. London: Longman.

Weingarten, H. & Deller, F. (2010). *The Benefits of Greater Differentiation of Ontario's University Sector*. Toronto: Higher Education Quality Council of Ontario.

Welch, I. (2014, May 9). Why Divestment Fails. *New York Times*. Retrieved Aug. 23, 2015 from www.mobile.nytimes.com/2014/05/10/opinion/why-divestment-fails.html?referrer=&_r=0.

Wells, D. (1995). Origins of Canada's Wagner Model of Industrial Relations: The United Auto Workers in Canada and the Suppression of 'Rank and File' Unionism, 1936-1953. *Canadian Journal of Sociology*. 20 (2), 193-225.

Westlake, D.E . (1997). *The Ax*. New York: Warner Books.

Wheeland, P. (2015). Montreal Cops Are Out of Control. *Quebec Ink*. Retrieved May 6, 2015 from http://cultmontreal.com/2015/05/montreal-police-are-out-of-control/.

Wilkes, R. (2015). Indigenous Resistance in Comparative Perspective: An Overview with an Auto-biographical Research Critique. In Coburn, E. (ed.), *More Will Sing Their Way to Freedom: Indigenous Resistance and Resurgence* (pp. 111-28). Winnipeg: Fernwood.

Williams, M. (2014). The Solidarity Economy and Social Transformation. In Durban, V.S. (ed.), *The Solidarity Economy Alternative*. Scottsville: University of KwaZulu-Natal Press.

Williams, R. (1983). *Towards 2000*. London: Chatto & Windus: The Hogarth Press.

Williams, R. (1989). *Resources of Hope: Culture, Democracy, Socialism*. Gable, R. (ed.). London; New York: Verso.

Wilson, J. (1989). Spousal Benefits Conference, Our Own Terms? *Rites*. (Toronto), September 4, 18.

Wines, M. (2014, May 6). Stanford to Purge $18 Billion Endowment of Coal Stock. *New York Times*. Retrieved Aug. 23, 2015 from www.nytimes.com/2014/05/07/education/stanford-to-purge-18-billion-endowment-of-coal-stock.html?_r=0.

Winter, B. (2000). Who Counts (or Doesn't Count) What Is Feminist Theory? An Exercise in Dictionary Use. *Feminist Theory*, 1(1), 105-11.

Wirth, L. (1938). Urbanism as a Way of Life. *American Journal of Sociology*, 44, (1-24).

Wolfe, R. (2012, Feb.). The Movement as an End-in-Itself? An Interview with David Graeber. *Platypus Review, 43*. Retrieved Aug. 23, 2015 from www.platypus1917.org/2012/01/31/interview-with-david-graeber/

Wood, E.M. (1995) A Chronology of the New Left and Its Successors, or: Who's Old Fashioned Now? *Socialist Register*, 31, 22-49.

Wood, L.J. (2014). *Crisis and Control: The Militarization of Protest Policing*. London: Pluto Press & Between the Lines.

Woolf, N. (2015, Apr. 17). Cornel West Warns of "Planetary Selma" at Harvard Fossil Fuel Divestment Protest. *The Guardian*. Retrieved Aug. 23, 2015 from www.theguardian.com/environment/ 2015/apr/17/harvard-divestment-protest-civil-rights-moment.

Workman, T. (2009). *If You're in My Way, I'm Walking: The Assault on Working People Since 1970*. Winnipeg: Fernwood.

World Bank. (2010). Global Economic Prospects 2010: Crisis, Finance and Growth. In *Through Public Opinion* (pp. 273-89). Washington: The World Bank.

Wotherspoon, T. & Hansen, J. (2013). The "Idle No More" Movement. *Social Inclusion,* 1(1), 21-36. *Wounds of Soldiers.* New York & Oxford: Berghahn Press.

Young, I.M. (1990). *Justice and the Politics of Difference.* Princeton: Princeton University Press.

Young, I.M. (2000). *Inclusion and Democracy.* New York: Oxford University Press.

Young, S. (2014). I'm not Your Inspiration, Thank You Very Much. [TEDTalk] Retrieved Feb. 13, 2015, from http://www.ted.com/talks/stella_young_i_m_not_your_inspiration_thank_you_very_much?language=en.

Zald, M.N & McCarthy, J.D. (eds.). (1987). *Social Movements in an Organizational Society.* New Brunswick: Transaction Books.

Zibechi, R. (2010) *Dispersing Power: Social Movements as Anti-Social Forces.* Oakland: AK Press.

Zippel, K. (2004). Transnational Advocacy Networks and Policy Cycles in the European Union: The Case of Sexual Harassment. *Social Politics: International Studies in Gender, State and Society,* 11(1), 57-85.

Zukin, S. (1991). *Landscapes of Power: From Detroit to Disneyworld.* Berkeley: University of California Press.

Zukin, S. (1995). *The Cultures of Cities.* Oxford: Blackwell.

Zukin, S. (2010). *Naked City: The Death and Life of Authentic Urban Places.* New York: Oxford University Press.

CONTRIBUTORS

BARRY D. ADAM teaches Sociology at the University of Windsor. His work on the subjectivity of subordination and on gay and lesbian movements (*The Survival of Domination*, *The Rise of a Gay and Lesbian Movement*, *The Global Emergence of Gay and Lesbian Politics*) documents how individual coping strategies can coalesce into collective mobilization and a transformative politics that restructure or revolutionize the conditions of subordination.

LAURIE ADKIN teaches Political Science at the University of Alberta. She is the author of *Politics of Sustainable Development: Citizens, Unions, and the Corporations*, and editor and co-author of *Environmental Conflict and Democracy in Canada*, and *First World Petro-Politics: The Political Ecology and Governance of Alberta* (forthcoming).

CLIFF (KAM'AYAAM/CHACHIM'MULTHNII) ATLEO is a doctoral candidate in Political Science at the University of Alberta and the 5th Annual Henry Roe Cloud Fellow in American Indian and Indigenous Studies at Yale University. His research offers a critique of "Aboriginalized" capitalism and seeks out alternative economic practices rooted in Indigenous teachings and traditions.

MICHAEL BUECKERT is a doctoral candidate in Sociology and Political Economy at Carleton University. His doctoral research explores the influence of financial activism, including divestment campaigns, on class power and social change. He has previously written on international development aid policy and the capitalist state.

WILLIAM K. CARROLL is a professor of Sociology at the University of Victoria, where he served as founding director of the Social Justice Studies Program. Among his recent books are *Expose, Oppose, Propose: Alternative Policy Groups and the Struggle for Global Justice*, *The Making of a Transnational Capitalist Class: Corporate Power in the 21st Century*, *Remaking Media: The Struggle to Democratize Public Communication* (co-authored with Bob Hackett) and *Challenges and Perils: Social Democracy in Neoliberal Times*.

ELAINE COBURN is assistant professor in the International Studies department of Glendon College at York University and is a researcher affiliated with the CADIS-Ecole des Hautes Etudes en Sciences Sociales in Paris, France. She is the editor of *'And More Will Sing Their Way to Freedom': Indigenous Resistance and Resurgence.*

MATTHEW CORBEIL is a doctoral candidate in Political Science at York University. His research focuses on social conflict and corporate power in Ontario's mining sector. He is also a member of the Industrial Workers of the World.

STEPHEN D'ARCY teaches Philosophy at Huron University College. He is author of *Languages of the Unheard: Why Militant Protest Is Good for Democracy* and co-editor of *A Line in the Tar Sands: Struggles for Environmental Justice.*

JESSICA DEMPSEY teaches Geography at the University of British Columbia. She works with the CBD Alliance, many NGOs and social movements to develop analysis and position papers on global biodiversity issues. She has published articles in leading geography and political ecology journals, including *Environment and Planning A*, *Geoforum* and *Progress in Human Geography.*

BETH DEVOLDER is a doctoral candidate in Interdisciplinary Studies with a focus in Critical Disability Studies at the University of British Columbia. She is the author of *The Faces of Disability and Disability Health Research: A Primer.*

CRAIG FORTIER teaches Social Development at Renison University College. He has participated in movements for migrant justice and in support of Indigenous sovereignty for over a decade. His PhD dissertation examined how radical anti-authoritarian movements learn, imagine and practice processes of decolonization through collaboration with Indigenous sovereignty struggles. He publishes in *Decolonization.*

PETER GIBBS holds a degree in Environmental Studies and Geography from the University of Victoria and was the lead organizer of Divest UVic. He was also the Director of Training at Dogwood Initiative. Peter is an organizer and trainer at Organize BC, where he runs training, coaching and capacity building programs for progressive organizers throughout British Columbia.

SAM GINDIN was the Research Director of the CAW (now UNIFOR) from 1974-2000 and an assistant to the President of the union from 1985 on. After leaving the CAW he taught Political Science at York University. He is the author of *The Canadian Autoworkers: The Birth and Transformation of a Union*, co-author with Leo Panitch of *The Making of Global Capitalism: The Political Economy of American Empire* and co-author with Greg Albo and Leo Panitch of *In and Out of Crisis: The Global Financial Meltdown and Left Alternatives.*

JORDAN HOUSE is a doctoral candidate in Political Science at York University. His research focuses on prison labour in Canada and labour movement renewal. His dissertation examines Canadian prisoner organizing and prisoner labour unions. He is a member of the Industrial Workers of the World.

CATRIONA JOHNSON is a doctoral student at the University of Victoria researching collective family governance. She was the Assistant Director for State and Federal Relations for the Maryland Developmental Disabilities Administration, a policy analyst with the Washington-based National Disability Rights Network, and Director of Public Policy Initiatives for the Maryland Developmental Disabilities Council.

GARY KINSMAN is a professor emeritus in Sociology at Laurentian University. He is the author of *The Regulation of Desire*, co-author with Patrizia Gentile of *The Canadian War on Queers* and editor of *Whose National Security?* and *Sociology for Changing the World.* He is a long-time queer liberation, AIDS, anti-poverty and anti-capitalist activist.

XAVIER LAFRANCE was a student movement activist in Québec for many years. He teaches Political Science at the Université du Québec à Montréal. His current research is on new radical left parties and social movements. His book, *Citizen-Worker: Rethinking the Transition to Capitalism and the Making of a Working Class in France*, is forthcoming.

WARREN MAGNUSSON teaches Political Science at the University of Victoria. His books include *The Search for Political Space: Globalization, Social Movements, and the Urban Political Experience*,

Politics of Urbanism: Seeing Like a City and *Local Self-Government and the Right to the City.*

DAVID MCNALLY teaches Political Science at York University. He is the author of six books, including *Global Slump: The Economics and Politics of Crisis and Resistance*, winner of the 2011 Paul Sweezy Award, and *Monsters of the Market: Zombies, Vampires and Global Capitalism*, winner of the 2012 Deutscher Memorial Award.

JACINTHE MICHAUD teaches Gender, Sexuality and Women's Studies at York University. She publishes in French and in English in *Studies in Political Economy, Politique et Sociétés* and *Conscience subalterne, conscience identitaire.*

PAMELA MOSS teaches in Human and Social Development at the University of Victoria. Her research coalesces around themes of bodies, power and knowledge production in numerous contexts. Her most recent book, co-authored with Michael J. Prince, is *Weary Warriors.* She is working on a book project entitled *Fatigue.*

MICHAEL J. PRINCE teaches Social Policy at the University of Victoria. He works with advocates and organizations in the disability rights movement including the Council of Canadians with Disabilities, the Canadian Association of Community Living and Inclusion BC. Michael is the author of *Absent Citizens: Disability Policy and Politics in Canada* and, with James Rice, *Changing Politics of Canadian Social Policy.*

JAMES ROWE teaches Environmental Studies at the University of Victoria. He works across the fields of political theory, social movement studies and political ecology. He is co-author with Ronnie Lipschutz of *Globalization, Governmentality, and Global Politics.*

KANCHAN SARKER teaches Sociology at the University of British Columbia-Okanagan. He also taught at the Dept. of Political Science, York University. He was a researcher at the Sociological Research Unit of the Indian Statistical Institute, Kolkata, from 1990-2001. He works on social movements, neoliberalism, inequality and India and publishes in national and international journals.

ALAN SEARS teaches Sociology at Ryerson University. His books include *The Next New Left: A History of the Future* and, co-authored with James Cairns, *The Democratic Imagination: Envisioning Popular Power in the Twenty-First Century.* He is an activist in anti-capitalist, queer and Palestine solidarity movements.

JILLIAN SMITH is a graduate student in Sociology at Memorial University of Newfoundland. Using an environmental justice lens, her research focuses on community interpretations and responses to the fracking controversy near the boundary of Gros Morne National Park.

MARK C.J. STODDART teaches Sociology at Memorial University. He is the author of the book *Making Meaning out of Mountains: The Political Ecology of Skiing.*

DAVID B. TINDALL teaches Sociology at the University of British Columbia. He is the co-editor of *Aboriginal Peoples and Forest Lands in Canada.*

HARSHA WALIA is a South Asian activist, writer and educator. Formally trained in the law, for the past fifteen years she has been active in grassroots anti-racist, migrant justice, Indigenous solidarity, anti-capitalist and anti-imperialist movements including through No One Is Illegal. She has worked with women in the Downtown Eastside for the past decade and is a member of the Febuary 14th Women's Memorial March Committee. Harsha is the author of *Undoing Border Imperialism.*

LESLEY WOOD teaches Sociology at York University. She is the author of *Crisis and Control: The Militarization of Protest Policing.* She is also active in the anti-poverty and global justice movements.